Goda

Sarnobat

Vadal

Vadal City

Marta Ban River

Red Lake   Apura

Thao

Somsak

Jharlang

Neeramphorn   Kharsawan

Guntur

Warun

kula   Akara River   Akershan

Nansakar River

e Hall of the
Protectors

MaDharvo

Bast   Fortress

HOUSE
OF
ASSASSINS

HOUSE
OF
ASSASSINS

LARRY
CORREIA

A Baen Books Original

Baen Publishing Enterprises
P.O. Box 1403
Riverdale, NY 10471
www.baen.com

ISBN: 978-1-4814-8376-6

Cover art by Kurt Miller
Map by Isaac Stewart

First Baen printing, February 2019

Distributed by Simon & Schuster
1230 Avenue of the Americas
New York, NY 10020

Library of Congress Cataloging-in-Publication Data

Names: Correia, Larry, author.
Title: House of assassins / Larry Correia.
Description: Riverdale, NY : Baen, [2019] | Series: Saga of the forgotten
    warrior ; 2
Identifiers: LCCN 2018047721 | ISBN 9781481483766 (hardback)
Subjects: | BISAC: FICTION / Fantasy / Epic. | FICTION / Fantasy /
    Historical. | FICTION / Fantasy / General. | GSAFD: Fantasy fiction.
Classification: LCC PS3603.O7723 H68 2019 | DDC 813/.6—dc23
LC record available at https://lccn.loc.gov/2018047721

10 9 8 7 6 5 4 3 2 1

Pages by Joy Freeman (www.pagesbyjoy.com)
Printed in the United States of America

To Jody

HOUSE
OF
ASSASSINS

Chapter 1

~~~~~~~~~

Twenty-five years ago

The children hurled rocks at each other until they got close enough to beat the other team with sticks. Whenever one of them got sufficiently hurt to start crying, the others would mock him, because they were children of the warrior caste and they had no time for babies.

"Savage bunch," said the first caste man. He was dressed in white and gold, which the warrior children knew was foolish, because how in the world could you hide in the trees to ambush your enemies while dressed in white and gold? The important visitor was standing on the observation platform next to the familiar figure of their leader, the phontho of the Vane garrison, Andaman Vane.

"What are they, six years old?"

"Six to eight. The older and bigger ones play at dirt war in a different field; keeps them from breaking the little ones."

"Play?"

"Yes. This isn't training. Training is serious business. Dirt war is just a chance for them to show their mettle. It is our way. Start them early. As soon as they can walk they can start developing a proper fighting spirit."

There was a *clonk* and a scream as a boy was struck in the side of his leather helmet by a rock. Dizzy, he tumbled down the

1

muddy hill. His friends immediately set upon him to *finish him off,* which meant putting bruises on him until he begged for mercy.

"Aren't you worried they'll die?"

"Ha!" Their phontho laughed at the absurdity of the idea. The first caste were *so soft.* "Once in a while accidents happen, but don't worry, Arbiter. You might not be able to tell from up here, but we've rules in place for their safety."

The rules were simple. When you picked your stick, it had to be pliable, nothing stiff enough to break skin on a thrust, and it couldn't be thicker around than their thumb. So it was more of a painful switch than anything. On the thrown rocks, they were supposed to stick with pebbles and never aim for the eyes... But in the heat of battle, everyone tended to go for bigger rocks, because all the children knew those flew better.

"Bruises make character. We have them fight like this now to weed out the snivelers. Those will do fine in support companies, obligated to the worker caste to raise funds, or married off to other houses, but the Vane barracks is allowed only five hundred active raiders, so I make certain that they're the best of the best. Five hundred elite warriors is what I promise your Thakoor, and what I always provide... If he changed the treaty and allowed me to form a second company, I could provide a thousand such men."

"I could make this suggestion, Phontho, but there are many within Great House Makao who feel that House Vane may already be *too* ambitious for a vassal."

"We are merely eager to serve. When your inspection is over, you can report back to your Thakoor that Vane remains ever loyal and ready to provide as many soldiers as he desires for his just and mighty cause."

"Don't worry. I have been most impressed by the tour. If the rest of our vassals had such discipline and spirit, we could conquer the whole of the west... Are any of these children yours, Phontho?"

"The girl." And the way her father said it filled Thera with pride.

"Really? You let your *daughter* out in *that*?"

Andaman Vane laughed. "You are new here. Welcome to Vane. Who do you think defends our lands while your Thakoor has sent me and my men off across the border? Our women don't march to war, but that doesn't mean war won't sometimes come to them. In the warrior caste, even our daughters are trained, not to the same level or intensity of course, but more than enough to defend themselves. Plus, when they're grown, they will have a better understanding of what their husbands and sons must do in order to better support us in our duties."

Since Thera could hear that her father and the important man from the Makao had their eyes on her now, she moved out from behind cover, braved the falling rocks, and screamed their battle cry, "*Behold, Vane is here!*" Her bold charge got her halfway up the hill before a larger boy on the other team intercepted her. Thera may have cheated by using a stick much larger around than her thumb, but she had the skinniest hands so it seemed fair to her. He was standing above her, she aimed her out-of-regulation stick for his legs. It was hard to defend yourself bending over. His toes were sticking out the end of his sandals, they made a great target. He yelped when she smacked them. As soon as he was hopping on one foot, it was easy to shove him down the slope.

Once Thera had taken the summit, all six mighty feet of it, the other team rallied to knock her off, but she had pockets full of rocks ready and an excellent arm. She began throwing rocks, aiming for their bellies, so even if she was off a bit, she'd still hit something that really hurt. "*Vane is here!*"

"Yes, but why is your daughter the only girl participating in this... dirt war?"

Her father laughed again. "She's the reigning champion. How else would she defend her title?"

Then Thera could no longer listen to her father's conversation with the important man, because she had to concentrate on holding her ground against the fierce counterattack.

An hour later, Thera's father came looking for her in the tall grass around the dirt war field. "Where are you, child? It's time for supper."

Her arms and legs were covered in welts, and it hurt too much to move, but that wasn't why she was hiding. She was in the tall grass because she didn't want anyone to see her weep. So she wiped her eyes and tried to look like she hadn't been crying. "I'm over here."

Phontho Andaman Vane dar Makao knelt down next to her. Even though he was the greatest commander their people had ever known, who'd led successful raids deep into the territory of three different great houses, his voice was always gentle when it came to his girl.

"What's wrong, Thera?"

"I lost." She sniffed. "I don't like losing."

"Anyone who enjoys losing isn't fit for our caste. But the good ones learn from their defeats so they can do better next time."

"But you never lose, Baba."

"I spent the whole day with my lips planted upon the buttocks of a soft-palmed bureaucrat who knows more about poetry than warfare, all in the off chance he'll make a nice report about us to the Thakoor. A few generations ago our house dominated the west, and now I have to beg for permission to field a fraction of the army we used to, in service of a house we used to boss around. No, Thera, there are different kinds of defeat, and I too know its bitter taste."

"It's worse because I got shamed in front of the high-status man."

His grin brightened her dark day. "He's a firster. They have no mind for tactics. He probably didn't even know the rules enough to realize your side lost—by the way, it was because the children who held your left flank, their arms grew tired. You should have rotated them out sooner—but all he'll remember is that you are the bravest little girl he's ever seen."

"I'm not little. I'm brave and *big*."

"True, and fearsome as a tiger. Now come on." He took her by the hands, hoisted her up, and swung her around, grass tickling her bare feet. "If we're late for supper your mother will be angry."

Thera giggled as her father put her on his back to carry her home, her stinging wounds and bitter defeat quickly forgotten.

Because of her father's rank, they had the finest home in the warrior district, but it was a long walk from where they conducted dirt war. They had to pass many other warriors' homes, and Thera would be embarrassed to be seen by her peers being carried.

"Put me down!"

"You're no burden. I've got helmets that weigh more than you."

"I can't look weak!"

"Clever girl," he agreed. "Even when you aren't feeling strong, you must never ever show weakness. Victims want pity. Warriors demand respect. Down you go."

It was a beautiful day. The sun shined. Butterflies danced between the leaves. Men came out of their homes to greet her father, always with great respect and devotion. She knew his warriors loved Andaman Vane nearly as much as she did. Many of the senior men asked her father how the arbiter's visit had gone. While they spoke, Thera wandered off the path, looking for a good stick to swing at the butterflies.

She looked up and saw something strange.

There was a black mark on the sky.

"Baba?"

Her father and the other warriors heard the alarm in her voice, stopped their conversation, and then followed her pointing finger with their eyes.

The mark quickly grew into a great black cloud, trailing fire. It was huge, but sped across the sky like an arrow. Dogs began to bark. Birds were flushed from the trees. Then it was over them, blocking out the sun, turning day to night, as the roar of thunder struck their ears. It was like nothing anyone had ever seen. It was a nightmare beyond understanding.

Some of the bravest warriors in the world quailed in fear. "It's the gods!"

"Silence with that foolishness," her father snapped. "There's no such thing as gods."

"What is it, Phontho?"

"Flaming rocks occasionally fall from the sky." Bold and somehow calm, he stared up at the terrifying thing that could squish them all. "That's just a really big one. Get up and show some dignity. It's not going to land on us. It's heading west toward the sea."

Thera watched in awe as the black thing trailed fire across the whole of the sky. Father was right. It was going to fall in the ocean and crush the demons instead. They were safe.

Then a bolt from heaven pierced her skull.

"Thera!"

She was lying in the grass again, only everything had turned red. Her father was kneeling next to her, but she couldn't understand what he was shouting. Then it went black.

There was bouncing. She was very confused. Thera was being carried in someone's arms as they ran across the warriors' district. The thing in the sky was smaller, further away, but people were still watching the smoke line that traced its path. Some of them gasped or shouted in surprise when they saw her. Why did they look so scared? Her vision came and went.

When she was awake again, she was being put on a table. Thera knew this place. There was one worker who lived in the warrior district who was loved and treated as one of their own, and that was the surgeon, because he put them back together when things went wrong. She'd been here before—for stitches in her arm—after a hard day of dirt war.

The surgeon leaned over her, but his normally kind face was distraught. Why was his apron covered in blood? She tried to tell him that everything would be okay, but her mouth wouldn't work. Why was he sticking a metal tool *inside* her head? *He shouldn't be able to do that.* The surgeon looked up at someone she couldn't see and shook his head sadly.

Asleep ...

Awake. Her mother was there but she was screaming and crying. Thera tried to call out to her, but she couldn't make words.

Asleep.

Then the pain came. She'd been spared it before. Maybe the bolt from heaven had been too sudden to hurt? Like being able to see the fireball in the sky before she could hear it, pain was like sound. And now the pain had caught up.

In and out, awake and asleep, darkness and light, Thera was too frightened to know what was going on. She was hurt and scared, so she slept.

Somehow she was back in her own bed and her parents were there. Father looked tired. Mother had been crying a lot. It hurt too much to talk, to think, so she went back to sleep, this time for a very long time.

The seasons changed. Sometimes the pain was worse, and sometimes when it was better she could hear what was going on around her. Her mother sang to her a lot, but after a while the songs stopped.

Her father was always there though. He didn't give up. He poured broth down her throat with a tube to keep her from starving. She heard him argue with people who declared that Thera was lingering between life and death, and that she would never wake up. Nobody could survive such a wound they said. She was dead, her body just didn't realize it yet. It would be merciful to smother her with her pillow and put her out of her misery. Thera was scared to die, but thankfully her father ordered those men away.

Eventually other men came, but these weren't warriors. They were of the first caste, and they told her father that he was needed on the border. He'd been gone from his post for too long. If he didn't fulfill his duty, then someone else would be appointed phontho in his place.

"She's in a coma. The only time she moves is when she has a seizure. Either kill her and end this pathetic existence, Andaman Vane, or turn her care over to a slave. The Thakoor has declared you are needed elsewhere."

"I will not leave my daughter. The bolt from the heavens broke her skull, but it hasn't broken her will. I know Thera will recover."

When one of the men told father that even if she did wake up, she'd be nothing but a useless drooling imbecile—nothing to ruin his name over—he had struck the man down and, from the noise, taken off his belt and whipped them with it until he'd driven the first-caste men from their home.

Thera didn't know how long she slept after that. It was rare when she could think, and that was when the pain was there. She was weak and useless, and at times she thought about giving up and drifting away, but each time she could hear the real world again, the pain seemed a little less.

Until the day she really woke up . . .

That was when the Voice first made itself known.

That had been a long time ago.

Father had kept her alive. She'd survived, but it had cost him his rank and ruined their family's status. The bolt from heaven had caused her so much trouble in the years since then that at times she wished the damned thing had just killed her and gotten it over with.

As the dream faded, Thera remembered that she wasn't a helpless little girl anymore, but rather a grown woman who'd made her own way in a very unforgiving world, and the second she got her hands on something sharp, someone was going to pay for knocking her out.

Thera woke up slowly, and as she did so, decided she must have been drugged. Head aching and vision fuzzy, she tried to move, but as a result had to fight off the sudden urge to vomit. She tried again, but slowly this time. Once she realized that she was being held down flat on her back with ropes across her chest and neck, it made her glad that she'd managed to keep the contents of her stomach down.

Her hands were tied. Her wrists hurt, skin rubbed raw against the cords. She couldn't lift her head enough to see her feet, but she could tell there were ropes around her ankles as well. When she wiggled her toes she discovered she was barefoot. Her clothing had been replaced with an unfamiliar silk gown. In the process of taking her clothes, she had been deprived of all the many knives she normally kept on her person.

The orange light told her it was nearing sundown. There was a window big enough to climb through—if she could just get free—only then she realized there were metal bars over it. Except this was no prison, it was more like a rich man's bedroom. There were shelves holding carvings of ivory and jade and even a few books. The bed beneath her was far too soft and smelled of perfumes. The walls were painted bright colors, and as her eyes focused she saw that they were covered in murals, though without rubbing the sleep from her eyes she couldn't tell what the art was depicting.

The ropes were so tight she couldn't even inhale fully. She struggled for a while, looking for any give at all, but there was nothing. She was stronger than most women, but this was enough rope to secure a team of horses. Whoever had put her here knew how to tie knots as good as any barge master. Pushing as hard as she could barely even made the heavy bed frame creak, and only seemed to make the knots tighten around her neck. Thera was stuck. After several minutes of futile twisting she let out a frustrated scream. Even that didn't work to her satisfaction because her voice cracked. It was unknown how long they'd kept her unconscious, but it had been long enough that it felt like a small animal had been mummified in her mouth.

"Get Sikasso. The witch is awake again."

Thera realized one of the mural walls was actually a sliding screen. The speaker was on the other side.

"Untie me!"

"Last time we did that you tried to gouge out my eye."

She didn't remember that at all. "Do you still have them both?"

"Despite your best efforts, yes."

"Then untie me and let's try again. This time I'll pluck them out and cram them down your throat. Come on, you fish-eating bastard! Let's go!"

"I swear she gets angrier every time she wakes up," the man muttered.

Thera couldn't remember waking up here before, or trying to thumb someone in the eye, though that did sound like something she would do.

"What do you mean? How long have I been here?" Despite a few other incoherent threats, Thera couldn't get the man on the other side of the screen to keep talking. So she quit struggling and waited for the room to stop spinning. Her head hurt too much to remember how she had gotten here. Her memories were as blurry as her vision. Eventually both of those began to clear.

There had been an ice storm. She remembered Ashok getting into a fight with the entire village, and the ensuing battle against the mountain raiders, the blacking out as the Voice came over her, and returning to herself with a mob of workers gawking at her, then finally wizards dropping from the sky around her in the forms of great black birds.

Oceans...

Now that she could remember who had taken her, Thera knew she was doomed. She'd done her best to keep her odd affliction a secret from those who practiced magic. These wizards knew she was special, and all wizards were curious and greedy. They would figure out the source of her abilities, then they would probably saw the top of her skull off to pry it out.

Vision slowly improving, now she could tell there were other shadows on the opposite sides of those screens, and, from the long shapes, the men were holding weapons, ready to strike the instant she appeared to be a threat. As she looked to the ceiling, she came to understand that the thing hanging directly above her, which she had first taken as some sort of decorative lamp holder, was actually a trap made of sharpened stakes, like you would drop on a tiger in the jungle. If she'd slipped her bonds someone would cut a rope, the trap would fall, and she would be almost instantly pierced and crushed beneath it... And she had thought the ropes had been heavy-handed.

They were scared of her. The wizards might not understand

what she could do, but they were taking no chances. Unfortunately for Thera, she was no real wizard, capable of amazing feats, controlling the elements, or changing her form. She was simply a woman with a curse that had brought her nothing but misery.

After an unknown amount of time, the screen slid open. The man who approached the bed was familiar, dressed in colorful silks, somewhere between young and old, neither attractive nor ugly, having a completely forgettable face, only he looked far worse for wear than when she had met him briefly in Jharlang.

"Where did your arm go?"

The wizard looked down at his empty sleeve, annoyed. "You've asked me that every single time we have spoken."

"I don't remember. Well, what happened to it?"

"Ashok Vadal cut it off with an axe."

"He does that sort of thing." Thera began to laugh at his misfortune.

The wizard backhanded her across the face. It stung.

"I already know you're a foulmouthed, belligerent woman, Thera Vane. You have wasted enough of my time." Despite striking her, his manner remained cold and aloof. "Let us begin again. I am Sikasso of the Lost House."

"I feel like we've done this before."

"Because we have, several times, and each time after we finished speaking I put you back to sleep. If necessary I will continue to do so, over and over, until I am satisfied I have the truth."

She didn't know how long that had been going on. Other than having what felt like the worst hangover of her life, she was fed and clean, but getting a limb removed with an ax was more traumatic than being knocked out and tied to a bed. Sikasso was walking around, but he still appeared weak, with big dark circles beneath those threatening eyes. So he hadn't been recovering for too long.

"How long have I been here? A week? Two?"

"Long enough for you to have told us about the bolt from heaven, and how it is through you the Forgotten has been providing prophecies to the Keeper of Names."

Thera hated the Voice. "I don't know if it's the Forgotten. I don't know what it really is at all."

"Your associates seem to think it is one of the old gods and you are its oracle."

"There's no god living inside me. It's a thing that got inside my head, and every now and then it takes control to spout some gibberish for the fanatics to fawn over."

"What sad manner of prophet doesn't believe in their own prophecies?"

"One who would be rid of it if I could. The damned thing has ruined my life."

"A tragedy," Sikasso mockingly agreed. "So tell me, Thera, if this thing is not a god, how can it predict the future?"

She had no answer for that.

"We have been paying little attention to the rebellion in the south since it has not directly concerned us. False prophets come and go. This one was more successful than most, sending forth prophecies to motivate even the dullest casteless, but it was still of little interest to my people. Only then I saw what you could do with my own eyes, heard the words inside my own mind, and I could sense the power within you. It's different than black steel or demons, and since those are the only two known sources of magic, what you did should be impossible. While you've been here, my people have searched out some of the prophecies you've given. They are surprisingly popular among the non-people. I was shocked to find that some of them have actually come true. How did you do that?"

"I don't know. I'm not a wizard. How do you turn into a giant bird?"

Sikasso had a malicious smile. "The Lost House does not share its secrets so easily."

"However shape shifting works, it must not help grow arms back."

This time when he hit her, it was much harder. Thera saw stars. That wasn't a warning like the first one. That was real anger.

She tried not to let him see her pain. She didn't cry out. Thera had grown up in the warrior caste, where only victims showed weakness. Her eyes sent a message of hate as she tasted her own blood.

"Sensitive topic, I see."

"Mark my words, Thera. I will find a way to repair this disfigurement, and once I do, I will take Ashok Vadal's limbs, one by one, until he is a pathetic, armless, legless, *lump of meat,* begging me for death. And only then will I kick him into the sea."

That wasn't idle talk. It was a vow. However, it told Thera a few things. Sikasso wasn't the kind of man who became loud when angry, but rather focused, which meant he was very dangerous. But more importantly, his reaction told her that Ashok had survived.

Not that she expected the living embodiment of the Law to go out of his way to rescue a criminal like her, but Sikasso didn't know that. "He'll be coming for me, you know. Ashok pledged his life to the rebellion." She still didn't grasp his reasons, because for a man with such a simplistic, straightforward view of the world, Ashok could be remarkably difficult to understand. "And there's no rebellion without the Voice."

"Yes, it has caused quite a bit of trouble, which is why if I can't figure out the source of your power, then I will sell you to the Inquisition to recoup our costs. Perhaps they will have better luck unlocking your secrets."

Thera felt a cold chill run up her spine. Whatever sad end she'd expected before, the Inquisition was worse. "I am more than happy to help you understand it."

"You don't even know who you would be helping."

"You're not the Inquisition."

"We've had this conversation already, Thera. You've repeatedly told me how you just want to walk away and disappear. You are a survivor. You care about no one other than yourself. We have come to this point before. And each time I've laughed at your pathetic bargaining and used my magic instead. Yet, I haven't been able to break through. I can't understand what is in *there*." Sikasso rudely stabbed one finger against her temple and pushed hard. Thera had to wince away.

"This mysterious power is tantalizingly close, but its true nature vexes me. If I thought dissecting you would give me its secrets, you would already be in pieces. Keeping you in a magical coma and combing through your memories doesn't seem to work either. I've already burned through several valuable demon pieces, and even a precious flake of black steel. Whatever is inside you is capable of defending itself. When I push, it pushes back."

"I'm not fond of it either. Why do you want it so badly?"

Sikasso seemed to think it over for a moment, mulling if it was worth giving her the truth, but it was hard to tell if that was just an act to make him seem more relatable. But he probably figured if he was going to put her back to sleep anyway, it wasn't like she would remember this conversation.

"A few generations ago, my people were nearly exterminated as punishment for delving into illegal magic. The only reason we survived at all was because our knowledge was valuable to a few important men. For a hundred years we've lived in the shadows of the Law. They know we exist, but pretend we don't. We live by their whim, and in exchange we occasionally serve as their secret killers. They pay us in magic, and the circle continues. We need them, and they need us, but oh...to break that cycle. A new source of magic could be the key. We want the same thing you want, Thera, the same thing your pathetic fish-eater rebellion wants. We merely want to be left alone."

"I'd give you the damned thing if I could."

"You've said that enough times I've begun to believe you. We've been treating you as if we've captured a mighty demon, but I've yet to see any sign that your mysterious gift can be used as a weapon. Repeatedly, you have tried to offer your cooperation for your freedom. So today, we will try this new approach."

Thera would have nodded if she could. As far as she could remember, she wasn't enjoying the old approach at all.

"If you are telling me the truth, and you have no desire to possess your odd magic. Perhaps together we can come to understand the source, so we can free you of it. Rather than being our prisoner, you shall be our guest."

Provided the process of taking the Voice away didn't kill her, being rid of the damned thing would be wonderful...But Thera simply said, "That sounds reasonable."

"Guests behave themselves...Do you agree?"

"It would be impolite to disrespect such hospitality."

Sikasso reached into the sash around his waist and retrieved a small piece of what appeared to be demon bone. All of the impossibly perfect knots simultaneously loosened by themselves. The heavy ropes slid off the bed. The odd fog that had been clouding her mind seemed to lift, and now the only pain she was feeling was from the back of Sikasso's remaining hand.

No longer nauseous, Thera sat up quickly. The shadows behind the screens tensed. A sword was raised, ready to cut the rope and drop the tiger trap on her. She didn't know what they expected her to do, unarmed, in a flimsy nightgown, but to show that she was no threat, rather than leap off the bed to try something stupid, she made a show of slowly rubbing the feeling back into her abraded wrists.

"Be warned, Thera Vane, I am not a tolerant host. Do not attempt to escape. Even if you could, we are in the wilderness far from civilization, beyond the reach of the Law. There is nowhere to go. Disobedience will be met with pain. Do you understand?"

"I do," Thera answered, already contemplating how best to murder a one-armed wizard.

"Then the House of Assassins welcomes you."

Chapter 2

Word of his rebellion must be spreading, because their arrival had drawn a curious crowd. Most of the residents of the tiny mountain village seemed welcoming toward the Sons of the Black Sword, except for the one angry man blocking their path, shouting threats, and swinging around by the hair a severed human head.

Ashok Vadal signaled for the column to halt. "What's that madman carrying on about?"

The young Somsak warrior who had been serving as their advance scout approached. "A warrior demands to fight you."

"Another?" He was getting tired of having to duel every ambitious member of the warrior caste they met along their way. At this rate it would take all winter to reach Neeramphorn. "That head looks fresh. Did it belong to anyone important?"

"I didn't get close enough to ask."

A multitude of non-people had watched them with wide eyes in their gaunt, half-starved faces as the Sons had ridden in. All religion was illegal, but the village had turned out to see their gods' supposed champion anyway. Because casteless could be killed with impunity by their betters, they were staying clustered around their pathetic shacks, far from the angry warrior, who had planted himself, defiant, in the middle of the road.

This road led to the nearest pass which would take them to

Neeramphorn and hopefully, their missing prophet. "I do not have time for this."

"I doubt he'll step aside. He's ranting like a lunatic." And that damning assessment came from a bloodthirsty mountain raider with a face covered in tattoos commemorating each of his many battles and murders. It said a great deal about one's state of mind to be labeled irrational by a Somsak.

"Return to your brothers, tell them to remain wary, but I will tolerate no repeat of yesterday's violence against the casteless."

"They put their grubby fingers on our horses. The fish-eaters are lucky all they got was a beating."

"Do as I say."

These particular Somsak were here because they had been secret believers in the Forgotten, and Ashok was the Forgotten's champion. Since he had killed scores of their brothers to prove it, the normally combative mountain folk never questioned his authority. "As you wish, General."

Ashok didn't like that title, a relic from the Age of Kings. *General.* It struck him of brazen criminality, boastful and arrogant. It hadn't been bestowed upon him by proper authorities, but rather by an illegal prophecy. However, he was oath bound to follow the edicts of the prophet, so he had no choice but to accept the archaic rank.

The scout began riding away, but thought better of it and hoisted his crossbow. "Want that I should stick him from here, and save you the trouble?"

"No." The Law declared any member of the warrior caste to be of higher station than he was, and thus deserving of his respect. "I will deal with the warrior."

He surveyed the village. It was mostly rough shacks fit only for casteless. Ashok saw no sign of warrior caste insignia anywhere, which was not surprising considering this place was of little strategic value and there was nothing worth defending here. The tiny settlement was too pathetic to be the home of even the lowest of the first caste. There were a few humble homes which would belong to low-status members of the worker caste, but no sign of the occupants. They must have been smart enough to flee into the woods when a large group of armed criminals were spotted riding in. All that remained in the village were non-people, their livestock, and the lone madman.

It was a sad little place, stinking of dung and smoke, but at least the casteless here had the good sense to hold back, not run up and mob them with religious fervor like had happened in the last village. The Somsak had reacted rather instinctively and viciously to that.

His second-in-command stopped his horse beside Ashok's. "You've got another challenger, I see."

"As long as people believe I still have the sword, the brave and the desperate will keep trying to claim it from me."

"I'm passingly familiar with the concept." Risaldar Jagdish chuckled at his own misfortune. "If I'd never gone to duel you, I wouldn't have ended up chasing wizards across half of Lok just to restore my name."

They'd been opponents once. Great House Vadal had needed to hold someone responsible for failing to stop the unstoppable, so noble Jagdish had received the blame. As a result, a desperate but honorable man had joined a very dishonorable group. Ashok was glad to have the assistance of a warrior of such integrity at his side, but it saddened him as well, because he could imagine no good end for the outcasts who had joined the Sons of the Black Sword.

"I can tell by that look on your face what you're thinking. Ashok Vadal may not be able to feel fear, but he bears guilt enough for ten. Don't worry about it." Jagdish grinned. "I've got a plan. When I get done with these wizards, Great House Vadal will welcome me home with a parade."

Ashok was unsure how much of that was bluster and how much was delusion. "I will trust your judgment."

They were joined by the *spiritual* and final leader of their tiny band. "We're stopping? Excellent. This settlement is yet another opportunity to teach of the Forgotten's return."

"You'll want to make it quick, priest," Jagdish said. "There's only one fool brave enough to challenge Ashok this time, so it won't be much of a delay."

"Eh, I'll take what I can get. More important than spreading the word is the opportunity to get off this damnable bony beast!" Unlike Jagdish—who was perfectly comfortable in the saddle—Keta was a terrible horseman, so the Keeper of Names practically fell off his mount with a pained groan as soon as it was holding still. Keta's horse swung its head and tried to bite him, but the priest of the Forgotten grabbed its ear and twisted hard to show it who was boss. "They're as surly as the Somsak who breed them."

The mad warrior hadn't moved from the road, but was still shouting something unintelligible, gesturing wildly, and brandishing his trophy. From this distance, his armor seemed well maintained, and he wore the white diamond symbol of Great House Kharsawan on his chest.

A multitude had died by Ashok's hand over the years, but those had been different than his more recent killings. Their deaths had happened because the Law required it. Deprived of that justification, Ashok was far less comfortable taking lives than he had been before. He would have gone around, but it was twenty miles to the next pass into Kharsawan territory, and that was on an actual trade road which meant it would have a real border checkpoint and soldiers posted. Hardly anyone bothered with this narrow, rocky goat trail. Additionally, this time of year, if they were unlucky enough to catch a big storm, the passes could be closed off entirely.

Assuming she'd not already been killed by the wizards who had captured her, Thera could afford no more delays.

"I'll take care of this so we can be on our way. Risaldar Jagdish"—it seemed a bit pretentious to use the rank for a leader of fifty warriors for their group of just over a dozen criminals, but it was Jagdish's legal rank—"see to resupply. And keep the Somsak on a short chain. They can't just loot whatever they feel like. We have no standing to requisition anything, so Keta will pay these people a fair sum in trade. I believe that is how the lower castes do it."

"It is, but the rebellion only sent me with so much money!" Keta protested. "I'll simply explain to them that we're servants of the Forgotten on an important journey. I'm sure the true believers will be moved upon to aid us."

"I'd keep those banknotes handy then," Jagdish muttered, having no patience for superstitious foolishness or faith in the generosity of hungry casteless. It was difficult for proud whole men to *ask* their inferiors for things they would normally just take, but Ashok knew Jagdish would follow his orders.

Ashok dismounted, passed his horse's reigns to Jagdish, and began walking toward the angry warrior. The non-people began to speak to each other in hushed tones as he passed by. Though he was dressed in a battered old coat taken off a dead miner in Jharlang, without insignia of station or house, everywhere he went now the casteless seemed to know who he was. Their whispers were a combination of awe, fear, and perhaps...hope? He called upon the Heart of the Mountain to temporarily sharpen his hearing. Faint sounds became sharp. They were repeating his casteless name, over and over, *Fall. Fall. Fall.* Not only did they know his identity, their conversations were about rumors of casteless quarters rising up, the slaughter of whole men, and the alien concept of *freedom*.

Rumor traveled fast among the casteless.

"Fight me, Ashok Vadal! Fight me so that I may claim the black sword!"

Ashok kept walking toward the warrior, opening his long coat as he did so in order to reach the inferior steel sword that had taken Angruvadal's place by his side. Whenever he thought of the loss of his ancestor blade, it filled him with anger.

"I, Fullan Apsorn dar Kharsawan, hero of Banjali, who drove the Thao from the walls of Neeramphorn, winner of five duels, champion of—"

"Yes, yes, you're most impressive. Save your breath," he shouted back. The polite thing to do would be to let the challenger go through his list of victories and accomplishments, but Ashok had a rebel prophet to rescue.

Fullan seemed a bit taken back, as if he'd been practicing his speech for this moment, but hadn't anticipated that particular response. His voice was hoarse from all the earlier shouting. "As a bearer you are obligated to duel me!"

"You are wasting your time and, more than likely, your life." Ashok continued to crunch along the road. There was a thin dusting of powdery snow over the gravel. It was a cold day, but to a fiery tempered warrior, it was never too cold for a fight. "Angruvadal is no more."

At last they were close enough, and the warrior lowered his voice to a more conversational, but still aggressive tone. Perhaps he wasn't so insane after all. "I don't understand. What do you mean?"

"It is gone. The sword has broken, shattered on the demon-possessed husk that was once Nadan Somsak in the town of Jharlang a week ago. I have no ancestor blade for you to claim."

"No! You're spinning lies, trying to save your miserable life. Your casteless trickery cannot save you from my wrath."

Now that they were close, Ashok was better able to assess his opponent. With long hair gone gray, his face darkened by the sun and crossed with many scars, Fullan was far past his prime. Normally the men who wished to fight Ashok were young, searching for glory, and stupid enough to think they had a chance. The elders were usually wise enough to know better, but this one wore an air of desperation as heavy as his armor. Upon his shoulder was painted the rank of risaldar, a captain of fifty, same as the much younger Jagdish. A rank of medium accomplishment, odd for one so proud, and unimpressive for a warrior of his age.

This was clearly a man at the end of his obligation to his house. Fullan should be spending his remaining years in peace, with his family, passing on his knowledge to another generation. It would be a shame to kill him. Then Ashok noticed the headless corpse lying in a nearby ditch. That one was dressed in the chain and plate armor of a Kharsawan soldier as well.

Apparently Fullan had already won one duel today.

"I am guilty of many terrible things, but lying is not among them. I will show you." Stopping twenty feet away, Ashok slowly reached for his sword. Fullan instinctively stepped back—because everyone in Lok had heard legends about the destructive power of an ancestor blade—but he didn't flee. Ashok slowly drew the Thao broadsword free, then held it up so the plain steel could catch the morning sun. "All I have is this ordinary thing. If this were Angruvadal it would devour the light and sear your eyes."

"So I've heard." Fullan snarled. "You're hiding it somewhere. You've got to be."

"I wish it were so, but Angruvadal is gone." It pained Ashok to say those words, still grieving for his oldest friend.

Fullan must have believed him, because as the truth sunk in, his knees began to wobble. "No. I need that sword. I can't return home without it."

"You have no choice."

Tears formed in the old warrior's eyes. He lifted the severed head by the hair. It slowly spun around until Fullan was looking at the dead man's face. The dead man stared back at him, judging. "Oh, what have I done?"

"Was he a friend?"

"One of my students," Fullan stammered. "Word reached our barracks you might be headed toward this pass, but we got orders from the Inquisition not to intervene. Those masked bastards be damned, I snuck out in the middle of the night to come here to confront you. Only Yash had the same idea, and he'd gotten here first. He was always an ambitious lad. But only one of us could take the sword from you. He didn't understand that I needed it more. I've nothing left to give. No honor left to claim. They're retiring me, putting me out. An old warrior is good for nothing but teaching children. This was my last chance! Yash was still young, with plenty of opportunities to earn his own glory still. Why wouldn't he listen? Why wouldn't he respect his place? I'm senior, the right was mine. Mine!"

This wasn't the first time desperation had moved a man to murder, and it wouldn't be the last. "I am sorry." And Ashok truly was.

"We fought to see who should have the right to challenge you. My wife died a long time ago, and they didn't bother to arrange another for me. I've no heirs. No one will remember my name. I gave my life to my house. I couldn't be usurped by a pup. I . . . I . . ." It was unclear if the warrior's compulsion to explain himself was for Ashok or the dead man. Either way, Fullan's naïve dreams of becoming a bearer had been destroyed. As he realized that he'd thrown away his honor for nothing, his fingers unclenched, and the head fell in the snow with a *thump*. Fullan reflexively wiped his hand on his sash. That hand had begun to shake. "What have I done?" Then he let out a wail of frustration and regret. Spittle flew from his lips as he shouted, *"What have I done?"*

"You made a terrible mistake which will haunt you the rest of your life. The only question now is how long that life will be. I have nothing you want. Step aside and go in peace. Or continue this challenge, and I will do what is required of me."

It took Fullan a few long moments to make his decision, the entire time staring at the head of the young warrior lying face down in the snow.

"Do not make me fight you, Fullan Kharsawan. I take no joy from it."

The old man didn't look up. "They say Ashok Vadal has killed a thousand men in battle."

"The number is higher now."

Fullan stared at his hands. "Look at me. I'm shaking like a leaf. I'm no coward. But if you've killed so many, then I suppose it's not shameful to be afraid."

Ashok's own ability to feel fear had been magically torn from him long ago. "I wouldn't know."

"If I can't return as the new bearer of an ancestor blade, then I'll at least return as the warrior who slew the foulest criminal in all the land." Fullan drew his sword.

Ashok was disappointed, but not surprised. "So be it."

He was casteless, not even a real person, outside the Law and certainly deserving no respect from a whole man, but Fullan gave him an official legal challenge anyway. "Offense has been taken."

"Offense has been given," Ashok gave a small bow as he officially accepted the duel.

With a roar, Fullan came at him, swinging wildly. The sword flashed back and forth, driven with fury more than skill. Ashok would never know if emotions had overcome his senses, or if this was simply the old warrior committing suicide... He simply reacted.

Sidestepping the attack, Ashok countered. With the turn of his wrist, he jabbed the point of his blade into Fullan's neck, just below the ear. He calmly stepped back to avoid the flailing which would result. Even deprived of the sword that could rout armies, Ashok was still one of the greatest combatants in the world. His duels seldom lasted very long.

Artery severed, the blood came rushing out. It took a few pumping heartbeats for Fullan to realize he'd been struck a fatal blow. The warrior crushed one hand to his neck, blood leaking between his fingers, and managed two halting steps before dropping his sword.

"Even if Angruvadal had not shattered, it wouldn't have found you worthy. You should never have come here."

Staring at Ashok, wide-eyed, Fullan dropped to his knees.

"I did not want this." Then Ashok turned and walked away, leaving the old warrior to die alone in the road.

The poor villagers had watched the duel from a distance. To them the warrior caste were a terrifying force, separate and unstoppable, yet Ashok had just eliminated one of them with ease. He could hear their whispers. *The stories are true. The Forgotten has returned. The gods have sent Fall to free us and terrible is his wrath. Fall. Fall. Fall.*

And he silently cursed Keta and his ilk for filling their stupid casteless heads with rebellious lies that would only get them
killed. Freedom was a myth. There was Law and consequences.
That was all.

It began to snow.

Jagdish met him on the way back and passed over a rag.
Ashok used it to clean the blood from his new sword. Unlike
the old one, this one could rust.

"That seemed to go well."

"It was a waste, like all the others." At times it seemed like
he was the only man in Lok who had been content to stay in
the place the Law had mandated for him, so it was ironic that
he was the only one denied that comfort.

"You could have told him the Sons of the Black Sword are
recruiting."

"He'd already made enough bad decisions for one day... Are
we ready to leave yet?"

"Keta is bartering for feed and rations now, but he got distracted telling stories of super warriors riding flaming ships made
of black steel out of the sky to smite demons because his gods
love us so very much."

Ashok snorted. "Have him make it quick. The Kharsawan
man spoke of something troubling. The Inquisition might know
we are here."

Jagdish flinched. "Oceans."

"It may be nothing. It may be something." Having worked
with Inquisitors in the past, he knew they could be very clever.
It was possible that they knew exactly where the Sons were, or
they could have been saying the same thing at every barracks near
every pass in the region just to check for potential collaborators.

"What'll we do?"

Individual Inquisitors weren't so dangerous—unless it was one
of their elite witch hunters—and neither could be compared to a
Protector, but any Inquisitor had the authority to draft as many
warriors as needed to fulfill their mission. "We will avoid them
if possible. If we cannot, my mission doesn't change. I must find
and protect the prophet, no matter what."

"I'll go tell Keta to wrap up his sermon. I'm in no hurry to
end up beneath the torturer's knives."

Ashok took one last look at the bodies. Fullan Kharsawan

had died on his knees and stayed balanced there, probably held up by the rigidity of his armor. Snowflakes were collecting on his shoulder plates. He knew what the warriors of Kharsawan would say. There was no shame in dying while fighting Ashok the Black Heart. That was a hero's death. But greedily murdering one of your students to prevent him from taking a chance for glory? Fullan's name would be forever worth salt water, his accomplishments forgotten.

"One last thing, Jagdish. Have Keta tell the villagers that when more warriors arrive to collect their dead, to say that I'm responsible for both deaths."

Jagdish stopped. He knew all too well what it meant for a warrior to lose his good name. "You would do that for this man?"

Ashok had meant it when he had said he was no liar. "It's true enough. In a way, my very existence killed them both."

He had no doubt there would be many more before this was through.

Chapter 3

The prisoner woke up gasping and choking. "Am I still alive?"

"Don't worry, old friend," Grand Inquisitor Omand said. "Not for much longer."

Khangani Vokkan was of the first caste and a high-ranking member of one of the Capitol's oldest Orders, but social status meant nothing once beaten, starved, tortured, and chained naked atop the Inquisitor's Dome. He had poured a cup of water down Khangani's mouth to wake him and to moisten his tongue enough to have this conversation. Rivulets were running down this filthy face, cutting tracks through the dirt and dried blood. Omand knew from long experience that if Khangani had realized that was the last drink he would ever have, he would have savored it more.

"I'm blind. Have you cut out my eyes?"

"Of course not. My men are not clumsy butchers. They only do what is necessary to ensure our subjects are telling the truth. You were telling them the truth, weren't you?"

Khangani wheezed, as he tried to breathe with broken ribs and through missing teeth. "Yes."

They had grown up together in distant Vokkan, been obligated to the Capitol at the same time, Omand to the Inquisition and Khangani to the Historians; one learned from trinkets collected from dusty tombs while the other learned from knives and confessing screams, yet they had remained cordial over the years. Omand did not really have friends, merely associates or contacts with varying degrees of usefulness. Khangani's usefulness had run out, which brought them here this morning.

"You still have eyes. It's just the swelling and dried blood, not to mention it's very bright here beneath the sun today, and we've kept you in a dark cell for a very long time." The fortress of the Inquisition was high on the slopes of Mount Metoro, the peak overlooking the entire sprawling magnificence of the Capitol. "Should you regain your sight before the buzzards pick the flesh from your face, it is a fine view from up here."

Khangani knew what that meant. "We're upon the dome." It was the dreaded final destination of the condemned. He pulled against his chains. They were so heavy, and he was so weak now, that they barely rattled. "Kill me, please, Omand."

"You are a confessed traitor. The Law declares the sun and desert wind will kill you... eventually."

The two of them were alone except for the dead. There were a dozen other corpses chained atop the dome in various states of decomposition. That smell, and the others like it—a red hot branding iron pressed against blood and bone, or burning hair, or bowels loosed by fear—was why Omand had begun smoking a pipe as a young man. The hot tobacco smoke provided a distraction from the unpleasant odors of an Inquisitor's duties.

Now, as the leader of the entire Order, he was above such petty dirty work, but he still retained the smoking habit.

"Omand, I beg you. Have mercy, please."

"You were a Historian. You must know how the tradition of the Inquisitor's Dome came about. Long ago, in the mad times before religion was banned, there was one small sect that neither buried nor burned their dead. They believed fire and earth should never be polluted with death—an absurd concept to a civilized Law-abiding man—yet this did force them to be creative. So when one of them passed away, they left their bodies atop a tower for the birds. Once they were picked clean and bleached white, the bones were simply swept into a central hole in the tower, forming a great ossuary."

Even beaten and broken, Khangani couldn't help but be the historian. "It was called the Tower of Silence, and it was a sacred place of respect—"

Omand had to laugh at the concept of *sacred*.

"—not this fiendish method of execution!"

"I believe the first Inquisitors adopted the tradition due to its public nature, because every now and then when the weather is just right, the proud residents of the Capitol will get just a hint of death on the wind. It serves as a reminder that the ever vigilant servants of the Law are watching, prepared to deliver punishment against all transgressors... Not to mention it's exceedingly efficient. You can't see it right now, but there's a hole only a few feet away. Eventually your remains will be hurled down that shaft to eternally join with the thousands of traitors who came before you."

"You're a demon!"

"Spare me. I've dealt with real demons. They are not subtle creatures. Now the question is how long will you last? If we were here in the summer the heat would already be unbearable, but even winter in the desert is hot. This time of year most will linger for several days, though I've seen proud warriors last nearly a week. Their skin is charred black by then. Whenever they move it cracks, but with no moisture their blood is too thick to seep out. It's like their veins are filled with scabs." Omand looked up at the circling carrion birds. He'd always thought that the token of his office should have been a vulture instead of the golden raven he wore around his neck. "Though sometimes the birds get a little eager and start eating your extremities before you expire. That speeds up the process, but in a most unpleasant way."

Khangani began to weep. That was a terrible mistake. He would soon regret wasting water.

Omand wiped the sweat from his brow with the sleeve of his robe. He wasn't wearing his Inquisitor's mask today, because there was no need to hide his face here. His assistant Taraba had thoughtfully left a stool for Omand to sit on, so he got comfortable, and began preparing his pipe with a pouch of fine tobacco he had brought back from his recent journey to Great House Vadal. He had forgotten just how much he disliked the smell atop the dome. The death stink would linger in his clothing all day.

"I suppose it doesn't have to be this way. We did play as children together... I can't believe that was nearly forty years ago. Can you?" Omand struck a match and lit his pipe, savoring the cleansing smoke. He got it started with a few puffs. *Much better.* "The Law is clear, but we're alone and I have a sharp knife. No one would ever know I sped you on your way. Despite what the other Orders say about us, Inquisitors don't enjoy being cruel. It's simply our obligation."

"You were always a monster, Omand. They whispered about some of the things you did as a child back home, about the tortured pets, and the missing servants. The Inquisition merely gave you an excuse to be what you really are."

"Every man has his place." Omand blew out a cloud of smoke. This was the best part, after the subject had been so broken they were no longer wasting his time with protestations of innocence, and once they accepted, even welcomed death, they could become rather pliable. "Answer a few of my questions and I will gladly end this."

"Anything. I'm tired of suffering."

The Grand Inquisitor smirked. This weakling knew nothing of suffering. It was a sad commentary upon the character of his caste that so many of the ruling class broke so easily. Omand glanced around to make sure they weren't being spied upon. Then he called upon a small fragment of black steel tied to a bracelet around his wrist to make sure no one was listening through magical means. Air whistled as a tiny portion of the ancient material was consumed. The world seemed to shake around him. The circling birds screeched and climbed away. Now he was certain they were truly alone.

"When you became aware of a plot within the Capitol to overthrow the judges and install a king in their place, who else did you tell?"

"I already told your torturers every name! That's all of them I know."

Omand had thought so. His men were extremely thorough. They'd been taught by the best. "These conspirators, they are hoping the chaos caused by the casteless rebellion in the south, and the rampage of the murderer Ashok Vadal and his ancestor blade, will make the Capitol look weak and ineffectual to the houses."

"I know nothing of that!"

"Of course not. Do you know of their plot to bring about the extermination of all the casteless?"

"They spoke of it with pride. The conspirators want all the non-people killed. In every land, in every house, slaughtered to the last."

"Do you know why?"

"I ... I don't. To cause a crisis in the Capitol somehow."

Of course Khangani didn't know, because the fool who had

approached him about joining their conspiracy hadn't really understood either. The Grand Inquisitor had told very few people about that part of his plan. Such sloppiness also demonstrated that Omand had been correct in insulating himself from his lower ranking co-conspirators. Even when someone did slip, the crime was simply reported back to the very Order that he controlled. Omand knew more about the crimes being committed than those he was torturing confessions from, because he was the one who'd organized them to begin with.

"Casteless uprisings happen periodically, but they inevitably fail. However, if one were to succeed, other non-people would be inspired to act. It would spread like wild fire to every house. Chaos would engulf Lok. Many of the great houses would be damaged from within. The others would take advantage of their weakness and attack. War would consume the continent. The Law itself would be threatened, as it only stands as long as the houses respect the Capitol. A committee of disharmonious voices would be insufficient to bring us back from this brink. A strong leader would be necessary to restore order, one powerful vision to unite us, and only he could institute the reforms to keep such turmoil from ever happening again. The conspiracy is prepared to offer such a man."

"They didn't tell me that much. I swear."

When you play the game, there are secrets within secrets, and lies on top of lies. Even the other members of Omand's dark councils knew little of what would come next. They thought ordering the extermination of the casteless was merely a distraction to exacerbate the rebellion. "Don't think as a politician, Khangani. Think as a Historian. Your Order is remarkably tight lipped. You were the first among you to accept an invitation into this conspiracy, a fact which should make you deeply ashamed. Think of the forbidden texts and the old sealed histories from the Age of Kings. Why would anyone want to exterminate all the casteless?"

"Historically? They're the descendants of the original first caste, the supposed Sons of Ramrowan, the Forgotten's warrior, and the former priest caste who served them."

"Indeed. Your Order was created to preserve history, and mine was created to protect us from the bad parts. Now this is the most important question of all. Who among the Historians is the caretaker of Asura's Mirror?"

Even after all the torture, Khangani appeared stunned at that question. "How do you know of that? My people never speak about the relics."

"I know everything. I know this conspiracy asked you the same question, but despite your predilection for treachery, you still honored this particular vow and told them nothing. You were fine with rebellion, but perhaps you felt giving up the ancient secrets of your Order went too far? Regardless, the criminals asked so the Inquisition must know. Your next few words will determine whether you die quick and painless, or with a buzzard's beak scissoring through your guts, so I would encourage you to answer truthfully."

Much like iron held in a fire, even the strictest vows of secrecy became malleable after a great deal of torture. "Ever since I was first obligated, studying that era was frowned upon. Only volunteers are assigned to safeguard relics. It's an insular section. Going down that path meant an end to your advancement in our Order, so that wasn't an area I paid much attention to."

"Who among you did?"

"Vikram Akershan is in charge of that section, but surely he has nothing to do with the conspirators. He has total dedication to his obligation."

"Anyone else?"

"Outside of Historians, Lord Protector Ratul used to inquire about the safety of the relics often, only he disappeared years ago. That device is a reminder of the evil times, when fools thought they were communicating directly with the false gods. But no one ever thinks about those old myths anymore."

"Some of us still do." And then Omand leaned over and sliced Khangani's throat wide open with his knife.

As his prisoner bled out, Omand finished his pipe and enjoyed the view. It was the only break he would allow himself that day, because the Grand Inquisitor was a very busy man.

From up here the Capitol truly was a marvel to behold. The greatest city in the remaining world, over half a million lives existing in a place so harsh nothing should live at all, as far from the corrupted ocean as possible. There were thousands of men equal to or of higher station than Khangani down there, all playing the great game. It was supposed to be the ruling class, but most of the first caste were gray, featureless bureaucrats, signing their forgettable names onto mandatory forms which would never be read by anyone, passing time until their inevitable demise, unmissed and unremembered, replaced with another unremarkable man, but among them were a few with vision. They were the real rulers, the ones who made things happen. Some of those were with Omand, others against him, most didn't even know they were involved yet. Momentous events had been set in motion, so they would all know soon enough.

It was getting uncomfortably hot, and that was only going to make the smell worse. It was time to get back to work. Omand felt the aches and pains as he got off the stool. You did not earn the reputation as the most successful witch hunter in the history of Lok without sustaining a great number of injuries in the process. He was paying for them now. Hopefully soon, if everything went according to plan, troubles of the flesh would no longer be an issue.

Inquisitor Taraba met him in the stairwell. He was a hard-working, meticulous young man, and just ambitious enough to make a good assistant. "You appear in a good mood, sir. I'm assuming the interrogation went well."

Taraba meant nothing of it, but his being able to read Omand's facial expression reminded the Grand Inquisitor that he needed to put his mask back on before dealing with any other subordinates. "Why wouldn't it have?"

"Forgive me. I simply meant that I knew the two of you had grown up together. Those of us lacking your experience and dedication might find such an interrogation difficult."

Omand waved one hand dismissively. "It was a very large house. Now I want to know everything there is about a Historian named Vikram Akershan, and this must be gathered with the utmost discretion."

Taraba knew better than to ask why. "I will see to it personally."

Good. Taraba was an excellent Inquisitor and Omand's right hand. There was no crowd he couldn't vanish into, secret he couldn't find, or back he couldn't stab. He was also one of the chosen few privy to *most* of Omand's grand vision. Taraba was very good at his obligation, but he would never be as good as Omand. He had the skills, but lacked the *detachment*. Taraba saw people. Omand saw things. Really, everyone might as well be casteless as far as Omand cared.

They began walking down the curving stairwell. It was much cooler in the shade.

"Tell me, Taraba, is there word from our agents in the east?"

"Nothing from Sikasso yet, which is odd."

The Lost House were a malicious, secretive lot. He fully expected them to betray him as soon as it was expedient, but he'd thought they would do so in a self-serving—thus predictable—way. "I assume that rather than following and observing Ashok Vadal as ordered, they simply decided to murder him, steal his ancestor blade, lie to me that he was still alive, and then go about committing atrocities in his name so that I will continue paying them."

"It sounds like they may have tried in a small Thao mining village called Jharlang. Only it resulted in a few dead wizards and a hundred dead Somsak raiders."

Omand nodded. "So Sikasso made some new friends, yet Ashok the Black Heart lived up to his fearsome reputation one more time. Good. We will see to it by the time the rumors reach the Capitol it will have grown to a thousand dead warriors and Ashok will have slaughtered the whole village and consumed their flesh in a cannibal frenzy. I need every judge terrified that Ashok will inspire the casteless in their homelands to rise up."

"Inquisitors have been dispatched to Jharlang to investigate, and we're watching every route through the region to pick up Ashok's trail. He either has forged traveling papers or is hiding like a bandit."

"Excellent." He needed to keep an eye on their symbol of rebellion. The Inquisitors had been ordered to observe, but not hinder. "What else?" Taraba was not wearing his mask either, probably out of respect to his superior, so Omand could tell that the young man was nervous to bring up the next part. "Spit it out."

"There are rumors that Angruvadal may have shattered."

"Ah..." If true, that was unfortunate. With that sword, Ashok could threaten armies. Without it, he wasn't nearly the menace. He had ordered someone possessing one of the most dangerous magical devices in existence to work for a religious lunatic. Omand had been hoping for so much more destruction.

"This is not yet confirmed."

"I knew it was a risk to put Ashok onto such a path. He was remade into a living embodiment of the Law, and thus perfectly obedient, but his ancient sword was not. Black steel blades are aware and their motives inscrutable. They've broken before when they didn't approve of how they were being wielded. Being used by a criminal must have been too dishonorable for Angruvadal to bear and it destroyed itself."

Ancestor Blades were one of the most precious things in the world. To lose one was a great tragedy. Omand probably should have felt something over the loss of such a valuable resource, sadness, or at least guilt, but mostly he wondered how much this complication would upset his current plans.

"If we were to leak this information in the Chamber of Argument, the loss of their sword would ruin the reputation of Great House Vadal," Taraba suggested.

"A bold move." Omand had already thought of that. Vadal was one of the strongest houses, militarily and economically, and one of the few powers which could thwart him. "But no, we will proceed with the plan. The important thing is for the great houses, and more importantly the non-people, to believe as long as possible that there is still an ancestor blade outside the Law. That will make the first afraid and their casteless bold. There are other ways to manipulate Harta Vadal to our side."

"When Lord Protector Devedas and his men find Ashok, they'll return to the Capitol, bragging, probably with his head held high on a spear. Then everyone will know the truth."

"Ah, Devedas." The man who would be king had recently gone from adversary to ally in the great game. Yet his hunt for Ashok was personal, and there would be no swaying a man so motivated by pride. "Leave him to me. We have come to an arrangement... And if he doesn't honor it, there are other ways to apply leverage."

"Speaking of which, Radamantha Nems dar Harban has not been fulfilling her obligation at the library."

So Devedas must have realized that having an object of affection was a liability and moved her someplace safer. Love was a weakness in the great game—whether it was for a person or an ideal, devotion was just another weakness that could be leveraged against you by the more morally flexible opponents. A clever move. Devedas was learning.

"How long since we've had eyes on her?"

"We have men watching their family estate, but she hasn't been seen since the Protectors left the city."

"Ah, that was my mistake then. I told Devedas I was willing to kill his woman. My brashness deprived us of a valuable bargaining chip. I should not have been so blunt in my threats."

Unlike most Protectors, who were rather direct in the application of force, Devedas had some political cunning. He would make a fine puppet king under Omand's guidance, and a much better friend than an enemy...within limits of course, because if Devedas ever found out that Ashok's rebellion was Omand's creation, the Lord Protector would most certainly try to kill the Grand Inquisitor. Such a development would be most unfortunate because the Capitol couldn't have the heads of its various Orders haphazardly murdering each other.

"I'd hope our potential future queen is refraining from any further meddling in our affairs, but if she does, I saw that there are several open spaces on the dome...No, we must keep it discreet. Put a bounty out for her safe retrieval. We'll place her in our custody somewhere nice, and return her after the coup, ensuring that Devedas keeps his bargain. However, I still must decide what to do about the Protectors until then."

With Angruvadal, Ashok could survive nearly anything. Without his ancestor blade, he wouldn't have a chance against his vengeful former brothers. He had brought great shame upon their entire Order and the Protectors were a tenacious lot. The rogue would be hunted down, the stain scrubbed from their honor, and then they would tell the whole world he was no more. If Omand was to get the most out of the Black Heart's fearful reputation, he needed to slow down his pursuers.

"I think that if something were to happen closer to home, something which would even come to the attention of the judges themselves, it will draw the Protector Order's wrath in the wrong direction and buy our sword-breaking troublemaker a bit more time." They had run out of stairs. This floor of the fortress should only be populated by loyalists, but Omand would take no chances, so he leaned in and whispered to his subordinate, "Send word to Javed that it is time to complete his mission."

He gave the order as casually as if he were telling his chef what to prepare for lunch.

Taraba's eyes widened, but then he responded with a grim nod. "It will be done, Grand Inquisitor." The young man turned and walked away, pulling his mask on as he went, probably because he was having a hard time keeping the emotions from his face. Not everyone could be as calm and casual about ordering the massacre of hundreds of innocents as Omand Vokkan.

Chapter 4

For the last six months, every single morning, Inquisition Witch
Hunter Javed would sit on a rock, high above the main trade road
south of the Capitol, eating his breakfast and watching.

His mask—the leering, fanged face of the Law—had been left
behind when he had been given this assignment, but he didn't
need a mask to hide who he really was, for Javed was a man
of many faces. Everyone in Shabdkosh believed he was merely
another merchant of Great House Zarger, with just enough status
to avoid the shakedowns of jealous warriors, but not important
enough to be of interest to the local arbiters and their political
machinations. So no one paid attention to Javed as he plotted
murder and counted wagons.

Every day he watched for a specific trading company. When
he saw them, he counted the wagons until he got to the fifth one.
That was the wagon which would be carrying his orders from
the Inquisitor's Dome. Merchant caravans always flew banners
advertising their wares. He didn't care about the words, just the
colors. Usually there was nothing new, just green, yellow, yellow. Sometimes it was blue, red, blue, which meant he needed
to walk up the road a bit to check for a coded note left beneath
a specific rock.

This was a common method of passing messages among the

secretive witch hunters. It made him idly wonder what they'd ever do with an obligation who was color blind? That could lead to some hilarious miscommunications.

This morning the slowly lumbering wagon bore three flags: yellow, red, yellow.

About damned time.

Javed left his breakfast unfinished on his favorite rock and climbed down the hill, excited to fulfill his mission. His house had obligated him to the Inquisition because he was a handsome, likable sort, easily trusted by others, but also an excellent liar untroubled by conscience. He was perfect for assignments like this. Javed began to whistle a happy tune as he walked. He only needed to go slightly out of his way to scratch a symbol on a door at the edge of the casteless quarter.

Shabdkosh wasn't much of a town. It existed as a way-stop for the important people traveling to and from the Capitol. They may have shared the same desert, but the Capitol was served by several mighty aqueducts that enabled it to sustain a huge population, while Shabdkosh had a few deep wells that could serve at most a thousand souls, after they had watered the caravan oxen and the carriage horses of the first caste of course.

So Javed's next stop was to poison the well inside the warrior-caste fort. It had been a long time since any criminals had been bold enough to threaten anything this close to the Capitol, so the guards here were complacent, and as the merchant who delivered their rice, Javed was a familiar face. Nobody noticed the always friendly rice merchant drop a clay jug down their well.

The formula was potent and often deadly even in small dosages. It was one of the Inquisition alchemists' more useful mixtures, because the victims would not usually experience any symptoms for six to eight hours after ingesting. By the time they knew something was wrong, other soldiers would have been drinking all day.

Meanwhile, he knew that the Inquisitors who had been secretly living among the casteless would have seen the mark he had left for them and begun their preparations as well. There were a large number of casteless living here due to the sulfur mine, a tedious, smelly trade that the worker caste thought beneath them. Javed had two other conspirators, one having taken the place of the overseer, treating the non-people with extra petty cruelty to make them bitter, and another playing the part of a casteless religious fanatic, nurturing hostility and fomenting rebellion. He didn't envy his brothers, living in filth and disease pretending to be stupid fish-eaters in order to accomplish their mission. Javed was looking forward to ending this charade and returning to the Capitol. His brothers had to be ecstatic, certainly hoping to never smell sulfur again.

Once the casteless started seeing warriors clutching their guts and collapsing at their posts, it would be hailed as a sign of the Forgotten's favor. The strong made weak, so the weak could become strong, and all that nonsense. His allies would kill a few warriors to show the rest how easy it was, and then the casteless's bloodthirsty nature would take over. Out of obedience or fear, most of the non-people would remain hiding in their shacks, but he had been assured that enough fools and hot heads would rise up to ensure quite a bit of bloodshed.

Casteless were violent, but untrained and stupid. They would squander their energy on the wrong targets, the workers who profited from their labors most likely. So Javed would personally make sure there were sufficient casualties among the important people to make this a notable act of rebellion. He would do so by setting the lone first-caste compound on fire, burning it to the ground while its occupants were trapped inside, and picking off anyone who made it out alive.

Javed returned to his shop and removed his bag of tools from where he'd kept it hidden in the rafters. There was one particular arbiter who had sneered at the quality of his rice. Javed didn't even particularly care for rice, but he took his cover identity very seriously. He would make sure that arbiter got a poisoned crossbow bolt to the face.

He never asked why the Law needed them to kill a town, especially one only a couple days journey from the most important city in the world. He had seen no more signs of wickedness here than anywhere else, but regardless of the reason for their death sentence, Javed was looking forward to carrying it out.

Chapter 5

The Sons of the Black Sword stopped and made an early camp. They could have pushed on, but in the dark even their surefooted Somsak horses were bound to break a leg on the narrow, rugged mountain path. If the big moon, Canda, had been up, perhaps they would have tried, but tonight only tiny Upagraha was rapidly crossing the sky, and it was nothing more than a bright dot, not much larger than a star.

Ashok had the fortitude to suffer through the cold night in nothing but a coat, but the others might have frozen to death, even huddled together beneath blankets, so he allowed them to build a fire. If the Inquisition truly knew which pass they were crossing, there would be no hiding. If the masks sent a legion of warriors after them, they might as well die warm.

As Keta preached of forgotten gods to the fanatics, their general sat alone, away from the others, sharpening his stolen sword on a whetstone. Ashok had heard most of the Keeper's stories by now. They were surely a mix of ancient truth and modern lies, but the telling made Keta happy, and it motivated his *army*. Ashok scoffed at the thought. His army was a handful of raiders and a few of the workers they'd been raiding. The only thing that united them was that they'd all worshipped the old ways in secret and had fallen into a religious fervor after seeing Thera's odd magical powers manifest in Jharlang.

A year ago he would have executed all of them as treason-
ous cultists without a second thought. Now he was supposedly
one of their leaders. *Truly, Omand Vokkan had a gift for creative
torments.* The Grand Inquisitor would have a good laugh if he
could see what indignities Ashok had been reduced to now.

He had once been numbered among the highest caste, the
bearer of an ancestor blade, and a senior member of the Protector Order. In a land where everyone had a place, his had been
near the top, and he'd done his best to keep everyone where they
belonged. However that had all been a carefully crafted lie. His
entire life he had been nothing more than an unwitting pawn in
a political game, all because for some mysterious reason mighty
Angruvadal had chosen a pathetic casteless boy to be its bearer.

Once informed of his true identity, Ashok had condemned
himself, exposed the guilty parties, and then turned himself over
for judgment. He would have taken his own life in shame, but it
was illegal for the bearer of a precious ancestor blade to perish
in such a dishonorable manner. So he'd sent himself to prison
and waited until the Grand Inquisitor himself had delivered his
final orders to Ashok's humble cell. To a man whose very foundation was based upon obedience there was no punishment more
humiliating than being banished to live the rest of his days as
a criminal.

Yet Ashok had still obediently set out to fulfill his new
obligation—find and serve the casteless prophet—for the Law
demanded it. And he had failed so utterly, that after only a few
weeks as a criminal, the prophet had been carried off in the
talons of a great black bird, and his precious ancestor blade had
been destroyed.

The only thing that remained of once mighty Angruvadal
was a single black-steel shard that was still lodged in his heart.
The sword had spared his life, and for that he was bitter, for as
long as he lived he was required to fulfill his mission, no matter
how terrible it might be.

While Ashok had been deep in thought, Keta had finished
his nightly sermon. Satisfied that the inferior steel was as sharp
as it could be, Ashok put his new sword away, and he listened
as the believers asked questions about their god.

For a bunch of fanatics, their questions seemed reasonable.
If the Forgotten was real, why did he abandon us for so long?

If the casteless were the chosen people, why did the Forgotten allow the Law to crush them into dust?

Keta acted as if he had all the answers, but Ashok could see that he was afraid. The Keeper did a good job hiding it, but without his prophet to guide him, he was lost. Ashok found the whole situation odd, because Thera herself seemed to be an intelligent, level-headed woman—for a criminal outcast—not a believer in Keta's wild stories.

When it came to Thera, Ashok was . . . *conflicted*. He had been torn down and rebuilt as a perfect servant of the Law. He despised rebels with every fiber of his being. Except he'd come to respect Thera's dedication and professionalism, and in an odd way, even enjoy her company. It was difficult, getting to know those you were supposed to hate.

The worker Gutch wandered over, stopped a polite distance away, and coughed to get Ashok's attention, even though one would have to be deaf to not hear the giant of a man lumbering through the trees, stepping on every crackable twig . . . Or perhaps he was loud on purpose, because Ashok had the reputation of not being a man you wanted to surprise on accident.

"Excuse me, General. Could you spare a moment to have a word with your humble servant, Gutch?"

Jagdish had warned him that the smuggler was often deliberately obtuse, and liked to play the jovial fool, but not to underestimate him. Gutch was the reason they were headed for Neeramphorn, because a faint hope was better than no hope at all.

"Of course."

"Heh . . . Seems odd, calling you *General*." Gutch squatted in the snow beside the log Ashok was sitting on. "I remember when we were both inmates in the same prison, and now you've got yourself a fancy title again."

"The title is only as good as the army it leads."

"Perhaps someday your ranks will swell into a mighty force, fit to take on the army of a great house or the Capitol itself."

Ashok shuddered at the thought. "I do not think we ever met at Cold Stream."

"Well, you were a bit more memorable than me, what with all the killings. Place got a lot safer after you arrived, once the uppity sorts became afraid to draw your ire. I did enjoy watching your many duels through a crack in the wall of my cell. Entertainment helped pass the time. As for me? Old Gutch prefers to stay out of the way and not cause trouble."

"Since you're too large of stature to avoid notice—an unfortunate trait for one who has chosen a life of crime—instead you play dumb and friendly so no one takes you as a threat."

They were far enough from the fire that Ashok could only barely see his features, but it was obvious Gutch's forced smile had died. As Jagdish warned, this one was smarter than he looked. Then Gutch chuckled. "Dumb, I take some exception to, and I don't *pretend* to be friendly. I truly like everyone, General. I just like them better when they're not informing on me. As the Law says, a man must recognize his place. My favorite place is outside the view of those in your former profession."

"Of course."

Gutch gestured rudely at where Keta was speaking to his faithful. "Not like those rabble-rousers. They're just asking for trouble. Can you believe the tales the skinny one is spinning? You'd have to be terribly gullible to believe such things. Only the fish-eaters can save us from the army of demons that are gonna rise up out of the sea? Not bloody likely. Surely you don't believe any of that?"

He had been taught the gods were a myth, created as a tool of the ancient kings in order to subjugate and abuse the masses, before the Age of Law had brought justice and reason to Lok. Exhaling, Ashok could see his breath. It was just vapor, visible because of the cold. There was no spirit inside like the fanatics proclaimed, and when it was gone, they were just dead flesh to be discarded in the most sanitary manner possible. However, a few recent events had made Ashok question his beliefs... Like Thera predicting the future, or ghostly beings speaking to him as he lay dying. So there might be gods—just in case he had warned them to stay out of his way—but he did not like to dwell on the idea.

So Ashok ignored the question, and focused on the real world. The worker was thickset, but it was not the lean, fast muscle of a combatant, but rather the big arms and chest which came from the repetitive movement of heavy weights. He might not have been a warrior, but Jagdish had said he'd seen Gutch crush a wizard's head flat with the giant iron beam they'd used to bar the front gate of Cold Stream prison, a beam that normally took two warriors to lift.

"I am told you were a smith."

"Forge master smith, first class," Gutch corrected, pride in his voice, but then it was obvious that the many convoluted ranks of the worker caste meant nothing to Ashok. "I was high status among my people, or was, until I got stuck in prison over a little misunderstanding."

Considering the usual penalty for smuggling unregistered magic was death, Gutch must have had resources sufficient to bribe a judge. "I assume you've come to speak about what we will do once we reach the city."

"Correct. My contacts in Neeramphorn have among their customers some wizards called the Lost House, a dangerous, secretive lot, always hungry for...certain goods..."

"You may speak freely. They're trafficking in illegal magic. A serious offense, but it's no longer my place to enforce the Law."

"Good. I prefer to speak honestly," Gutch said, but Ashok doubted that very much. "I'll level with you. I was merely a tracker. We're a rare breed. There aren't many of us who've got the gift of sensing magic over distance."

His old sword master, Lord Protector Ratul, had also had such an affinity, and could even sense when things had been previously manipulated by magic. Ashok wondered if that extraordinary vision had contributed to Ratul's descent into traitorous madness and religious fanaticism. "I am familiar with it."

"That's how I can tell you've got magic in your blood. Every Protector I've ever come across has. You've all been changed, whole men turned into something more."

The Heart of the Mountain was the Order's greatest weapon and most precious secret. "That is none of your concern."

"Concerned me enough that when I sense one of them coming, I run for my life. Though none carry more of it in them than you, and I'm not talking about that shard stuck in your chest either. Far as I can tell, magic has been twisting you since you were a child."

The worker was correct. After Angruvadal had chosen a casteless child to be its bearer, Vadal wizards had broken his mind, erased his memories, and rebuilt him as the perfect servant of the Law, but even thinking about Bidaya's conspiracy filled him with disgust. "You were speaking of your contacts."

"Understand...Back to business, men like me find the bits.

Sometimes part of a demon corpse will wash up on shore, or an old chunk of black steel will get unearthed. Now we're supposed to report such finds, but civic responsibility doesn't put food on your table. Legal magic is expensive and the Inquisition controls who gets access to how much. People always want more. So I get those magic bits to my friends—think of them as a loose organization whose job it is to know people—then they sell to wizards, great houses, ambitious Thakoors, whoever, all off the books, with the Capitol and its tax collectors none the wiser. Everyone profits."

Such flaunting of the Law offended Ashok to the core of his being. It was a testament to his absolute dedication to his new orders that he didn't strike the brazen criminal down on the spot. Instead he just nodded. "I see."

"It may take me a few days to put together a meeting, they're careful like that. It can't be rushed, but I'll approach my old friends. Then we'll see about how to find this Lost House who stole away your false prophet. However, you've earned a certain reputation among my business associates. You're what we'd refer to as a *detriment to commerce*. As in you've massacred large numbers of them over the last twenty years."

Ashok shrugged. "Then they should not have been Law breakers."

"If they smell a Protector coming, they'll run."

"That is no longer my station."

"Regardless of your current legal troubles, the name Ashok Vadal might as well be a synonym for Protector. All my people tell stories about you to scare our youngsters so they don't get sloppy. Cover your tracks, lads, lest the Black Heart finds you out. You can't be anywhere near. If my friends discover I'm working with you, I'll get a knife between my ribs, and then they'll disappear down a hole so deep and dark you'll never find them."

He found it interesting that Gutch said working *with*, rather than *for*, but the worker and Jagdish had come to a mutually beneficial arrangement. A *partnership* those two had called it. Jagdish wanted revenge on the wizards who had murdered the Cold Stream guards, and Gutch would help find them in exchange for any magical fragments recovered from the wizards. Though Ashok did not himself fully grasp the intricacies of *profit*, it was a supremely powerful motivator to those of the worker caste.

"I will defer to your knowledge on this topic, Gutch."

"Good. Jagdish said despite your tendency for abrupt decision making, you were a thoughtful sort."

"I am. Which is why I will be sending Jagdish with you into the city."

"What?" Gutch sputtered. "I assure you, that's not necessary. Once a worker shakes on something, the deal is sealed. Gutch is no betrayer of trusts!"

Ashok had been condemned to live the rest of his life as a rebel, not a fool. "During those twenty years I spent hunting down criminals, I learned a few things about them. They have no honor and they will turn on each other for the smallest reward."

He let that hang there, purposefully unclear if he was speaking about Gutch or his associates. The last bounty he'd seen offered for his head had been a vast sum. He didn't know what it would be in these lands, but it was surely more than enough to tempt a greedy worker.

Gutch slowly nodded. "Of course. I'm certain honorable Jagdish will be of great assistance in this endeavor."

Informing on him to the authorities would even be the proper legal thing to do. It annoyed Ashok to no end that he was being placed in opposition to his beloved Law and everything he'd ever worked for, but he couldn't fulfill the Grand Inquisitor's commands otherwise.

"I, too, prefer to speak honestly, worker. Be aware, I do not care about your petty crimes or what you intend to do with their treasure after I have dealt with these wizards. My only purpose left is to find and protect the prophet of the Forgotten. To do this, I will do whatever is necessary. If you are faced with any difficult choices in the city, I would advise choosing the wiser path."

"What do you mean by wiser path?"

"Take the one that does not place you as my adversary..." Gutch had seen the pile of corpses Ashok had left in Jharlang, so he paused to let his words sink in. "That'll be all."

Gutch stood up with a grunt. "Night, General." This time when he wandered off through the trees he forgot to make a good show of blundering through the dark. In fact he didn't so much as step on a single twig.

Chapter 6

As the runner delivered his message, Devedas grew angrier and angrier, until the muscles of his jaw had clenched and he caught himself grinding his teeth together. He tried not to let his fury show. As a Lord Protector of the Order, it wouldn't do to let his composure slip in front of his men.

When the warrior finished his report, Devedas thanked him for undertaking such a long journey and told him to go and get some food, drink, and sleep. The Order had requisitioned the entire inn for the night, and kicked everyone else out. Most of the Protectors were out questioning the locals, so the messenger could take whichever bed was free. The exhausted man was happy to comply.

When only Protectors remained, they were able to speak freely.

"Where the hell is Shabdkosh?" asked Ishaan Harban.

"Just within the northern border of Makao, in the desert west of Akara. I was born near there," said Teerapat, the youngest Protector present. "He's attacking my house!"

"I know this place." A map of Lok had been unrolled on the bar, and Karno Uttara stabbed one thick finger into a spot south of the Capitol. It wasn't important enough to warrant a dot on the map. "Approximately there."

While they'd been heading east to search for him, Ashok had somehow slipped past them and traveled west. *But why?* The

Inquisition had witnesses claiming to have seen Ashok Vadal there, clear as day, and the high body count certainly made it sound plausible.

"It makes no sense," Karno muttered to himself.

None of it made sense. The last time Devedas has spoken to Ashok, he'd seemed content to voluntarily rot in a prison cell, yearning for execution.

"He's gone to war against the Law," Teerapat said. "Of course he'd strike near the Capitol."

"This doesn't feel like Ashok's work. Poisoning wells? Burning homes with people trapped inside? No. That's too impersonal. Ashok has killed multitudes, but most of those face to face."

"The revelation he was casteless drove him insane. You can't expect logic from someone like that."

Karno shrugged. "I've known Ashok longer than you."

"I wouldn't brag about being friends with the most infamous traitor in the world!" Teerapat snapped.

Karno frowned at the insult, but the big man was slow to anger. Devedas on the other hand, was not.

"That's enough, *two*-year senior. I was closer to Ashok than anyone. I loved him as my brother. None of us knew who he really was. He didn't even know who he really was. So be very careful who you may be giving offense to by suggesting we should have somehow known better."

Teerapat swallowed hard. The Lord Protector had no patience for offense. The long scar down Devedas' face was a reminder that he had once even been willing to duel the bearer of an ancestor blade. That event had become legend among the younger members of the Order. The Protector gave his superior an apologetic bow.

However, Devedas knew that Teerapat wasn't entirely wrong... "It brings embarrassment, but it does no good for us to pretend Ashok wasn't one of us. When Ratul betrayed the Law and went to live among the fanatics, Lord Protector Mindarin's strategy was to act as if Ratul had never existed at all. He went off to die in obscurity, and Ratul Without Mercy was forgotten. Even among our brothers we seldom acknowledge him. But Ashok is not Ratul. Ashok will not be ignored. He is a man of singular purpose, even if we no longer know what that purpose is, he *will* follow it. And as long as Ashok lives he will bring shame to this Order."

"We'll find him," Ishaan stated.

"We'd better. Men wearing *our* armor, carrying *our* insignia, claiming *our* name, helped Ashok escape. Why? Who were they? I've accounted for the whereabouts of every one of us during those dates. No Protector was involved but the judges consider my word tainted." Devedas had a difficult time hiding his disgust for their supposed betters. "There are forces within the Capitol who think we were at best incompetent, and at worst, complicit. They would have us all held accountable for his crimes."

In the flickering candlelight of the dreary inn, the men in the silver armor faced the grim truth. Failure to apprehend the traitor Ashok threatened the very existence of their entire Order.

"I agree with Karno about this attack," said Ishaan. "I remember one time when Ashok wouldn't even wear an executioner's hood at a beheading because it struck him as dishonest."

"Regardless. Even if this latest slaughter wasn't his doing, the Capitol thinks it was, and thus we must be seen responding." Like most men who'd actually accomplished things in their lives, Devedas had a great deal of contempt for politicians, but his office was forcing him to learn to think like one. "I'll go to Shabdkosh myself. Ishaan, as the other Protectors return, divide them into groups of at least three, and assign them search areas. I want to question every settlement expanding outwards from our two potential sightings in Jharlang and Shabdkosh. The winter has been mild so far, so most of the routes are still open. Obligate the local warriors to serve as our runners so we can stay in contact. Cooperate with the Inquisitors, but don't trust them. Their Order has much to gain if ours fails."

"It'll be done, Lord Protector," Ishaan assured him.

"We'd cover three times as much ground working alone," Teerapat suggested.

All of the older Protectors who had actually fought alongside Ashok looked at each other incredulously, and then burst out laughing.

"Oceans, to think that I was that young and stupid once," Karno declared.

Devedas knew there wasn't a single coward among them, and that made him afraid of how many of them would die before Ashok was stopped. "This is no mere criminal. He's a force of destruction. I send three at a time, because if they're unfortunate enough to have Angruvadal drawn against them, then *one* might get away to warn the rest of us. With each reliable sighting, we will tighten the noose until we can bring our full might to bear. You're dismissed."

The Protectors began to leave. They were all good men, some of the finest the Order had ever seen. But some of them were sharper than others. For his special assignment he needed someone both capable and loyal to a fault. "One moment, Karno. I need to speak with you."

The big man waited while his brothers went to their duties. Between the bulk, the huge beard, and the unkempt mane of hair, Karno looked like some forest beast they'd managed to dress in armor. He was a man of few words, and when he used them, they were always painfully to the point. "What?"

"Sit down." Devedas gestured toward one of the bar stools. "I've got a different assignment for you."

The poor stool creaked beneath his weight. Wearing his armor, Karno probably broke a lot of chairs. "You should send me wherever you think Ashok's most likely to go."

"I wish I could. We both know there's only a few of us who'd stand a chance against him in a fair fight."

"If your fight is fair, then your tactics were stupid."

Devedas chuckled. As much as they'd tried to forget Ratul, the old sword master's lessons had stuck with them. "Sorry, my friend, but I have need of your wisdom elsewhere."

Karno scowled at the mention of wisdom. He was known for being good at two things. Solving crimes, and then bashing the criminals responsible with his war hammer. He preferred the latter to the former.

"I've got an important witness, who has information concerning a conspiracy within the Capitol, but recent events have left me wondering if she is sufficiently hidden."

"As you know, I will always do as I am commanded, even if it's wasting my time bodyguarding your lady friend."

"Karno . . ."

"Who you shouldn't have feelings for anyway, seeing as we're one of the few Orders where marriage is forbidden until after our obligation is fulfilled. That's the kind of thing I should have to tell first year acolytes, not Lord Protectors."

"In this case, Rada is just a witness. Nothing more."

Karno snorted. "I'll admit, the librarian is rather clever, and lovely too, but you should make do with pleasure women like the rest of us. If you've got no attachment they can't be used against you. I never even bother to learn their names."

"It's not like that."

"Obviously. I could see that every time you looked at her. They call me Blunt Karno, not Blind Karno."

He'd never intended to fall in love. He'd worked far too hard to attain his current rank to jeopardize it over something as childish as romance. And though he could never confide his plans in a man as Law abiding as Karno, he intended to use his current position to attain a far greater status. Even if his gamble worked and he became king of Omand's usurper government, then the logical thing to do was marry a high-status woman from whatever great house he needed to shore up an alliance with.

Yet, Devedas had willingly walked into this trap. He'd known many women, but none of them were like her. Even though it complicated matters politically, he was determined that Rada would be his wife. And once Devedas set his mind to something, he saw it through.

"It is what it is." Devedas reached over the bar and pulled out the first bottle he found. Then he found two glasses. He pulled the cork with his teeth.

"Allow me to set aside our relative ranks for a moment and speak freely, Lord Protector."

"A horde of demons couldn't stop Blunt Karno from speaking freely," Devedas said as he poured them both a drink.

"If you truly care for this woman, do the right thing. Twenty-three years now you've served the Law. You've more than fulfilled your obligation. You've seen more bloodshed and awfulness than most warriors can even imagine. You deserve to retire in peace, make that pretty librarian your wife, and raise a gang of good-looking children."

"It's not that simple." He pushed the drink over to Karno.

"Everything is simple. You just insist on making it complicated."

There was nothing simple about becoming a king.

"I still have work to do."

"I swear, Devedas, you are the most ambitious man I have ever known."

You have no idea. "These are perilous times."

"Truth. We were just planning on how best to hunt down and kill someone I respect more than anyone else in the world." It was interesting that Karno used the present tense rather than the past for *respect*. "I'm guessing since you two were so close, you feel compelled to stick around, denying yourself happiness, until you feel things have been put right."

The theory was incorrect, but Karno would surely try and kill him if he knew the truth. Protectors were supposed to put the Law ahead of personal ambition for a reason. "You're a perceptive man, Karno."

"Ashok's not your fault you know."

"Perhaps he is. I tried and failed to take Angruvadal once."

"And nearly got your face cut off in the process."

Devedas laughed. "Ashok and I were only children. But how different would everything have turned out if that sword had found me worthy?"

"You can't dwell on the past."

"Oh, you're wrong about that, brother." He'd had another opportunity to challenge Ashok for the sword, not too long ago, confronting his old friend in his prison cell after learning the truth about his origins, but he'd hesitated—for reasons he still couldn't fully grasp—and his chance for an honorable duel had been lost.

He'd made a vow after that. There would be no more lost opportunities. Unjustly deprived of his father's ancestor blade, his family lands, his birthright throne, he'd then been given to the Order, which had told him how to live, who to kill, and it wouldn't even allow him the woman he loved.

Devedas was done being the servant of lesser men. It was his place to rule.

"There are things I cannot tell you, Karno. You must understand that there are forces who would use Rada against me. I'm not commanding you to do this as your superior. I'm asking you to do this because I trust you more than anyone else. Protect her. Please."

Karno sighed. "For how long?"

"Once Ashok is dealt with, I'll reassess the threat."

"Very well." Karno was solemn as he picked up his glass to make a toast. "To an old friend."

"To an old friend." Devedas raised his glass. "May we kill him speedily."

Chapter 7

"Behold, Risaldar Jagdish. I give you Neeramphorn!" Gutch declared as they rode around the bend. "Three Corners City, the jewel of the mountain on a mountain of jewels."

The warrior stood up in his stirrups to get a better view. All he could see were the outer walls, and they weren't even a true city wall, just one massive gatehouse blocking a narrow mountain pass. From here Neeramphorn didn't look like much.

"Come now, Gutch. This can't be all that. You're from Vadal City, the only thing fancier than it is the Capitol."

"True, true. Vadal is the greatest house in Lok, with the nicest weather, the best food, and the prettiest girls, without doubt, but it's said a city where the borders of three great houses intersect, there's three times the risk yet three times the profit." Gutch inhaled through his nose, taking a massive breath, and expanding his already gigantic chest theatrically. "You smell that?"

"Coal smoke?"

"Opportunity!"

Jagdish pulled his precious pocket watch from where he kept it safe inside his coat and checked the time. It had taken an hour of calm riding from where Ashok and the others were encamped. The locals kept the snow tramped down, so they could probably make it back in half that time if their lives depended on it. This

particular entrance to the city was supposedly the least used of
the three gates, and the only things they had passed on the way
in were side roads leading to various mines and miners on their
way to deliver wagons of ore. To Jagdish, who had been raised on
horseback beneath the sun in a land of plenty, everyone in this
part of the world seemed to want to dig in the dirt like a mole.

The air was tinted brown from the smoke. Mountains which
should have been beautiful and crystal clear appeared fuzzy to
the eye. Gutch had said it was because in the winter the air got
trapped in the valleys and that this wasn't even that bad yet. It
would grow worse and worse until cleaned out by a storm, and
that some days it was like walking in a caustic fog, but coughing
fits and runny eyes were a small price to pay for such *industry.*

"We're in luck, from the yellow sun on that flag, this is still
the Thao gate. They're the easiest to work with."

"You didn't know for sure?"

"I haven't been here for years. This gate will be boring and
staffed by dullards. The Kharsawan gate will be manned by
sticklers for good paperwork, and the Akershan gate is always
run by greedy pigs. But don't worry. Regardless of which house
is controlling which gate now, the tax collectors and guards all
bribe the same." Gutch laughed. "Don't let that hurt your feelings.
Most folks don't take their honor as serious as you do."

Low-ranking warriors were underpaid and underappreciated, of
course they tried to make a few extra notes off the weaker castes
whenever given the opportunity. Some graft was to be expected.
Jagdish didn't care how bad other houses' soldiers were about it
because they weren't under his command.

"Now swallow that Vadal pride and try to look like an outcast,
booted from his army and making his way as a poor disgraced
bodyguard—"

"Such a far-fetched act."

"A bodyguard serving a magnificent merchant of wealth and
distinction."

Jagdish snorted. "Where are we going to find one of those
at this hour?"

"Kiss my vast buttocks, fish breath! I am too a merchant of
wealth and distinction, or at least the man at that gate stamping
these traveling papers I forged had best believe so, or we will
have a very exciting time."

A half an inch of fresh snow had fallen during the night. They had been following hoof and wheel tracks all morning. Ahead of them a wagon, heavy with coal, had been stopped and was being searched by a pair of guards.

"What do you suppose they're looking for?" Gutch asked.

"Ashok, more than likely."

"There is quite the bounty on the head of our illustrious general."

Jagdish glanced over at his traveling companion. "Don't even think about it."

"Me? I'm above temptation, even though that money would go a long way toward my goal of buying my own palace. But I'm still unclear why you'd throw your lot in with him anyway. You want to clear your name and go back to your pretty worker wife, joining up with the most wanted criminal in Lok isn't going to help. Me and you could find those wizards just fine on our own."

It was a valid point. "I'm a good soldier, but killing powerful wizards is Protector work, and do you know any other Protectors who are going to go out of their way to help the likes of me? Besides, you speak of honor, but in his own peculiar way Ashok is the most honorable man I know. He may be a criminal, but because he was betrayed by fate, not by any failure of character."

"Like the Law gives a damn. I'm just saying—"

"And I'm saying that I'm beginning to enjoy your company, so it would be a real shame to have to run you through with my sword for wagging your big mouth."

Gutch sighed. "Fine, be that way."

"Just remember our deal, I restore my name and get a new command, you get rich and do whatever it is rich workers do."

"Pleasure women." Gutch muttered under his breath. "Lots and lots of pleasure women."

Then they had to be silent because they were nearing the cluster of haphazard trade stands that inevitably sprang up outside any city gate. Merchants whose papers were denied for whatever reason simply set up shop outside until their wares were gone or until they'd sold enough of their inventory to afford the entry bribes. It was early enough and cold enough that there was little traffic yet, so most of the hawkers were still warming themselves by their fires.

A single casteless woman was pouring out a piss pot by the

side of the road. For a moment Jagdish was worried that she would somehow recognize them, like the many casteless they'd seen on the journey here, but their celebrity must have been limited to Ashok and Keta, because she kept her eyes averted to avoid offending the whole men.

The guards were still listlessly poking spears into the coal pile, so Jagdish and Gutch dismounted and waited their turn. There was a water trough for the horses. Somebody had even broken the ice already, so they let the animals drink their fill.

Jagdish did his best to look like he didn't care, but inside he was judging the Thao soldiers, from their sloppy uniforms, to their unpolished boots, to their careless demeanor. It was one thing to be slow but good, or fast but sloppy. But slow and sloppy was simply unforgivable. He could have snuck a sea demon in under that coal from how little effort they'd put forth searching it. If they'd been his men, he'd rip them, and then have his havildar, Wat, make them unload and load the whole wagon, coal by individual painstaking coal, until they learned their lesson. Except Wat had been murdered by wizards, the poor dead bastard, which was what brought Jagdish all the way here to scowl disapprovingly at these Thao amateurs.

Thao liked to brag about how they were one of the few landlocked Great Houses, like their distance from the evil ocean somehow made them better than Vadal men with their long coastline, but whenever their warrior castes clashed in a raid, Vadal always won. That's what happened when trumped-up terrace farmers clashed with professional soldiers. His people might not be proud of him, but Jagdish was still exceedingly proud of his people.

When the gate opened, Jagdish got his first real look at Neeramphorn. This part looked like a bunch of shoddy buildings stacked on top of each other, climbing up the mountainside, all connected by walkways held together by chains, rope, and faith. There were smokestacks everywhere, and a multitude of workers were moving about, probably burning things or melting things, or whatever it was workers did here. Once the wagon was through they were signaled to approach.

Sadly, the gate closed. These Thao weren't *that* lazy. "Traveling papers, please."

"I'm a forge master smith of Great House Vadal, here to

arrange the purchase of ingots." Gutch handed his forgeries over. That soldier carried the papers through the small side door to whatever minor official was stuck manning this post.

"Do I look like I care, worker? You. Bodyguard. Come here."

Jagdish obediently approached. Since he was no actor, he was still wearing his battered traveling uniform, in the blue-gray and bronze of Great House Vadal. It wasn't like he could fake the accent of a different house anyway, but he had removed his rank and insignia. It was common for warriors unwanted by their house to hire themselves out in the service of workers. Even the lowest of warriors still had to eat.

Two Thao soldiers studied him. Proud Jagdish knew he could beat them both, but he let them sneer. They weren't Vadal men, so their opinions were basically worthless. They looked to Jagdish, and then to their sheet of paper which had obviously come off a printing press, then back to Jagdish.

They were trying to decide if he matched the description of Ashok.

He couldn't help himself. "Don't worry. You'll know the Black Heart when you see him."

"How do you know that's who we're looking for?" asked the older of the two, who was about Jagdish's age. He wore the rank of a havildar.

"That's who everyone is looking for nowadays, greatest criminal in the land and all that. But he's a tall fellow, few inches taller than me, lean but strong as an ox, and faster than a tiger. They say he's killed over a thousand men in combat, and brother, when you see his eyes you know it's true."

The younger soldier was barely more than a boy. "You ain't met the Black Heart."

He was tempted to tell them that the Black Heart had once broken his leg in a duel that had since become famous. There weren't very many men in the world who could claim to have fought Ashok Vadal and lived to tell about it. Only Gutch had been taken off to the other side to be questioned as well, and he was silently pleading for Jagdish to keep his mouth shut. One of the hardest things in the world for a warrior was to refrain from bragging, especially when he'd actually earned it.

"I only met him in passing once, Nayak, but he makes an unforgettable impression."

"Yeah, yeah, sure you did. We need to see your sword," the havildar ordered. "Draw it, slowly."

Jagdish did as directed. If they were still checking swords, then the soldiers here had not yet heard about the destruction of Angruvadal. That was good. Ashok may have been painfully honest, but Jagdish liked the idea that anyone tempted to hunt them would do so fearing certain death. That was just good tactics.

They stopped him when it was half free and obviously made of plain steel. "That's fine. Sheath it and wait here for your charge." The havildar took a deep breath, then delivered a list of rules in a manner that suggested he had given this speech hundreds of times. "The city is divided into three sections. Warriors may travel freely within the section controlled by their house. Members of the warrior caste not obligated to those three houses—that means you—must remain close to whoever holds their contracts at all times. Unaccompanied warriors not of the three houses are subject to penalty."

"Flogging?"

The nayak chuckled. "For a Vadal man in these mountains? More like hanging."

"Ha! I like your attitude. When I was a nayak I thought I knew everything too. You come to Vadal City sometime and I'll buy you a drink."

"If I ever visit the land of the northern swine herds it'll be because I'm leading a raid."

The havildar just sounded bored as he ignored the back and forth. "No unsanctioned dueling. No fighting or drunkenness outside of sanctioned venues..."

While the list of prohibitions and punishments droned on and on, he noticed that a few more warriors had come out of the side door and escorted Gutch inside. "Where are they taking my merchant?"

The havildar obviously had no idea, but had at least gotten through the memorized portion so he could speak normally again. "That's no concern of yours. Stay with your horses. If the Inquisitor needs to question you too, they'll send for you."

"There's an Inquisitor here?" Jagdish tried not to show any reaction, and failed. *Damn it, Gutch...*

"Not a friend of the Law, Vadal man?"

"Oh, I love the Law, brother. I've just learned it's best for a simple soldier to keep his head down when its chief servants are around."

The older of the pair appeared to appreciate that sentiment. "You and me both." It didn't matter what house you served, all soldiers shared that opinion. Sometimes the question wasn't so much who was guilty or innocent, but who was in the wrong place at the wrong time. "I can tell you've not always been stuck serving portly merchants. What was your rank?"

In reality, Jagdish had been of greater status, but he lied. "I was a havildar like you, before my risaldar made a bad decision and needed someone to blame for it."

"That's what we're here for, making officers look good... But you understand that when the first caste who wear the Law over their faces or their hearts ride into town, nobody tells us why."

"There's Protectors here as well?"

"Three of them arrived yesterday," said the nayak. "Never seen more than one at a time before."

"It must be something serious then." Jagdish looked toward the door. Gutch was still in there. A criminal being questioned by someone who made his living catching liars? This was bound to end badly. Would the worker talk? Would he sell them all for a fistful of notes? "Three Protectors... What manner of hard bastard criminals do you grow in these mountains anyways?"

"As if you can talk! It's your Vadal criminal whose got the Thakoor so worked up they've got us searching every single cart big enough to smuggle a goat in. Sure, we got crime, but it isn't like our house gave its ancestor blade to a casteless so he could go about massacring whole villages."

That was rather insulting, even if true. "Come now, friends. It could be worse. At least the criminal you're on the lookout for isn't from House Sarnobat. Then he'd massacre the village *and* molest all the livestock."

The three soldiers had a laugh. "You're alright for a Vadal thug," said the havildar.

Jagdish liked them too. So he was really hoping he wouldn't end up in a sword fight with them in the next few minutes.

Other travelers arrived, so Jagdish had to step aside. Still no Gutch. But also no Inquisitor coming outside and ordering his arrest. He checked his pocket watch. The one hand was still ticking along. Trying to act nonchalant was making the tension worse. If something happened he had to decide whether to run or fight. The answer depended entirely upon the unknown of whether Gutch was busy betraying him or not. How did real criminals do this sort of thing? At least battle was honest. After what felt like forever, Jagdish checked his watch again, and found that only a few minutes had passed.

Gutch came back outside, his expression unreadable. There was no one bellowing for his arrest though, but knowing the sneaky Inquisition they would probably just surprise him with arrows to the legs so he couldn't escape, then torture him at their convenience. His fake merchant waved for him to approach the gate. Still no shouts or arrows, so Jagdish took hold of the horses' bridles and walked them over.

The havildar looked at the fresh stamp on Gutch's forgeries. "Everything seems to be in order and your taxes are paid. Have a pleasant stay in beautiful Neeramphorn, merchant."

"I'll pass on the beauty as long as it is a profitable stay," Gutch responded. He gave Jagdish a nod as if to say everything was fine. Jagdish would believe that once they were through.

The gates were opened. Gutch went through, acting casual as could be. Jagdish followed. The stonework inside was even shoddier than expected. A proper battering ram would make short work of it.

The havildar caught his look of disgust. "Don't judge, Vadal man, the city just keeps growing so fast and filling new canyons, we just keep adding new gatehouses to accommodate it. By the way, if you've got any pride left after having to serve a worker all day, Canda's Favor is the best place in the city for you to lose all your notes in a game of dice. And it's one of the few establishments those colors you still wear won't get you stabbed."

"Thanks for the warning, Havildar. May your mandatory wagon searches bring you great glory."

The Thao gave him a profane gesture indicating where Jagdish could stuff that opinion, but he did it with a smile.

Once on the other side, there was still no alarm, no waiting paltan of deadly Inquisitors, no trio of merciless Protectors, just hundreds of workers doing worker things. The narrow streets were snow churned into mud, and around them were a multitude of buildings constructed of wood and brick, belching smoke from great round chimneys. They walked for a time without speaking.

Like every worker's district Jagdish had ever been in, there was a great deal of hammering, banging, shouting, and haggling. All the noise was making their horses nervous. Once Jagdish was certain they weren't being followed and no one would be able to hear them over the racket, he asked, "What happened inside the gatehouse?"

"Even when being questioned by a fearsome Inquisitor, Gutch remains a man of his word. Don't worry, Jagdish. I honored our bargain."

Jagdish noticed that Gutch was looking a little flushed and, considering the cold, sweatier than usual. "You'd better not be lying to me. You were in there a long time."

"Sitting on a bench, waiting for a high-status man to finish his tea." Gutch looked around nervously. There were many people going about their business, most of them avoiding the mud by walking on wooden boardwalks. "I think someone recognized me...Don't worry, I'm not talking about the masked buffoon, he only wanted to know if we had heard of any sightings of the Black Heart. I told him no. Since Ashok Vadal is not known as a master of disguise, and it is unlikely he's recently put on a lot of weight, I wasn't that interesting. Ah...Wait here a moment."

Gutch turned to the left and went down an alley between two brick buildings. Broken barrels and trash were piled up, and the walls were covered in graffiti. Gutch skipped most of it and went to one design in particular, a yellow hand with a black eye in the palm. It had been painted over what had probably been a blue elephant. The paint had been applied recently enough that it had not weathered away, but Jagdish could decipher none of the messages around it. The letters were so stylized they looked like gibberish to him, but it seemed to mean something to Gutch.

"Oh, this is not good. Not good at all." The big man hurried back out of the alley and climbed back onto his poor, overburdened horse. "We must hurry, but don't look like we're in a hurry."

"What's not good? Who recognized you?"

"There was a stone mason in there doing repairs. He looked familiar when I walked in. By the time I came out, he had run off."

"So what? Another member of your caste recognized you. You said you've been here before. I say this not to give offense, but a man of your rotund nature is bound to be remembered."

"Rotund? I should have just informed on you and collected

the reward. Look, I told you I have friends here..." Gutch sucked on his teeth, as if he was taking a moment trying to decide on the right way to phrase it. "I may have not been entirely forthcoming about the nature of my associates. It's not really one big happy family. There are as many competing gangs outside the Law as there are castes and subcastes within it. Some are friendlier than others..."

"And?"

"Some want to kill me...Oh, don't give me that look! Like you've never hurt anyone's feelings in your line of work. Just keep walking. I didn't know this section had changed ownership."

"You said you expected the Thao to control this part of the city!"

"I'm not talking about the houses. I'm talking about the *real owners*."

Chapter 8

It didn't take long for Jagdish to meet the real owners.

They didn't even have a chance to make it into a different district. Since most of the city was a disorganized mess crammed into a bunch of small canyons, the roads were neither wide nor straight. Because of the crowds the horses were limited to a slow walk. Running down a worker in a worker district was a great way for a warrior from a distant house to get beaten to death by an angry mob.

The mason who had spotted Gutch must have had friends nearby, because there were already six ruffians blocking the road ahead. They were workers, wearing leather aprons and thick gloves. All of them were carrying hammers, pipes, or chains. things which were legally considered tools rather than weapons, because a worker had to receive a special dispensation to carry a weapon—not that there was a lot of difference between getting your head smashed with a war hammer or a sledge hammer. They were obviously up to no good, and heading directly toward Jagdish and Gutch.

"Cocky bunch. Doesn't this damned city have any watch patrolling it?"

"If there were warriors here they would look the other way, same as back home, Risaldar."

"That's a filthy lie."

But Gutch had already turned his horse and was heading back the way they'd come, only he pulled up short when he saw more men coming from behind them. When a group of burly, determined sorts are walking with purpose, they stand out from the crowd.

The locals realized what was going on, and began clearing off the streets. Mothers dragged their children away. Everyone got out of the gang's path. Nobody protested. Nobody asked questions. It was very odd to Jagdish, because these men had no legal authority here, but they were as sure in charge as any man of status.

Jagdish had been a cavalry scout, so he knew how to fight on a horse. "I'll make us a hole."

"No! I promise there are more you don't see, and any watch who do respond will be on their payroll. If we're arrested we won't live to see a jail...Oceans," Gutch swore as he tried to pick another route. "There." He thumped his horse with his heels.

"You're just going somewhere there's fewer witnesses to restrain them!"

"Nobody here reports crimes," Gutch called back over his shoulder. "Ride!"

Jagdish followed. The men had given up on acting casual and had begun running after them. Rather than fear, Jagdish found that he was angry. He was a warrior. Who were these scum to threaten him?

But that was the pride talking, and he knew it. There were many of them and one of him. A lucky swing with a pipe and Jagdish would never kill those wizards, never clear his name, and his unborn son would grow up in the wrong caste, sent back to his mother's people, to end up like these slobs.

They made it across the alley, between two factories, their horses nearly crushing some casteless who were trying to stay warm next to a steam vent, and then they were out the other side. Only there was no street, just an open area between two massive brick buildings. It looked like another building had stood here once, but from the crumbling pillars, it had burned down long ago, and later they had turned the space into some sort of junkyard or trash dump. Before them was a maze of broken barrels, piles of rusting metal, and garbage. There were windows far above, and terrible metallic noises were ringing through them. The walls were so tall that they were blocking most of the sunlight. Jagdish was completely lost.

"Ah damn...Wrong way," Gutch appeared terrified, and he was normally level headed. It made Jagdish wonder what he had done to anger this gang so much. "We've got to find a way out."

Gutch's poor horse tripped on a wire. It was too tight to maneuver the animals through here quickly. "Abandon the animals and go on foot." Jagdish smoothly turned his horse back toward the alley, dismounted, and smacked it on the rump so it would run. The alley was narrow enough that it would at least cause their pursuers some trouble.

"We need to hide," Gutch said as he rolled off, missed his stirrup, and flopped into the mud.

"Which way do we need to go?" he asked. Gutch pointed. Jagdish grabbed him by the collar and dragged him upright. The man really did weigh a ton. "Keep your head, and we'll be fine."

"The problem is they want my head!"

There was an echoing crash from down the alley. A man screamed, then Jagdish's horse screamed. That was a very unpleasant sound.

The two of them ran through the junkyard. Over the years the scrap had been piled higher and higher until there were only tight winding paths through it. It was hard to tell what the rusty stuff even was, since plants had grown over it, died, and then been snowed on. Jagdish tried to keep them going in the direction Gutch had indicated, hoping to find another alley, or a fence low enough to climb over, but the paths kept ending, forcing them to backtrack. Some of the walls of the old factory were still standing, making it even more confusing. He could hear men cursing and barking orders. Their pursers had entered the yard as well.

Everything around them seemed to be sharp. Jagdish caught a jagged edge, ripped his sleeve, and cut his arm. He tripped and bumped into some rotting beams. Unfortunately they fell over with a crash. Somehow the workers above must have heard that over the noise of their workplace, and curious, soot-covered faces appeared in the windows above to see what was going on in their junkyard. Those workers must have recognized their local gang, and took no pity on the strangers, because they immediately began shouting directions.

"Inhospitable bunch," Jagdish muttered as crouched down. Gutch was right behind him.

One of the unseen gang members called out. "Might as well give up, Gutch. There's only one way out and I'm standing in front of it. I never thought you'd be dumb enough to show your face in Neeramphorn again."

"That's Bajwa," Gutch whispered.

"Friend of yours?" Jagdish whispered back.

"Used to be."

"I'm gonna skin you for what you did to my brother. I'm gonna make a rug out of your hide and render candles from your fat!"

"Well, not very good friends."

A worker came around the corner ahead of them, carrying a club. "Found th—"

In such tight quarters, Jagdish didn't bother with his sword. He used his dagger.

Crashing into the man, he smashed one hand over his mouth while the other plunged the blade into his guts, over and over. Jagdish pushed him back, sliding through the snow, until they crashed into an abandoned machine. His hand slipped. The man screamed for help as he fell.

"Follow me," Jagdish snapped. He didn't know where he was going, but a moving target was harder to hit. Gutch only paused long enough to pick up the dropped club.

The workers in the windows above saw one of their caste stabbed by an outsider and howled for blood. Bottles and bricks were hurled downward to shatter against metal.

The gang was all around them, swarming through the yard. Jagdish caught glimpses of them through the gaps. With a roar Gutch flung himself against a lopsided stack of parts, knocking it over onto some workers in the next aisle. It made a terrible crash, and men bellowed in pain.

Jagdish kept moving until he spotted a wooden fence in the distance. Whatever was on the other side had to be better than this. "That way." And then he nearly got his head taken off by a pry bar.

He hadn't seen that worker coming. The bar clanged off some wooden beams, flinging snow. Jagdish responded by slashing him across the belly. Only this one was wearing one of those thick leather aprons, so that accomplished nothing. He jabbed for the man's neck, only he'd already spun around with the bar. Their forearms collided as the worker blocked, and the dagger went flying from Jagdish's hand. Then from out of nowhere the worker's elbow connected with the warrior's skull.

Stumbling back, blinking in surprise, his first coherent thought was *workers aren't supposed to know how to fight.* Before Jagdish could get hit again, Gutch flew across the aisle and tackled the worker. They landed so hard it had to be like getting trampled by a bull.

More of them were coming. Gutch struggled to his feet. The man beneath him was flopping around and gasping for breath. Jagdish grabbed Gutch by the arm as he ran past. "Get to that fence!"

One of the workers above got lucky, and a brick hit Jagdish in the arm. He winced. It hurt like a bastard. A bottle whistled past his ear and shattered at his feet. Then they were out of throwing range of the windows, and all he had to worry about was the score of criminals nipping at their heels.

There was an open area between them and the fence, a mere twenty feet not yet filled with junk. It was just dead grass and room to swing. *Good.* "Keep running," Jagdish snapped, as he drew his sword and spun about.

The hounds hadn't expected their rabbit to turn. The first to reach him was a worker wildly whipping a chain about his head. Jagdish went beneath it and Vadal steel cut the worker's thigh until it clipped bone. He went down flailing.

Jagdish came up and slashed at the next purser. He was a bit far, so the worker was able to squeal and leap back. That one dropped his hammer and ran. *That's right. A worker might learn how to throw a punch, but only warriors know how to face steel.*

Unfortunately, there were at least a dozen more where that one came from, and they'd slowed up as they'd come out of the scrapyard and were approaching as a mass. The one he'd cut was crying and thrashing, which was giving the rest pause, but there was courage in numbers. Jagdish knew he was good, but he wasn't that good.

Risking a quick glance over his shoulder, he saw that Gutch was trying to climb over the wooden fence, but since the fence was tall, and Gutch was very large, it wasn't pretty.

Escape that way wasn't looking likely. That meant he just

needed to kill enough of these that the rest would leave them be. Jagdish shifted his stance to a defensive one, weight on the balls of his feet. He'd cut and retreat, cut and retreat. Hopefully they'd run out of blood before he ran out of yard and ended up beneath a pile of angry workers.

One of the workers approached slowly. Jagdish shifted the point of his sword in that direction, and the worker flinched. But to his credit, he didn't run, rather he nodded his head at his wounded comrade. "Can I get him out of the way?"

"Be quick about it."

Jagdish's eyes flicked back and forth, watching all of them, as the worker took hold of the wounded man's coat and dragged him back, leaving a wide red trail in the snow.

Jagdish spoke clearly so all could hear. "You'll need to put a tight knot around his thigh to stop the bleeding if you want him to live. Trust me, friends, he's not keeping that leg. Now ask yourselves which parts you're willing to leave behind before you try me."

They got ready to charge anyway. *Brave bunch.*

"Hold on." A short, stocky man shouted as he made his way through the crowd. "Timo, get that man to the surgeon. Should anyone ask, it was an unfortunate industrial accident." He was dressed better than the others, with a fine coat, and on his chest was a purple flower. Like most warriors, Jagdish had never bothered to learn the worker castes' symbols. "As for you, stranger, one small act of mercy deserves another. We can end this without further unpleasantness."

"What are you supposed to be?"

"He's an apothecary, among other things," Gutch shouted, as he tried one more futile leap to try and catch the top of the fence, and failed miserably. "Like a lying, backstabbing cheater!"

"Such slander coming from the likes of you, Gutch? My brother died atop the Dome because of you."

"Your brother was an idiot!"

"I'll deal with you in a moment!" he shouted back. "Now, listen to me carefully, warrior. I am Bajwa and I run this town. You're obviously a bodyguard of some skill, but this treacherous pig is not worth dying for. You stabbed one of my boys to death and crippled another, but I'll keep your horses and call that a fair trade. There's only one way your employer is getting out of here. But you? You can just walk away."

Jagdish didn't budge. "Then I wouldn't be much of a bodyguard."

"A man who actually knows the value of a contract is a rare thing. What's this fool paying? I'll beat it, because I could use a swordsman like you."

"It's sad so many of my caste can be bought so cheaply that you take it for granted." Jagdish studied the faces of the workers waiting to kill him. Whatever Bajwa was paying, it was motivation enough. "I'm sorry, but you can't have him. I need him first. If you want Gutch, you have to go through me."

"Thank you!" Gutch shouted.

Bajwa ran one hand through his sparse hair, frustrated. "You know why men of honor are so rare these days? They all die pointlessly for no good reason. Kill him, boys."

The gang began their approach.

"A Protector!" The one who had been sent to drag off their wounded man came running back through the junkyard looking like there was a sea demon on his heels. "A Protector's coming!"

These criminals had no problem fighting Jagdish, but when they heard one of the ultimate servants of the Law was on his way, their eyes widened in terror.

"I probably can't beat all of you, but I swear I'll last long enough for him to see you strike me down," Jagdish declared. "Then you can try and explain it to the Law."

"We're not done, warrior," Bajwa snarled. Then he raised his voice. "Fortune favors you again, Gutch."

"Your sister favored me once too, Bajwa! Now run like the cur you are."

"Let's go, boys. We'll catch Gutch and his friend later." The gang leader spun one finger in the air. The workers immediately began to disperse. Jagdish hadn't even noticed that there were side doors into the brick buildings, but they would have done them no good. It wasn't until the gang pounded on them with an oddly cadenced knock that they were unlocked from the other side.

If the Protector went looking for them, the criminals would probably just blend in with the regular workers. From what he'd seen earlier, the locals would cover for them. The Protector would never know that they hadn't been there, innocently lifting heavy things or whatever pointless business it was workers did all day.

Sadly, Jagdish and Gutch weren't getting out that way, and none of the locals would lie for outsiders. Even though they could claim to just be the victims of a robbery, they couldn't afford the attention of a Protector. They needed to get out of here *fast*. He sheathed his sword and ran to the fence.

Gutch was red faced and out of breath from trying to grab the top.

"Can't you just crash through?"

"I tried. I bounced off!"

Jagdish looked it over. Gutch could boost him to the top, but there was no way he'd be able to pull up the giant. That left one option. Jagdish sighed as got on his hands and knees. If only his family could see the lengths he was going through to save their name ... "Stand on me. Hurry." Gutch didn't hesitate, and immediately planted one big boot on his back. "Ooof." It had to be what getting stepped on by an elephant was like. Jagdish wanted to curse Gutch for being so damned large, but there wasn't time. It was painful, but it worked, and this time Gutch caught the top of the fence and struggled up. He swung one meaty arm down. Jagdish grabbed his hand and was hoisted up as if he weighed nothing.

They dropped onto the other side, Jagdish silently, and Gutch with a bang and a flop. But there was no time to catch their breath. An unseen dog was barking at them. They ran down tiny, filthy alleys, avoiding everyone. Once it felt like they weren't about to be set upon by the gang or the Law, they slowed to a cautious walk until they found a dark corner beneath a warehouse to hide in. It was so secluded an old casteless woman had died here, a month before judging by her desiccated condition, but nobody had even noticed.

As he was reduced to hiding beneath the flea-ridden blankets of a dead casteless, waiting for it to be dark enough to try and sneak away, Jagdish had to laugh at his misfortune. Their mission to track down the Lost House was off to a fine start.

Chapter 9

Six years ago

"You seem troubled. What are you thinking about, mistress?"

"I'm thinking about what's the best way to kill my husband and not get caught."

Thera Vane's arranged marriage was not a happy one.

"Ha ha, yes, such a sense of humor." Her personal attendant glanced around nervously, but they were alone in the bed chamber. Then she went back to brushing out Thera's long hair. "You are most amusing, mistress."

"Of course," Thera muttered as she looked at her troubled reflection in the mirror. "I was only joking."

Arranged marriages were the norm among her caste. The higher the status, the more likely your family would marry you off for political reasons, sealing contracts, creating alliances, and so forth. That was just the way of things. It was the one time you were better off being unimportant. Low-status warriors could often marry for love. Nobody cared about them enough to use them as bargaining chips.

Thera had thought her odd reputation would spare her from being used like that. Normally the daughter of a war hero would be in great demand, but Andaman Vane had been demoted and punished for his disobedience. They no longer had an estate or riches. Though her family had managed to keep Thera's occasional seizures a secret, everyone knew about the injury in her youth and the many years it had taken her to recover. What warrior in his right mind would want to marry a poor girl from a bad line, with bad luck and bad health, to bear their sons?

Sadly her low status had merely delayed the inevitable. She was no first choice, and to present her as such would be an insult, but the great house had decided she would do as a widower's replacement. She had married late. People often said better late than never, but for such a wretched man, she'd have preferred never.

"Life would be simple if Dhaval would just get himself killed in battle, but he's too much of a coward to lead from the front."

The slave girl was growing nervous. "You shouldn't make such jokes, mistress. The roik is not a kind master."

There should have been some measure of pride, being married to a leader of one hundred soldiers, but Dhaval Makao was a petty, bitter man, rotten to his core. "The only reason he attained that rank is because of politics. He's a warrior in name only. In House Vane he wouldn't be worthy to dig latrines." Thera sighed. "But I suppose I'm not in Vane anymore. I'm in the great house that conquered it."

"If Roik Dhaval heard you say such things, he wouldn't see the humor. He would take great offense."

"I'm aware." Thera was Dhaval's third wife. The first had died in childbirth, as had the baby. She suspected the last vestiges of his humanity had died along with them, if he'd ever been human at all. Dhaval's second wife had *fallen* down the stairs and broken her neck. Or at least that's what he had told the judges, because beating your spouse to death during a drunken rage was illegal. The Law was rather clear on that.

The slave kept brushing the tangles from her hair, while Thera cursed herself for saying anything at all. Opening up had been foolish. She had slipped, but that's because she had no one else to talk to. She had no friends here. The slave girl would rat on Thera in a heartbeat if Dhaval knocked a month off her obligation.

Loneliness was making her desperate. The women of Vane had quite a bit of autonomy, and could even serve as karta and head a household. In Makao, a wife was expected to be a silent trophy that produced babies, more of a beautiful pet than anything. Thera wasn't good at silence, and thus far, had no luck getting pregnant. She suspected her long illness had left her barren. So far

her marriage had been a year of uncomfortable silences punctu-
ated by Dhaval's angry, drunken outbursts. He was too proud to
ask a judge to grant a divorce, and she'd already vowed the day
that he lost his temper and tried to toss her down the stairs like
her predecessor, she'd stab him in the throat, Law be damned.

The slave had stopped combing.

"What is it?"

"Sorry. I didn't mean to stare, but this scar on top of your
head...It's from the thing that fell from the sky?"

"You've heard about that?"

"We all have. There was a boy in my village, got kicked in
the head by a horse, broke his whole skull. He wouldn't wake
up, but the surgeon told us about a girl from Vane who'd been
hurt far worse and how she'd eventually healed. He didn't make
it. It's a miracle you survived."

"Miracles aren't real. I survived because Vane blood doesn't
die easy. Thankfully it healed without being a misshapen mess."

"You can't hardly tell your head was ever broken, and you
can hide it well. You are very pretty, mistress."

So was the slave, which explained why her wretched husband
had claimed the poor girl. Dhaval liked to collect pretty things.

"Lucky me." Thera had never taken much pride in her appearance, but she recognized that she was decently attractive, though
a bit strong and plain by Makao's snooty standards, but good
enough, which was why Dhaval had accepted when the Vane
arbiters had offered her as a wife. She suspected the reason his
powerful family had approved the contract was the women of
Vane had a reputation for toughness, so she'd be more difficult
to break on accident should their barbaric son lose his temper
again, and thus spare them future embarrassments in court.

"It could be worse, mistress."

"I do not disagree." Dhaval had only tried to strike her once.
It had been over dinner, but she'd threatened to stab him with
her fork, and they hadn't eaten a meal together since. "He's at
least smart enough to know when to back down."

"I meant that he doesn't beat us slaves...Often."

Thera didn't like having slaves. The whole concept bothered
her. They were just regular people, temporarily deprived of their
status as whole men because of some violation of the Law. Thera
could take care of her own affairs, comb her own hair, fix her

own clothing, and fetch her own food. But whenever she tried to do anything on her own, her husband became offended. Dhaval loved having slaves do all their menial tasks. It made him feel important. This particular girl had been a worker in one of the villages his garrison protected, so she'd been obligated to his estate to make up for their unpaid debt.

"He's not so bad, as long as you don't upset him." The girl seemed hesitant to continue. "But it's like you're determined to upset him, then he takes his anger out on us. Perhaps if you weren't so obstinate?"

Thera was growing annoyed. "Just comb it so the scar stays hidden and quit talking."

"Yes, mistress."

By the time she was done dressing in the silly bunch of colorful silks, jewelry, and headdress that her useless husband insisted was appropriate attire, another slave arrived to announce the arrival of a visitor.

"Does Dhaval wish for me to stay hidden in my chambers, or does he wish to parade me about like a show pony to impress his friends again?"

This slave was an old man, who'd once been a cobbler in the city of Kanok, before he'd been punished for overcharging the army on a shipment of boots. "Neither, mistress. Roik Dhaval has gone to a meeting at the great house. The visitor is here to see you."

Thera was suspicious. *Who would want to see her?* The other wives ignored her. She was a social nobody here, but since she had no use for the vapid, useless beauties the other officers were married to, Thera was fine with being ignored. Hopefully it wasn't Dhaval's family. They either barely tolerated her, or held her in outright contempt.

"It's a risaldar from Vane, who says he was in the city on business. He didn't wish his arrival announced to the entire house, but asked to speak with you alone."

There was only one risaldar of House Vane who would go out of his way to visit this particular estate. Thera rushed past the slaves and practically ran for the stairs. From the balcony she saw him, a bit more wrinkled and grayer around the temples, but still as powerful a presence as ever.

"Baba!"

Andaman Vane grinned when he saw his daughter. "Hello, Thera."

"I'm so glad you're here." Overjoyed, she had to hold onto her ridiculous frilly dress to keep from tripping on the stairs, but when she got to the main floor she leapt into his arms and hugged her father tight. It was the happiest she'd been in ages.

"I didn't know you were coming to Kanok." Then she realized he was still standing in the entryway, wearing his boots. In Makao it was rude to enter a home without taking your shoes off. The slaves hadn't even invited him inside! Her own father! That was insulting, but he seemed so glad to see her he hadn't taken offense. "What're you doing here?"

"I had to deliver some reports to the great house. I don't have much time." He glanced at the two slaves still watching curiously from the top of the stairs, then whispered, "We must speak privately."

"Of course, this way." Barefoot, she led him out the door. There was a large garden in the middle of Dhaval's estate where Thera spent many hours because it was quiet, secluded, and enabled her to avoid her new family. "I have a garden where I like to pass the time."

The bushes had once been carved into animal shapes—a fashion copied from the warmer houses in the north—but Dhaval had eventually given up on the tedious practice, so now the central garden of their estate was more like a small overgrown forest. When they arrived at the quietest part, her father took in the wooden targets that Thera had tied to the decorative fence, with the thousands of notches left upon them from her throwing knives, and nodded appreciatively.

"For a moment I thought maybe you'd taken up gardening."

"I try to stay in practice. Apparently being able to pin a running rat with a spike at twenty paces is considered unladylike in these parts. How was I to know that?"

"The Makao are rather flamboyant and impractical. They've got you dressed like you're about to lead a parade."

Thera laughed. "They consider *this* casual. Can you believe it? I couldn't even kick a man above the knee in this frivolous outfit if my life depended on it. And these are their warriors. You should see how their first caste dress. They walk around like puffy, embroidered, giant flowers."

Speaking of clothing, her father was wearing the drab uniform of a risaldar, nothing like back when he'd been a mighty phontho, covered in bright ribbons and clanking medals. He wore only one medal now, a simple bronze medallion in the oval shape of a banyan leaf, awarded for courage in battle. It was the first award he had ever earned decades ago, and when she'd once asked about it, he'd told her it was the only medal that had ever really mattered to him. That was just how her father was. In all the years since his fall, he had never once acted bitter or resentful for choosing to stay by her side, but had instead rejoiced daily that she lived.

"So how is life among the perfumed fops?" her father asked, still smiling.

She almost told him the truth. He had no idea what manner of monster their house had married her off to, but she didn't have the heart to tell him how miserable she was. Andaman Vane was a proud warrior, driven by honor. He'd probably challenge Dhaval to a duel...Only Dhaval came from a powerful family, and her father had very little status. Her husband would just dismiss the challenge. If Andaman Vane angered Great House Makao again, this time they would surely take his life.

"It's fine. I'm doing well."

"What of your health?"

There had been one seizure, but it had been here in the garden, and there had been no witnesses. She'd woken up lying in the dirt, aching from violent muscle spasms. If the Voice had spoken that time, there'd been no one around to hear. It had left her weakened for several days afterward, but she'd blamed it on a fever and Dhaval had believed her.

"I have been well."

He looked around to make sure no one was eavesdropping on them. "And the Voice?"

She shook her head. Only Thera and her father knew about the Voice. Not even her mother had known about it before she had passed away. If news of her curse got out, marrying well would have been the least of her worries. The Voice was the sort of strange thing that would attract the attention of Inquisitors.

He sighed in relief. "Thank goodness. My greatest fear is that it comes upon you again, and I won't be around to protect you."

"It's been years since that...thing...last spoke. I think it's gone."

But her father didn't look so sure. "May we be that fortunate.

Now, I apologize for being so abrupt, but I have little time. I'm not supposed to be here at all. I'm merely serving as a guard for our delegation, and if they find out I left my post, I'll be severely reprimanded."

Thera was shocked, it wasn't like her father to shirk his duty. He'd only done that once before, and it had cost him dearly. "You should go before you get in trouble!"

"Seeing you is worth the risk. We traveled for a week to get here, yet our arbiter wouldn't even give me the smallest courtesy and allow me to visit my only child, who lives right down the street. To the ocean with him." He took hold of her arm. Somehow his hands of stone were always gentle when it came to her. "You must listen carefully, Thera. I've come to warn you. A house war is coming."

"What?" There hadn't been a house war in the west in her lifetime.

"The raids between Harban and Makao have been escalating. They've kept Vane very busy. I must say, your father has regained quite a bit of his old glory recently. I've led three raids already this year, looted two towns, and captured a whole garrison. It's certainly reminded the men how much better things were back when I was in charge."

"I hadn't heard about any of this. Has the Capitol authorized it?"

"Not at all. In fact, they've denied both great houses requests for reprisals, but things are spiraling beyond the first caste's control. There will be house war... No more raids. I speak of full-fledged warfare, the total might of both sides brought to bear against each other. It'll be glorious. I'm surprised your husband hasn't spoken of it. Your new family is in the thick of things."

She let that pass. They rarely spoke at all. There was no way to explain her relationship that wouldn't put her father in a difficult position. "Are they mad? If the Capitol doesn't approve, they'll set an example. I don't know how many times you told me that growing up. Don't enrage the Capitol. They'll send the Protectors in and kill everyone."

"They probably will, but in times of great strife comes great opportunity."

"Wait... What're you plotting?"

"It's best if I not say, and safer if you're not involved. You have a comfortable life here. I don't want to disrupt it."

Thera laughed. "Oh, I know you too well. You're up to something. Please, disrupt this comfortable life. I'd rather know the truth."

"It would put you in danger."

"As if I've never had to keep a secret before!"

"You're as stubborn as your mother."

"She was soft hearted. You mean as stubborn as you, old ox."

"You have me there, little tiger... However, this would test your loyalty, your new family versus—"

"Vane," Thera stated without hesitation. "I choose Vane."

None of that seemed to surprise him. He chuckled. "Very well... In a total war, if Makao is too busy fending off Harban, whose warrior caste is nothing to scoff at, then Vane has an opportunity to be a vassal no more. We'll break off, and declare ourselves free of Makao. We're tired of bleeding for them. Let the fools fight, and once they're fully committed, then we would have the chance to reclaim what is rightfully ours."

Thera was shocked by the audacity of the idea, and she had just been plotting how best to murder her husband. "Rebellion? Who is with you?"

"All of my old officers will follow me, and their men will follow them. Among the first caste, the name of Andaman Vane is worth salt water, but those who matter will still follow me into battle. The first hand out ranks and titles like holiday treats, but they don't understand real authority only comes when soldiers respect their commander. The Capitol won't care, as long as we pay our taxes and obligations. Our arbiters won't like it, because they never like when warriors take the initiative, but once I secure victory and we achieve great house status again, they'll be quick to act as if it was all their idea and claim the glory for themselves."

"And if you fail, they'll heap blame on you alone while they plead their ignorance." Her head was swimming. Thera had to sit down. She picked the closest bench, heedless of the dust on her fine dress. "This... this is..."

"Bold," he finished for her. "Of course, if I go through with it, you'll either have to deny me and pledge your undying loyalty to Makao, or you'll have to flee this place and return home. Even if you did forsake me, they still might try to use you as a hostage in negotiations. That's why I came here today, to warn you. Vane means everything to me, but I am not some Capitol politician who will use my own flesh and blood as a pawn. I willingly risk my own life, but that is my choice. I will not force that upon you."

This was a lot to absorb. "So you've come to ask your daughter's permission . . . to rebel against the Law?"

"When you put it that way, it doesn't sound particularly dignified. I wanted your opinion."

"Really?" Her father was one of the greatest war heroes in the west. "My opinion?"

He smiled. "I've missed having my best advisor by my side. And also I wanted to make sure you have an honorable way out first, so if I fail I don't drag you down with me."

Thera was quiet for a long time. She had a question, but she was afraid that she already knew the answer. "Who gave you this idea?"

Andaman Vane took a deep breath. "It is my own."

"No . . . It isn't."

"Then why ask the question if you already suspect the answer? It is my own *now*."

"This is what the Voice told you the last time it spoke. You never told me what it said. You declared it to be nonsense, and said not to dwell on it, but I could see it in your eyes. You were scared, but you were intrigued too. This was it, this was what that thing told you about, wasn't it?"

It was obvious where Thera had gotten her stubborn nature from. "I may not know what it is, where it comes from, or what it wants, but I know a good idea when I hear it."

"What did the Voice say? What've you been trying to protect me from?"

"I am out of time. I must go now." He began walking away.

Thera reached beneath her many silks, pulled out one of her hidden throwing knives, and hurled it end over end, planting it into the wooden target in front of her father's path with a solid *thunk*. And then she demanded with all the authority she could muster, "What did it tell you?"

He stopped and gave a resigned sigh. "Oh, my tenacious child, how I have missed you."

"I have to know. Please. I beg you, Baba. Tell me the truth."

Her father regarded her solemnly. "It said it kept you alive for a reason, to deliver its message. It said everything is going to change soon. I didn't believe it, but it predicted this war. It saw the future, and I didn't believe it until I saw those things with my own eyes. Specific things, during the chaos of battle, random events you . . . *it*, couldn't have known about years before they happened."

When the Voice came upon her, she couldn't hear it, as if she was sent someplace else, but it was loud and clear to those close enough to listen. "How can it tell the future?"

"I don't know. But it did, I swear to you it did."

"Did it say how the house war ends?"

"In a great bonfire, a thousand bodies piled high, while the Protectors watch them burn."

"Are you among them?" she asked, hesitant, afraid to know.

"It didn't say who was on the grisly pyre, but the Voice declared the time of rebellion to be at hand. *The time of rebellion,* Thera. Who else could it be speaking of other than Vane? This is our chance!"

She could see the gleam in his eye, the new energy he possessed. For the first time in many years, Andaman Vane had *hope.* She couldn't take that away from him, not after all that he had sacrificed for her.

"If you think this is for the best, I trust you. Do what you must."

"I promise that I will. The Voice said *you* would be the instrument that brings about this rebellion. Now I am certain. Thank you, Thera. We will not fail," Andaman Vane declared with all the sincerity of his great heart.

Thera dreamed of long forgotten gardens and foolish promises. The Voice never lied, but it was easy to misinterpret, and it made no allowance for wishful thinking. It gave hope, but hope could kill sure as an executioner's blade.

It had taken several slaves to remove the tiger trap, but after that Sikasso had let Thera keep the room. Once her head had cleared from the spell she'd been under, she'd been able to take in just how luxurious her surroundings were. The murals had been painted by a master: serene scenes of nature and bright, colorful recordings of great battles. She knew from the many burglaries that she'd committed that any of the sculptures here could be moved for a fortune. The value for just the jade and ivory in weight alone was impressive, let alone what collectors would pay for the illegal antique statues of old gods. The carpet was softer than the best bed she'd had as a child of the warrior caste, and the bed . . . well, once freed of the ropes, it was so indulgent it was like lying on a cloud. Truthfully, these were the nicest quarters she'd ever slept in, and Dhaval's family had been pretty rich.

All that luxury didn't keep Thera from trying to figure out how to escape. A nice prison was still a prison. She may have been untied, but the door remained locked. There was a window, with glass so fine that there wasn't so much as a hint of distortion or discoloration, but she was blocked from opening it by solid iron bars. The view outside was nothing but low, fat trees and fog, providing her with no clue as to her actual location.

For the first day after their agreement, Sikasso had left her alone, saying that she'd need time to recover her faculties from the invasive magic that he had used on her before they began work. Slaves had returned her rough traveling clothes, all freshly washed and repaired, though they didn't give back any of her many knives. She'd have to improvise something else for stabbing people in the meantime.

Then they had brought her a feast. At first she'd thought the slaves were preparing a banquet there was so much, but it was all meant for her, and it was all wonderful, with enough spice to bring tears to her eyes. One downside of living outside the Law was that you often ended up living off slop fit for untouchables. Eating well again was a bit overwhelming. Sikasso must have been trying to impress her.

It was said a leopard didn't change its spots, and a cruel assassin wouldn't suddenly become a friend. Even if Sikasso could free her from her curse, she had no doubt that he'd kill her the moment she was no longer of use. Deal be damned, she was getting out of here.

Whenever the slaves unlocked the door, she noticed that a wizard remained in the hall, watching. Or at least she assumed he was a wizard. They all looked like normal men, but this fellow kept one fist clenched, hiding something between his fingers the whole time. More than likely a piece of demon, and he was certainly ready to set her on fire, or whatever it was wizards did, should she try to run out.

Though she tried, the slaves wouldn't speak or even make

eye contact when they delivered food or removed dirty plates. Whenever she spoke to them, they'd ignore her until the task was complete, then look back at the wizard in the doorway, and he'd dismiss them with a nod of his head. She didn't even know if they were actually condemned slaves, or just very unlucky workers to have such odd and dangerous masters. At least they looked healthy, clean, and well fed.

She'd eaten enough at lunch to survive the week, but they still brought her dinner anyway. Luckily the locking mechanism was rather loud, so she was able to hide what she was working on before they entered. Previously, she'd decided that this time she would try to make conversation with the wizard. Thera would even attempt to be charming. As a product of the warrior caste, she wasn't very good at *charming,* but she knew that she was attractive, and there were times a smile and batting her eyelashes got her further than threats and sullen glares.

"There's plenty here if you'd like to share." She held up a bowl full of lamb in a thick red sauce.

"I do not." The wizard was a handsome man, thickly bearded, with strong features and broad shoulders, everything that his superior Sikasso was not.

"No need to stand there in the doorway. I'm not going anywhere."

"I'm to make sure of that."

"I'm Thera. What do they call you?"

"My name is not your concern." Even though he was probably several years younger than she was, he had one of those deep voices, where everything he said was conveyed with gravitas. He should have been a judge.

"No need to be rude."

"There was no need for you to cut Vilsaro's throat in Jharlang."

Thera lost her fake smile. "Vilsaro, huh? I didn't catch his name at the time."

"He was my friend."

"Well, your friend shouldn't have put his hands on me." While the wizard snarled at her, she stuck a big piece of lamb into her mouth and began to chew. "Mmm. That's good. Your loss."

He obviously wanted to say more, but apparently he had more respect for—or fear of—Sikasso than he had desire to avenge his dead friend, because he said nothing else on the topic.

"I am Kabir."

"See? Wasn't that easier? It is a pleasure to meet you, Kabir."

When the slaves were done serving, the wizard closed the door and locked it.

As soon as they were gone, Thera pulled out the thin piece of iron from her sleeve and got back to work. It had been a decorative end cap for one of the shelves until she'd pried it off. Then she retrieved the statue from beneath her pillow and went back to sharpening her shiv while she ate. The man with extra arms sitting cross legged must have been a common image back during the Age of Kings, because despite the Inquisition's best efforts to destroy all images of illegal gods, she'd seen quite a few of these around. Hopefully whoever he was, he wouldn't mind her using his base as a whetstone.

Chapter 10

The lock rattled again before sunrise. It was probably the slaves bringing Thera her breakfast.

The night before she had stuffed her pockets full of naan so she'd have something to eat while crossing the wilderness, and most importantly she'd gotten a decent edge on her improvised blade. It was nothing to be proud of, but it was thin enough to slip between ribs and sturdy enough not to snap on the first thrust. She'd use some excuse to close the distance, surprise the wizard, stab him a few times, and then flee. Simple.

Only it wasn't the young wizard at the door this time, but the far more dangerous Sikasso. At least she assumed the younger one was less deadly. It seemed like magic was the sort of thing where experience mattered more than physical strength.

"Good. You already have your boots on. We're going on a walk."

"Oh?" A different wizard didn't change her plans. At least he was alone, so there would be no slaves calling for help.

"It's good you have fashioned yourself a little knife and hidden it up your sleeve. It can be dangerous outside these walls."

Now *that* changed her plan. "How did you know?"

"You are in my house now, Thera. I see everything. You should know it insults me as a host that you would doubt my ability to keep you safe from harm." His voice grew cold and dangerous. "Leave it."

Thera sullenly pulled out her shiv and dropped it on the bed.

Sikasso had a malicious smile. "Don't worry. I have not taken offense. Only those who show initiative ever successfully learn to use magic. Now come along. It is not far, though if you get hungry you can always snack on some of that bread in your pockets."

Thera followed Sikasso. It was the first time she saw what was beyond her room. The walls were stone, but uniformly fitted and polished better than in any warrior's keep. The floors were hardwood, with different colored rugs every few feet. Her room had not been an anomaly. There was art everywhere, tapestries, paintings, and sculptures—some of which were far too big to steal easily. There were many other rooms, some doors open, revealing more rooms like hers, some closed, their contents a mystery.

The building was not nearly as large as the great house in Kanok, but if anything, it was finer.

They reached a large central hall. From up on the balcony, Thera could tell this was where the wizards dined, and home to even larger pieces of statuary. There was a great fireplace big enough to cook a whole cow in . . . She wasn't sure these wizards ate beef, traditionally some houses didn't care for it, but regardless, they could fit one in there if they wanted. A fire was going inside, sufficient to ward off the chill.

Adorning the walls were faded green banners featuring a red symbol which Thera had never seen before. These were obviously old, tattered and stained. A few of them even looked as if they'd been scorched in a fire.

"Who does that symbol represent?"

"House Charsadda."

"Never heard of it."

"Few have. That was what the Capitol wanted. It wasn't enough for us to be destroyed, but also removed from history. The judges are very good at erasing the past."

Houses were defeated, but they never really went away. Their people and holdings would be taken over by another. She knew that life well. "It's a vassal now then?"

"Like your own family, Vane, was conquered by the Makao long ago? Houses come and go, gobbling each other up, or civil wars split them in two, but this was nothing of the sort. When we fell, no neighbors wanted to take this place over. It was a house of lepers, and the others wouldn't risk contamination."

That made no sense to someone raised by warriors. When borders changed, new territory was valuable, and the towns inside, their workers could be taxed in exchange for protection. "Surely someone claims this land?"

"By the lines on a map, yes, though only wild men and feral beasts live nearby. Here? This house, once the seat of our power, it was to remain abandoned. To the Capitol we were a piece of gangrenous flesh, amputated, and the stump cauterized with a branding iron..." Sikasso paused, frowning. "Strange. I've used that analogy while showing people around many times before, but this is the first time I've been able to understand such pain on a personal level. It...hurts."

She hurried and changed the subject from the wizard's missing limb before it put him in a fouler mood. "You have a beautiful home."

"It has taken great effort. When our house fell, the only thing left standing of this place was the walls." Looking smug, Sikasso led the way down the curving stairs. "We may have been forsaken by the Capitol, but my predecessors decided there was no need to live as barbarians. What you are seeing now is the result of five generations of repair and rebuilding."

Thera understood money better than most from her caste, because she'd spent the last few years of her life stealing it in order to survive. What she was seeing here indicated a vast amount of wealth. "You make your way as assassins. Good money in that, I take it?"

"Not everyone can afford to pay us in black steel, yet there is always demand for our services. There are other forms of compensation."

Thera knew a man's life was only worth however many notes it took to bribe an untouchable to stab him. "You didn't build this palace off murder alone. Killers come cheap."

"We don't."

"What makes you so valuable?"

"That requires a broad answer," Sikasso said as they reached the main floor. "If you need a wizard to do something inside the bounds of the Law, there are far more economical options than the Lost House. Outside the Law, however, when powerful men need things done in secret, no one else can offer what we can. Enough talk of business, I must show you something."

As they walked along, Thera was able to figure out what was bugging her about this place. The building was large, but felt relatively empty, more museum than home. She saw two or three of the silent slaves, heads shaved and clothes plain, for every person she suspected from their finer dress was a wizard. Those all seemed to watch her suspiciously. None acknowledged her, but all of them were deferential toward Sikasso.

It took her awhile to realize that all of the wizards were men. The only other women she saw were among the slaves. There were no children at all. Did the wizards keep their families elsewhere? But before she could ask, they had reached the main doors.

In a normal estate of this size, warriors would have been obligated to guard such doors, but these wizards didn't seem to have any warriors. Maybe they thought they were too good for her old caste? Sikasso casually waved his hand toward the doors and they were flung open as if by a mighty wind. Thera corrected herself. They *definitely* thought they were too good for the warriors.

Outside the world was wrapped in a thick gray fog. Frogs croaked and unfamiliar insects buzzed. She could barely see the tops of the trees—old, wispy things—and glowing bugs flying between them. There was a cobblestone path lit with glowing braziers burning every twenty feet. Sikasso began walking down the illuminated pathway. It was chilly out, so Thera pulled her coat tight about her. She still didn't know where in Lok she was, but if the whole region was cloaked in this damnable fog, it would make navigating difficult. Though it would make escape easier, assuming wizards didn't have a way to see through it.

When she turned back to look at the great house, it was a solid construction, but nothing that could resist a siege. It looked like there had been more walls once, but they were toppled now. A few towers rose through the mist, but they were broken and covered in moss. "You've no outer defenses."

"We've no need. The only things we have to defend ourselves from here wouldn't be stopped with mere walls."

The stones were also covered in moss, so their steps were muffled. Everything here seemed soft and green. They walked through the mist for a few minutes, before Sikasso asked, "Do you know how magic really works?"

"I've seen what it can do."

"I'm not speaking of the effect, but how it is accomplished. Do you know what magic *is*?"

"Magic is just magic."

"Only a simpleton defines a word with that same word. Don't be a simpleton." Sikasso halted in a slightly wider spot in the road. "Magic is all about energy and elements, force and patterns. Look around you. Air, earth, life. What you see is not really what it is. The whole is constructed from various elements, billions of tiny pieces, smaller than the eye can see, compacted together to form different types of matter."

All Thera could see was fog. It smelled like rotting plants. "Sure."

"Magic is simply a different kind of matter, also made up of minuscule elements, only it is unique in that it can be controlled by one who has the will to do so. All matter exists in various patterns. Magic simply allows me to direct it into a new pattern."

As Sikasso spoke every one of the lanterns went out, plunging them into darkness.

"What's happening?"

"I have taken us outside the waking world so you can see things as they truly are."

Thera didn't move. It was black as coal. She could no longer feel the clammy fog clinging to her skin or hear the frogs or smell the decay. There was nothing at all. All she could hear was the pounding of her heart. Sikasso had killed more than the lights. It was as if he'd closed off the entire world. She was afraid to move. If she took a step would she become lost?

Except the wizard's voice still reached her. "We are now *outside* the patterns. A useful space for when I wish to travel somewhere without being seen, or walk through a wall, or bypass a lock, but that's not why I brought you here. This is a test to find out if you can see magic at all."

She couldn't see a damned thing, and frankly it was terrifying.

"Most can't. Open your mind to the world around you. If you were born with the gift, then you will be able to sense the patterns. In order to change the structures you must understand them first."

She tried, she really did, but it was like being buried alive. "I've got nothing."

"You have no inclination toward wizardry. Unfortunate." Sikasso then demonstrated that he was no regular teacher. "If you can't, then I suppose I'll just have to sell you to the Inquisition."

That was almost as scary as being stuck on this...outside. She thought about lying, and declaring that she could see, but then he'd probably ask her to describe it, and her lies would fall apart.

Then Thera could vaguely sense *something*. She couldn't see it exactly, but it *felt* like it was there. Only it wasn't *here*, it was back in the waking world. She couldn't tell what it was, except that it felt old...and dangerous. It felt like she'd walked into a cloud of molten sparks. "There's something coming, Sikasso. Take us back. Take us back now!"

"Ah, you're not completely blind then after all. One of the Dasa has sensed us and come to investigate. Back in the waking world all it will see of you is a shadow. When the superstitious cry about seeing ghosts from the corner of their eye, they probably caught a glimpse of a wizard skulking through this realm."

The cloud of sparks was hovering over her. Past that was a heat, like an open flame, no, more like a blacksmith's forge, hot enough to soften steel. It seemed more curious than malevolent, but she feared that was about to change. "Let me go!"

"Alas, I have twisted the world into this state, but I have no more magic left to get us out."

As the heat closed in, Thera closed her eyes, but that made it no darker. "Surely you've got some demon on you."

"I was curious if you became desperate enough, if you could call upon your magic to set you free."

She suspected the Voice was worthless for that, as it had never helped, only caused her trouble and then left her stranded in dangerous situations. "You're a liar. Even if I could, I might free myself and leave you trapped. You'd have brought magic at least enough for yourself."

"See? I knew you weren't a simpleton." As Sikasso said that, her senses quickly returned. The lights flickered back into existence. Insects chirped. The smell of a swamp assaulted her nose.

And a monster was standing right in front of her. Thera gasped in surprise, reached for a dagger that wasn't there, and nearly tripped over her own feet as she tried to get away. She crashed against the nearest pole, causing the brazier to tip.

The creature was the size of a man, but built like someone

had draped a blue sack over a skeleton and then pulled it tight. It had a head, but no face. No mouth, no nose, just an indent where eye sockets would have been in a skull. The creature was dressed in unfamiliar armor made of round plates connected by mail, and it carried a battle axe in its thin blue hands. The steel was speckled with rust.

"Demon!"

"Hardly. It's merely one of our Dasa, a guardian servant... Continue your patrol." Sikasso made a dismissive gesture, and the thing began shuffling away.

"What sort of witchcraft is that?" As she asked that, she realized she must have sounded like Ashok.

"They are a relic from the old days, before the Age of Kings even. The template to create them has long been lost to us. They are resilient, but there are very few left in the world. Sometimes one is found inert in an ancient ruin, and fools smash them open to get the chunk of black steel inside, but we pay a good price for them to be brought here instead. Once agitated, they are far more dangerous than they appear...I suppose they're like a wizard in that way."

She watched in stunned disbelief as the thing plodded off down the path back toward the house. "Is it alive?"

"No more than a worker's machine made of gears and levers is alive. It is powered, and thus moves. They neither eat nor breathe. They have no desires or intellect beyond that required to obey basic commands."

She'd been raised to mistrust magic. They had no use for a wizard's tricks in Vane. The darkness and the monster had unnerved her more than she wanted to let on. It was a lot to take in so quickly. She wanted to get out of this nightmare place. "Is that what you wanted me to see?"

Sikasso smiled. "Neither of those were the purpose of our little walk, just distractions along the way. No, come. It is a bit further."

Now chilled to her core, Thera followed him in silence. So wizards could see all those little bits that made up the patterns of everything, but for her to see anything at all it had taken a walking relic with black-steel guts to be breathing distance away. Earlier she'd been worried about escaping through the fog, but the Dasa didn't even seem to need eyes to see, and had found her when she wasn't even really there. When Sikasso said it obeyed commands, she was certain he wasn't talking about hers. The presence of the guardian servant complicated matters, but that didn't mean that escape was impossible.

Sikasso seemed to be enjoying their stroll and one-sided conversation. "You asked earlier about how I change form? Those are simply other templates we've mastered. The bird, the snake, the swarm, the tiger, and more, all of those were handed down by the ancients. The elements that make up my body are redistributed accordingly. Yet each time, there is a cost. When we use magic, some fraction of it is consumed in the process. The tiny particles do their work, then expire. The greater the feat, the further you shift the pattern, the more magic dies."

That she knew. There was a good criminal trade in demon parts. "Which is why the things that hold it are so costly."

"It's simple economics. Great demand, limited supply. Real magic comes from only two known sources, black steel and demons. The uneducated call the fire and thunder the fanatics of Fortress make magic, but they're simply utilizing natural processes. Black steel is finite and irreplaceable. What the ancients left behind is all there is, but it is dense with extremely powerful magical elements. The magic harvested from sea demons is weaker, but replaceable, albeit with extreme difficulty."

"I'd guess it's a bit harder than shearing a sheep." Thera laughed.

Sikasso did not. "And now there is a possible third kind . . . We have arrived."

The cobblestone path abruptly ended at a chasm. It dropped a long way, and the bottom was obscured by the mist. The ground seemed torn, as if there had been a violent upheaval which had split it apart long ago, but now every edge had been softened by moisture and moss. Due to the fog, Thera couldn't see what was on the other side.

Then she heard a distant, rhythmic noise that made her stomach clench with dread. She had not heard that sound for a long time.

The crashing of waves. The smell of salt.

"Are we by the *ocean*?"

Sikasso gave her a grim smile as he sat on a nearby rock. "Now you will see why you shouldn't be so quick to refuse my protection."

The sun was just beginning to appear, the top of an orange ball over the too-flat horizon. The fog glowed with reflected light. It took a while, but Sikasso seemed to be enjoying her growing discomfort. She watched in horror as the sun gradually burned away the mist. They were on a cliff top, overlooking hell itself.

To the east was the sea, vast, unending, and filled with evil. She began to catch glimpses of other buildings, but they were ruins, fallen towers and broken walls that had collapsed during whatever cataclysm had torn this ground apart. Then with a gasp she realized that some of the rocks that were splitting the waves below were actually the roofs of now submerged buildings. The land to the north of them was visible now, and it was water and marshes as far as her eye could see.

The palace that had become the House of Assassins had been built on a bluff overlooking a city. They were standing on the only part that hadn't been flooded.

"The other sides are the same." Sikasso could tell exactly what she was thinking. "And it is as infested with submerged demons as you imagine. There are a few safe paths through the flooded forest to get back to the Law-abiding world, but you would never find them on your own."

Demons were a nearly unstoppable force of hunger and destruction. Pass too close to a lurking one, and you'd be torn to pieces and crammed into its jaws before you even knew it was there.

"No whole man would willingly live this close to hell. What is this place?"

"Before the demons rained from the sky, man crossed the sea in mighty ships. This city was what they called a *port*. The ocean was not always this close. The ancients had built dams big enough to control the flow of the River Nansakar, and levees, canals, and huge walls that held back the sea. Even after the demons turned the ocean into hell, long after every real ship in the world had been rent apart by their claws and sent to the bottom, man still lived here. It was said it was too beautiful to abandon.

"We survived here for centuries, but when the combined wrath of the Capitol was brought to bear against us, even the earth trembled at their will. They shattered those ancient dams, the waters came rushing in, our people were devoured by demons, and House Charsadda was consumed by hell."

Thera shuddered at the thought. Over the last few years she

had spent a great deal of time on the rivers of Lok, far more than any whole man would consider sane, and was even brave enough that she had learned to swim, but that was in fresh water, and only a long way from the sea. It was rare for a demon to travel very far up a river, but entering salt water meant almost certain death. She'd only been in the ocean once, briefly, and that trespass had nearly cost her life.

"What crime was so terrible for your people to enrage the Capitol so?"

"The Law cannot tolerate equals, only subjects... But the past isn't why I brought you here, Thera Vane. You need to understand there is no reason for you to continue damaging my furniture, snapping off pieces to fashion into knives. Attacking my people is futile. There is no escape, because there is nowhere to escape to. Fulfill your bargain, and after that I will guide you through the flooded forest. Until then we will show you how to use magic. You saw the Dasa, so you've got some minor ability. Perhaps learning to control traditional magic will enable you to unlock this third source."

"Me? You would teach *me* to be a wizard."

"I have more important duties. I will obligate someone else to be your teacher. Be warned, many of my brothers disagree with my decision. They think we should have already sold you to the Inquisition, or that we should simply avoid any risk, kill you, and be done with it. It is only by my whim you still live."

Thera stepped to the edge of the cliff and looked down at the ruins far below. "And if I can't learn?"

Sikasso was completely sincere yet threatening at the same time. "Then it would be better to leap over the side now and spare yourself the suffering."

Chapter 11

~~~VVV~VVV~~~

Three days had passed since Jagdish and Gutch had entered the city of Neeramphorn. Three days without word... Ashok had grown restless.

They had taken over an abandoned mining camp, and there they had hidden like criminals, avoiding all contact. They had gathered wood and taken several deer for meat. By day Keta would tell his made-up stories, and how soon they would recover the prophet, their magnificent army would journey south, join with the rest of the rebellion, and go forth righting past wrongs, so that the gods would once again smile upon the land which had forsaken them. So on and so forth. Ashok suspected that if he had not been present to frighten them, the Somsak raiders were restless and bored enough they'd have turned to banditry. Even fanatics could only take so much preaching.

The first day he had been annoyed by the delay. So he had found an old wood cutter's ax and split enough logs to last a small village the whole winter, thinking the entire time about how if he was still a Protector he could have just walked into Neeramphorn and started executing criminals until someone drew him a map to the Lost House.

It was exceedingly difficult. He had only one reason to live, one goal to focus upon, and no good way to achieve it. He *hated* depending on others. Protectors usually worked alone. Ashok had enjoyed that.

The second day, he decided that he needed to do something useful to keep from dwelling on his oath. He had passed the time in prison by training with Jagdish, so Ashok decided to do the same thing here. The Somsak were fearless as normal men could be and didn't need much encouragement. They considered it an honor to spar against the man who had defeated their army by himself. Even though this time he was armed with a stick rather than Angruvadal, they still hadn't done much better than they had in Jharlang.

By lunch time all the Somsak were exhausted, nursing bruises, and putting snow on their swelling joints. So Keta had approached Ashok with a bizarre request.

"It's nice you're sharing your knowledge with the warriors."

Ashok didn't know if it was *sharing,* so much as pummeling them gave him something to do. Except he knew from his own time as a student of Master Ratul that there was a lesson to be learned from every beating.

"They are fierce, but clumsy. Their house has not trained them sufficiently. They expect aggression to carry the day. It can, until it does not. Determination rarely beats skill, and determination alone *never* beats skill and determination..." Ashok stopped, not sure why he was explaining the martial philosophies of the Protector Order to Keta, whose knowledge of combat was limited to swinging about a meat cleaver with wild abandon. "What do you want, Keeper?"

"A small request, nothing more." The middle of the old mining camp was open. The snow had been trampled flat by shuffling feet and falling bodies. Keta gestured toward where the rest of his new followers were repairing an old shack so they'd have a warmer place to sleep. "What of them?"

"What of them? They're worker caste. They're doing what they're supposed to. As are the warriors."

Keta was a thin, balding man. He had a love of rhetoric, more passion than sense, and was too clever for his own good, a terrible combination of traits for one born casteless. If he'd been born of first-caste parents he probably would have wound up an arbiter by now. "Come now, Ashok, you are still trapped in your old way of thinking. The castes are a lie, created to keep everyone inside a fence that does not really exist. We are not cattle to be herded."

"Every man has his place. To break that fundamental truth is to endanger all of the Law."

"Where is your place then, Ashok?"

"Here." He frowned. "Apparently."

"That's right. Outside the stifling confines of your Law, where free men are able to choose their own way. Their fate decided by the sweat of their brow rather than the station of their birth. Those men aren't just workers any more than I'm just a casteless butcher."

"How joyous. We can all be criminals together."

"I think some of Thera's sarcastic nature rubbed off on you during our journey. Though it's an improvement over when we first met and you were continually threatening to kill me, and that one time you nearly strangled me. But think of it, the gods want you to lead the rebellion's army, but that army will not be made up of just warriors, it will be made up of *everyone* who desires freedom."

Ashok had his reasons. Anyone else who chose this path willingly was a fool. He had no desire to be a curator of fools. "Once I have found her, I will do as the prophet orders. Nothing more, nothing less. If I'm told to train workers or non-people to fight—disgusting violation of the Law that may be—I'll do what is commanded."

"You shouldn't do it because it's ordered, but because it's right! You're a free man now. You need to learn to understand that."

He had spent his entire life being told what was wrong and right, first by the Law, and now he was condemned to be told the same things by the supposed voice of the gods. "Tell me your request so that I can be spared your philosophy lesson."

"Teach those workers to be soldiers. I know we are few here, but there are a multitude waiting at our hidden fortress in Akershan. It is still small, but the rebellion is growing. The seeds you plant now will someday bloom into mighty—"

"All this talk makes me want to return to the days of threats and choking. Fine. You are the representative of the prophet I must serve. Send over those workers, I will teach them."

Keta grinned. He seemed to savor these small victories.

"But I warn you now, Keeper, everyone has a place for a reason. We are only what we are."

The odd little man seemed to thoroughly enjoy these talks. "Yet before me stands arguably the greatest combatant in the world, who was once a little starving casteless blood scrubber. So much accomplished from so very little. Your very existence disproves the basic premise of the Law. From nothing you rose to the top of an elite order of the highest caste."

Ashok ground his teeth. "Now I'm back to nothing. Like everything which strays from the Law, the aberration was corrected. And when the time comes for your rabble to face a real army, made up of warriors who've trained hard their whole lives, then your people will fail and they will die. That will be on your head, not mine."

"Don't worry. There is already a prophecy about that. When we truly go to war I know that the Forgotten will provide the weapons necessary for us to prevail."

"So your god is going to just give us weapons?"

"He gave us you, did he not? Have some faith, Ashok!"

He could not say it aloud because of his vow of secrecy, but Ashok's thought was *Grand Inquisitor Omand and a group of vengeful judges assigned me to you, not your god.* "Send them over, Keta. Let's get this over with."

So on the afternoon of the second day, Ashok tried to teach the workers. It went far worse for them than the Somsak. They at least knew how to hold a sword. But the workers were tough and could deal with more pain and discomfort than expected, he'd give them that. They'd all been miners, and swinging a pick all day had given them strong arms, but they had a long way to go before they would ever be anything beyond an embarrassment on the battlefield.

Though deep down, Ashok had to admit that if given time they did not have, then there was potential. Realistically, he was not the man to teach them how to be soldiers, because Ashok was not himself a soldier. Protectors were an elite group of specialists, not the rank and file spearmen who took and held ground. The Order did not have its own army. It did not know how to build or maintain one. When a Protector arrived somewhere they simply commanded the local warriors to obey, and they did, or they'd face the full wrath of the Law. Nobody could outfight a Protector, but there was far more to soldiering than being good with a sword. It was about discipline, responsibility, and accountability. These men would be far better off with someone like Jagdish to guide them, not that he thought Jagdish would dishonor himself by giving warrior secrets to a lower caste.

On the third day, Ashok continued working with his army.

He made them fight so he could observe. The warriors embarrassed the workers, easily defeating them, but then Ashok in turn embarrassed the warriors. As his own sword masters had taught, humility was vital. A student was more likely to listen when they knew their teacher could destroy them with ease. And Ratul had beaten Ashok, many, many times.

One part of him wanted these men to fail because they were enemies of the Law. Only in the moment, when sticks crossed, and the combatants were struggling for breath, muscles aching, being thrown down over and over, he didn't think about such high-minded things. There was just the repetition, the violence, and hopefully, improvement.

For the first time, Ashok bothered to learn all of their names.

Though, he still did not want to hear their stories. For whatever reason whenever there was a lull, one of them would always feel compelled to try and explain why they had chosen to join the Sons of the Black Sword. Something about how they truly believed in the Forgotten, or they had somehow been wronged by the Law, or whatever their justification was. The miners talked about being down in the dark, with tons of rock creaking over their heads, and praying to gods begging not to be crushed. They didn't know these gods, but the Capitol couldn't save them down in their holes. Only gods could keep them from being buried. So gods *had* to be real, because the miners *needed* them to be real.

Whenever they started talking like that, Ashok took that as a sign that they'd caught their breath, and then put them back to practicing their forms again. The only way they would receive his approval today was through their efforts. No matter how much they implored their gods for mercy, Ashok would give them none during training.

As the sun went down, they gathered for the dinner that Keta had prepared—venison again—and ate in exhausted silence. Ashok was thankful for that. It reminded him a bit of his time as an acolyte, when they'd been pushed so hard all day that there was no conversation over meals, just tired children inhaling their rations as quickly as possible, afraid that the masters would decide to interrupt their meal time in order to send them back out. Only the winter was far milder here in the east than in the high mountains of Devakula.

The Keeper was smart enough to spare them a sermon that night. If he had tried, Ashok would have made sure Keta participated in training the next day. They'd see how much energy he had to preach then. Ashok decided he might just do that anyway, the Keeper might as well learn how to use that meat cleaver he always kept hidden in his coat.

Dinner was interrupted by the return of their lookout. He heard the scuff of boots on rocks, and the creak of a crossbow on its sling, long before the returning Somsak reached the shack. It was Shekar's turn on watch, but he should have waited out there for his relief. He had been stationed where he had a good view of the main road. Something must have happened.

Ashok stood and opened the door, filling the shack with freezing wind. Everyone else quit eating to see what was happening. "What is it, Shekar?"

He was the oldest of the Somsak, but that wasn't saying much. The mountain raiders tended to die young. "A rider carrying a lantern passed on the road. He barely slowed as he reached our trail, but it was obvious he was looking for the sign for this old mine. He paused just long enough to drop this in the middle of the road where it would be seen." The warrior handed over a wooden tube. "I didn't want to abandon my post, but I figured you would want to see it right away, General."

Ashok took it and removed the cap. There was a sheet of paper rolled up inside. "It's almost time for change of watch anyway. Get some food and warm yourself by the fire. Who is next?"

"I am, General," said a worker named Gupta.

"Then go before we are overrun with Inquisitors."

The men laughed. Ashok's scowl told them he wasn't joking. Gupta picked up his gloves, wool hat, and still-unfamiliar spear and hurried into the dark. "Try to at least scream a warning as you are murdered!" one of his friends shouted after him. In answer, Gupta waved his hand as if it were a swimming fish, an extremely rude gesture among the lower castes.

Ashok removed the letter and silently read it by the light of their fire. The men went back to their exhausted chewing, but they were curious.

"What is it?" Keta asked.

"A message from Gutch..."

"Is all well?"

To answer truthfully would demoralize the men. "Let us speak outside, Keeper."

✧   ✧   ✧

It is with great sadness that I write this letter, for I, your loyal servant Gutch, am in need of assistance. Upon arrival it was discovered that my former associates have had a falling out and are engaged in a gang war of the utmost brutality. I have been captured and am being held for ransom.

The bodyguard you so thoughtfully provided kept me safe for a few days, until this morning, when we were inadvertently separated. I do not know his location or condition. However, I was unable to escape.

My capturers originally intended to execute me as punishment for some perceived wrongs made against them many years ago. However, once I explained that you, my noble employer, were a rich and powerful high-status arbiter come all the way from the Capitol seeking the discreet purchase of certain items, they changed their minds and have decided to ransom me back to you for the paltry sum of five hundred notes. This is a truly humble amount considering the value I bring to your estate.

My capturers are watching as I write this, and helpfully suggested that I should include the fact that if you do not pay this ransom, I shall be killed in an extremely gruesome manner, which they are now describing to me with great zeal in excessive bloody detail.

Please bring the ransom to an establishment called the Face of the East, in the pleasure district of Neeramphorn, by midnight tomorrow, or I shall die. They now add that it only takes one servant to make a delivery, and if more are seen, I shall die. It seems that the longer I write the more caveats they are adding, all of which result in my death, so I shall cease now.

Sincerely your ever faithful servant Gutch

A hasty post script! Because I know my master values his privacy, he should be aware that some of his old friends from the Capitol are here in the city, and it would be best if he avoided them.

Keta finished reading the letter. "He's a long-winded sort."

That comment showed a remarkable lack of self-awareness. "Without the smuggler, our only path to find Thera is closed."

"But, Ashok, what if he's turned on us? This could be a trick, luring us out to be captured."

"A possibility, though by the mention of old friends, I believe Gutch speaks of Protectors in Neeramphorn." Very few people could ever be accused of being Ashok's *friends*. "If it was a trap, why warn me of their presence?"

"I don't know. He's an untrustworthy worker. They lie and cheat each other constantly!"

"Only yesterday you were lecturing me about how the castes were a fabrication."

"That was before I was worried about the possibility of walking into a trap! We're criminals because we're standing up against an oppressive regime. Gutch is a criminal because he's greedy... But we have to find Thera. Ah!" Keta threw up his arms in frustration. "I don't know what to do."

That was because Keta was more of a talker and a thinker than a man of action. Ashok didn't have that problem. While Keta had been reading the note, Ashok had begun strapping on weapons and gathering supplies from the packs outside. Their tiny building was too small to hold them and their equipment. "Do you have five hundred notes left?"

"Not even close at this point."

"Then a trade is not an option. I shall go into the city to find Gutch and Jagdish. They gave us until tomorrow, so they will not expect me tonight. If it is a trap, I will kill everyone involved. Then I will find the illegal magic–smuggling gang, on my own if necessary, and make them talk."

"That's madness with Protectors there."

"I will find a way. However, regardless of what happens in Neeramphorn, you must take these men and go south. It is time for you to return to your rebellion."

"What? No. Not as long as Thera—"

Ashok held up one hand. "Do you trust me, Keeper?"

Keta hesitated a bit too long. "Yes... Mostly."

"Then understand, if the Protectors discover I am here, escape will become very difficult. The rest of you are not fast enough. They will find you and kill you."

"She's the prophet, Ashok. I can't just abandon her."

"You're not. I will find her. The rest of you will only slow me down."

Keta was obviously torn. He suspected that the little man cared for Thera as a woman, and not just as his prophet, but Ashok also knew that he had been agonizing over being away from his rebellion for so long. He babbled perpetually about how good life was in their hideout. Keta had been sending them secret messages through a network of casteless insurgents, but coded notes were not the same as real leadership. He had inspired them, guided them, and kept them alive despite being hunted by the forces of the Law, and now he was worried they were falling apart without him.

"Promise me, Ashok, that you won't give up on her."

"Do you question the word I have already given?" Now *that* was insulting, but Ashok kept his anger in check. For a fanatical criminal, Keta meant well. "I have already given an oath more powerful than anything you will ever understand. I have sworn to protect her, so it will be done."

"Poisoned, half drowned, and delirious you mentioned this oath. I know you made one to somebody, but I don't know to who or why. You've never spoken more of it."

"And I never will. Now I must go. In the morning, ride south. I'd suggest avoiding the city. It may be in turmoil."

The Keeper of Names paced back and forth as he ran his hands through his wispy hair. "Fine! The Sons of the Black Sword will ride for Akershan. After you find Thera, please, you must bring her back to our hidden fortress."

It was hidden well enough that even the Protectors had not found it despite searching for a couple of years. Thera knew the way. Ashok did not. They had wisely kept that secret from him. "And if she is already dead?"

Keta cringed. He'd been avoiding thinking about that all-too-likely possibility. "Then you can still join us. The Forgotten chose you. The rebellion still needs you. I will tell you how to find the secret entrance."

Ashok shook his head. "No need. If the prophet is gone, then my duty is finished. Principle demands I avenge her and punish all responsible, but then I will gladly walk into the sea and trouble this world no more. Farewell, Keeper." He started toward the road.

Keta called after him. "I know she lives! The prophecies are not yet fulfilled. We will meet again in Akershan, because the gods are not done with you yet!"

Ashok did not give a damn about gods' opinions on the matter.

Chapter 12

He ran all the way to Neeramphorn. Using the Heart of the Mountain he could see in the dark better than a horse and was nearly as fast. The air was thin and foul, and his exertions required him to breathe more of it. When he saw the lantern light of a gatehouse, Ashok slowed to a walk and then moved off the road and crouched behind a tree.

Counting the guards, even if there were double their number inside the gatehouse, he could kill them all without too much trouble, but hoped that would be unnecessary. Ashok preferred being direct rather than subtle, but he could not afford to attract the attention of the Protectors. And truthfully, he found himself troubled by killing outside the justification of the Law.

Luckily this time there was another way. There were many stalls and wagons to provide cover, and since the gates were closed for the night, the proprietors were gathered around their own fires, eating, talking, or in some cases, already snoring. There were a few lanterns hanging around the gate itself, but the edges were cloaked in shadow. The stonework was rough, and that meant there would be hand holds. It looked like it might be a difficult climb...but not for one who had touched the Heart of the Mountain.

Calling upon its magic to make his senses sharp, Ashok snuck to the wall, darting from shadow to shadow. He was in a long dark coat and hood, with his weapons secured beneath so they wouldn't rattle. He breathed through his scarf so they wouldn't spot the rising breath. Some of the merchants were keeping an eye out for trouble, but they were concentrating on protecting their goods from robbers. Luckily there were no dogs to start barking at him.

A few times he made a small bit of noise, but the encampment here more than covered it. Not to mention the guards weren't paying that much attention, and the city on the other side of the gate was exceedingly loud. Then someone began plucking the strings on a veena, and a woman began singing a song. Another merchant joined in with a drum. No one would hear him over that racket.

Reaching the wall, Ashok scanned for solid holds, then shifted the power of the Heart to strengthen his limbs. He jumped and caught a ledge ten feet up. Dangling there, fingers locked like a vise, he waited to see if the guards had heard, but they were still continuing their conversations. So he began to climb, shifting the Heart's magic from his limbs to his eyes whenever he needed to spy a new hold, and then turning back to make leaps that would leave a normal man broken on the rocks below.

Sensing no guard posted at the top, Ashok made it through the battlements. Below him stretched the smoky chaos of Neeramphorn. The other side of the wall was better lit, but nobody was looking up, so Ashok leapt down and landed crouched, absorbing an impact which would snap a regular man's legs.

Ashok hadn't seen the soldier because he was lying in a pile of straw, nearly empty bottle of wine in hand. The warrior's eyes widened when he saw the man in black fall from the sky. Before he could shout, Ashok was leaning over him, hand crushed over his mouth, eye to hooded eye.

"This is only a bad dream," Ashok whispered. "Go back to sleep. You would not want to meet me in the waking world."

The warrior nodded vigorously. When released the man didn't cry out. In fact he made a great show of crunching his eyes tight shut and curling into a ball on the straw. Some of the warrior caste were certainly braver than others.

Ashok was so quick that he was two streets away before the frightened warrior opened his eyes, realized he was alone, and tried to raise the alarm. Hopefully enough wine was gone from that bottle that when his fellows heard the report of threatening figures materializing from the night sky, they'd dismiss it as drunken nightmares.

It had been many years since he'd last been to Neeramphorn, but the city had experienced such rapid growth that this area had not even been inside the walls then. It was so industrious that even after dark in the winter, the streets remained busy. Once he was certain he was away from suspicion, Ashok got out of the shadows and onto the boardwalk. His coat was long enough to hide his sword. With his hood up and scarf pulled over his face, he didn't look too different from the locals. Since these were by nature a busy people, even his quick, determined walk was not out of place.

The crowd surged around him as shifts changed, tired workers going home and fresh workers going in. When he began spotting familiar landmarks, Ashok set his course toward the pleasure district. Industry gave way to the businesses that served them. There were a multitude of food stands, and a great many workers were on their dinner break. The coal smoke was replaced with smells of frying dumplings and curries, far more appetizing than yet another serving of Keta's gamey deer.

Ashok himself did not understand commerce. It had always been beneath his station. When a Protector needed something, he simply requisitioned it in the name of the Law. Now he found himself wishing that he'd taken some of Keta's banknotes in order to buy a decent meal. But that was just weakness speaking, because a criminal did not deserve a good meal, so Ashok ignored the delicious smells and refocused on his mission.

He began seeing red lanterns. The pleasure district was on the border between the Thao neighborhoods and those controlled by Kharsawan and Akershan. This was where most of the legal casinos, fighting arenas, brothels, and opium dens were located. It was open to everyone but the non-people. There would even be members of the first caste here, though they would more than likely be in disguise.

As the city had grown, the pleasure district had needed to expand, but trapped in narrow valleys, there was nowhere to go but up. The mountain was not too steep here, so they had built up the sides, driving pilings into the rocks. The buildings had gotten taller and taller over the years, and then they'd been connected by catwalks, to smoothly move customers from their betting to their drinking, all out of the weather. If you hit someone in the face with a cold mountain wind they might sober up enough to want to keep some of their notes. Ashok may not have grasped the intricacies of commerce, but the merchants of Neeramphorn certainly did.

The Face of the East was a large four-story building, connected to all the other buildings around it. According to the signs and what he could see through the windows and balconies, it catered to workers of wealth and warriors of low to medium status, and it offered gambling, alcohol, poppies, and pleasure women. Judging by the crowd outside, it was a popular place. Well guarded too, judging by the armed men controlling the door.

A few warriors tried to enter, but they were stopped and told they couldn't come in wearing their swords. Drunken brawls were one thing, but drunken sword fights could be incredibly destructive. It was an insult to ask a warrior to give up his sword, and offense might be taken, but the clever merchants had found a way around that custom. Right beside the entrance was a sword polisher's stand. It was a polite lie which enabled the warriors to say they weren't being disarmed while they drank themselves stupid. Instead they were having their weapon professionally sharpened, cleaned, and secured until they returned to claim it with a ticket.

If this was where the bounty was to be delivered, then Gutch was more than likely being held inside, or at least somewhere nearby. If he'd still had the full authority of the Law, Ashok would have walked right up to the door, announced himself, made his demands, and then cut down anyone who disagreed. Such behavior now would only bring the Law down on his head. He had to find Gutch another way, but after twenty years as one, it was hard not to think like a Protector.

He kept his head low so the hood would cover most of his face, in the off chance someone here might recognize him. He pulled up a stool at a noodle stand across the road in order to watch the comings and goings. The proprietor asked what he wanted.

"May I have a cup of water?"

"No noodles?"

Ashok's stomach growled. It had been a long run. "I have no money for noodles."

"Then go!" the man shooed him away, waving his hands like Ashok was a troublesome monkey. "Get out, bum."

It was difficult to be snapped at by someone who would have once been as insignificant to him as a flea. Ashok inadvertently slipped, forgetting his current status, and lifted his head. He looked the man in the eyes and, without raising his voice, said, "*I thirst*. Clean water. *Now*."

The noodle man, or whatever title was fitting for a worker of his rank, nodded fearfully and scurried away. Ashok had been told by many a criminal that he was intimidating. He'd always assumed it was just due to his office. *Apparently not.* He went back to observing the Face of the East and tried to think like a criminal.

In the worst possible scenario, he would leave his sword with the polisher to gain entry, find Gutch, then kill whoever was guarding him with his bare hands and take their weapons to fight his way out. Or perhaps he would enter through one of the other establishments around it, then try to find an unguarded catwalk? One side of the building was not as busy as the others, so it looked promising. There was no street below there, only rocks. It was rather dark, and the building it was connected to on that side was rather close. There were rain gutters which would make for an easy climb, and he could enter through a window on the top floor, unseen.

Noodle man returned and offered him a whole jug of water. "Fresh from the tastiest natural spring on the mountain just this morning, then kept cool in the shade all day. There might even be a little ice in it."

Ashok took the jug and drank the whole thing. When he was done he wiped his face on his sleeve. "Ah. Much better."

"Of course, noble sir. We often get men of the highest caste who wish to experience the joys of the pleasure district, but who dress humbly to avoid attention. Please forgive my earlier outburst. No offense was intended."

"No offense was taken. Thank you, merchant."

"Enjoy the stool as long as you wish." Then he went back to his paying, and far less threatening, customers.

Ashok found the whole exchange curious. Even without status, he was treated with deference, just because he acted like he deserved it. It was fascinating . . . yet led to uncomfortable conclusions. He went back to watching the building, just in time to see a familiar face.

Jagdish?

He almost didn't recognize him since he had shaved his beard off, but he was fairly certain it was Jagdish who had just walked past a balcony on the fourth floor. Only he had been wearing the wrong uniform. Unless Jagdish had a twin brother in the army of Great House Kharsawan, the good risaldar was in disguise.

Gutch's letter claimed they had been separated. Jagdish must have followed Gutch's captors here, and now he was on the same mission as Ashok. Considering this place had to be swarming with criminals, it was a remarkably brave, yet probably foolish move. It made sense though. Jagdish was not the sort inclined toward hesitation.

Before Ashok could decide how to proceed, another complication presented itself. There was some commotion near the entrance. A man in a gray cloak had been stopped at the door, apparently refusing to give up his sword. His view was blocked, so Ashok couldn't tell what it was the man showed the guards, but by the way the warriors immediately shut their mouths and scurried fearfully out of the way, he could guess.

That was a common reaction when a Protector displayed the token of his office.

No gleaming, intimidating armor. No show of force. No loud declaration to strike fear into the hearts of the lawbreakers. It was rare for a Protector to be so discreet. The only time Ashok had ever behaved that way was when he was worried about frightening away his target.

The cloaked man walked into the Face of the East, still armed. A guard ran off, probably to alert his employer that one of the ultimate enforcers of the Law had just entered the premises. He knew from experience that now there would be a great rush to hide any illegal activity, and once word got out, anyone who was wanted for a crime would leap out the nearest window and run for their lives.

The subtlety of the Protector suggested he was more than likely here looking for Ashok. His presence somewhere one, or possibly two, of Ashok's associates were was no coincidence. Somehow the Order knew of their fellowship. Jagdish had disguised himself, but a Protector learned to read faces, separating out the general unease everyone felt around them from the dread of the guilty. Jagdish would be found, and since he was a man of character, would likely fight to the death rather than allow himself to be captured. He was skilled, but would have little chance against a Protector.

It was difficult to think like a criminal. The smart thing for a criminal to do in this situation would be to abandon his companions, avoid the Protector, and flee... Luckily for Jagdish, Ashok still struggled with such concepts.

Trying to appear nonchalant, he walked across the busy street and then around to the rear of the building. The backside had even fewer potential witnesses than expected. There were a few sleeping drunks, and one soldier lying so still he might actually be dead. It stunk, as this was where they threw out their waste when they were too lazy to walk to the proper disposal sites, but Ashok wasn't here to serve citations for minor violations of the Law concerning sanitation and public health. He got a running start, leapt, and grabbed hold of the second-floor balcony. Pulling himself up, he made sure no one was looking out that window, but the curtain was closed. Then he tested the rain gutter and discovered it was solidly mounted. He began to climb.

Chapter 13

Before leaving on this foolish errand, Keta had told Jagdish that the gods would bless and aid him in his search. *Such lies! More like a curse than a blessing.* The way things had been going, if Jagdish lived he was going to horsewhip Keta, and then if the priest had any idols or graven images—he didn't actually know how such things worked—but if he did, then Jagdish would piss on his gods!

For three days he and Gutch had been pursued by gangs. Each time they'd made it to a different neighborhood, they'd found out that Gutch's old friends had retired or been murdered, and replaced by greedy scum without a scrap of loyalty. All the smugglers would rather sell them to the apothecary Bajwa than speak of the Lost House. Over the last few days Jagdish had been chased, bruised, battered, slept in a hole, and he'd killed at least six men, maybe more, depending on how good their physicians were at stitching up lacerations in this blasted, soot-encrusted city.

He was only *here* because Gutch was a big stupid idiot who had run left when he should have turned right, and wound up cornered by a bunch of Bajwa's men. It would serve Gutch right, leaving him to die, but Jagdish was terribly loyal, so abandoning a comrade—even a foolish one who had drastically underestimated his popularity—seemed dishonorable. His lovely wife Pakpa had told him many times that he was too dependable for his own good.

He had tailed them to the Face of the East, easy enough to do, since they'd just put ropes around Gutch's ankles and dragged him the whole way behind a horse. They'd gone right past a group of warriors obligated to the city watch, and they'd simply averted their eyes, pretending not to see a thing. If Jagdish ever found out any man under his command had ever ignored such brazen criminality, he'd punish them so harshly they'd envy the lifestyle of the casteless.

Knowing that he'd be recognized by Bajwa's men, upon arrival in the pleasure district he'd grabbed a new uniform from a hanger. The junior nayak it belonged to had been too distracted by a pleasure woman to notice, and was sure to get ripped when he returned to his barracks naked, but that's what he deserved for not keeping an eye on his issued equipment. He'd changed his appearance as much as possible, shaving and cutting his hair with his knife, but upon inspection in a mirror Jagdish decided that even though the Kharsawan warrior caste were wretched excuses for real soldiers, their uniforms were nice, and he did look rather dashing in red.

Then he'd gone after no-good Gutch, into the nest of vipers, hoping that his friend's quick wit and smooth talk would keep him alive long enough. He'd been forced to leave his sword with the polishers, but he still had his ceremonial knife beneath his sash, a dagger hidden in his boot, and a length of sturdy wire taken from a junk pile for strangling.

The Face of the East was a popular destination. It was crowded, so packed with warm bodies that even though it was cold out, the balconies were all kept open. Good, otherwise they would have all choked on the pipe smoke and perfume. There were many women here, some slaves obligated to the establishment, but a lot of them were young worker women who came here in giggling groups, probably looking to catch the eye of a rich man from their own caste, or to have a brief fling with a warrior—if they were lucky.

The metals were painted to look like gold or silver. The wood was all carved, albeit clumsily. There were paintings on every wall, though Jagdish was willing to bet none of them would have been considered good. Not that he knew a thing about paintings of course, but he had been on the Personal Guard of Great House Vadal, so he knew what real wealth looked like. This was not that. Though it was a reasonable copy, more than good enough to fool most warriors into thinking they were living like the first caste for a night.

If the owner hadn't been trying to kill him for the last few days, Jagdish probably would have enjoyed the visit. If he ran into Bajwa or any of the men he'd fought with, he would just have to hope they didn't recognize him.

Jagdish had slowly made his way through the crowd, searching each floor, looking for some sign of where they would hold a prisoner. There was no basement that he could see, rock was too hard, probably not worth the effort. There were areas for different games, and some of those rooms were by private invitation only, with a guard keeping out unwanted guests. Gutch might be in one of those, but there were too many, and Jagdish couldn't start strangling people until he'd narrowed it down.

There were musicians on each floor, each group playing different kinds of songs depending on what was being sold. The gambling areas were playing raucous folk songs, about bravery and heroes, better to motivate warriors to keep throwing dice or drawing cards. The third floor was the brothel, and they kept the music poetic, romantic, and also thankfully, very loud, so as to drown out the moaning. The top floor was for drinking, which was clever, because once filled with wine and lacking sense, the warriors would have to try and make their way back down through the gauntlet of temptation without losing all their notes. The music here was happy, and sung by beautiful women, because nobody wanted a bunch of warriors to become morose while intoxicated. Surely Jagdish wasn't the only man who'd snuck in some knives.

Once he had reached the top, Jagdish stopped to think. And it was better to think while sitting at a table with a drink in his hand. To keep wandering would be to attract suspicion. So he ordered a cup of sunda, a local drink made from fermented rice buried in a mud pot, and found a place to sit away from all the other red uniforms in the room. If they tried to make conversation, he was far too ignorant of their ways to pass for one of them. Luckily, he wasn't the only obvious veteran sitting alone, looking bitter, and nursing a drink. Apparently that behavior was common across every house.

He had walked by six locked and guarded doors. Approximately half of those had been quiet, the others had sounded like gambling had been going on inside. There were more private rooms in the brothel, but those were for paying customers. First, Jagdish was far too loyal to Pakpa to think of such a thing, and second, he didn't have enough money to buy his way in there anyway.

There was no choice. He would simply have to pick a door and hope for the best. It was just another game of chance in a palace full of them. Maybe Keta's gods would guide him to the right one? That thought made him laugh, so he finished his sunda and gagged on the taste. He had no idea how the warriors of Kharsawan drank the stuff. In Vadal they'd use it to strip paint from armor.

Before Jagdish could stand, he realized something was wrong. Soldiers were shouting for more drinks, but getting no response. The service had gone from speedy to nonexistent. Jagdish noted both bartenders were gone, their aprons untied and discarded on the bar. He glanced to the door, where two large guards had been waiting with clubs to bust open the head of anyone who got too drunk and started a fight. They were also gone.

A man in a gray cloak was walking among the patrons. He wasn't going out of his way to be rude, but he was also not meek about it. He simply pushed them aside, indifferent. A few warriors looked to take offense, but when they saw what was beneath that cloak, their expressions turned from annoyance to fear, and they quickly stepped aside. Between the bodies, for just a moment, Jagdish saw the flash of a golden symbol, hanging from the man's neck by a chain. With pointed teeth and eyes that never closed, it was the leering face of the Law.

Oh no.

He lowered his head and stared at the table. Jagdish didn't dare move.

The Protector slowly made his way around the room, glancing briefly at each man, judging them for a moment, and then moving on. As he did so, the warriors who'd seen him began to whisper warnings to their companions. Even men who had broken no Law were right to be terrified of its enforcers. The nervousness spread, but nobody left the bar. To do so at this point would be to attract attention.

The rich workers seated behind Jagdish began to speak nervously to each other. *What is one of them doing here?* He could hear the open fear in their voices. The warriors were all trained to have brave faces or risk disgrace. Killing a warrior would at least require some explanation to their commanders about why the Law was depriving them of assets. If a Protector killed a worker he probably wouldn't even have to do any paperwork.

Someone must have told the band, or maybe they just realized that something was amiss, because they stopped playing their instruments. The woman quit singing. The sudden quiet made everything worse.

The Protector paused in his search, looked to the stand where the musicians were seated, and spoke loud enough for everyone present to hear. "Why did you stop?"

The singer gave him an abrupt, fearful nod. "Forgiveness, Protector. I was afraid—"

"Only lawbreakers need fear." He pulled his hood back, revealing sharp, angular features. His hair was long, tied in a knot on top, but shaved on both sides, a style common among the warrior caste in the western houses. "I like that tune. You were doing fine. Please, continue."

It was rather awkward, but the band began to play it again from the beginning. The woman sang, but there was a bit of a crack in her voice this time. The Protector resumed his search, far more overtly now, eyeing each of them one by one. Jagdish just kept trying to memorize the pattern of the wood grain of his tabletop.

If it came to a fight, he had fought a Protector before, perhaps the greatest of them all, but Jagdish had lost badly. All of his sparring with Ashok had made him a better swordsman, but that meant nothing without a sword, and he knew damned good and well there was no way a Protector cared about polite fictions enough to be unarmed. That man certainly hadn't left his sword with any damned polishers! If the Protector's sword was drawn, he certainly wasn't going to block it with a claim ticket. Jagdish knew he would have better odds of surviving a leap off the fourth floor balcony than fighting his way out.

The Protector stopped in front of Jagdish's table, and just... stood there.

Beneath the table, his fingers were resting on the knife hidden beneath his sash. Jagdish's mouth was suddenly very dry.

"Your mug is empty."

"It is."

"Unfortunate."

The unfortunate part was that if he'd known this was going

to be his last drink, he would have ordered something decent. He wished the Protector would move on, only he remained in place, looming over Jagdish, judging. He didn't dare speak. You couldn't lie to one of these men. They had all traveled across the whole of Lok. They'd know, just hearing his accent, it would be obvious he wasn't from Kharsawan.

"You could order another, but it appears I have scared off the servers."

"Uh huh."

Several heartbeats passed. "Look at me, warrior."

If he was about to die, he would do so with courage. Jagdish lifted his head.

The Protector had cold, dark eyes. His gaze was unflinching as winter. "What's your name?"

He was no coward. "I am Jagdish."

"You are not from here, are you?"

He didn't answer. Instead he slowly curled his hand around his knife.

"I believe you lost something along the way, Jagdish."

He had lost many things, his friends, his command, his good name. "You'll have to narrow it down for me."

The Protector reached into his cloak and pulled out a dagger. He held it up by the blade, so that Jagdish could clearly see the hilt, capped in horn, and wrapped in blue-gray cord, the colors of Great House Vadal. The last time Jagdish had seen that blade had been when he'd lost it fighting Bajwa's thugs. The Protector held it out, chest high, then dropped it on the table. The metal made a loud noise when it struck the wood. Every head turned their direction. This time when the band abruptly stopped playing, the Protector didn't order them to start over.

Jagdish stared at his lost dagger for a long time. If he'd been able to check the little watch ticking away in his pocket, surely at least a minute passed. It felt like an eternity. The room was deathly silent as everyone waited, relieved they weren't the one under suspicion. They'd all heard stories about Protectors dispensing cruel justice, and now they'd get to see it firsthand.

"A Vadal man of your description is said to be traveling with Ashok the Black Heart." There were many gasps around the room when the Protector declared that. And here they'd been expecting a regular criminal.

There would be no surrender. He would flip the table and slash for the Protector's throat. Who knew? Maybe Keta's gods would find his efforts amusing enough to reward him.

The Protector must have seen Jagdish tense up, and the hint of a smile crossed his thin lips. So inhumanly fast, he wasn't even concerned. If anything, he was looking forward to this. "This is the part where most criminals beg for mercy. You are bold, Vadal man, I'll give you that. But first... tell me where Ashok is."

"I am here."

If the room had been quiet before, now it became like a tomb. The Protector slowly turned his head to the side, eyes narrowed and the muscles of his jaw tightening. Jagdish had to look over his shoulder, but he'd recognized the voice. Sure enough, Ashok Vadal had appeared seemingly out of nowhere and was standing in between several workers, a mere twenty feet away.

"Hello, Ishaan."

The Protector had been so confident a moment before, but his manner changed. It wasn't outright fear, oh no, they were far too hard an order for that, but a knowledge that the stakes had changed. Despite his professional demeanor, Jagdish could tell this man was as certain of his impending doom as Jagdish had been about his own only a moment before.

The Protector nodded. "Greetings, Ashok."

With that, the workers standing around Ashok realized who he was, and recoiled as if someone had dumped a basket of cobras at their feet. All of the lower caste bolted for the stairs. Some of the warriors did too. Who could blame them? Drunks stumbled, tripped and fell, but most stayed frozen in place, too frightened to look away.

Jagdish was forgotten as the two unnatural killers stared each other down.

"How did you find this one?"

"Among the Black Heart's company seen traveling south of Jharlang, were a Vadal warrior and a worker of great stature. A few days ago a Vadal warrior and a very large worker entered this city, and immediately afterwards were involved in a street fight. There were several altercations and murders since, all involving those two. A man matching the worker's description was seen being dragged into this establishment against his will."

"I taught you well, Ishaan."

While he'd been speaking, the Protector had begun a slow walk. Not toward Ashok, but across the room. Jagdish realized that Ashok was doing the same. Each time one of their boots touched the wooden floor, it was gradual, as if they were testing their footing, like two circling tigers about to fight. The warriors around them, surely normally brave men, were trying to squeeze themselves back against the walls, making themselves as thin as could be. Nobody was about to interrupt this duel.

"Where are your brothers?"

"The entire Order searches for you. Many of us rode to Shabdkosh."

"Never heard of the place."

"No? An Inquisitor reported you were seen there, right before a casteless mob rose up and murdered everyone there in your name."

"That was not my doing."

"The judges disagreed. It's only a short journey from the Capitol. A great many important people rode past in their carriages and saw the carnage with their own eyes. They were rather cross. Devedas has gone to placate them."

"Is Devedas well?"

"Well as can be expected, considering the shame you brought to this Order. He did as the judges wanted, but he thought it was unlikely you would go west from Jharlang, so he sent some of us in every direction. I came here."

Jagdish interrupted. "There's two more of them in town, Ashok!"

"Silence, you," Ishaan snapped.

"So that's why you converse so freely with me, with brothers near they will see people fleeing this place and come to your aid. A wise decision, considering how dangerous this criminal can be."

"As you said, you taught me well." Ishaan stopped circling. "The Law was everything to you. We all wanted to be like you. I tried to emulate your manner. How could you, of any of us, not be a whole man? How could *you* be a traitor to the Law? When I received word of your fall, I couldn't believe it. I still can't. I plead with you, Ashok, surrender, so we may end this."

"I wish I could, but I cannot."

Ashok stopped walking as well. He had picked his spot. The lines were drawn. The battle would commence. Jagdish realized then why Ishaan was desperately waiting for reinforcements. He didn't know Angruvadal was gone. Deprived of his ancestor blade, Ashok would be in an even fight against another Protector. He would be destroyed by three.

"Gutch is on the third floor, west wall. I caught a glimpse as I climbed past that window." Ashok directed that to Jagdish. Then he spoke to the Protector again. "Who are your companions?"

"Bundit and Teerapat."

"Good men." For someone who was supposed to be so merciless and cruel, Ashok sounded resigned. "It would sadden me to kill them."

"We've got no choice, Ashok."

"I know...Neither do I."

Both men moved so fast it was difficult for the assembled warriors to follow. Ashok launched himself at the Protector. Ishaan drew his sword, expecting to counter mighty Angruvadal. Only Ashok didn't even try for his blade, instead he dove right into the Protector, encircled him about the waist, and drove him back. The move took Ishaan by surprise, and before he could slash Ashok's spine, they'd gone across the balcony, crashed through the wooden railing, and both men fell into the night.

Chapter 14

Ashok knew that he couldn't fulfill his duty and protect the Prophet if they didn't recover the smuggler who had a way to find her. To stand and fight Ishaan—an exceedingly skilled swordsman—meant that the warriors present would be moved from their stupor. In order to escape, Jagdish needed a distraction. Taking their battle elsewhere was the best option.

But sometimes the best option was still extremely painful.

They didn't fall all the way to the ground. Instead they impacted the walkway between buildings at the second level. Ishaan shattered the roof tiles with his back, then they were separated as they collided with a heavy beam hard enough to snap it. Ashok went rolling one way, Ishaan the other. Some workers had been walking across the catwalk, all of them were knocked off their feet, and one poor fellow went screaming over the side.

Tasting blood and dust, Ashok got to his feet. Luckily, he'd broken no bones. Ishaan however, was on his hands and knees, violently coughing up blood. Such was luck. He had either snapped ribs and driven one through a lung, or he had been pierced through the back by the broken beam. Either way, it would take even a mighty Protector a moment to recover from such an injury. This was Ashok's chance to finish him. Ishaan realized that as well, since he tried futilely to stand and defend himself, but the Heart couldn't bring back his breath in time. Even the best swordsman couldn't fight without air.

It would be foolish to leave such a deadly hunter on his trail. Ishaan wasn't helpless, but close enough against someone as lethal as Ashok. Not even the Heart of the Mountain could save you from having your head lopped off or your heart cleaved in half. It would be so very easy.

Only he had no desire to kill a former brother. It was not his place. It was not just outside the Law, but *wrong*. Instead Ashok turned back toward the Face of the East to make his escape.

"Halt!"

Ashok had nearly run directly into Senior Protector Teerapat Makao. His blade came so close to removing Ashok's head that it left a thin red line across his throat as it whistled past.

"Ashok!" Teerapat brought his saber back around and took up a defensive stance. "Surrender or perish."

This time Ashok did draw his sword.

Teerapat cringed as metal struck metal, but they parted, with the Protector appearing shocked to still be alive, and his sword not blasted into pieces by legendary Angruvadal. He was a young man, barely two years at senior rank, but Ashok had helped train him, and knew that he was a solid fighter none the less.

"What? Why do you not use the black sword?"

They clashed again, Teerapat with a quick lunge, followed by a cut aimed for Ashok's abdomen, but he had seen it coming, intercepted it with the flat of his blade, and countered with a thrust that pierced nothing but fabric.

"Am I not worthy of fighting Angruvadal? Do you insult me?" Men from Great House Makao were notoriously prideful.

"Shut up and fight."

Ashok went in swinging, but it was a ruse to draw his guard high so he could kick Teerapat's leg out from under him. But the Protector leapt over the kick. Teerapat slashed again, but Ashok moved into the swing, caught the blow with his hand guard, and twisted his wrists, using leverage to capture and drive his opponent's blade down. Then he elbowed Teerapat in the face. The Protector responded, and just missed driving his fingers into Ashok's eye.

They parted to assess. The workers they'd knocked down were crawling for their lives. A man who was lying at their feet decided a one-story fall was preferable to being trapped beneath flashing razors, and rolled under the railing to drop into the mud. Behind him, Ishaan had managed to contort his arm until he could grasp and pull a massive pointed piece of wood from his back. He dropped the bloody chunk, and a look of concentration came over his face. Ishaan was calling upon the Heart to close the sucking hole in his lung. He'd return to the fight soon. The final Protector would be nearby. Ashok had to hurry.

He attacked. Teerapat was good, but Ashok was better. They exchanged several furious blows, until Ashok shoulder rammed him against the railing, drew back, and thrust his blade deep into Teerapat's thigh. The Protector gasped in surprise and pain, but did not give up. In that split second, Ashok knew he was a hair away from the artery, if he twisted and ripped the sword free, then Teerapat would be gushing blood everywhere. Experience had taught him that once severed, if that artery climbed back into the pelvis, such bleeding was difficult for even the Heart of the Mountain to stop.

Ashok pulled the steel straight out.

The curved sword came back around, but slower this time, so Ashok blocked it, and slammed the ridge of his hand into Teerapat's throat hard enough to crush his larynx *flat*. The Protector gasped futilely for air. They still struggled, but that blow had knocked most of the fight out of him. Before Teerapat blacked out, Ashok grabbed him by the cloak, dragged him close, and said, "Calm, Senior. Just as we trained, focus on the Heart and it will keep you alive until your breath returns. Do you understand?"

Eyes wide, face turning different colors, Teerapat nodded desperately. Then Ashok hurled him over the side.

Looking back, Ashok saw that Ishaan was up, but not yet recovered enough to fight. In this moment, it was a good thing the Heart of the Mountain could only be directed toward one task at a time.

"I beg you, Ishaan, do not follow me. I've broken the Law enough." Ashok began walking away. "Don't make me take its servants' lives too."

Chapter 15

~~~~~~~~~~~~~~~~~~~~

The warriors had momentarily been too stunned by Ashok and the Protector falling off the building to react. Jagdish used that to his advantage and ran for the stairs. Most of the Kharsawan men were far more interested in watching two Protectors fall to their death, so they ran to the windows to look down, but a few remembered the petty criminal who had started it all and tried to intercept Jagdish.

A man stepped into his path, and without slowing, Jagdish kicked him in the groin hard enough to lift him to his toes. Another tried to intercept him, but Jagdish's hand flicked back and forth, and the little ceremonial knife left a cut across his forehead just over the eyes. Another grabbed hold of his sleeve, but Jagdish sliced open the back of that intruding hand. When that warrior flinched and let go, Jagdish shoved past and leapt down the stairs. There was no time to look back, but he heard them give chase. He yanked the gaudy paintings off the walls as he went, hoping the warriors would trip over the frames.

His boot slipped and he took the last ten steps bouncing on his chest and hands, but at least the floor on the brothel level had rugs thick enough to cushion the fall. Jagdish got up and sprinted in the direction he'd been previously denied entrance to. He turned a corner, thought better of running, and stepped behind a heavy curtain.

Jagdish waited until he heard several angry warriors rush past. Once he was certain it was clear, he left his hiding place and continued on. Men and women in various states of undress pushed past him trying to get out. They probably didn't even really know what was going on, but some woman was yelling about how the Black Heart was here to slaughter them all, and someone else was shouting about Protectors looking for criminals to execute. When you heard either of those things being screamed by someone obviously in fear for their lives, it didn't matter how distracting your current activity, it could be postponed.

Luckily the guards who had been stationed here earlier had fled like the rest of Bajwa's men, so Jagdish was able to walk right in. This area was reserved for the wealthy, high-status customers, and the art here wasn't cheap. Certainly, neither were the very beautiful young women who ran past him while pulling on tiny silken gowns. Jagdish noticed that. He was loyal to Pakpa, but he wasn't blind.

A stern-looking, yet still attractive, older woman was taking handfuls of banknotes out of a drawer and stuffing them into hidden pockets inside her elaborate robe. "Out!" she ordered when she saw Jagdish. "I'll call the guards!"

"They're long gone. I don't care about your money. I'm here for Bajwa's prisoner."

"The fat one?"

"How many do you people have, woman? Yes! The fat one!"

"Far end of the hall. Take him and be gone!" She pulled a key out of the same desk drawer and hurled it at Jagdish. "Bajwa sticks his ransoms here because we've got the most guards, but this one's been more trouble than he's worth. Only one day here, he already charmed the slave girl assigned to feed him, got loose, then upset some of my customers while trying to escape."

That certainly sounded like Gutch. Jagdish took the key, went down the hall, and unlocked the door. Sure enough, Gutch was inside, a great snoring lump in the middle of the bare wooden floor. "Wake up! It's time to go."

The sleeping had been an act. "Jagdish?" When Gutch sat up, it revealed that he had pried up a board from the floor to use as a makeshift club. He was covered in bruises, welts, and scratches, and one eye was swollen shut, indicating he'd received a good beating, but he grinned anyway. "You're a resourceful one. And here I was thinking I was going to have to get the jump on them and fight my way out."

"Ashok's here."

Gutch limped for the door. "Excellent. My plan worked. Then all is well!"

"What plan? There's Protectors here too."

"Oceans! Why didn't you say that first?"

By the time they got out, the madam was gone, though in her hurry to escape she'd dropped many papers and a few banknotes. Of course, Gutch picked them up.

"There's no time for that."

"There's always time for money, Risaldar. But that's not what I'm after." He held up one page that had come from a ledger. "Ah, here we go."

"What're you doing?"

"I'm seeing which establishments Bajwa's favorite girl keeps getting sent to, so I can find where that miserable wretch sleeps. Then I can come back later and smash his teeth in."

"Good man, Gutch! We'll find those wizards yet."

"Sure. That's why I want to find him so badly. *The wizards*," Gutch muttered through badly split lips. "Just remind me to ask Bajwa about wizards before I beat him to death."

"Noted." From the noise in the Face of the East, it sounded like everyone was trying to leave. If the Protectors were raiding an establishment it could only mean that criminal activity was afoot. Nobody wanted to get caught up in that. If something illegal was found here, even if innocent, the lower-status bystanders might accidently end up among the executions, and the higher might become embroiled in a scandal. "Let's go."

The guards had taken most of Gutch's clothing and his boots, but luckily a customer had left in such a hurry they'd forgotten their fine sandals. They must have come from someone who'd ridden here on a rickshaw or carriage, because they weren't fit for the winter, but Gutch took them because it beat running through the frozen mud in bare feet. Another customer had left behind a fine silk cape, which Gutch threw over his shoulders. It was comically small, but would have to do.

They made it down the next flight of stairs without incident. Nobody noticed them. Judging by the large number of people who'd rushed to the windows shouting about watching a sword fight, Ashok and the Protector had survived their fall and had gone about trying to murder each other.

"I should help Ashok."

"No offense intended, Risaldar, you're good, but even if you had your sword, in a Protector fight you'd be as useful as tits on a boar."

Gutch was as insulting as he was correct. Besides, Ashok would want him to focus on their mission. If he'd wanted Jagdish's help he wouldn't have jumped off a balcony where Jagdish could not follow. "Come on. We'll try to sneak out in the confusion."

The first floor was chaos. Customers, eager not to be caught up in Protector business, were trying to push and shove their way out. But some of the watch had heard the commotion and were trying to keep people in until they could figure out what was going on. Only all of the watch obligated to this district were of Kharsawan's warrior caste, as were many of the customers, so lots of them were escaping as the watch allowed their brothers to pass. To be fair, none of them had been implicated in whatever law breaking had attracted the Protectors... Yet.

The workers were not so lucky. Warriors loved any opportunity to put what they considered the uppity caste back in their place, and there were already a few broken noses on workers who'd overstepped their bounds. Jagdish felt pity for any warrior who mistook a disguised firster for a lesser man. Bloodying a high-status nose would probably result in a hanging.

Jagdish had an idea. If nobody recognized him from upstairs it might actually work. He dragged Gutch along toward a side door where the watch was letting their fellow warriors escape. "Hide your face. Act like you don't want to be recognized."

"What?"

"Do it!"

Gutch used the cape to cover his face. He looked absurd.

Jagdish cleared his throat as he approached the watchmen. "Let us through."

A Kharsawan soldier stepped in front of the door. He let his cudgel land in his open palm with a menacing *thump*. "I don't know you, brother."

Even though he was only wearing the insignia of a lowly nayak, Jagdish carried himself like an officer as he got right into the guard's face. He kept his voice low, as if he didn't want anyone else to hear. "Listen carefully. This uniform was borrowed for the night. I'm a risaldar of the Kwang garrison." Jagdish picked the most distant and obscure Kharsawan holding he could remember from a map. "Some of our officers wanted to inconspicuously taste the pleasures of Neeramphorn, and we were invited here by Bajwa himself. *This* is our phontho." He jerked his head toward Gutch, who didn't look like a warrior, let alone a leader of an entire garrison, but at that level appointments were more political than anything, so it was possible. "He is an extremely important man. If his wife finds out he was seen in a brothel, she'll rip him, he'll rip us, and when he gets angry my whole garrison gets flogged. Then he'll probably come looking for you."

"I can't—"

"That woman is practically a sea demon, Nayak! He will need someone to blame and it will be you if you do not *step aside*."

It worked. "All right, hurry."

"Good decision. This favor will be remembered." They made it onto the side street. The crowd was scattering. Jagdish noticed one of the warriors he'd slashed, holding a bandage on his hand, as he explained to the watch what had happened. "Keep your head down and keep walking, Phontho."

From the noise around the corner, people were shouting about a battle. The crowd was of two minds: get out, or get a good vantage point to watch. Even if Ashok beat the Protectors, every warrior in the city would attack him as soon as they figured out who he was. Ashok had provided a good distraction for Jagdish, it was only right to return the favor. So as they walked through the crowd, Jagdish casually grabbed an oil lantern from a peg on the wall of a food vendor and tossed it into a nearby wagon full of straw.

In a place like this, with so many sprawling wooden buildings stacked right on top of each, fire was a terrible danger. It was the only thing he could think of that would be of more interest to the witnesses than a sword fight. They'd walked another twenty feet before anyone noticed and began to shout "*Fire! Fire!*"

"I hope that works." Gutch lowered the cape so he could see better. All eyes would either be on Ashok or the fire. Nobody would be paying them any mind. "The fastest route to a gate is that way..." He trailed off as he saw something interesting. "I'll be damned."

Jagdish followed his eyes. A hundred feet away, the fine coat of the apothecary stood out in the drab crowd. "Well hello there, Bajwa."

The chief criminal of Neeramphorn must have been alerted that one of his holdings was being raided by Protectors, and had come to see for himself. He might have bribed every official in the city, but Protectors were outsiders, and so devoted they couldn't be bought. The smart thing for Bajwa to do would be to run and hide. Only members of that deadly order of Law enforcers were rare, so Bajwa must have thought the alarm to be wrong or exaggerated.

Bajwa was busy listening while one of his men who had fled the Face of the East gave his report. There were a great number of workers rushing to and fro, trying to organize a bucket brigade before the fire spread, so between the distance and the commotion, Jagdish couldn't tell what was being said, but Bajwa looked very upset as he began walking away from his establishment. *Yes, the Law is really here. Now go run and hide.*

The criminal only had two burly workers as bodyguards with him, and they were heading down a narrow lane filled with many shadowy alcoves, perfect for murder.

"You thinking what I'm thinking?" Gutch asked.

Jagdish began following them with malicious intent. "I was supposed to remind you, don't forget to ask about the wizards."

Chapter 16

After crossing back through the casino, Ashok searched for an escape route. He was spotted by a few warrior customers, but with their swords left at the polishers, they were wise enough to not get in his way. There was another walkway to a different building, so he took that one. Only the instant he closed the door behind him, he glanced around, decided it was momentarily clear, and then vaulted over the side to land in the road. There were people here, but they were far more worried about a rapidly spreading fire than any fleeing lawbreaker. So Ashok put his hood up and began walking away.

More city watch were rushing toward the Face of the East to see what the commotion was about. Someone began ringing an alarm bell. That would rouse the fire crews—the Law was very specific about the minimum percentages to workers who had to be obligated and trained for that additional duty—and they would only add to the commotion. His best chance to escape was before the fire was contained.

Running would only draw attention, so he walked a block. It seemed as if all of Neeramphorn was perpetually under construction, old buildings being torn down, with new taller ones raised in their place, so a nearby construction site looked like a good short cut out of the district. Many workers were still toiling here even at this late hour, but when they'd heard the alarm bell they'd rushed to help. In a dense wooden city, fire was everyone's problem, and obligations aside, their families lived here. As they hurried outside, Ashok slipped in unnoticed.

As he crossed the cluttered construction site, he marveled at their efforts. Once finished this building would be impressive. It was vast already, not quite big enough to equal one of the smaller palaces in the Capitol, but still a testament to the industry of the worker caste. It was hard to imagine they could accomplish such a thing without being directed by their betters.

The skeletal frame stretched high above, a multitude of floors, all connected by bamboo scaffolding. Many workers were still up there, comfortable in that dangerous environment, but they'd all started climbing down when they'd heard the bell. Five or six stories up was a terrible place to be in case the fire spread this direction. It was actually impressive how some of the workers seemed able to climb down the poles and ropes as effortlessly as monkeys.

There was a loud *crack* behind him. Without looking, he could tell it was the sound of a metal capped shaft striking stone. It was a noise anyone who'd trained in the Protectors' Hall recognized immediately, a sound of challenge.

Ashok turned.

He had been followed. It was Protector of the Law, ten-year senior, Bundit Vokkan. He was dressed as the other two had been, plain as a Protector could manage, but was armed with a very intimidating weapon. The pole arm was six feet long, with the last foot being a blade heavy enough to easily take the leg off a horse. The back of the blade had a spike for hooking or piercing armor. They called such a weapon a reclining moon blade in northern lands, though Master Ratul had told his students the old name for it was *guandao*. Either way, he had made sure all of the Protector acolytes had been taught in its use.

Most Protectors preferred swords due to the convenience, but Bundit had taken to fighting with a pole arm as naturally as the monkey workers here took to climbing ropes. He was one of the more effective combatants in the entire Order, so Ashok had sparred with him many times.

Bundit was a round-faced, solemn man, given to little conversation even in the best of times.

"Give up."

"I can't." Ashok drew his sword.

"Very well."

The Protector charged.

The blade came at him, striking fast as a cobra. Ashok darted to the side, knowing that attack was just the beginning. Bundit liked to overwhelm his opponents with a flurry of unexpected attacks. The steel came back around, from below, then from above, always twisting, ready to slice him wide open. Bundit was a master. He kept back, using his superior reach, one hand on the metal cap on the end, using that to steer the blade with precision, or with a sudden shift, a great deal of force.

Ashok struggled to stay ahead of the blade. If he'd still had Angruvadal a single blow would have pulverized the shaft into splinters, but all he had was this ordinary sword. Fighting in the open, with room to work, the advantage belonged to Bundit.

They fought back and forth across the stone. Ashok continued to parry, but the attacks just kept coming. Whenever he tried to capitalize on turning aside a blow, Bundit simply danced back until he could bring the blade up between them again. The instant Ashok focused too much on the blade, the shaft spun about, and the hardwood clipped his leg. A savage minute of this back and forth and Ashok's arms were burning as much as they had after a whole morning of practicing against his Somsak followers.

They were both breathing heavily.

"Your footwork is the equal of Master Ratul's. He taught you well."

"Thank you." Bundit nodded at the compliment, and then went back to trying to decapitate him.

Only this time, Ashok moved to the side, running toward the scaffolding.

Bundit realized what he was doing and tried to intercept him, but it was too late. Once Ashok was between the bamboo poles, the Protector lost his ability to swing wide. But he could still thrust, and Ashok narrowly avoided being pierced through his sternum.

Going ten feet to the side and it was as if their battle had moved from the plains to the forest. Now their movements were restricted, and Ashok had the advantage. A sword could be maneuvered in far tighter quarters than a reclining moon blade. Bundit struck, but the haft skidded off some bamboo, slowing him just enough for Ashok to step around and slash. The Protector grimaced as a long cut appeared on his shoulder. It was Bundit's turn to retreat.

No fools survived the Order's program, so Bundit didn't charge back in blindly. Instead he stepped out from beneath the scaffolding, cocked back his arms, and struck directly at the poles. Protectors kept their weapons sharp enough to shave their faces. With the momentum at the end of a pole driven by super-human strength bestowed by the Heart of the Mountain, the blade tore through the bamboo like it wasn't even there. Several poles were sliced in half. Bundit swung again, and again, like a farmer threshing a field.

Ashok looked up. There was a long *creak*, and then a cascading series of *cracks*. Dust rained down as the scaffolding above him began to collapse. A worker screamed as he plummeted to the ground. Ashok moved back. Bundit followed, still cutting, as the canopy of Ashok's temporary forest came crashing down.

A board struck him on the side of the head hard enough to break skin. He was separated from Bundit by clouds of dust and falling objects, but the Protector was willing to bring this whole place down on top of them. Ashok no longer possessed the ability to feel fear, but he retained a perfect understanding of his situation and mortality. It was dive back into the open or risk being crushed; neither were good options.

When Angruvadal had been in his possession, it had given him access to all its former bearers' combative memories. In desperate moments like this, it would suggest courses of action or warn him of dangers. An odd—yet somewhat familiar—sensation came over him. Time seemed to slow, and an instinct that was not his own told him to *reach out*.

Angruvadal?

It couldn't be.

But Ashok obeyed the instinct, and reached with his open hand into the cascading dust and debris. As the scaffold above him collapsed, the items the workers had left behind came crashing down. Something solid fell, two feet long, metallic and deadly.

Ashok caught the heavy saw by the handle, spun about, and aiming purely by instinct not his own, hurled it back through the dust. The saw whipped through the air, end over end, to hit with a tooth-snapping *crack*.

Leaping through the falling boards, he saw Bundit was still

reeling, spitting blood. The saw had slashed through his cheek, laying it wide open, before breaking his jaw. Aiming his sword for Bundit's fingers, Ashok's strike exposed bones and tendons. The Protector lost control of his pole arm and fell sideways. He immediately began to rise, but Ashok kicked him violently in the side of the head. Bundit flopped over, and rolled down a ramp.

He stood there, panting, as the scaffolding continued to collapse and shake the place to its new foundations. Bundit had landed on his back, eyes closed, skull broken. Blood was coming from his mouth and leaking from one ear. Ashok had felt the skull give beneath his heel, so he was unsure if he'd killed his brother . . . former brother. It would depend on if—or how deeply—fragments had been driven into his brain.

Damn it. Ignoring the falling catwalks, the snapping ropes, and the screaming workers, he went toward Bundit. If he was still breathing, then the least Ashok could do was pull him out of the way so he wouldn't be crushed.

He could feel heat radiating from the shard in his chest . . . Part of Angruvadal still *lived.* A small measure of its ability to guide him had returned. And in the very instant it had come back, he had used that assistance to murder a loyal servant of the Law.

But if Angruvadal still lived, it wasn't nearly as prescient as when it had been whole, because the instinctive warning of danger came too late.

Ashok sensed someone running through the dust from behind him, but before he could react, hot pain pierced his body. He looked down to see the bloody tip of a sword sticking out of his abdomen. A boot landed on his spine, and he was shoved forward. The sword cleanly slid out of his body.

He landed on his knees but immediately rolled to the side. The swing that had been meant to remove his head whistled uselessly through the air.

Even run through the guts, Ashok got right back up to meet the new threat.

It was Protector Ishaan Harban, injured, but unbowed. Ishaan was a westerner, so he preferred to fight with the two-blade style, in this case, with a sword in one hand, and a dagger in the other. The sword was red with Ashok's blood.

The Heart of the Mountain did not favor one and deny the other as they fought to the death. It didn't care about right or wrong, it simply gave its energy to any who had touched it. Blood ran down Ashok's belly, quickly soaking through his shirt. Ishaan was ashen faced. The Heart would allow both of them to fight on despite their wounds.

The Protector attacked, guiding his sword with perfect control. The second blade would be used to intercept Ashok's strikes, but it could kill just as easily. Swords flew back and forth. Steel struck steel. Edges chipped and cracked. Cloth parted. Skin split. Blood flew. The two master swordsmen moved between the poles, up and down ramps, across boards precariously balanced over deep trenches. There were no words, only constant movement, advancing, retreating, circling, always striking. Afterward, the workers who were trapped and unable to flee would describe the clash as like watching two bloody whirlwinds collide.

Since both were using the Heart to control their bleeding, neither could increase his strength or speed. This was a contest of muscle and will. But even without magic, these were two of the most dangerous men alive.

With both of them balanced atop a plank, Ashok trapped a downward strike of Ishaan's sword, but then the Protector lunged inside, trying to finish the fight with a rapid series of stab wounds from his dagger. Only perfect coordination allowed Ashok's free hand to grab Ishaan's wrist. Ashok was sliding around in a puddle of his own blood, but as he shoved Ishaan's sword away, he brought his own down, turning into the cut.

That slash opened Ishaan from shoulder to chest.

The Protector roared, and then he did something desperate. Ashok felt the change as Ishaan let go of the Heart of the Mountain for just a moment, directing it away from controlling his injuries, to providing him with brute strength instead. It was a suicidal move, but if a Protector was about to die, he would always try and take a criminal with him.

"Ishaan, no!"

Despite Ashok pushing down with all his might, the dagger came up and pierced his side. The steel was winter cold, but the pain was like fire around it. Ishaan began to lift him so that Ashok's own body weight would split him open around the blade like a butchered pig.

Ashok lifted his sword, angled the tip down, and drove it through the top of Ishaan's chest and into his heart.

The two men fell, crashing into the trench.

They hit the rock hard, and lay there for a moment. Slowly, Ashok managed to get back up. Ishaan didn't.

The Protector was on his side, blood covering half his face, sword sticking out of his chest, but he was still alive . . . for a moment. They had fought together, bled together, and served the Law as brothers, and now he had killed him.

Ashok was in agony, and not just from the two massive holes in his abdomen. Blood flew from his lips as he shouted, *"Why didn't you quit when you had the chance?"*

His response was barely a whisper. "You wouldn't have."

Then Protector of the Law, fifteen-year senior, Ishaan Harban's eyes slowly unfocused until he was staring at the great nothing.

Chapter 17

Ashok stumbled into the darkened street, hands keeping pressure on his side and stomach. He could do nothing to staunch the blood running from the entrance wound on his back. He needed to stop moving to give the Heart a chance to work, but if he stopped here, he would be found.

The bell was still ringing, which meant the fire still burned. Ashok could barely hear the bell over the noise in his head, like the buzzing of bees. He was losing too much blood. He needed to rest, focus, and slow his heartbeat before he pumped all of his life into the snow.

A nice carriage stopped before him. It was pulled by two white horses, and they shied away from him because of the smell of blood. Ashok was so dazed that for a moment he couldn't understand why some high-status man was stopping for the likes of him, but then he realized the driver was Jagdish.

The door swung open and Gutch extended a hand. "Get out of sight. Hurry."

The inside of the carriage was opulent, all silks and pillows filled with soft feathers. Ashok was hauled in. He lay down, pulled open his shirt to see how bad his wounds were—very bad—and as soon as he'd taken his hands away, began staining the fine carpet red.

There was a small window so the important riders wouldn't have to stick their heads out into the weather to give directions to their driver. Gutch shouted through it. "It looks like he's been stabbed a bunch!"

"Try to stop the bleeding." There was the snap of a whip, and the carriage began to roll.

"I don't think I can. It's right in his stomach."

"I'll be fine," Ashok said as he jammed a piece of silk against the hole. He just needed to rest and be still for a while. The Heart would do the rest.

"I've seen gut wounds like that. I'm sorry. Even if they don't go right away, they always sicken and die in terrible pain."

"Protectors can't get sick." Then Ashok realized he'd spoken as if he still were still one of them, not some criminal dog. He'd stolen that ability from the Order, just like he had stolen his entire life. That gift had been meant for better men. He wasn't even a whole man. "Never mind."

The illness Gutch spoke of, the battlefield surgeons called it sepsis. When certain organs were pierced, they would release poisons into the body which would fester and rot. Protectors did not die of sepsis. They rarely died from any kind of poisoning at all. In fact, when any of them was exposed to a new poison, it was as if the Heart learned from the experience. The next time any Protector was exposed to that same poison, the Heart was prepared to counteract it. Like whatever had been on the poison arrow that had struck him at Sutpo Bridge, all Protectors would be immune from it in the future.

Ashok went back to putting pressure on his wounds, closed his eyes, and concentrated on the pain. His agony was a useful indicator of damage, but it took some practice to sort out the useless pain that radiated outward from a wound, with what was actually important. Only this time he found a new pain, deep in his chest. Though Ashok had been physically injured far worse than this before, it turned out *guilt* left a more fearsome wound than being run through with a sword.

"Is there anything I can do for you, General?" The way Gutch asked that, he probably meant, like make him comfortable before he died.

"I must focus. Be silent."

Ashok only understood how magic worked well enough to

fight against its illegal users and to take advantage of the gifts the Order had bestowed upon him, but he was one of the few who knew that the power within the Heart was finite, and every time one of them drew hard from it, the Heart became a little weaker. One day it would expire, and when it did, the Protectors would be no more. It angered Ashok that any of that precious magic would be wasted on a wretch like him.

Only the Law had spoken, and he still had a prophet to serve, so Ashok used that precious magic to seal his wounds and keep his blood pumping to his vital organs instead of all over the interior of the carriage. But he would try to use up only enough magic to save his miserable life, none to dull the pain, and the rest could heal on its own time.

After a long while, there was a rattle as Gutch opened the small window to speak to the driver. "I think Ashok has stopped breathing."

"I'm not dead. I'm meditating, you fool."

"Oh . . . Never mind, Jagdish. He's alive and pleasant as ever."

Ashok opened his eyes. He was unsure how long he had been out. He was still in terrible pain—stomach wounds were the worst—but nothing he couldn't fight through. The worst of the bleeding was stopped and the rest had slowed to a trickle. The carriage had continued moving the whole time. Ashok couldn't tell in which direction they were heading, but he could no longer hear the fire bells.

"Whose carriage is this?"

"His." Gutch nodded toward the unconscious man sprawled across the other seat. Ashok had been so light-headed from his injuries that he'd not even noticed they weren't alone. To be fair, Gutch's prisoner was a small man, who did not take up much space. He was wearing a white coat, splattered with fresh mud, and his wrists had been bound with cords taken from the carriage's curtains.

"Who is he?"

"That's Bajwa and he runs this town. Isn't that right, Bajwa?" Gutch leaned over so he could kick the man in the leg. Their prisoner groaned. "Hopefully, he's the man with the answers to all our questions."

The ringing in his ears had died enough that Ashok could think clearly again. "Where are we going?"

"We're back in the Thao district, but I don't know where we're going to end up. Because of this nasty bastard, I'm fresh out of friends. The watch is sure to be out in force, so Jagdish is trying to find a place to abandon this thing so we can hide."

Teerapat was still alive. Ashok had crushed his larynx, but that was simply a hollow tube of muscle. He would already be fully recovered, and if he followed protocol for this situation he would order the city sealed and searched, house by house if necessary. From Ashok's own investigations, he knew that wanted criminals never lasted long without allies to hide them, especially among a populace eager to inform on them.

"Head for the nearest gate. We're leaving tonight."

"It'll be closed until dawn."

"And heavily reinforced by then as well." If they were going to escape it was now, or not at all. "Tell Jagdish to make haste."

"They'll stop us!"

"I will not let them. Do it."

Gutch hesitated, surely because Ashok looked more corpse than man, but he did as he was ordered, opening the window and nervously passing on the directions.

Ashok closed his eyes. "Wake me when we arrive."

Chapter 18

Like all honorable warriors, Jagdish was not a religious man. Belief in gods was banned by the Law for the moral good of all the people, so on and so forth—he'd never cared enough to understand why the Capitol felt so strongly on the matter—but it was hard for a warrior to not develop an almost, dare they say, *superstitious* belief concerning luck.

A veteran quickly learned that sometimes no matter how skilled you were, or how clever your tactics on the battlefield, sometimes luck was just out to get you. Turn left instead of right, die. Look up instead of down, die. You could do everything right, be unlucky, and die. You could do everything wrong, get lucky, and live. In the warrior caste there was no shortage of old cowards with chests full of medals, and graveyards filled with young heroes.

So there were probably no such thing as gods, but *fate*... A warrior knew that fate was real... She was a stone-hearted bitch. And judging by the full paltan of guards already standing around the Thao Gate, Jagdish had really done something to anger her.

"Whoa," Jagdish told the horses as he pulled back on their reins. There was no place to turn the carriage. The hour was very late, their mere presence would be suspicious. Thao warriors were already moving to intercept them. There were more men atop the walls, and surely more inside the gatehouse.

These men looked like they had just gotten out of bed. Uniforms hastily thrown on, sleep still in their eyes, told to assemble, and rushed into position, Jagdish had looked that way himself many times over the years. Grumpy and tired, it was what all soldiers looked like when roused by an alarm in the middle of the night that they knew would probably turn out to be nothing.

Four men approached the carriage. Behind the battlements, bows were being strung. The rest of the warriors stayed in positions of relaxed alertness around the gate. Perhaps it was just the laconic, disheveled nature of these jumped up half-farmers, but the Thao warriors were taking their midnight alarm far more seriously than Jagdish had expected them to. He had drastically underestimated their professionalism a few days ago.

Two of the four warriors were carrying lanterns. The others had spears. "Ho, Kharsawan. What's all this?"

Jagdish remembered he was still wearing a red uniform. They meant him. "Good evening. A bit of bodyguard obligation is all. I've got an important man here and he wishes to go outside."

"Everyone knows the gates are closed until dawn."

"But my employer is very rich." When they'd searched Bajwa after clubbing him over the head, they'd found a folded roll of banknotes on him, big around as a fist, perfect for bribery. "Perhaps *arrangements* could be made."

"His wealth won't make the sun rise any faster. I know the apothecary's carriage." As the lanterns got closer, with a terrible sinking feeling, Jagdish realized that the speaker was the same havildar who had greeted him upon arrival. Once again, fate held a grudge against poor Jagdish. "Everyone in this part of the city recognizes that gaudy thing. Perhaps another time, but unfortunately for your master there was some sort of altercation in the pleasure district earlier. We are locked down."

Jagdish nodded, not daring to say another word, and hoping they wouldn't recognize him in the dark. Unfortunately, they kept getting closer. The soldiers didn't stop until he was within the circle of flickering yellow light ... and spearing distance.

"Hang on," said one of the spearmen. It was the junior nayak who had questioned him a few days ago. At some point Jagdish must have given a grave insult to fate, because she certainly hated him with a burning passion. "You look familiar."

Jagdish shrugged. Hopefully a clean shaven face would make the difference. Pakpa certainly thought it made him look younger.

But the havildar was a sharp one, and more observant than he looked. He squinted suspiciously in the lantern light. "Your master couldn't leave the city without stamped traveling papers, let's see them."

A cold bead of sweat ran down Jagdish's neck. He tried to keep his words short. "Forgot them."

It didn't work. "I thought that was you . . . but you're in the wrong uniform, Vadal man."

"That's where I know him," exclaimed the nayak. "It's the one I was telling you boys about, the one who claimed to have actually met Ashok Vadal!"

Oceans. "For your sake, brothers, open that gate and get out of our way, or you'll get to meet him too."

The warriors laughed.

The door of the carriage opened and a blood-soaked nightmare got out.

The warriors stopped laughing.

Ashok strode right up to the four men. Before the havildar could shout a warning, Ashok was on them. He kicked a soldier in the chest, hurling him into another. One of the lanterns hit the cobblestones and exploded. A spear descended, but Ashok effortlessly ripped it from the warrior's hands and smashed him in the face with the butt of it. Then the spearhead flicked around, knocking the other lantern from fumbling hands to fling it against the gatehouse, where it shattered and bathed the walls in flame. Then spinning the spear, he swept the havildar's feet out from under him, sending him flying. He finished by jabbing the blunt end hard into the nayak's stomach.

All four were down in the blink of an eye.

Walking toward the gate he bellowed, "*I am the rebel Ashok Vadal!*"

One of the archers let fly. Ashok simply *caught* the arrow before it could strike him. Jagdish had never seen anything move that fast before. Ashok threw the arrow down in disgust, and then hurled the spear. It struck the battlement next to the archer like it had been fired from a ballista. Bits of stone flew as the archers took cover.

There could be no doubt in their minds that it really was the legendary killer in their midst. In the light of the broken lanterns, Ashok delivered his ultimatum. "I just murdered Protector of the Law Ishaan Harban, who I loved like a brother. Yet I stabbed him in the heart because he got in my way. I care *nothing* about any of you. *Now open this gate or I will tear it down!*"

It was as if Ashok's anger had silenced the perpetual industrial racket of Neeramphorn. All that could be heard was the nervous stamping of the horses, the moaning of the injured warriors, and the crackle of flames. The rest of the soldiers readied their weapons. *Oh, they were all awake now.*

The door to the gatehouse opened and a man wearing the golden mask of an Inquisitor stepped out. Ashok and the masked man stared at each other for a long time. The mask made it hard to tell what the Inquisitor was thinking. He had to be afraid. Only a fool wouldn't be in this situation. Finally, the Inquisitor raised his hand. Jagdish got ready to dive off the seat, hoping to take cover before the arrows hit.

Instead of ordering them to attack, the Inquisitor loudly declared. "Open the gate. Let them go!"

The Thao seemed stunned by this, but they did as they were told. Iron bars were lifted. It took two of them to push the heavy door wide. Then the warriors pulled back, terrified that this was all some sort of elaborate trap. They still expected a fight.

Ashok walked directly toward the Inquisitor, right past a line of spears and arrows. He paid them no heed, because all of his focus was on that golden mask. He stopped, a mere foot away from the Inquisitor, as if daring the man to act. To the Inquisitors credit, he didn't turn and run, though from the trembling in his legs, he was surely tempted to. A mask can't hide the shakes.

The most terrifying criminal in the world slowly raised one red hand. "Protector blood has been spilled. Loyal servants of the Law have died." And then Ashok pressed his hand against the Inquisitor's mask. Ashok cruelly pushed against the metal, grinding it against the Inquisitor's face. "Tell Omand that this is his doing, as much as it is mine."

Then Ashok dragged his palm away, leaving half of the leering visage of the Law smeared with blood and the Inquisitor quaking in his boots. He nodded toward Jagdish. "We are done here."

Fate may have had it in for Jagdish, but she had no hold over Ashok Vadal.

Jagdish flicked the reins and made a clicking noise with his tongue. The horses obediently began to pull. As they rolled past, he looked down at the poor nayak lying on the cobblestones, holding his stomach, gasping like a fish. "I warned you he makes an unforgettable impression."

It wouldn't take long for them to be followed. Inquisitor be damned, the warrior caste of even the easygoing Thao were too proud to absorb that level of insult. Jagdish had no idea what the Inquisitor had been thinking, letting them pass, but he knew that as soon as an officer with any sort of pride arrived at the gate, there would be a pursuit organized. That's what he would have done.

So Jagdish pushed the carriage horses hard. Except this path was rutted and covered in snow. These poor animals had been chosen for their beauty, not their stamina. The carriage was an ostentatious show of wealth, from a worker who was far too proud for his own good, and now it was being rattled to death. It had been built for parading through the city so a criminal could pretend to be first caste, not for bouncing along rough mountain roads. They had one small lantern, but it was mostly for decoration. He could barely see the road ahead of them, and was trying to remember if there were any sudden turns terminating in steep cliffs through here.

After a few miles, Ashok got out of the cabin, stepped carefully over the spinning wheel, and up to the driver's seat next to Jagdish. He raised his voice to be heard over the wind and the rattle. "The warriors will give chase."

"If they didn't they wouldn't be fit to be called warriors," Jagdish answered, as he cracked the whip again to keep the horses motivated. "There's just enough new dusting of snow there's no way they can miss our tracks. They'll catch us eventually. Assuming this delicate piece of porcelain doesn't crack an axle, and then they'll catch us soon."

"We can abandon the carriage and go through the trees. If we find a steep enough cliff to scale, they won't be able to track us."

"An hour ago Gutch thought you'd bled to death."

"I am fine." Ashok didn't look fine. Even in the poor light, Jagdish could see that his bloodstained face was haggard. He didn't know what it took to kill a Protector—correction, former Protector—but if they kept pushing he figured he would find out.

"Good for you, but Gutch is wearing sandals that probably came off a dainty pleasure woman. He'll be frostbit in no time. And we have to carry Bajwa. I didn't get chased across Neeramphorn for three days to leave behind the man who knows where those wizards are."

"A quandary," Ashok agreed.

Jagdish snorted—what a master of bloody understatement.

Then Ashok's eyes narrowed. "There are men waiting in ambush ahead."

He could hardly see a damned thing past the rumps of two white horses. It was said Protectors had the eyes of a hawk, but that was absurd. "Where?"

But rather than answer, Ashok stood up and shouted, "Sons of the Black Sword!"

Ahead, a match was struck and a torch caught. That Jagdish could see. Someone walked into the middle of the road and waved the torch back and forth overhead. Jagdish tried to stop the horses, but they were too frenzied to heed the pull, so he had to use the carriage's hand brake. It turned out the ride became much worse when the wheels weren't allowed to spin and this thing turned into an awkward sled. He'd never understand why rich men felt the need to travel in wheeled apartments filled with pillows.

The ambushers had heard Ashok's greeting, and risen from their hiding places. As an accomplished scout himself, Jagdish had to admit that the Somsak were very good at camouflage. He would have ridden right into a bunch of crossbows and never even known they were there. It turned out the man waving the torch was Keta, their so-called Keeper of Names. Jagdish had no idea why Ashok put up with the odd little fanatic, but he was still glad to see him right then.

"Damn that Keta, I told him not to wait for me. He was supposed to take the men and go south."

"You expected someone who started a rebellion to be good at following orders? Be thankful he didn't listen, we may still survive."

Ashok must have been in more pain than he let on, because normally he would have just leapt down from the seat, but instead he climbed carefully, using the steps like a normal man, and winced when he reached the ground. It was one of the only times Jagdish had ever seen him show weakness. It didn't last long.

There was no time for greetings or pleasantries. "Soldiers will be following. If you have a way to escape, we must take it. If not, then prepare to fight."

Shekar of the Somsak ran up to them, but stopped at the edge of the road, so as to not leave any extra footprints in the snow. "Raiders always know how to disappear, General. Come. The horses are this way. There's a downward path we can take. We'll send this silly cart on its way. By the time they discover it is empty and backtrack, we'll be long gone."

"Brilliant," Jagdish said as he hopped down. "There's a prisoner inside. We need him alive."

"Of course, Risaldar..." Then Shekar snapped at his brothers. "Deng, fetch their prisoner. Abor, take the rear. Cut a pine bough and brush our tracks. Move!"

The Somsak immediately did as Shekar directed. If their little army lived through the night, at least Jagdish knew who to appoint as their first havildar.

Despite the darkness, they found a good trail and made decent time. It helped to have experienced mountain raiders to lead them. The Somsak were vassals to the Thao, but like many vassal families, they weren't too fond of their masters. They seemed to take great joy in the idea of losing their pursuers and causing them even further embarrassment.

They couldn't return to the shack they had been using. Gutch had given that location to Bajwa so his ransom note could be delivered. It was doubtful the gangs would willingly tell the warriors where they had been hiding, but the Protectors or the Inquisitors would easily make them talk. So they simply kept moving, the further away from Neeramphorn the better.

Jagdish was exhausted, but he was doing better than some of the others. Gutch was on a Somsak pony that was far too small for him, and he was wrapped in curtains stolen from Bajwa's carriage to keep from freezing. The crime lord of Neeramphorn had been laid across a pack horse like a piece of baggage. Jagdish was beginning to worry that he'd clubbed Bajwa far too hard, but he suspected much of his lack of consciousness was feigned, and he was just waiting for a chance to escape. Only with his feet tied together and surrounded by bloodthirsty Somsak, Bajwa wouldn't make it very far.

Ashok now...He didn't look well at all, and Jagdish didn't know if it was from his wounds, or from the night's events. Normally, there was a certain way he carried himself. Not prideful, no, he could even be humble if the Law was involved at all, but always assured. Not the swagger of a young warrior, but rather possessing a confident certainty that if a thing could be done, then he would do it. Tonight though, he was swaying atop his horse. So weak that a few times Jagdish looked over expecting to see an empty saddle because Ashok had finally passed out from blood loss and fallen into the snow. But their general stayed mounted, though he hung back, alone, and did not speak.

When Keta had asked Jagdish what had happened to Ashok, he told him that he truly did not know, but that he had shouted so loudly that the whole city must have heard about how he had murdered one of his former brothers. Keta's reaction to that news showed that he truly was concerned about Ashok—as a friend and not just as a weapon of rebellion—and that revelation made Jagdish dislike Keta *slightly* less.

Just before dawn they came upon a settlement so pitiful that Jagdish hesitated to call it a village. There were three tiny dwellings, constructed from garbage leaned against trees in the rough semblance of a house. They looked too sad to live in, but smoke was rising through the hole in the roof that served as the chimney on one of them. No whole man would live like this. The inmates in his prison had lived better than this. Something this pathetic could only belong to the casteless.

They were alone in the forest, nowhere near a road, and far from any real settlement. There were no banners indicating ownership, no insignia of an overseer, nothing.

Jagdish rode up to Keta. "Who do these untouchables belong to?"

"No one. I'm betting they're runaways."

"You'd know about that."

Keta scowled, obviously biting off a sharp retort. "Regardless of where they come from, we need to rest. I'll speak to them about camping here, and make sure they're not inclined to tell anyone about us."

"Just tell them we're stopping and if they don't like it—"

"No, Risaldar. Despite their poverty, these are whole men as much as you are, and they'll be treated with respect."

Jagdish was badly outnumbered by religious fanatics who thought the little man spoke to gods, so he didn't bother to argue. "As you wish, Keeper."

"If we stay here, it'll be as their guests. I hope they don't mind the intrusion. We may be here for a while." Keta looked back toward Ashok, the concern obvious on his face. "I think our general needs time to recuperate."

"Yes, the blessings of your gods only carry one so far... Speaking of which, tell those useless bastards thanks for nothing. They were of no help in Neeramphorn."

"Yet despite the odds you escaped with your lives and miraculously captured the man you sought in the process. But I'll be sure to pass on your concerns." Keta thumped his heels into his horse and started toward the sad little dwellings. "Just don't cry to me to intercede on your behalf when the gods curse you with festering boils."

"That would be impressive, considering they're imaginary," Jagdish muttered.

Chapter 19

When dawn arrived on the mountain, a cock crowed, and Ashok awoke inside a casteless hovel that stank of dung and smoke. His wounds were healed enough that he could move without tearing them open again, but not healed enough to be free of agony. He could have called upon the Heart more, but he left the pain alone. He deserved it.

Ashok remembered a time when Ishaan Harban, having barely attained senior rank, had assisted him in arresting a corrupt arbiter in Zarger. They had pursued the man for a week across the desert before being ambushed by bandits. Together, they had slaughtered all the criminals, executed the arbiter, and restored the Law. *Good times.* Despite intense heat, dehydration, stinging scorpions, and a violent close-quarter battle, Ishaan had never once wavered, and had remained perfectly dedicated to the Order ever since. Ishaan had been as reliable as the sun.

This morning, the world felt diminished.

Careful not to step on any other sleeping bodies, Ashok took up his nicked and battered sword, and went outside.

The forest was very still. A bit more snow had fallen during the night, so even the casteless huts looked almost clean. There was a pen filled with oinking pigs, and a chicken coop as big as the untouchable's shack.

Several others were already awake and about. Keta was sitting on a log next to the chicken coop, speaking to the casteless who made their home here. Only this time, the Keeper wasn't the one talking. It was an old man speaking, skin-and-bones thin, and oddly enough Keta wasn't just listening, he was taking notes on a piece of paper.

Keta saw him. "Ashok. How are you feeling? Allow me to introduce you to the free man who built this settlement. He is a guru, a wise and holy man."

His natural inclination was to dismiss them as mere runaways who were hiding in the forest like animals. Only they were not so different than him now, reduced to begging untouchables for a place to sleep next to their fire. He supposed that made him even lower than they were. "Thank you for your hospitality."

Despite his attempt at politeness, the ancient non-person still seemed frightened of him. "For the Forgotten's warrior, my home is your home. This is a very secluded and safe place, very hard to stumble upon. You are the first outsiders who have found us in many years. Surely this is the will of the gods."

"If you would excuse us, guru... is it? What are you doing, Keta?"

"Taking their names."

"Why?"

"For the genealogy."

"Why does that matter?"

Keta seemed a bit indignant. "I am the Keeper of Names."

"I have never given the nature of your title much thought." When they had first met, Keta had known Ashok's casteless name, and even the name of his real parents, but Ashok had never concerned himself about *how* he had known.

Keta blinked a few times, caught unprepared to explain his calling. "These people are not recorded. I will write them and their ancestors in the sacred book once I return home. It was one of the very first responsibilities of the priesthood started by the Sons of Ramrowan to ensure that their bloodline endured forever. Even after their reign ended, we have kept these records in secret."

If true, that was quite the achievement. Legally, the caste-less were property, not people. They had no family name. But perhaps it was not so odd. Whole men took great pride in their ancestors. Maybe untouchables felt the same compulsion to know where they had come from too. Only Keta would surely fill their heads with nonsense about how the casteless were all descended from priests and kings, so they could get themselves worked up over it until they got put down by their betters.

"Very well." Ashok left them to their fantasies. He saw no sign of a stream, so he went off into the trees, found a snow drift, and stripped naked. Taking up handfuls of snow, he scrubbed the dried blood from his body until he was clean. The snow left his skin red and burning, but it woke him up and focused his senses.

By the time he dressed and returned to the village, the others had risen. Keta had finished recording the untouchables' genealogy, while Jagdish and Gutch had dragged their—now conscious—prisoner out for interrogation.

The four of them gathered around the sullen, silent Bajwa.

"Are you ready to begin?" Jagdish asked.

"I am. Keta, send your supposed descendants of mighty Ramrowan away. What they do not hear, the Inquisition cannot make them tell." Ashok sincerely hoped they weren't tracked here, but he could take no chances.

The Keeper did as he was told. Ashok studied their prisoner. Bajwa had been beaten, tied up, degraded, and was sitting in the snow with a sack over his head. This was a man who had used guile and ambition to gain far more wealth and power than the Law had granted him. Ashok knew criminals well. He would either break easily, or not at all.

Gutch cracked his knuckles.

Keta returned a moment later, having shooed away the residents. "Look at us, four individuals, one from each of the great divisions within our society, yet here we stand, putting aside our differences of caste and status, choosing to work together in pursuit of a common goal. The worker, the warrior, the untouchable, and even a man of the ruling class—"

Ashok scowled at Keta.

"Sorry, *formerly* of the ruling class, but all of us *united*, not coerced by Law, but rather each motivated by their own free will to come to this juncture! Surely the gods will be pleased by such cooperation."

"We're only here because we need to torture information from this man."

"Well, the gods have to start somewhere!"

"Yes, but it's hardly worthy of another of your boring sermons," Jagdish said as he pulled off the sack they'd kept over their prisoner's head. Bajwa had been tied to a post, and gagged so he couldn't speak, but he looked suitably terrified.

"Unless of course your Forgotten was one of those old dark gods. I've dealt with cultists who believed their gods demanded human sacrifice," Ashok said.

"Oh no, of course not. The Forgotten expects his servants to get their hands dirty, but nothing like that."

"Good." Even forced outside of the Law, Ashok still had to draw the line somewhere.

"Enough of your mad babbling, false priest. Pass me that meat cleaver I know you keep hidden in your coat," said Gutch as he approached their captive. Their worker had a nasty black eye left over from Bajwa's thugs. "Let's get to it."

As soon as Gutch ripped the gag from Bajwa's mouth, the bargaining began. "Hold on now with the cutting. My people will pay a good ransom for my return."

"By now your people—whichever ones the Protectors didn't execute at least—have already forgotten about you and rallied behind a new boss. Your business won't even know you're gone."

"Shut your fat face, Gutch. Unlike you, my men know the meaning of the word loyalty. The rest of you, don't listen to this fool. He did me wrong and wants me dead. Everyone else here I can make rich!"

"I do not care about your notes." Ashok squatted down next to Bajwa, tilted his head, and looked the criminal in the eyes. "Do you know who I am?"

"No, but from the look of you, you're the leader of this gang, trying to move in on Neeramphorn. What do you want? A cut of the profits? Your own territory? We can deal, boss to boss, you and me can talk this out and—"

"I am Ashok Vadal."

That hung there for a long time. Bajwa trailed off, then licked his lips, nervous. "Oh no. Apologies. I didn't intend offense."

Ashok did not raise his voice. He didn't even try to be threatening. "I am seeking the location of a group you have supplied with illegal magic. You will provide this location to me. If you attempt to lie, I will know, and I will hurt you until I am satisfied you speak truth."

"Giving up customers? So what's in it for me if I talk? You don't kill me?"

"If you're lucky," Gutch interjected. "We're looking for the Lost House."

"What?" Bajwa sputtered. "They're not real. They're just a story to scare kids!"

"Don't deny you know how to contact them. Whenever I brought your brother a piece of black steel, he'd brag about reaching out to the Lost House first, because they'd pay with buckets of gems or sacks full of banknotes. And Ashok here knows they're real because he's already killed a few of them... Oceans, they aren't so hard. I killed one myself."

Jagdish folded his arms. "By yourself?"

"Eh, you distracted him."

Bajwa scoffed. "Betray the assassins? They'll destroy all of you and then come back for me!" He tried to force a laugh to drive home his point, but he was too scared of Ashok, so it was more of an awkward wheeze.

Ashok gave Bajwa the back of his hand hard enough to bounce his skull off the post. "I have no patience for evasion. Tell us what you know of this Lost House."

That blow had knocked the blood from Bajwa's nose and the truth from his mouth. "They're real all right, but they're ghosts. There's nobody they can't murder. They walk in one shadow and come out another. They can change into beasts and fly on the night winds. Even the Inquisitors leave them be."

"Where do they dwell?"

"I don't know!"

Ashok lifted his hand to cuff him again.

"Down the Nansakar! I mean I've personally never been, but I'm told if you follow the river all the way to sea, it turns into a swamp, Bahdjangal, the flooded forest. They're somewhere out there. I've been told they've got this magnificent palace, practically a whole castle, all to themselves."

"Rubbish," Jagdish said. "I've seen the raid maps. The Nansakar river basin is nothing but a wilderness. There's not so much as a town there."

"No, really. I swear to you. Back in my great-great-grandfather's day, there used to be a city way out there, but something bad happened to it. It's just ruins now. That's where the assassins live. The Lost House only use a few trusted couriers, but I've sent them magic, and they've sent back treasure. They've a man in Haradas, runs the barges there, named Chattarak. My men deliver the magic to him, he takes it the rest of the way."

"You never thought to follow him home to see about robbing his masters?" Gutch asked incredulously.

"Of course not, you imbecile. *They're killer wizards.* You don't rob someone with a reputation like they've got. Is that what you intend to do? Rob the Lost House? You were always too greedy for your own good, Gutch. My brother was an idiot to trust you."

"There's a long list of reasons your brother was an idiot, but trusting me wasn't among them."

"Enough," Ashok snapped. He had never been to the region Bajwa spoke of, and knew little of it. There were so few people living in the eastern wastes that it was rare for Protectors to be dispatched there. However, he remembered the ancient world map that was inside the structure which held the Heart of the Mountain, and there had once been a large city at the mouth of the Nansakar long ago, so that much was true. Only in all his education, there had been no mention of this place still existing only a few generations ago. "If these assassins have their own palace, then surely it would have come to the attention of the Law by now."

"Some of them know about it, but they've got some sort of deal with the assassins. I heard it from one of them with my own ears. He said their master, Sikasso, has gotten them special favors from the Inquisition. They trade, murders for amnesty."

"You really expect us to believe that the Inquisition would use criminals to do its bidding?" Jagdish said. "The Inquisition? The men with the scary masks and the sticks up their asses over the tiniest infraction, consorting with shape-changing killers? They've got their own wizards, and secret witch hunters hiding in every closet."

A year ago Ashok would have been incredulous as well, but he was a living example of Grand Inquisitor Omand's strange policies. "Continue, Bajwa."

"That's all I know. When a tracker brings me magic, I'd send a runner to Chattarak to negotiate the price. They paid good, fast, and more than fair. Never once broke a deal, and I was smart enough not to cross them. Any other smuggler who did cheat them, shorted them on weight, or tried to pass off empty bones, wound up dead within days, usually strangled inside his room with the door still locked from the inside. You go after them, you can't say I'm the one who told you."

Satisfied that Bajwa was telling the truth, Ashok looked to his companions.

Gutch obviously still wanted to murder Bajwa, but even he seemed convinced by his story. "I've heard rumors about where the Nansakar meets the sea. The south is the Akershan wastes, but the north is thick timber clear to Guntur. There's a maze of small rivers that come together there, and lots of old ruins up those rivers. I mean really old ruins, from before the demon rain. Places like that often hide black steel, but the trackers who go searching in those parts never come back. It's got a real bad reputation. Could be wizards don't like competitors."

"You were a lazy and incompetent tracker anyway, Gutch," Bajwa said.

The big worker gave the crime boss a swift kick to the stomach.

While Bajwa gasped and wretched, Ashok looked to Keta, who'd been silent for most of the interrogation. "Keeper?"

"He could by lying, so that we blunder through the woods while the Lost House is really a thousand miles in the other direction. *But...* I think the Forgotten delivered this man into our hands for a reason."

Jagdish snorted. "I delivered him with a blow to the head."

"I believe the gods want us reunited with Thera. We must work with what they have provided. I see no other way."

"Jagdish?"

"This smuggler is probably as trustworthy as Keta's useless gods, but it sounds reasonable. Wizards need a place to hide in order to work their illegal magic. A swamp in the middle of nowhere's got to be a damned good place to hide."

Ashok mulled over what to do. He didn't want any more delays, but after the events in Neeramphorn, the Protectors would expect him to try and make as much distance as possible. The idea of fighting more of his former brothers sickened him, and he couldn't rescue the prophet if he was killed before he could get to her. It had snowed enough last night that their tracks would have been covered. They would be relatively safe here for a time.

"We will camp here a few days while they widen their search for us. Then we will slip past our pursuers and go south toward the river to find their runner."

Gutch jerked his head at Bajwa, who was still coughing. "What about him?"

"I told you what you wanted to know," he gasped.

"Ashok told him to cooperate. He did," Jagdish said. "Letting him go is the honorable thing to do."

"What? No!" Gutch shouted, spittle flying from his split and scabbed-over lips. "This isn't one of your fellow warriors, Jagdish, to be bound by a concept as tenuous as *honor*. Yesterday he was bragging about how after he robbed and murdered whichever poor servant delivered my ransom, he was going to castrate me and force feed me my own testicles. We let him go, he'll return to Neeramphorn and tell the Protectors right where we're heading. Or worse, get word to the wizards so they can ambush us on the way!"

"I said honorable, not wise."

"Gutch is right. The important thing is getting our prophet back," Keta seemed uncomfortable with his agreement. He had started a rebellion, but Keta didn't delight in shedding the blood of someone who had never wronged his people. He sighed. "We can't risk it."

"No. I'll keep quiet! Really I—"

Ashok reached out, took hold of Bajwa's head, and with a violent twist, snapped his neck. Gutch leapt back and Keta gasped.

It happened so suddenly that even Jagdish was taken by surprise. "I suppose that settles the debate then."

Ashok stood up and dusted off his hands. Their assessment of the danger had been correct. The criminal's fate had been sealed. Once decided, there had been no need to make Bajwa linger on in fear after that. It spared them all the indignity of begging. Ashok was a pragmatic man, but he was not a cruel one.

Gutch spit on the corpse. "Don't let this wretch trouble your sleep, Keta. Believe me, the world is a far better place without Bajwa in it. He hurt a lot of people who didn't deserve it. Good riddance."

Ashok looked toward Keta, who seemed a bit shaken, but determined. For some odd reason, it made him glad that the priest was not *too* comfortable with casual executions. "You said your gods expected their servants to get their hands dirty, Keeper." He showed Keta his palms. "These are what dirty hands look like."

Ashok walked back to the shack. By the time he got there the casteless had already stolen all of Bajwa's fine clothing and tossed his body over the fence to feed their pigs.

Chapter 20

Grand Inquisitor Omand watched with glee as Ashok Vadal fought a dozen Great House Vadal warriors to the death in a knife fight.

"Oh, this is truly fantastic," he said as an actor was hurled over the dinner table and another had a wooden blade trapped in his armpit. Fake warriors tumbled from the stage or writhed around on the stage, feigning fatal wounds. It was a crescendo of violence. The audience would love it.

"During the actual performance the stage hands will be throwing cups of fake blood on them," Artya whispered back to him.

Omand had always enjoyed the theater. "Brilliant, my dear. Brilliant."

The actor they'd chosen to play Ashok was physically imposing, but also very dramatically talented. The speech he had given after kicking in the doors to interrupt Bidaya's banquet had given Omand chills. The lines about how the old gods had sent him to destroy the Law had been extremely well done, with just the right touch of fanaticism. Omand had said that he didn't just want Ashok portrayed as a brute, but rather someone who fit the part of a hero turned to darkness, evil, yet still intelligent.

Great houses didn't fear brutes. Brutes were simplistic and easily defeated, but everyone feared a visionary. Their villain needed to be seductive. So Artya had hired one of the most respected actors in the Capitol to play the Black Heart.

During rehearsals the amphitheater was usually empty. Opening night there would be thousands of high-status guests gathered to watch the premiere, but not counting their nearby bodyguards, there were only four people in the audience today, a tiny island in a sea of empty seats.

Grand Inquisitor Omand Vokkan was the honored guest of Artya Zati dar Zarger, Arbiter of the Order of Census and Taxation, who had funded the production of this new play, *The Black Heart's Rebellion*. It was sure to be huge success. Artya had not been obligated to the Capitol for long, but had already become a force to be reckoned with among the social circles of the city's elite.

It was said by many that young Artya was charming, beautiful, and threw the best parties. It was also said by a few that she secretly worked for the Inquisition, but whenever Omand found out someone was actively spreading that rumor, he promptly had them killed.

The last of the Vadal warriors had been fake stabbed to death, and now a shirtless giant walked onto the stage. "Oh, this is the part where Ashok faces Bidaya's champion. What was his name?"

"Sankhamur," said the man to sitting to his left. "I knew him."

"Really, Javed? I did not know that."

Inquisitor Javed had recently returned from his secret mission in Shabdkosh, and surely had no idea why his superior had invited him here. Witch hunters were weapons of guile and deceit, reserved for missions of infiltration and assassination. It must have seemed odd to him, inviting a vicious dog out of his kennel to go among polite society.

"Yes, sir. We met once when I was on assignment in the north. Sankhamur was a supremely skilled bodyguard, keen eyed, and steady with a blade."

"Yet, I heard Ashok gutted him like a pig. I hope this version at least puts up a good show."

And indeed, he did. The actor playing Sankhamur was very imposing, shaved and oiled, a walking wall of exaggerated muscle. No real warrior looked so puffy, but what did most of the first caste know of such things? They were so insulated from strife that what they knew about war came from plays like this. Artya had explained that she'd picked this actor specifically to symbolize the physical might of the warrior caste. So when Ashok killed even this mighty specimen, what hope could their real warriors have against such a monster?

"What do you think of all this, Taraba?"

His assistant was sitting on the row behind them. "Very impressive, sir. I'm sure it will be the talk of the Capitol."

"And you, Javed?"

Since they were nominally in public, the three Inquisitors were all wearing their masks, so Omand could not read the hardened witch hunter's expression, but Javed sounded amused. "I don't know. This is all so flamboyant."

"It is effective," Artya insisted.

"What I do, what the Grand Inquisitor once did, that's real acting. Not this exaggerated business. We blend in and become someone else entirely. We change personalities as easily as these fops change their costume, only we wear them for months at a time, becoming whoever necessary to complete our mission."

"Remarkable..." she murmured. "I did not know our Grand Inquisitor had such an exciting background."

"He rooted out subversives for years. From the jungles of the north to the icy south, the triumphs of Omand Vokkan are legend."

Omand enjoyed the flattery, but even the members of his own order had no idea just how much he had accomplished during his time in the field. In the darkest corners of Lok he had witnessed things seen by no other man since the Age of Kings. The world had given up its secrets, and he had tasted power beyond imagining.

"Perhaps you could teach me more about what you do later, Inquisitor Javed?"

"Maybe. You seem like a quick learner, Arbiter Artya. But back to this play of yours, I can't tell if it's supposed to be a tragedy or a comedy."

"It's a serious drama," Artya snapped, since she took great pride in her propaganda.

"It's certainly a tragedy for Great House Vadal," Omand said, silencing his subordinates.

With all of the warriors dispatched, and the actors playing the party guests cowering in terror, Bidaya Vadal came back onstage and gave a speech about how the great houses would never stand for such casteless butchery. Omand found the actress to be a bit shrill, but considering the real Bidaya, that was accurate casting.

She walked to where the prop of Angruvadal had been stuck in the floor, declared that the first caste could never fall as long as they had black steel on their side, and dramatically lifted the sword into the air.

"This is the best part," Artya whispered as she leaned forward.

The actress began to tremble. *"It guides my hand toward evil! What madness will result when even our ancestor blade turns against us? With such power in filthy untouchable hands, nothing will stop their evil! Nothing!"* And then she screamed as she struck herself in the head and fell, seemingly lifeless, to the stage.

Taraba began to clap. "Well done."

Artya was rather pleased with herself. "During the actual play, she'll have a sack filled with fake blood hidden in her wig. It'll burst when struck and she'll be positively drenched."

Omand would make certain his opening night seat was located somewhere that he could see the look on Harta Vadal's face, as he watched the reenactment of his mother's death. That would be a good opportunity to judge a potential opponent's state of mind, and also be amusing at the same time. But Omand wasn't completely satisfied yet.

"It isn't quite right though. This actress is too sanctimonious. I don't want anyone rooting for Ashok. He cannot be sympathetic in any way. Have her replaced with a younger, prettier actress, so there is a greater feeling of loss."

"Of course, Grand Inquisitor. I was thinking the same thing. I have a few others in mind already." As the false Ashok cruelly stepped on the bodies to walk off stage, the curtain fell. "Now will be the intermission while we change the set. Next is the scene where Ashok murders his way out of the prison, demonstrating his complete disdain for the Law."

One of the bodyguards approached and handed Taraba a note. He read it, and then passed it to the Grand Inquisitor without comment. It was in a cipher that only a select few within their Order could understand.

The historian Vikram Akershan has been found.

That was splendid news. Omand passed the note back to Taraba, who would burn it at the first opportunity.

"Sadly, we must return to our duties. I will watch the rest opening night, but fine work, Artya. Between this and the recent unpleasantness in Shabdkosh, the Capitol will be speaking of nothing but the untouchable menace. I've found most judges to be remarkably pliable once you set the tone of the conversation. During the next open session in the Chamber of Argument I would have you once again propose a great extermination of the casteless. You are seen as eloquent and passionate about the topic."

Artya really did have a charming smile, even as she contemplated genocide. "I shall prepare my remarks."

"Good. Be aware that I just received word this morning by magical courier that Ashok murdered a Protector in Neeramphorn. Be sure to include that in your list of outrages. By next week the rest of the Capitol will have heard as well. Shabdkosh hit close to home. The judges know that could have just as easily been any of them who had stopped there on their way from the Capitol back to their homes. And if the Protectors can't save them, who can? Important people do not like feeling unsafe. Now they are imagining what it would be like to wake up, surrounded in fire, the victim of rebellious arson."

"Unfortunate business," agreed the witch hunter who had burned them.

"Use their fear to your advantage, Artya. That will be all."

Artya made her farewells and then went to replace her actress. Omand watched her go. "If I had ten more like her, I could rule the Capitol through dinner parties alone."

"A capable woman," Javed agreed. "A man could go far with her at his side. Is she in need of a husband?"

"She's too high status for you," Taraba said.

"Then I shall have to earn more promotions." It was unwise to speak in such a brazen manner in front of the Grand Inquisitor, foolhardy even, or was that just the role he had chosen to play today? "May I ask why you brought me here, Grand Inquisitor?"

Javed was one of their most accomplished witch hunters. After his performance in Shabdkosh, Omand had welcomed him into the conspiracy. As suspected, Javed had no issue with the idea of the Inquisition secretly controlling politics—better them than anyone else—and he seemed to find the idea of ridding the world of untouchables to be a worthy one. After all, they were just more mouths to feed. The witch hunter had talent, but more importantly Omand sensed that like him, Javed possessed *detachment*. He suspected Javed only felt truly alive when given a challenge. Omand could use such a man to accomplish great things.

"I have an exceedingly difficult assignment for you."

"I am honored to be chosen."

"Ashok Vadal is in the east, somewhere near Neeramphorn, and it sounds like he's building an army. Those I originally tasked to observe him have proven unreliable. Your new assignment is to infiltrate the so called Sons of the Black Sword."

"Do you wish Ashok dead?" Javed asked.

"Not yet. He is a useful asset, but he is proving to be an unpredictable one. I want a spy in his camp. When the cost outweighs the benefits, I will have you eliminate him. But remember, though exaggerated, this play is based upon true events. Ashok is deadly to his enemies, so if you are to have any chance, he must see you as an ally until it is too late. Taraba will provide you with any resources you need, banknotes, traveling papers, our files about these cultists, and even a poison capable of felling a mighty Protector. How are you with magic?"

"I have mastered three patterns."

That was extremely impressive for someone who wasn't licensed as a wizard, but Inquisitors were given a pass when it came to such things. Omand himself knew fifteen. "Then Taraba will issue you plenty of demon as well. Time is of the essence. You will leave in the morning. Ride your horses to death and confiscate new ones in each town."

"It shall be done. Thank you for this opportunity." Javed sounded sincere, but with a witch hunter, who could tell?

"I am leaving now," Omand stood up and Taraba followed. "Feel free to enjoy the rest of the play."

"Perhaps the lovely Artya would watch it with me...I must admit, I am curious how it ends."

Omand knew the finale of the play featured an orphaned daughter of the first caste singing a poignant song, while in the background Ashok and a casteless mob slaughtered the good people of Sutpo Bridge. The girl was considered the finest vocalist in the Capitol, and it had cost a great deal to secure her contract. The message was rather blunt by his standards, but the judges in the audience needed to leave with the feeling that *they could be next.*

But instead the Grand Inquisitor smiled beneath his mask and said, "The saga of the Black Heart ends however I say it ends."

Chapter 21

~~~~~~~~~~

Radamantha had no desire to go on adventures. She'd never wanted to stumble across a conspiracy, get threatened by wizards, or dodge assassination attempts by Inquisitors. At no point had she ever thought it would be fun to be rushed from her family estate in the middle of the night, disguised as a lowly worker, and smuggled out of the Capitol on a caravan. Nor had she wanted to spend the weeks since hiding on a goat farm, bored out of her mind.

All she had ever wanted was to fulfill her obligation, working tirelessly in the Central Library, doing vital things like preparing research papers, and taking care of the precious books. She'd been content to read about political intrigue and adventures. Only an imbecile would actually want to participate in such things!

Though she did have to admit she'd rather enjoyed the romance part. That was the one thing she'd discovered where reading about something just wasn't as nice as real life. The only good thing that had come out of her stumbling into the plot against the casteless was that she'd met Devedas. Even with the fear, and the running for her life, he actually made it all worthwhile. She'd never known anyone like the handsome, brave, confident Lord Protector. Only duty called, and he was away, thwarting conspiracies and valiantly upholding the Law. Rada had always thought of herself as the rational and pragmatic one, but when she thought about Devedas, the voice in her head sounded like her little sister pining on about true love.

Rada sighed and went back to staring out the window at the unending vista of scrub brush, sand, and goats.

The goat farm was a hideously smelly, boring place. There wasn't anything to read, not so much as a single book. The closest she'd come to reading material was a mass-printed notice from the Order of Agriculture and Irrigation about various livestock diseases and their methods of treatment. She'd already read it sixteen times. If she'd known Devedas was going to hide her in the most uninteresting place in the entire Zarger desert, she would've at least insisted on bringing some proper reading material.

The workers who lived here barely spoke to her. She tried to be friendly, but mostly they acted nervous around her. Though she was dressed in humble clothing like theirs, they all knew she was really of the first caste, and insisted on acting accordingly. Her caste weren't beloved by the inferior castes, but rather feared. She was staying here because these people were beholden to Devedas for some reason. She didn't know if he was paying them to hide her, or if he'd spared them from some punishment once, but it was apparent they weren't enjoying the presence of their house guest.

When she had asked why he couldn't put her someplace among her own kind, Devedas had patiently explained that was the first place the conspiracy would look for her. The first caste was so used to living in idle comfort that to most of them the idea of living among the lower classes was inconceivable. Only Rada's life had been spent in the austere Capitol Library. Unlike most of her peers, she didn't care about riches or comfort, so she'd be fine.

There was safety in obscurity, he'd declared, but sadly, it turned out obscurity stunk of goat piss. However, Rada trusted Devedas, probably more than she had ever trusted anyone else in her life, and he had assured her that he was putting some mysterious plan into motion which would secure their future.

She hated to admit it, but it made her a little giddy to think about how he had spoken about *their* future.

After the first few days, she'd been so bored that she'd lowered herself and offered to help the workers with the chores. By then she'd read that pamphlet so many times she was practically an expert on diseases of the goat—not that she'd ever actually touched one of the furry things—but the workers had gently turned her away. It seemed they were afraid that if a daughter of the first caste broke a nail doing manual labor, they'd all be flogged, or worse.

Rada rather hated being treated like a piece of delicate porcelain. The lower castes were terrified they'd accidently give offense to someone from the Capitol. And what made it worse was that people in the Capitol came from every single great house, with their many conflicting traditions, so it was virtually impossible to not give offense somehow.

She noticed that the workers were trying hard to never point their feet directly at her, because that was supposedly an insult... In Sarnobat maybe! Her family was from a vassal house inside Harban lands, on the opposite side of the continent! So these poor workers were walking about with feet splayed like exaggerated crows, trying not to anger her with pointing toes, because at some point in their past a different member of her caste had taken offense at how his inferiors were standing.

Sometimes people were just ridiculous...

Yet her exile beat being arrested and tortured by the Inquisition, so Rada simply passed the time looking out the window. With no books to read, she'd even thought about trying to write her own. After all, someone should document this incident. Except she didn't even have any paper, a decent pen, nor ink, so she'd given the farmer a few notes to purchase her some the next time he went to town for supplies. She'd been directed to avoid purchasing anything which would raise suspicion, which meant no books, but even workers needed to write things down. Surely there was some manner of goat inventory to be conducted.

What should I call my book? Her working title, *The Testimony of a Senior Archivist Concerning the Plot to Bring about the Genocide of the Casteless*, wasn't particularly pithy. Titles were hard.

Rada's thoughts about her incipient foray into authorship were interrupted when two men on horseback appeared along the road, riding directly toward the farm. From the dust cloud kicked up behind them, they were riding very fast. That was unusual. As they got closer, she could see their horses were powerful Zarger steeds, nothing like the tired old things the workers rode about on. Their clothing consisted of voluminous black robes, and they had curved swords sheathed at their waists.

There was some shouting in the yard. The dogs began to bark.

Rada pulled herself away from the window. She'd heard about the infamous desert raiders, but Devedas had promised this place was too close to the Capitol to be troubled by such criminals. Perhaps it was just the local warriors, come to tax the workers for the protection they provided. Either way, Rada didn't want to be seen by strangers so she decided to stay out of sight.

There was a quick knock on her door, but before she could respond, someone rudely opened it anyway. Her space was humble, and she was just a guest here, but that sudden intrusion offended Rada anyway.

"Mistress,"—it was the farmer's wife, Diya—"you must come out. There are men coming to see you."

"You know I'm not supposed to talk to anyone. Where's your husband?"

"He's gone to the market. Hurry. You must come," Diya insisted, looking very nervous. "They're important men and you don't want to be rude."

Rada had never really liked Diya. She seemed too fretful, and she'd never really talked to Rada at all, despite her best efforts to be friendly. Not to mention a few times she'd overheard her through the thin walls, angrily berating her husband for taking in a house guest.

"Who are these riders?"

"Important men!" That was not a sufficient answer. When Diya sensed Rada's hesitation, she quickly added, "Friends of Lord Devedas. Hurry. Come quickly."

Something was wrong. Devedas hadn't sent those men. He'd promised that when he sent for her, it would be someone she knew, or an obvious Protector. They rode around dressed in gleaming silver, not black robes. No one else could be trusted. As soon as her husband had gone off, Diya must have informed on her. *That rat!*

But Rada kept a polite smile on her face. "Certainly. I'll be right out. Please, give me a moment to gather my things."

"Good, good." Diya responded with her own forced smile, and the instant she closed the door Rada headed for the back window.

Hours of boredom had given her plenty of time to imagine and prepare for various terrible scenarios. She'd kept her pack from the caravan ready, with clothing, food, and water jugs she'd refilled fresh from the well every morning. She opened the shutters, looked around, saw nothing but sand and more goats, so tossed her pack onto the ground with a *thump*. Since it got really cold at night in the desert this time of year, she pulled on the coat and scarf she'd used to disguise herself when she'd fled the Capitol, and then climbed silently out the window.

Again, this just illustrated that adventure was for fools. Rada was terrified. There was nothing charming about climbing out a window. Once she was down safely, she pulled the pack straps over her shoulders, and began sneaking away. From the sound of horses stamping, and excited dogs barking, the two warriors were still at the front of the house. They began shouting demands.

"Where is Radamantha Nems dar Harban? Send her outside! Honor your bargain, woman."

She was no warrior-caste scout, but she'd read books written by them, so she'd taken their advice and paid careful attention to her surroundings on the ride in. Beyond the goat pens was a ravine, which would hide her movements until she reached the base of a nearby rocky hill. Unfortunately Rada had to climb over a fence to get there, and it turned out goats make a terrible noise when disturbed. The little ones sounded like wounded children screaming. The old ones sounded the same, but angrier. And these goats were exceedingly upset that the unfamiliar Rada was crossing their pen.

"Shhhhhhh." But they just stared at her with their horrible yellow eyes and kept making awful noises. They stuck their terrible snuffling noses against her pants. "Eww!" She realized they weren't trying to sound an alarm, they just thought she might have food for them. So Rada reached back into her pack, found the sack of dates she'd been hoarding, and dumped it on the ground. That silenced the damnable creatures and they immediately began gobbling up her food. If she starved to death while crossing the desert, it would be their fault.

Rada climbed over the back fence and ran for the ravine as fast as she could. There wasn't much athletic competition among librarians, so her run wasn't pretty, but it would have to do.

Only one of the riders had circled around the edge of the farmhouse and spotted her. He shouted a warning to his companion, then took off after her. His powerful horse leapt the fence like it wasn't even there. He immediately began to close the distance.

And because Rada was looking back over her shoulder while trying to run, she tripped over a rock and fell hard, skinning her knees, elbows, and hands.

The horseman slowed as he approached, having a good laugh at her misfortune. "Stop before you hurt yourself, girl."

She shrugged out from under her heavy pack and got up. The horse was watching her with angry eyes. Now that was a powerfully muscled beast which had surely run down many people. There was nowhere to flee where the rider couldn't easily cut her off, so she reached into her pack and pulled out the big weapon she'd taken from the caravan. Rada knew nothing about fighting, but it seemed like a cross between a knife and a hatchet, so she at least hoped it was intimidating as she brandished it before her.

"A cane knife? There's not much sugarcane to be harvested in Zarger." The warrior seemed to be having a jolly time as his horse stamped back and forth with heavy hooves that could easily kick her to death. His robes were black to absorb the merciless desert sun, yet baggy enough to keep the heat from reaching his body. The only thing she could see were his eyes, amused. "You're the librarian, aren't you?"

"I don't know what you're talking about. Stay back!"

"The Inquisition put out the word they'll pay good money for you. We agreed to split it with that farm wife, but don't worry. The masks want you alive. Now drop the knife and come along."

"I'm not going anywhere with you."

"It wasn't a request." He drew his sword. All Rada knew about swords came from books. The only one she'd ever really seen in action had been southern, which curved forward for more effective chopping, a fact which Devedas had demonstrated on some Inquisitors. The desert riders' swords were curved back for slashing from horseback. Either way, it turned out that in real life any sword was incredibly intimidating when pointed at you. "Inquisitors' notice said alive, not unharmed. Put it down."

"No!"

She didn't even see it coming. The sword dipped and flashed. Her big knife thing was struck from her hand so hard that it left her fingers stinging. Then just by moving his knees a bit, he directed his horse to bump into her. Its big chest knocked her right back into the dirt.

"Sorry about that, but I couldn't risk you accidentally cutting my horse. Now come on. You can either surrender peaceful like and ride with us back to town, or we can drag you along behind with ropes. It's not so far you'll die, but at the pace we set your feet will be bleeding by the time we get there."

Rada was furious as she stood up and dusted herself off, but she couldn't fight a warrior. "I've done nothing wrong."

"Everyone I've ever found for the Inquisition says that. Look, I don't care about the Law. I'm here because we make more off collecting one bounty on the side than our phontho gives us to live off of for a year."

"Whatever they're paying, I can pay more. My father is the head of an Order in the Capitol. And I am a close personal friend of Lord Protector Devedas."

He laughed again. "Sure you are, and I'm Thakoor of Great House Zarger and my horse is the bearer of our ancestor blade. I'm trying to be polite out of respect to your caste, but you're a defiant one. Ropes it is then. Just don't complain to me when the soles of your feet rub off. Maybe after a few miles you'll reconsider my earlier offer."

He reached for the curled rope at the back of his saddle, but then he stopped, puzzled by a noise, and looked back toward the farm house. A moment later the other Zarger horse appeared, galloping off across the desert, riderless. "What the—"

Then a huge man came walking around the side of the house, dressed in tan desert robes, with a great big hammer resting over one shoulder. A big straw hat was covering most of his features. Only between the beard sticking out and his imposing size, Rada recognized him immediately.

"Karno!" She waved. "I'm so glad to see you!"

"Who's the giant?"

"I'll have you know that's Protector of the Law, Karno Uttara, and his obligation consists of smacking miscreants with that hammer. I warned you I was close personal friends with the Lord Protector."

"That ruffian's no Protector." From the way his manner changed, that warrior had merely been toying with Rada. He shifted his grip on his sword, and suddenly it seemed far more dangerous. Even the horse's attitude changed. When it snorted and turned to face Karno, it made the way it had knocked her over seem almost playful in comparison. All mirth gone, the warrior called out, "What did you do to my brother, stranger?"

"He'll live." Karno just kept walking toward them, seemingly without a care in the world. "Are you alright, Rada?"

"I'm fine. What're you doing here?"

"I was asked to keep an eye on you. Hold, rider, I am who she's declared me to be. My armor is packed, but I can show you the token of my office."

Only he didn't wait to see if Karno was telling the truth or not. "This is my bounty!" The warrior made a clicking nose with his tongue, and the horse charged.

"Karno! Look out!"

Her warning was completely unnecessary. It was hard to miss a warhorse thundering right at you, or a curved sword rising into the air to cut you down. Karno just stopped, calm as could be. Standing in the path of destruction, seemingly heedless of danger, he took the hammer from his shoulder, extended it in one hand to the side, and then flicked it toward the horse's legs.

With perfect aim, it spun through the air, wooden shaft hit bone, not nearly hard enough to do a great deal of damage, but then it was twirling between the legs, and the animal tripped. It stumbled hard. The momentum turned into a slide, which turned into a very painful looking crash. The rider was thrown off, black robes turning brown as he rolled through the dirt.

Karno went over and casually picked him up by the throat. The horse thrashed around, but none of its legs had been broken. It managed to get up and run off.

The warrior struggled, but Karno was unmoved. He'd lost his sword on impact, but reached for a dagger on his belt. In a blur of motion, the Protector had locked onto that wrist and twisted it in a painful-looking direction. The warrior dropped the knife, then Karno dropped him. It happened so fast that Rada wasn't even sure what had happened, just that Karno had effortlessly tossed him on his face.

The warrior sprang back up, attacking with his fists. Karno seemed almost bored as he blocked the shots with his forearms, and then he took hold of a handful of black robe and was choking the warrior with his own clothing.

"Calm down, Zarger. I have questions." But the warrior tried to hook his thumb into Karno's eye. He was having none of that, so he spun the warrior around fast, and caught him by the throat with one big hand.

Since his arms were so much longer, the warrior could no longer claw at his face. He kicked Karno in the leg, but all the Protector did was turn his hip into it, and the soft leather boot bounced right off that wall of meat. Karno squeezed hard, cutting off the warrior's air. He made a panicked squeaking noise, and that seemed to take the fight out of him.

"Who sent you?" Karno relaxed his grip enough so the warrior could speak.

He gasped. "Inquisitors."

"I take it this was an unofficial obligation."

"Yeah. Lots of folks who get in trouble in the Capitol think they can hide in Zarger lands. Official criminals get posted, but sometimes the Inquisition wants to be discreet, like for high-status people who've not been charged with any crimes yet. If we find them, we collect them, quiet, and hand them over. We get paid. Nobody ever knows it's the Inquisition who got them."

"Interesting. My Order is more direct in our approach."

"I swear I didn't know you were a Protector!"

"Of course. Continue."

"They're usually rare, but we got two unofficial bounties this month to watch for. Then some farm wife started complaining about this one here, and she matched the description." He twisted his head a bit to look at Rada. Karno had knocked off his turban and scarf, so she could see his face. Thin and sharp featured, he was much younger than she'd expected. "Sorry. Nothing personal, miss."

"Indeed. This is nothing personal." Karno cocked back his other huge arm to deliver a mighty blow. The warrior cringed and closed his eyes tight.

"Wait!" Rada cried. The warrior had at least tried to be courteous in the collection of his bounty. She didn't want Karno to execute him on her behalf. "Please don't kill him."

"I didn't intend to. He's broken no Law."

The warrior opened his eyes hopefully. "That's true! I'm very fond of the Law."

Then the Protector crashed his meaty fist into the warrior's cranium, and dropped him in an unmoving heap. "But I don't want him following us either."

"I asked you not to kill him!"

"He'll wake up with a headache is all. In my experience a warrior can be knocked out like that several times before they begin to forget their letters and colors." Karno began walking away. "Let's go."

Rada picked up her pack and knife, then stepped over the unconscious warrior. She almost felt sorry for the fellow. "Where are we going?"

"I've got to find someplace safe for you. I have a few ideas." Then Karno paused. "Hmmm . . . Wait." He returned to the warrior and crouched next to him. For the briefest moment, she thought that he might have changed his mind, and he'd gone back to finish off the poor man, but then Karno began searching through his robes instead.

"It hardly seems fair to rob him. These warriors wouldn't be collecting secret bounties if they weren't so poor to begin with."

"That is kind, but no. He mentioned two of you." Karno pulled out a scrap of paper, unfolded it, and began to read. Rada couldn't make out the words without her glasses on, but it had been mass printed. She'd not known the Inquisition had its own pressing machine. It seemed everyone was copying her order now. "They provided a very thorough description of you."

"Oh?" Rada was curious. "Did it say I was pretty?"

Karno gave her an incredulous look. "No." Then he went back to reading. "Curious. They're looking for another member of your caste as well, Vikram Akershan, Senior Historian."

"Really?" Rada hadn't heard that name in a long time. "I know him."

"You are both to be taken alive. I wonder if he's another witness to this conspiracy."

"I doubt it. Vikram's something of a hermit. My father consulted with him once, library business. I was very young, but he dragged me along to his estate . . . Well, I wouldn't call it an estate. More like a fort in the middle of nowhere."

"Interesting . . . Do you recall the location?"

"I'm a Senior Archivist. Our minds are honed through rigorous training. Of course I remember. It was on the north slope of Mount Metoro, near where the Astronomer's Order built their observatory." Rada pointed toward what she thought was east.

"You mean that way?" Karno nodded in a different direction.

"I was close."

Chapter 22

Five years ago

There was a glow on the horizon.

They were miles away, but the great funeral pyre still lit the night. It was just as the Voice had prophesied. The house war had ended with the Protectors burning the bodies of the multitude they had slain. Only Andaman Vane's uprising had failed. His promise to her had been broken.

The Makao warriors watched that distant orange light in silence, as it consumed the bodies of their brothers and friends. The ones who could stand, did. Every one of them was covered in dirt and dried blood, many were wrapped in bandages stained red. Several of the soldiers couldn't stand at all. Their injuries were too great. All they could do was lie there and moan about their broken or missing limbs. Thera could tell some of them wouldn't live through the night.

She knew she probably wouldn't either, but she'd be damned if she went out without a fight. Thera had been thrown on the ground with her hands tied behind her back, but she'd found a rock or shell with her fingers. Whatever it was, it had a rough edge, so she'd been trying to use it to saw through her ropes. Only it was taking forever. The muscles of her hands ached and cramped as she worked, continuing to gnaw away at the rope. It was difficult with her hands trapped beneath her, but she didn't dare roll over, because Dhaval had left a guard to watch over the *traitor*. It was dark, and the warrior was too exhausted from the day's fighting to pay much attention to her, but he was sure to notice if she moved around too much.

The camp was too far away to hear the crackling flames or smell the smoke of the great corpse fire, but they could hear something far worse, and smell something far worse. There was the sound of crashing waves and the stink of salted rotten hell. Not only had they been defeated, but they'd been hounded so hard that they'd fled until they'd reached the seashore. There was truly no dignity in defeat.

Thera heard the sound of a horse galloping up. Whoever it was, the arrival caused a great deal of commotion in the camp.

"A Protector!"

There was the rattle of metal and creak of leather as soldiers took up arms.

"Lower your spears. If one of you fools breaks the truce, I'll kill you myself!"

Thera recognized her husband's voice. She'd not seen him for hours, since his men had found her, and she'd been dragged from her hiding place by her hair and mercilessly beaten. He'd been too busy fleeing the Protectors and the army of Harban to deal with her since, but she knew Dhaval. Simply killing her would be too easy. He'd want to humiliate her first. It took a special kind of man to remain so petty and petulant, even while in the process of losing a war.

She couldn't see the Protector from her position on the ground, but she heard his voice, clear and strong. "Your Thakoor has already given me his surrender. I am here to accept yours." Someone must have done something threatening, because the Protector drew his sword. "Pride makes you stupid, warrior. I may look like a tired old man, but I killed ten of you in this morning's battle. The hour's late, but I've got the energy to do a few more."

"Stand down!" Dhaval barked. "Bow your head!"

Of course, the one time Dhaval actually managed to sound like a leader was while surrendering... *Oh, Thera, you married* so *well.*

"Welcome to our humble camp, Lord Protector. I am Roik Dhaval Makao. This is all that remains of the Kanok Fourth Garrison. The Law has our full obedience. We lay our weapons at your feet and plead for the Capitol's mercy."

A horse whinnied. The Protector's sword was sheathed. There

was the creak of a saddle as he dismounted. "Dhaval, eh? Your name isn't on my list. You must not be important enough."

"List, Lord Protector?"

"The stooges your house is pinning the blame for this war on. The judges have to hold someone responsible. I've been executing men all afternoon."

Thera glanced over at the guard. He was distracted by the Protector, so she rolled over to get a better angle, and worked furiously at the ropes. She wouldn't have a better chance to escape than this. Her father's forces were still out there somewhere. If she could find them, she might still have a chance.

The Protector obviously didn't approve of their location by the seashore. "Demons might be attracted by the smell of blood or the cries of your wounded. What imbecile decided this was the best place to make camp?"

Dhaval muttered something in response.

"Of course. I should've known. Look at you. Twenty weary men here, sullied by battle, and yet you're the only one with a perfectly spotless uniform. That tells me everything I need to know about you." The Protector so thoroughly insulting her worthless husband's honor made Thera want to cheer. "Oh, I'm sorry. Does my observation offend you, Roik? Just say the word."

Duel him! Duel him! Thera thought to herself.

There was a long silence. "No, Lord Protector."

"I thought so." It sounded like he was getting closer to where they'd left her, so Thera had no choice but to roll back onto her hands to hide her frayed ropes. "What's this over here?"

"Merely a prisoner, Lord Protector."

"If that prisoner is from Harban, then the truce requires you to let him free."

"No, sir. Harban has no claim. *She* is one of ours, of Great House Makao. Or, should I say, *was* one of us."

They had nearly reached her. The ropes were frayed and close to breaking, but Thera had no choice but to stop moving. She tried to look harmless and pathetic. Since her fine clothes had been ripped and dragged through the dirt, and she was covered in bruises and welts, looking pathetic was easy.

The Protector stopped next to the guard and glanced down at her. His hair was long and white, his skin as weathered as a saddle bag, and despite his impressive armor, it was obvious that beneath all that steel and leather he was very thin. The leering face of the Law was on his chest. That symbol meant he possessed the authority to kill them all on a whim.

"Who is this? Bring over that torch so I may better examine her."

"She's a traitor," Dhaval spat.

"I'm no traitor! I'm his wife!"

The old Protector looked at her, then looked at Dhaval, then back at her, perplexed, then he gave a cruel bark of a laugh. "What?"

"She betrayed House Makao. She was caught sending messages about our war plans to one of our vassal houses. They intended to rebel while we were busy fighting Harban."

"That's not true, Protector. It's just an excuse to murder me, like he did with his last wife!"

The Protector sighed. "As amusing as this is, I've no time for family drama. I've still got officers to track down and execute. Either way, traitor or spousal murder, this is an internal matter, best for a judge of your house to decide. I'm leaving." He began walking away.

"Protector, please. He'll kill me before I ever see a judge."

"Shut your lying mouth!" Dhaval shouted.

"Please. My father is a respected man, formerly the phontho of Vane garrison. At least send him word that they're holding me prisoner, I beg you. His name is Andaman Vane."

"Ah..." The Protector paused. "Unfortunately that name was on my list."

Thera's world flew into pieces. "No! No! It can't be!"

The Protector was obviously a harsh man, but he delivered his next words with great sincerity. "If it means anything, Andaman Vane was a man of honor, and met his punishment with a courage and dignity that I have seldom seen. I do not know how he lived, but he died a credit to his caste."

Her father was gone. Her hope was extinguished. "Wait! He'll kill me! I'll never have the chance to plead before a judge. Dhaval is cruel and cowardly. He'll slit my throat as soon as you le—"

Dhaval brutally kicked her in the head.

It was an explosion of pain. Lights flashed behind her eyes.

"What is wrong with you?" the Protector demanded.

Only Thera could barely make out his words. She could hardly hear anything over the ringing in her ears. The blow had driven her face into the sand. There was blood in her mouth. The pain was unbearable.

But worse, a strange fire was building beneath her scar.

It had awoken the Voice.

She never heard it. When it came upon her, it was as if her consciousness was roughly shoved to the side. The last thing she saw was a pale light filling the camp, illuminating Dhaval as his expression turned from sneering hate to fear, until the light consumed everything and Thera could sense no more.

The pain came rushing back.

She didn't know how much time had passed, but she had been pulled roughly to her feet. Dhaval had her by the arms and was violently dragging her toward the edge of the cliff. He was shouting in her face, but she couldn't make out the words through the ringing. She struggled against him, but he was a stout man, and she was too dazed from the blow to the head to do much.

Looking back over her shoulder, Thera begged the Protector for mercy, but the man seemed to be stunned, his mouth hanging open, eyes staring right through her. The soldiers were terrified. She saw their mouths moving. The word... *witchcraft.*

Then they were at the edge. Below them was the dark ocean. Dhaval's eyes were bulging. His teeth were snapping together like a mad dog, completely consumed by rage.

Desperate, Thera twisted hard against her frayed ropes.

She began to hear again as Dhaval bellowed and spit in her face. "—a cultist in my own home! Bringing shame upon my name! I'll never live down this embarrassment! Let the demons take you!"

The rope snapped. Thera reached out, swept the dagger from her husband's belt, and slashed it across his eyes.

Dhaval screamed as he hurled her into the sea.

"It is vital that you think back to the greatest fear you have ever experienced," the wizard Omkar told Thera.

"I was," Thera answered. She remembered what it was like, thrashing around in the ocean, trying not to drown, as her blood and terror drew forth a demon from the depths. There was nothing worse.

"Good. Recall the sensations. Focus upon those," Omkar directed. "Sights, sounds, smells."

The water had shocked her body, cold, as sudden as the bolt from heaven. It had tasted like salt. She had been half blind from terror, but she'd still seen the demon coming out of the waves, nothing but a sleek black shadow. Years later and it still made her stomach hurt from fear.

The wizard must have heard the change in her breathing. "Do you have it now, Thera?"

"I do."

"Good. Once you have the scene clear in your mind, the emotions you experienced will naturally follow. There is clarity in context." The two of them were sitting on the floor, cross-legged, facing each other. Thera was blindfolded. "A memory is merely an imprint on a pattern. Now take that pattern from your mind and imagine it flowing into the piece of demon bone you hold in your hand."

Thera tried, she truly did. They had been over this a hundred times. A dead demon was just a container. Messages could be recorded on the magic within, and then a wizard could do several useful things with them. Like send them instantly and invisibly through the air, to be received into another container hundreds of miles away, to be viewed by another wizard, or passed on to the next.

"This is no different than using ink to write words on paper, Thera, just finer. Concentrate."

Only none of this was simple. The wizards kept prattling on about patterns, and waves, and how everything was tiny particles—some of which could be stuck together in spooky and interesting ways—but she couldn't see a damned thing. The piece of bone clenched between her fingers caught on fire. She yelped and reflexively dropped it. "Oceans!"

Her teacher sighed, annoyed. "Remove your blindfold."

The bone was lying on the rug. It hadn't burst into flame, and when Omkar snatched up the precious material in his bare hand, that proved it hadn't even gotten hot. She could have sworn it had been like red-hot molten metal, searing through her skin.

"It felt like—"

"Like another miserable failure," he snapped.

She had intended to say *a premonition,* but she remained silent.

Omkar was the eldest of the Lost House wizards that she'd seen, maybe even sixty, which was ancient by the standards of her caste, and he had gone to fat in his old age. She suspected Sikasso had given him this duty because he was too old and fat to go out and murder people in exchange for magic and treasure like the rest of them. But as her father had told her many times, never underestimate anyone who got old in a job where most die young.

"This was the simple part. The easiest memories to record are the ones with the greatest personal weight. Nothing stands out like your most terrifying moment, or the instant of your greatest achievement, or the happiest time of your life."

She had volunteered to share her most terrifying memory. She wasn't fond of it, but she wouldn't give these scoundrels access to her happiness. "I tried, but—"

"Silence."

Thera was not officially a prisoner. They no longer locked her door. Why bother? Where would she escape to? The demon infested swamps? But she wasn't made to feel welcome either, and she was certainly not one of them. She was a freakish anomaly to be studied, nothing more. If she proved useful, she'd live, and if not, they would dispose of her.

It was rather a lot of pressure to be under.

"A wizard who is skilled in this aspect can record and send messages as mundane as columns of numbers, or maps with troop movements marked upon them. Powerful men will pay great sums of money to send vital messages that would take days by pigeon, or weeks by horse." He held up the demon chunk she'd been using, and then showed her the one he'd had in his hand all along. "These are from the same creature, adjoining vertebra even, sending between the two would be child's play, or should have been if you could even get the first part right!"

Omkar was growing angry, and though he wasn't as threatening as Sikasso, no good could come from angering a magical assassin. So she tried to placate him by feigning humility. "I apologize, Master Omkar."

"My patience wears thin, woman, and I am probably the closest thing you have to an ally in this house."

As sad as that statement was, it was also true. Sikasso had ordered him to teach her how to use magic, and though he obviously didn't like it, at least he would speak to her. The others ignored her, or actively threatened to kill her as soon as she was no longer under Sikasso's protection. She needed to stay on someone's good side.

"I will try harder."

"You had better. Your list of failures grows daily. You have no talent for shape changing, manipulating the elements, or even giving strength to your own limbs. If you were one of the children, I would declare you unteachable, so we didn't waste any more valuable demon on you."

Curious. She had not left the great house since Sikasso had shown her the sea, but in that time she had only seen wizards and their oddly untalkative slaves. There had been no sign of their families. "Where are your children?"

"There is no class at this time, only a few hopefuls. There is a cap. We are never to exceed a certain number... Never mind all that. There will surely be a new crop soon to replace our many recent losses caused by your associate, Ashok."

"No... I mean, *your* children. Surely, you have families here. A man of your status must have a wife and heirs."

Omkar scowled. "That is none of your concern."

"For their sake I hope they live further inland."

"There is much you do not understand, Thera. I have little time to teach you. If you do not show some improvement soon, Master Sikasso will become annoyed and have you killed. Do you wish to waste our limited time speaking of these frivolous matters, or would you rather unlock the secrets of your power?"

It was time to get back to work. Sikasso was probably going to murder her anyway, but until that happened or she found a way out, Thera would play their game. She took back the demon bone and got ready to relive the worst moments of her life.

Five years ago, the ocean had rushed up to meet her.

She fell for a long time before the water hit her hard as packed clay. *Smack.* Her whole body crumpled around the impact, and overwhelmed with pain she curled into a ball. But that only lasted for a split second before fear of drowning overcame the agony and she forced her muscles to struggle for the surface. The waves were fierce and made a terrible roar as they crashed violently against the rocks.

Thera hadn't known how to swim back then. She'd confronted that fear later, while she'd been living as a criminal among the lowest workers along the rivers, and had no choice. She would have drowned that night, except Dhaval had thrown her into the shallows. The nicest thing he had ever done for her had been on accident.

Her fine clothes, once sodden, were heavy as armor and tried to drag her down, but her wildly kicking sandals hit something solid. The waves hurled her against the rocks at the base of the cliff. Somehow she grabbed hold, incoherent with terror, knowing only that she had to get back onto land as fast as she could. No one could survive if they were caught trespassing in hell.

Scrambling for purchase, her hands were clumsy and shaking. Desperate, she tore at the rocks, trying to hold on as another wave engulfed her, greedily trying to suck her into the deep. She was bleeding profusely from where Dhaval's boot had split open her skin, and from new cuts as she was bashed against the rocks. Thera called out for help as she tried to climb, but nobody was coming to save her. The soldiers above probably couldn't even hear her over the crashing of the surf.

Then from the darkness, it rose.

The demon had no eyes. Its face was just a smooth black lump. Unfeeling. Blank. Terrifying.

She screamed and tried to climb higher.

It slowly swam toward her. The powerful waves didn't seem to move it at all.

Somehow Thera scrambled on top of the rocks. "I'm on land! I'm on land! I'm not trespassing!"

Insufficient. The demon disappeared as a particularly massive wave rolled over its head. Then that wave hit Thera and knocked her off her seat.

She landed with a splash on the other side. Thrashing, panicked, she immediately sat upright. There were rocks beneath her bottom. It wasn't very deep. She moved strands of wet stringy hair from her eyes. Canda had come out from behind the clouds, stark and white, and Thera could see that she was in some sort of little pool, sheltered beneath the cliff she'd been thrown from.

Thera stood up and tried to wade to the side, slipping on moss and slimy underwater vines, hoping to find a path out, but another wave came over the rock and swept her off her feet. She screamed as something moved beneath her, thinking it was another demon. She kicked it, but it was only one of those disgusting water beasts the casteless ate. Later she would learn they called it a *crab*.

The demon followed her.

It climbed up onto the big rock she'd just been on, just a blacker spot than everything around it, malevolent and silent. She'd been told demons could be gigantic, but this one wasn't much bigger than she was. Yet the strongest warriors spoke of demon strength in awed whispers. Even a little one could pluck the legs off a horse like children pulled the wings off bugs. The sharpest spears glanced off their nearly indestructible hide. And their hunger was legend.

"Go away!" She needed a weapon. She'd lost Dhaval's dagger on impact. Thera found a stone the size of her fist. It would have to do. "Leave me alone!"

The demon slipped over the rocks and into the pool. Death was coming for her.

She would die like she lived. *Defiant.* Her aim was true, her arm strong. The rock hit the demon right in the center of its featureless head, hard enough to crack a man's skull, and bounced off uselessly.

It struck. Thera was hurled against the cliff. Unseen claws had parted her silks, and nearly opened her guts. She could see her belly exposed in the moonlight. Where its hide had brushed against her, the skin was scraped raw and bleeding. Salt water burned.

The featureless head split open, revealing rows of pointed black teeth. It twisted toward her as the mouth somehow hinged open wide enough to bite off her entire face. She struck at it with her fists, but all that did was split open her knuckles. It exhaled, breath strangely hot and dry as it closed in. She closed her eyes.

The jaws snapped closed. There was no blast of pain. No endless nothing. Somehow, it had missed, but had been so close the teeth brushed her cheek. Thera opened her eyes to see that the demon's sleek head was tilted upwards, as if something had distracted it.

Then the Protector hit the water next to them.

Even though he landed on his feet, the impact still made a great splash. The fall should have broken the old man's legs, but he immediately sprang up and launched himself at the demon, sword flying.

The creature lifted one arm and the sword rebounded off the eerie black hide. It spun, swinging its other arm, but the Protector caught that with his blade. Glowing sparks flew, not from the metal, but from the creature's claws.

"You can't have this one. Back to hell with you!"

They were about the same size, but the demon moved with blinding, unnatural speed, so fast it was hard to track the movements in the dark. Yet, the Protector seemed just as inhuman, just as unnatural, as they traded lightning-quick blows back and forth amid the crashing waves. She had seen the best warriors in Vane sword fight. They looked like children playing Dirt War in comparison to this man. Claw marks and dents appeared on his silver armor. He grimaced as a claw ripped deep through his side, but then he rammed his armored shoulder into the demon, knocking it over the rocks and back onto the ocean side.

A moment later the black thing slithered back atop its perch on a boulder, studying them. Thera's heart was pounding so hard she thought it was going to explode. She grabbed another rock to throw.

"Go on, demon. There is no easy prey for you here." The old man was breathing hard through the wet white hair hanging in front of his face. Far too much blood was pouring from his side, slick and red in the moonlight. "We apologize for entering your realm and will return now to ours."

Then Thera realized there was a white milky liquid running down the Protector's sword. *Demon blood.* One of his strikes had pierced its hide after all. How incredibly strong was this man?

The demon had no face to hold an expression, but she could tell it was thinking. Then with the crash of another wave, it was simply gone, vanished back into the darkness below.

She splashed over to the Protector's side. "You came for me!"

The Protector stayed watching the sea, sword raised, salt water up to his knees. "I had to." Satisfied the demon had truly left, he turned to look at her. "When the Forgotten spoke, I was momentarily taken by surprise."

"What? The Forgotten? No." Whenever a Protector thought someone was speaking for the old gods, executions followed. She was still badly shaken, but was coherent enough to hope that she hadn't been saved from a demon just to be killed because of the Voice. "Come, hurry. Please, you're badly hurt."

They made their way across the slippery rocks toward where the rugged cliff gave way to a sandy beach. The Protector was much older, wearing heavy metal, and had a wound that would have been quickly fatal on any normal man, but he still made it across the treacherous terrain far easier than she did. Thera was not content to stop on the sand. Instead she kept walking until there was grass underfoot, and the awful ocean was far behind them, and only then did she stop. Her legs were shaking so badly she had to kneel. And then she threw up.

In a grassy field, beneath a million stars, overlooking the hell that had just tried to bite her face off, the Protector declared, "After all this time, after all my searching, I've finally found you. I have finally found the *prophet*."

Thera had no idea what he was talking about. She'd just been kicked in the head, slashed her husband with a knife, and almost been eaten by a demon. Her father was dead. *Oceans.* This man had *executed* him.

Despite the terror that had robbed her limbs of strength, and the waves of throbbing agony in her head, that realization crowded out everything else. Andaman Vane was gone and this was the man who had taken him.

"You killed him!" Thera struggled to her feet, and then hurled her body at the Protector. She struck him in the face and tried to claw out his eyes. If she'd had a weapon she would've sliced him to ribbons.

But this was a man who could hold off demons, so he easily stopped her. "Calm yourself, please." Finally the old man knocked her hands away, spun her around, and grabbed her around the arms, pinning them. Incredibly strong, he hugged her tight, steel plates jabbing her in the back. Thera kept struggling, kicking and thrashing, except he was unbreakable. The Protector could have snapped her in half, but he just held on, like a patient parent with a toddler having a fit.

The futility made it even worse.

"Shhhh. Listen to me. I didn't know. I was following the Law."

"Damn you! Damn your Law!"

"That may be what it takes. Please, I beg you. Calm yourself."

She'd never been so completely overwhelmed by sorrow before, and she was in too much pain, both emotional and physical, to continue. Thera began to sob. When it was obvious that the strength was fleeing her limbs, the Protector slowly let go of her. It took everything she had left in her just to stand.

The Protector's face was wracked with guilt, his voice earnest. "I truly am sorry. Great and terrible offense has been given, and for that, I must atone."

"I, I don't know—"

"I do. I know what to do. I've been preparing for this moment for many years, I suppose in a way, my whole life." Then the strangest thing happened. One of the highest status servants of the Law in the entire world humbly bowed to her. When he looked up there were tears in his eyes as well. "I am Ratul and the gods have commanded me to serve you."

Chapter 23

〰〰〰〰

After many grueling hours of being insulted and berated by Master Omkar, Thera walked back to her room. Wizardry wasn't very physically demanding so far, but it was mentally exhausting. Her lack of achievement made it worse. Normally when she worked this hard she at least had something to show for it. Thera had been good at most everything she had ever put her mind to. As a woman of the warrior caste she had done more than what was expected, and once she'd forsaken the Law, she'd been an excellent criminal. When it came to magic, she was rubbish.

She was also, frankly, a terrible prophet. But she'd never asked for all that. She'd been forced into that role by the damnable bolt from the sky. Claiming to speak for the gods had been Ratul's idea. And after he had disappeared, it had been Keta who had taken over spreading the Voice's message to the people.

Sometimes it was like her whole life was similar to being in the ocean, pushed and dragged back and forth by powerful forces, and all she could do was keep her head above water.

Before she could make it back to her room, she was intercepted by a wizard in the hall. It was the handsome one, Kabir, who had been friends with the man she had killed in Jharlang. Every time Thera had seen him, his behavior had been malicious and threatening. When she'd asked about him, Omkar had warned it would be in her best interests to avoid angering Kabir because he was very dangerous. She wondered what manner of evil it took to gain the reputation of being a dangerous man among a house of assassins.

Regardless, Kabir was standing in front of her door, eating a piece of strange-looking eastern fruit, and blocking her way. "Good evening, Thera."

She gave him a polite nod. "Excuse me. I have had a long day and wish to retire."

"I've heard you've been making real progress. You recorded some fuzzy images of sea demon teeth and sent them to another bone a whopping two feet away. You're practically a master wizard now." He took a big crunching bite of the fruit, but didn't move aside.

"What do you want, Kabir?"

"Don't be so defensive. If I desired harm to come upon our esteemed guest, there are a thousand ways I could achieve that without something as simplistic as threatening you in the halls. Poison in your food most likely."

As he said that, the door to her room opened, and a slave carrying an empty serving tray walked out. Her dinner had been delivered. This slave was another tall man, nearly as big as Kabir, with a patch covering one missing eye. The timing was rather suspicious, almost as if the wizard had timed it to unnerve her.

"Poison is a tool for cowards."

"Spare me the warrior-caste sanctimony. We both know there is no such thing as bravery or cowardice. There is only risk and reward, success or failure, life or death. Goals are more important than methods." With his deep voice and smooth delivery, Kabir sounded like he was either giving some profound lecture, or trying to sell her something.

"Did he put something in my dinner?" she demanded of the slave. All of the slaves were dressed in drab colors, with shaved heads and faces. Except for the eye, this one was no different from the others, and like them, he just stood there, staring off blankly into space. She'd never heard any of them say so much as a word.

Kabir finished the fruit, dropped the core on the slave's empty tray, and wiped his hands on his baggy pants. "That will be all, Dattu." The one-eyed slave lowered his head in acknowledgement, and obediently began walking back toward the kitchen.

"Your slaves never talk back. You wizards must be harsh masters."

For whatever reason, Kabir seemed to take that as a personal insult. "I've done him no harm."

"I meant no offense."

"Of course... I've been giving some thought to your predicament. By now you must realize that once he gets what he wants from you, Sikasso won't just let you leave. The existence and nature of the Lost House must remain a closely guarded secret."

"The thought has crossed my mind. I assumed you would be fine with that, considering what I did to your friend."

He shrugged, as if his earlier anger had been exaggerated. Only Thera was certain it had been real, and his current nonchalance was the act. "I've had time to mourn Vilsaro's passing. I have come to terms with his loss, and I know he would approve of my current ambitions. Your presence here presents a great opportunity. Don't worry. You may speak freely. You are almost always being spied on, but unlike you, I'm extremely talented with magic. For a moment at least, Sikasso can't hear us."

Was this some sort of test? "Are you here to conspire against your master then?"

Kabir spread his hands apologetically. "It is our way. How else do you think assassins choose their leader? We're not some pathetic house where leadership is decided by heredity. We pick our governors based upon who benefits us most. Sikasso was the most dangerous among us once, but now he is distracted by his studies, trying to rediscover the pattern which will allow him to magically replace his arm. He might even succeed. He's rather tenacious that way. However in the meantime, his injury has caused him to neglect our greater purpose and to lose sight of our goals."

"And those are?"

Kabir smiled. "None of your concern."

"I swear, the next one of you vipers that tells me that, I'm going to cave his head in. Speak plain, wizard. I'm tired."

"Very well. Sikasso's deal with the Inquisition has made us richer, but he is content to bide his time while we continue to serve as mercenaries for the very system that wronged us. Some of us feel he has lost his way and forgotten our true purpose. And that purpose is righteous vengeance. Vengeance upon the

Law which condemned us, and vengeance upon the houses who fulfilled the Capitol's commands."

He hid it well, but this was a man driven by anger, and he meant every word of what he'd just said. Thera was no stranger to a desire for revenge—she had her own list of names—and she could see the truth of this statement in Kabir's eyes.

He stepped away from the door, and came toward her, stopping only when his lips were right next to her ear. "I dream of blood and fire. The Capitol in ruins and the bones of the judges being picked clean by vultures. But that is not enough. The very system they represent must be destroyed. They must pay for what their ancestors have done. So we've waited, and watched, taking their assignments, committing their murders, learning their secrets, all while secretly growing our power and influence in the hope that someday the Lost House would return to the light. That is our goal. And as I said, methods matter not. Each of us has sworn a blood oath toward this end."

Uncomfortable with his proximity and his fervor, Thera stepped away from the wizard. "Let me guess. Some of you think the time to strike is now, but your master urges patience."

"Sikasso is content to make secret deals for us to serve as Omand Vokkan's deniable thugs in exchange for scraps from the Inquisition's table. He is so blinded by habit that when a glorious opportunity presents itself, all he thinks of is cracking it open to see if there is treasure inside. I speak of you, Thera. Sikasso wants what's inside your head, hoping he can turn your gift into a weapon. He does not realize that you already are a weapon."

She had heard the same thing from Ratul all those years ago. It was odd that two men so very different could arrive at the exact same conclusion. "You mean the rebellion."

"Exactly! Over the last few years your words have inspired the non-people to rise up like never before."

"They aren't my words."

"Fine. The *Forgotten*." Kabir laughed at the absurdity of the idea. "Wherever the words come from, they inspire hope and courage, dangerous high-minded ideas unfit for casteless. Things are precariously balanced. It wouldn't take much to incite blood-shed sufficient to crack the very foundation of the Law. You could inspire all of them to rise up, in every land, all at once."

That annoyed Thera. She had no particular love of the casteless, but she'd lived among them, and for some bizarre reason, they believed in the Voice, and loved it. The rebellion was really Keta's, not hers... but she did feel some loyalty to them.

"You listen to me, Kabir, the casteless aren't just a pack of dogs you can sic on your enemies. They're people too. Fighting against the Law will get them slaughtered."

"You are the one urging them towards violence, not me."

Thera had no good response to that. "Yeah, well I still don't want to see them all get killed."

"Perhaps they wouldn't, *if* your rebellion had the wizards of the Lost House on its side."

Now it was Thera's turn to scoff. "A bunch of powerful wizards, going to pledge their swords to aid the plight of the untouchables? That'll be the day!"

"The casteless would be aiding *us*. We share a common enemy. We have eyes in every great house, within every Order of the Capitol, and when the time comes for us to strike, there will be a night of bloody knives the likes of which the world hasn't seen since the Age of Kings. But to truly win, and to overturn the Law once and for all, what we don't have is several million foot soldiers. If you help me further our goals, I can help you further yours."

Thera could feel the waves again, pushing her back and forth. She didn't like it one bit.

It was time to learn to swim.

"What do you propose, Kabir?"

"You help me, and I help you. Sikasso's dog Omkar is teaching you about the fundamentals of magic, but he's a terrible assassin. I spit on him."

"Did he get too fat to be a good murderer or something?"

Kabir was incredulous. "He's always been obese. Omkar's not a good assassin because he's too cruel. He gets caught up in making targets suffer, needlessly prolonging their deaths, and endangering the mission."

"Oh... Damn." It was a good thing she'd been trying to avoid provoking her teacher.

"Regardless, they wouldn't dare teach you the real secrets of our house. We are outside the Law, but we have our own very strict rules. I can teach you those things, so when the time comes, you can use that knowledge to secure your fate and help me overthrow Sikasso. Once I am in charge, we will gladly aid your rebellion."

He seemed so smug, but the offer was intriguing. "What's to keep me from betraying you?"

"The fact you are intelligent enough to weigh your options and see that I have reasons to keep you alive, but Sikasso does not. Plus, you must realize that I would deny your allegations and then murder you somehow."

And she had thought the politics of Great House Makao had been disgusting. They had nothing on this nest of vipers.

Kabir extended his open hand, to shake on their agreement, as was the style of a southerner. "Do we have an alliance?"

Was it better to take the word of an assassin who laughed at the very concept of honor, or trust in the mercy of the killer who had abducted her to begin with? Her father had told her that when faced with a choice that had to be made quickly, to always go with her gut.

"Only on the condition that you tell me everything. If you leave me floundering in the dark, then I will find a way to make you regret it."

"Agreed." They shook on it. Kabir had strong callused hands worthy of a warrior. "The pact is sealed... I must go. We will speak soon."

"I have questions now."

"And I have almost used up the piece of demon which is allowing us to keep this conversation private." Kabir began walking away.

Thera just shook her head as she opened the door to her room. Damn these waves, once again caught between a demon and a rock.

Kabir stopped at the end of the hall, as if he had just remembered something important. "I almost forgot, that food which was left on your table. I would advise you not to eat the fruit."

She sighed. "You poisoned it in case I was disagreeable."

"No. I was merely hungry and ate one. They're out of season and sour. I thought I'd spare you the misery. But it is good that you are starting to think like an assassin, Thera, because *everything* here can kill you... Sleep well."

Chapter 24

His pattern was flawed.

Sikasso tried to manipulate the elements into place, but they refused him every time. Logically, it should have been easy. When a wizard changed form, the tiniest fragments of their bodies were rearranged into new patterns. Arms became wings, toes became talons. Skin could stretch into scales. The same tiny elements that made his hair and fingernails could just as easily be condensed into a talon hard enough to pierce a shield. Or he could divide his matter into a million living pieces, a swarm that was still united by his consciousness. A wizard was only limited by his ability to master the patterns the ancients had left behind.

His basic lessons, received in this very room nearly thirty years ago, had sounded so very trite. His master had told him *a wizard is like water.* Young Sikasso had not cared for this comparison, because he had been raised by parents who talked about water as a necessary evil, for drinking, cooking, and legally mandated bathing, but let it collect into a body and it became an extension of hell.

Be like water... A lesson can be trite and offensive, yet true. A wizard was very much like water. If it was held in a bucket it was in the shape of a bucket, but pour it into a vase and it took on that shape. It was in a new pattern, but it was still water.

Energy could boil water into steam and taking energy away could freeze it into ice, but it remained water. In the end it could all be poured back into the same bucket it started as.

Provided a Protector didn't take an axe to your bucket...

His experiment failed again.

"Damn you!" Sikasso shouted as he burned up another piece of valuable magic. He dropped the now empty chunk of bone on the stone, and then smashed it beneath his boot. Drained of its magic, the piece of demon crumbled into dust. Only that petty act of destruction didn't satisfy him, and with an angry roar he used his remaining arm to sweep all the ancient books and scrolls from his desk. He hurled the candles against the wall. And then he made a fist and slammed it against the wood, over and over, only stopping when he thought he might break the bones of his hand.

Now, a fracture he could heal. Magic could mend bone and knit flesh, but no one knew the pattern for replacing an amputated limb. Of the secrets given by Ramrowan to the ancients, among them had been such a formula, but that pattern had been lost during the great upheavals.

With Sikasso's body damaged, its pattern so fundamentally altered, he could no longer use half of the abilities he'd learned, and the remainder were flawed. It made him *vulnerable,* and that, he could not tolerate. All predators sensed weakness, and it was in their nature to make the weak into prey. His assassins were no different than any other pack of hunters. They would not long be ruled by *prey.*

The fury caused by yet another failure was so great that his vision was tinged red. Veins throbbed in his forehead. If there had been someone here to kill, he would have done so. At least he could still do *that.* But luckily for the wizards and slaves of the Lost House, Sikasso was alone in the vault. The partial demon corpses hanging from meat hooks were his only company. At some point of his rampage he must have collided with one, because it had started swinging.

Sikasso watched while it swayed. This one was missing its head and lower body. Parts of it had been skinned, and incisions made to carve out chunks of precious meat.

The hook next to it held just an arm.

His eyes lingered on that limb... It would be so easy to take that and press it against the stump that Ashok had left him. No one understood how or why, but demon parts could be grafted onto a human, reanimate, and become functional. It also came with a perpetually refilling source of magic that was always in reach. It was incredibly powerful.

However, this came at too great a cost, as the bonding would turn the host into a dreaded hybrid. The demon wasn't just an attachment, their tissues would intermingle, and man and demon would gradually become one. The resulting creatures were more dangerous than either of their original species.

He shook his head in disgust, having recently seen that kind of degenerate magic in action, and he would rather die than end up an abomination like the thing he had turned Nadan Somsak into. It had been eight hundred years since a wizard had last regrown a limb, but no wizard *ever* had become a hybrid without eventually being driven mad with bloodlust. With certain medicines and alchemical treatments, the intermingling could be slowed for a time... But Sikasso was not that desperate.

Yet.

There was a knock at the door. Sikasso composed himself. He ruled because he was effective and coldly terrifying. Having an underling see him being neither would not help maintain his tenuous position. He picked up the scrolls and returned them to the desk, and then went to the door.

"Good evening, master."

It was only Omkar, a loyalist who lacked an imagination sufficient to aspire to Sikasso's office, so he spared no time on vapid pleasantries. "What do you want?"

"It concerns your project." The vault was kept unnaturally cold to better preserve their demon stockpile, so Omkar folded his thick arms as he entered the room. "Her talents are severely lacking. If she was one of my regular charges, I would waste no further magic on her. She has such a stubborn and rebellious nature I don't know if the treatment to make her a slave would stick. I'd have her beaten for her insolence but I suspect that would just make her even more obstinate. She feigns compliance, while her eyes plot murder. It would not come as a surprise if she attempts to kill me soon."

Sikasso scowled. He had no time for this foolishness. If he couldn't regain his abilities, he at least needed something to show his brothers for their losses in Jharlang or some of them might rise up against him. When the chief assassin was removed from office, it was never because of a willing retirement.

"It is vital that we understand what forces are at work. I would see to the oddity myself, but I am occupied. You will continue to train her until her power shows itself again, and when it does you will document everything. Understand?"

Omkar nodded. "It will be done."

"I don't believe this gods nonsense, but there is something there. I'm having her watched in case it manifests when she is alone. If this method doesn't work, then we will switch to more extreme measures. If mercy will not unlock it, then perhaps stress and danger will. If there is a third source of magic we must claim it for ourselves."

"What about your promise to sell her to the Inquisition?"

"A hollow threat. I would not give the Capitol another power to eventually use against us. Omand is one of the few men in the world who knows more about magic than I do, and he's got more secrets than we can even begin to guess at. We will continue, and the Inquisition must never know we've seized her."

"As you command, master."

He could tell there was more. "Speak, Omkar. I've work to do."

"It's our brothers. There's been some murmuring. The alchemist Hemendra is the most vocal, but there are others. Your presence has been missed. Some are worried . . . I mean no offense, but they're wondering why you've given them no new orders, or why you've not responded to any of the Inquisition's recent messages."

Sikasso's lip curled into a snarl. It was truly bad if his potential usurpers were talking freely in front of a loyal brute like Omkar. The predators had caught his scent. They would isolate him, and then they would move against him. Sikasso had done the exact same thing to their former leader when he had seized control of the Lost House many years ago. He had maintained his status by keeping his brothers content or afraid. They wouldn't backbite him so brazenly if they didn't think he was vulnerable.

"Tell them it is under control."

Omkar's eyes narrowed when he noticed that there were already at least a hundred ash piles on the floor, all that was left of the bones consumed in his master's futile quest. "Is it though?"

That demonstrated the danger of whispers, when even loyal

Omkar would dare question. Sikasso thought about killing him on the spot for his insolence, but the act would be wasted without witnesses, and then he'd have one less ally. He'd learned a long time ago that if you were going to murder a subordinate, to do it in a manner that sent the most effective message.

"Provided you complete your assignment and get inside the oddity's head, it will be."

"Of course, master," Omkar nodded. "One last thing. During today's session Thera revealed another memory to me. I don't know if this will be of use, but the one who first taught her about her gift, who introduced her to the casteless as the prophet they've been waiting for, was none other than Lord Protector Ratul."

"The heretic?" *Curious.* Before he had gone mad and abandoned the Protectors, Ratul had also trained Ashok Vadal in that Order's secret rites. Could there be some connection? He would dwell on that later, for now he had more pressing matters to attend to. "Be gone, Omkar. No further interruptions unless you have something important."

The other wizard appeared happy to flee the chill of the vault. Sikasso made note of that. The next time the fat man annoyed him, he'd be sure to give him an assignment someplace cold.

Sikasso picked up another piece of bone, crackling with energy, and prepared to try again. He had become the greatest assassin in the world and earned his place. Whether they realized it or not, the Lost House needed his leadership. *His.* This was the most power they'd had since the days before the ocean had swallowed House Charsadda, and it was all because of Sikasso. Ashok Vadal had taken his arm, but Sikasso would not let him take everything else he'd worked for all these years. He'd sacrificed too much to give up now.

Only the predators were circling. The sick and weak would be culled. His time was running out.

Before he tried changing the pattern again, Sikasso's eyes lingered a bit too long on the dangling demon arm.

Chapter 25

Several day's journey from Neeramphorn lay the town of Haradas, on the Kharsawan side of the River Nansakar, where the rugged mountains gave way to forested hills, and the wizard's secret courier lived as a humble barge master. However, before Ashok could find this man and force him to reveal the location of the Lost House, he had to deal with the matter of their new recruits.

Their advance rider had spotted nearly a hundred people waiting along the road south. Ashok had crept forward to observe. They were in a clearing in the middle of nowhere. From the hasty condition of their camp, they had not been there for long. Since they were obviously armed, his first assumption was that they were warriors sent by the Inquisition to find his criminal band, only they were flying no heraldry. They could be warriors from a neighboring house on their way to raid Haradas, except they were making no attempt to conceal their presence, and there were too few horses. There were a couple heavily loaded wagons, but fully half of their number had to be on foot. It was too deserted a stretch of road to support such a large number of bandits. The only thing that frequently traveled through here was shipments of lumber toward Neeramphorn and there were far easier things to steal than logs.

Ashok had temporarily called upon the Heart to improve his

vision, and had been confused to see the warriors were wearing the colors of three different houses. Most of their number were dressed like workers, and there were even a few in casteless rags. There was a surprising number of women and children among them. It was odd to see people of such disparate status thrown together without an obvious reason. He thought they might be refugees from some conflict he was unaware of, but they looked relatively clean, fed, and as far as he could tell, happy, so that made no sense.

He'd returned and told the others about the strange group. Going around would have required a significant detour, and time was of the essence. It didn't feel like a trap, and if it was, it wasn't a very good one. So he had admonished the Somsak to ready their crossbows, but to keep them down unless ordered, and then they had continued along the road.

The Sons were spotted and an obvious ripple of excitement went through the crowd. People rushed about, alerting each other, and they began to prepare, not for battle, but more like they were going to watch a parade. Two of the group broke away from the camp and approached the road. One was a warrior, wearing the insignia of Kharsawan, the other was a female worker in a long black coat. Both raised their hands in greeting.

"Hello, Sons of the Black Sword," called the woman. "We've been waiting for you."

Curious. Ashok raised his hand and everyone brought their horses to a stop. They were spread out enough it would be hard to take them all in one volley, and if anyone tried he would turn his Somsak loose.

"Who are you people?" Jagdish demanded. "And how do you know who we are?"

"Forgive our insolence. We're fellow servants." The warrior spread his hands apologetically. He was maybe twenty years old, a gangly, awkward lad, who wore the rank of a senior nayak. "We are all followers of the Forgotten just like you."

"Speak for yourself," Gutch muttered from the back of the column.

"We come from a few different groups who have gathered in secret. Most of us had never met before today," said the woman with a great deal of excitement. She was perhaps thirty, not unattractive, but tanned and weathered from some manual labor obligation toiling beneath the sun. "But we were all told that the time has come to leave our homes to join your mighty army."

Jagdish laughed out loud. "That's just what we need, more fanatics!" Keta and the Somsak all scowled at him.

The woman looked a little hurt, and the warrior seemed confused. "We mean no offense. We presume too much. We merely present ourselves, and the Forgotten's great servants will decide if we are worthy to join their cause."

Ashok felt ill. More people were turning against the Law, and it was his fault. They were dooming themselves to a short life of suffering and unhappiness until their disgraceful execution, and he was their sick inspiration. He glanced over at the mob. Their children were smiling and laughing, blissfully unaware of the dark path their parents had put them on. There was no good end for those who chose to pit themselves against the Law.

"Why do you do this?" Ashok demanded.

"Because it is what the gods want us to do," the young warrior answered with pride.

"You are willing to kill for these gods, and die for them?"

This time it was the woman who answered. "My people have passed down the old ways from generation to generation. We've lived in fear and silence the whole time. Killing and dying can't be much harder than that."

"Shows what you know. Dying is remarkably easy," said Jagdish.

The warrior looked over at Jagdish, and wrongly assumed because of the stolen uniform they were of the same house and status. "I've probably seen as many battles as you."

"Don't let this silly outfit fool you, pup. I am . . . *was* a decorated risaldar of Great House Vadal. I've killed more men than you have *met*."

While the young man hurried and apologized to Jagdish, Ashok whispered to Keta, "Did you know of these cults?"

Keta shook his head in the negative. "I was told nothing of more worshippers in these lands, but it isn't like we speak freely to each other. The faithful hide in the shadows, in fear of the Law. There could be ten thousand of us in the Capitol for all I know."

"I doubt that very much. We would have rooted them out and killed them." It was one thing to be a fanatic out on the edges of civilization, it was quite another to practice illegal religion in the birthplace of civilization. Ashok turned back to the two messengers. "How did you know our location?"

"The same way we knew the time had come, we were told by Mother Dawn," said the woman.

That was the name of the ancient woman he had met in Jharlang. "That can't be."

"Who?" Keta asked.

"An oddity, apparently with more to her than I first assumed," Ashok replied. "How do you two know this old casteless, Mother Dawn? She is from a mining village in Thao lands."

"Casteless? I don't understand. Mother Dawn is warrior caste," said the nayak. "And from the distant west."

The woman looked at her companion, confused. "No. She's a worker. Originally a baker from the north. She's been stopping in my town for a few days every other year as long as anyone can remember."

"She's no baker!" the warrior scoffed. "She can throw a razor sharp chakram as accurate as any warrior in Guntur. She appeared to us two weeks ago and told us we needed to gather here by today. A few of us had the faith to heed the call."

"What?" Two weeks ago Ashok had never even heard of Haradas, let alone known he would be on the road traveling there. "That is impossible."

"It is true. I swear it," said the warrior. "My brothers and I just arrived this morning."

"They did. We got here last night," the worker said. "She drew us a map and told us to be here by today, ten days ago. We're from some nearby villages, but have few horses and mostly walked. If anything my people made a much bigger effort to be here than these warriors."

"Hardly!"

Ashok didn't care who had sacrificed more in service of their illegal gods. From Jharlang to Gunter to Akershan so quickly during the winter would be impossible by normal means. The religious fanatics seemed sincere, but for their messenger to get around like that was either trickery or witchcraft. There had to be several different women claiming to be Mother Dawn, or one who had access to powerful magic that enabled her to travel great distances. Neither possibility explained how she could have known their current location so far in advance, with such specificity.

Of course, Keta had a different interpretation. "The Forgotten has placed more of his servants in our path to aid us!" he declared with great joy. "Truly, this is a miracle."

Jagdish looked over at the motley encampment. Half of them appeared to be women, children, or casteless. "If your god is handing out miracle armies, seems a shame not to send us a proper one."

"If I may," the woman asked timidly. "Which one of you is Ashok Vadal?"

"I am Ashok Vadal."

"You're real! The stories are true!" Both of them went to their knees in the snow and lowered their heads as if he was the Thakoor of their house. From the gathered mob, he heard them repeating his name in awe, most of the whole men calling him *Ashok* and the casteless saying *Fall* and others speaking of the *Forgotten's warrior.*

"Enough." Such deference offended him. He was just another criminal, nothing more, and he would be damned if anyone should take pride in that. "Get up."

They did. And from the way he snapped the frustrated command, they felt chastened as they brushed the cold slush from their knees. The woman hurried and spoke first. "Mother Dawn told me to tell you that the two children you carried to her are safe and well."

He'd once shown a small mercy and nearly condemned an entire town because of it. Yet news that they lived was a relief. He hadn't seen their bodies in the aftermath. It pleased him to know that some good had come from that day. Unless of course, Mother Dawn was a liar and in actuality she'd plucked out their hearts on some dark altar for a witch's ritual.

"Thank you. That is good to know."

The soldier interjected, "She wanted me to say that if you stack enough pebbles they can even stop a rolling boulder. She will continue sending you pebbles, but it is up to you to turn them into a wall. I don't know what this means, but she said you would understand."

At the time she had been warning him that powerful forces within the Capitol intended to massacre all of the casteless once and for all, and that most of them would be helpless to do anything about it. "It means she is some sort of witch who pretends to know far more than she should." The two seemed shocked when he said that, but Ashok had lived this long speaking plainly, he wasn't about to change now.

He turned to his second in command. "Jagdish, question all these volunteers and see what their skills are. Those who can be of use against the wizards may join the Sons of the Black Sword. There is no place for the weak where we are going. Any who seem untrustworthy, send them back to their homes."

"They're fanatics, Ashok. Untrustworthy would be the lot of them."

"It may be a fine line. Have Keta help you. If they seem even more irrational than he does, send them away."

Keta looked like he was about to argue with that, but then he must have decided that was, in fact, a reasonable barrier. Not all fanatics were created equal. "I will gladly help the risaldar judge their worthiness."

"Sorry, if I may interrupt?" the worker woman had raised her hand trying to get his attention.

"What? Speak."

"If you send anyone back to their homes, they'll surely be in danger. Some of them may have...well, been a little excitable about the gathering and talked too much."

"What manner of imbecile would brag about violating the Law?"

The warrior looked down at his feet, embarrassed, when Ashok asked that.

The worker tried to explain such foolishness. "Some of us may have spoken more than we should have about our secret beliefs to try and get our loved ones to come with us. It's easy to get caught up in the fervor. By now, Inquisitors will have been informed. To return would mean torture and death. But this is good. There's no turning back, so we're truly committed to your cause."

Ashok was growing frustrated. The Protector Order had to be searching the entire region around Neeramphorn. It was by luck alone that their small, fast-moving group had avoided being spotted. This haphazard wagon train would be easily discovered.

"We have no time for this."

"Wait. A suggestion, if I may?" Keta obviously knew what Ashok was thinking. "They can't go with us, and they can't go home, but I know where to send them. The hidden place I've told you of—the journey south is difficult, especially this time of year, but if the weather holds it is doable. The rebellion can take them in. It will be safe. There is room to grow there, and much work still to be done."

The south was far colder than what they'd just experienced around Neeramphorn. Ashok had no love for fanatics, but that didn't mean he wanted to see them snowed in and starving until spring. "You can't cross the Akershan mountains in the winter, Keeper."

"We don't go *over* them, Ashok. . . . Just trust me. It can be done."

"Mother Dawn didn't speak of any such thing." The worker woman sounded hesitant. "We were to help the Forgotten's warrior by joining his army."

"Ashok will lead the rebellion's army too. Soon we will be so strong the Law will have to leave us be. We've been building something marvelous there, where everyone is free to make their own way. We grow plenty of crops, have clean water, and you can practice your religion openly. I am the chief priest of the Forgotten, Freeman Keta, the Keeper of Names."

"Who?"

"Keta . . . I serve the prophet. I'm the one who has been recording the prophecies and directing the rebellion."

"Wait." The warrior sounded hopeful. "There's a *prophet*?"

Ashok just shook his head. The Law had done a fine job keeping Lok's fanatics isolated in their own dark little corners. "Keta, Jagdish, you two figure this out. I will continue on with Gutch to locate the courier."

"A wise decision. Too many newcomers at once might spook him." Gutch had been hanging back, amused at the spectacle. "Don't worry, if there's magic being smuggled in that town, I'll find it."

"I'd rather go with you," Jagdish said. "I'm here to hunt wizards, not order around kids and casteless."

"You once told me even a sad army needs officers."

Jagdish sighed. "I'm regretting my choice of words now."

"Good. Get this rabble organized and then join us in Haradas as soon as you can."

Chapter 26

~~~~~~~~~~~

Once they arrived in town, it didn't take Gutch long to catch the scent of magic, but it was not his tracker's gift that showed them the way, but rather a few friendly conversations. Since Chattarak was the master of all the barge traffic along the Nansakar, everyone in Haradas knew of him. During the day he conducted his business out of a small office near the river, and after sunset he could usually be found at a worker pub called the Black Sheep, where he rented a small room in the back, and generally kept to himself.

That was where they first caught sight of their target, eating supper and warming himself by the hearth. Chattarak was a small, wiry man, with a long unkempt beard, and a mane of wild hair. Despite the crowded, noisy room, Chattarak was alone at a table. Ashok noted he kept his back to the wall, and continually watched the other patrons through narrowed eyes as he chewed.

Haradas was the last real settlement in the southeastern Kharsawan lands, but it was a nothing town. It existed primarily to cut lumber to send up river for the needs of ever growing Neeramphorn, or south by wagon to the Akershan plains, where the winds were too strong for straight trees to grow. The town had been built on the banks of the river, which must have made their whole men uncomfortable, but they were far enough from the ocean that demon attacks were rare. There was a paltan of warriors stationed here to ward off border raids, but the security was so lax that there wasn't even an arbiter to check their forged traveling papers.

It seemed like the whole world was searching for Ashok Vadal, but nobody had bothered to tell poor Haradas of this fact. It was a forgettable sort of place.

They had borrowed clothing from the new volunteers, so were wearing long winter coats bearing the insignia of Kharsawan workers, Gutch a tree cutter and Ashok a miner. This was a trading town, so strangers were common. They fit right in as they ordered food and drink—it was the best meal Ashok had eaten in quite some time—paid for with a banknote taken from Bajwa. Each house minted their own coins, but Capitol banknotes had become commonplace wherever there was trade.

While they ate, they watched their prey, but it appeared Chattarak was truly alone. Even the hungry pleasure women avoided his table. He was known, but his reputation was not a pleasant one.

As always, Ashok's initial inclination was for the direct approach, dragging Chattarak from the place by the hair, and cutting fingers off until he told them where to find the wizards. But Gutch urged caution, because this was no mere servant of the Lost House. From the many pieces of demon Gutch sensed hidden upon his person, Chattarak was a full-fledged wizard, and a potent one at that.

"You go to stabbing in front of all these witnesses, fifty warriors will descend on this place. You may enjoy such things, but personally I'm tired of having to flee towns in the middle of the night." Gutch continued shoveling food in his mouth while he spoke. "You let me handle this one. Everyone loves Gutch. I'll share a bottle of wine with him, and soon we'll be the best of friends."

"What do you intend to do?"

"I will be my charming self, and engage in lucrative commerce." Gutch continued chewing loudly. Ashok marveled that the man could still speak with half a chicken between his teeth. Gutch had ordered a bottle of the establishment's finest wine, all the way from Vadal. When it was delivered, he grabbed it up, and made a big show of smelling it. "Ah, reminds me of home. How about you?" He shoved the bottle toward Ashok.

Most of the real memories he'd recovered of Great House Vadal involved scrubbing blood from stones, and the rest were fabrications. "I would not know. I was very young when I left."

"Well, trust me, it surely does. I used to drink this vintage all the time, oh, but not when I was young. I had to work long and hard before I could afford such things."

"I thought you were rich."

"I wasn't born with status, and even after I earned the rank of forge master smith, I didn't *feel* rich. More like I was a poor man who temporarily had money. But someday I'll return, so fabulously wealthy that I shall buy my own palace there, overlooking a vineyard of Vadal's finest grapes, and I'll have a hundred slaves to pick and stomp them into this delicious nectar, or however they make this stuff. That's why I've come all this way. Your reasons for doing all this, I still haven't figured out. The woman you seek must be rather lovely."

Ashok scowled. Gutch had talked his ears off the whole way here, and Ashok had said almost nothing in return. His duty to the prophet was a punishment mandated by Law. Officially he had no obligation to Thera beyond that...Except when he told that to himself, it no longer felt like the truth.

"You are too familiar, worker."

"See that insignia you wear on your sleeve? It says that I can be familiar as I want, my equal worker brother...So she *is* pretty. Good. If Keta's fake gods picked a lady prophet, I'd hate to see you put forth such effort for a homely one."

"My reasons shall remain my own."

"Nonsense, but noted." Gutch wiped his mouth with the back of one hand, and took up the wine and two cups. "Now, I go to be diplomatic. But would you kindly mind keeping an eye out, and in case he goes to turn me into a frog or some such, stepping in? I shall shout for help, or croak, as appropriate."

"Of course. Good luck to you."

The big man grinned. "Humble Gutch needs no luck." He made his way through the crowd toward Chattarak.

The Black Sheep was the most popular worker establishment in town, and thus crowded. There were many simultaneous conversations and arguments going on, most rather loud and drunken. The workers seemed to enjoy debating about everything, from Capitol politics they obviously didn't understand, to the quality of the tobacco they were smoking in great copious amounts. There were several games of chess being played, and some of them were interesting enough to attract a betting crowd. Ashok called upon the Heart to sharpen and focus his hearing until he could pick out Gutch's voice across the room. It was hard, since they were right next to the crackling fireplace.

"Hello, my friend. Busy night. Mind if I sit here?"

"I wish you wouldn't." Chattarak had an angry growl of a voice to match his rough appearance. "I prefer to drink alone."

"But then who would I share this with?" There was a *clunk* as Gutch put the wine down. Then the scraping of a chair as the big man took a seat. "Ah, that's better... Come. Drink. I'm celebrating."

"What's there to celebrate?"

"Exciting new business ventures and huge profits. Speaking of which, I was told that you're the man to talk with about hiring a barge to go down the Nansakar."

"You mean *up*, stranger. There's nothing downriver from Haradas except wilderness."

"That's not what I've heard."

"Then you heard wrong." Chattarak was growing suspicious. Ashok readied himself to act. He would try to remove the wizard from the room as quietly as possible.

Yet, Gutch was such a good liar that he managed to calm the wizard. "No need to be wary, friend. My associates spoke highly of you. I'm Vinod, a tracker of certain specific goods. I often sold things to a fellow in Neeramphorn by the name of Bajwa, but unfortunately he's no longer with us."

"Oh? I hadn't heard."

"It was a terrible accident. I'm afraid Bajwa's body was devoured by pigs."

"Appropriate. They're cannibals."

"I know! That's what I thought too. A toast!" Ashok could hear the wine being poured. "To cannibalism!"

Chattarak actually laughed. "To cannibalism." There was the clink of glass against glass, and a pause as the men drank. Gutch was even better at this sort of seedy business than Ashok had expected. "Ah, that is good."

"Indeed." More wine was poured. "But now I'm in a quandary. While the bosses of Neeramphorn fight to see who will take the apothecary's crown, in the meantime I've got no one to sell my goods to, and I find myself in need of notes. So I thought to myself, why not dispense with the middleman and meet Bajwa's best customers myself?"

"What goods do you speak of?"

"It is the strangest thing. I was walking along the beach minding my own business—"

"The border of hell is an odd place for a whole man to take a walk."

"I was enjoying the sunrise. But then I nearly tripped over a dead demon washed up on shore. Not a large one, and it had been nibbled upon by fishes, but still about three hundred pounds of useable flesh and bone."

"You don't say? That's quite the find. I've heard certain men would pay a lot for that sort of thing...But you didn't mention where you found such a prize."

"Don't worry. I'm sure I can find my way back to where I hid it. I had it packed someplace cool so it will remain in excellent condition while I am away."

"Three hundred pounds...I must warn you, Vinod. The scales we have at the dock here are very accurate."

Gutch laughed. "Forgive me. I tend to exaggerate. If I was going to negotiate such things, I would have to call it exactly two hundred and eighty-seven pounds of prime demon, practically bursting with useful magic."

"A significant treasure." The greed was apparent in Chattarak's tone. "Most off-books wizards would only be able to afford, at most, a few pounds at a time."

"A tooth here, a finger there, spreading it out over that many customers means a significant risk of one of them getting caught by the masks and telling them about me. So you can see why I'm seeking Bajwa's favored clients. I can think of no one else who would be prepared to purchase in such quantity right away."

"A tracker could retire a wealthy man for such a sale. To do you such a favor, it would be wise to grant these customers a bulk discount."

"How much of a discount do you think would be appropriate, my new friend, Chattarak?"

"Since they don't know you? Twenty-five percent less than what they'd pay Bajwa, at least."

Gutch groaned. "For such quality? That's robbery!"

"Such is the cost of building new relationships."

While the two criminals haggled over the price of Gutch's imaginary demon, Ashok continued watching the room for any other threats, but the local workers seemed to be having a merry time. Those who practiced magic in secret needed to be cunning in order to survive, but maybe Chattarak had become complacent here? It seemed to be going well, but he remained wary, waiting for the wizard to spring a trap.

"You know what? I like you, Vinod. I've decided to introduce you to my friends. I'm sure they'd love to hear your offer. Come, now. We must go if we are to catch them still at the docks..." Chair legs scraped across the floor. "Mind if I carry the wine?"

"Drink all you want. I'm happy to share."

Gutch was tall enough that it was easy to see his head above the crowd. Ashok watched them from the corner of his eye as the wizard walked out the front door. Gutch was clever enough not to get caught looking around, and wise enough to know that Ashok would follow. He waited long enough to not be suspicious, then got up, and weaved his way through the crowd.

The night air was much cooler and cleaner than the stifling, smoky interior of the Black Sheep. Chattarak was leading Gutch toward the river and now that any random passerby could clearly overhear their conversation, they'd stopped talking about their Law breaking. Ashok leaned against the wall and waited for them to get further ahead so he wouldn't be caught following. The workers of Haradas seemed to be of a cheerful disposition. Everyone who walked past Ashok gave him a nod of greeting, as was their local custom. He returned the greetings, but tried to keep an expression that showed he did not wish to engage in conversation. That particular expression came naturally to him.

Once they were a hundred feet ahead, Ashok followed. Chattarak was heading for the docks. Even if a river was free of demons, only the poor lived close to bodies of water. It was inconvenient to have your water delivered, but displaying your status was more important than convenience. Besides, if you were truly important you could afford to dig a well. Walled family estates gave way to humbler homes, then to lower-status worker dwellings. They walked past warehouses, storage yards, and workshops. There were fewer people here, and far fewer lights.

The docks were a simple wooden affair, just big enough to give the bargemen something to tie to for the night. There were fires burning beside some shacks on a mud bank downstream. That's where the casteless would live. After the people of Haradas dumped their waste and trash in the river, the untouchables could drink their fill. It may have been customary to show kindness to strangers here, but people rarely showed any mercy to their casteless. It was often easier for whole men to forget they existed at all.

There were a few stands and small buildings around the docks, but no lights were burning. There were no guards posted because there was nothing worth stealing. Only a fool would want a *barge*. Ashok had learned about barge work only recently from Thera, before that the whole endeavor had always been beneath his notice. It was one of the most degrading positions a worker could be obligated to. Most of the labor would be performed by casteless under their supervision. It was hard to imagine any whole man living out their days floating atop water, but trade demanded that someone do it.

For a powerful wizard to pretend to such low status, Chattarak had to be an exceedingly dedicated criminal. Gutch's new boots echoed as they walked across the wooden planks while Chattarak's simple shoes made no sound. Laughing loudly, he directed Gutch toward one of the shacks built over the water. Ashok sharpened his vision. There was no sign of Chattarak's supposed friends. In fact, there were no witnesses at all. It could be that Chattarak simply wished to continue their negotiations in secrecy, but it was a fine place for a murder.

Ashok focused on his hearing and began walking faster.

The wizard opened the door and gestured for Gutch to enter the shack. "In here."

Gutch hesitated. "It's awfully dark. Are you sure this is where your friends are?"

"I know where my friends are, but do you know where yours are, Vinod? Like the wizard who has been stalking us through the shadows."

"A wizard?" Gutch sputtered. "I don't know what you mean!"

"Who else would have such a potent piece of black steel hidden beneath his shirt?"

"Easy now, Chattarak, my friend, I didn't realize you could sense magic too. I guess you're not as good at it as I am though.

That black steel's not hidden on his chest, it's *in* his chest. Long story, but—"

Chattarak smashed the wine bottle over Gutch's head. The big man collapsed into the shack. "Shut your fish hole, tracker. I'll deal with you later." The wizard closed the door then turned to meet Ashok. "Greetings, newcomer."

Ashok had reached the dock and begun walking across the planks. Standing over the river made him uneasy. Canda was bright tonight. The moon gave them more than enough light to fight by, but not so much that any passerby would notice them and alert the watch. He stopped ten feet away, opened his coat, and placed his hand on his sword.

"I have some questions for you, wizard."

"I may have answers, but that depends on who is foolish enough to think they can deceive the Lost House." Chattarak reached beneath his coat and drew forth a pair of katar. Each push dagger had a foot-long triangular blade. He aimed one at Ashok's face and snarled, "You know my name, but I don't know yours. Speak, before I carve it from you."

"I am Ashok Vadal."

"Really?" Chattarak tilted his head to the side. He obviously hadn't been expecting that, but his lack of fear indicated that he was a dangerous opponent. "Well, this is an honor, meeting the infamous Black Heart. I marvel at your persistence, but I have no quarrel with you. What do you want with me?"

"One of your kind took someone I have sworn to protect, a woman named Thera. She will be returned to me or else."

"I know of her. She was brought through here by a brother wizard, Yuval, but she was drugged, so I never spoke to her. Though Yuval told me of Sikasso's recent misadventure. Most unfortunate that."

"I cut off his arm. How many of your limbs will I have to remove before you tell me what I want to know?"

Keeping one katar up, and the other cocked back by his side, Chattarak slowly backed away, further over the water. "I understand why Sikasso took that contract. It should have been a simple job, keeping an eye on you. When it was over we would receive your sword in payment. I warned him that was too good to be true. Sikasso should have known that to offer such an incredible prize, the job couldn't be that easy."

How *dare* someone offer these criminals Angruvadal? "Who arranged that payment?" Ashok demanded. "Was it Omand?"

But Chattarak only smiled. Ashok would have to wring the truth from him.

"Instead of gaining an ancestor blade worth of fragments, we lost several brothers, and the only prize received for our efforts was yet another puzzle. You've left Sikasso in a precarious position, crippled, frustrated, and failing to deliver on his great promises. I suppose I should thank you for that, because his discomfort does amuse me greatly."

Apparently this wizard did not care for his humiliating posting. Ashok drew his sword and started toward him. "Where are they?"

"Sikasso is not a patient man. Your woman is probably already dead. You threaten me for no reason, but you're not so fearsome without an ancestor blade. You've done me a favor coming here." Chattarak's voice had become a dangerous hiss. "I suppose with the glory I gain for avenging our fallen brothers, I'll get out of this dead-end obligation."

He struck, katars moving so fast they were nothing but a blur of steel. Wizards didn't fight like normal men. Their bodies moved at speeds which left warriors baffled, then pierced and bleeding. But Protectors trained to fight wizards, and Ashok had killed more of them than anyone else. He was not easily impressed by their tricks.

The blades darted in, lightning quick, driven by demonic energy but Ashok countered, moving his sword and his body to turn them aside at the last instant each time. Chattarak adjusted, and began slashing, extending his arms and whirling about. Using up so much valuable magic, the wizard became a force of nature. The blows just kept coming. Ashok attacked, trying to strike him in the arms, but they retreated faster than a cracking whip.

The assassins of the Lost House were good fighters. He'd killed some, but by surprise and overwhelming them quickly. In a straight fight, they were remarkably skilled. Ashok smashed one of the katars down, but before he could cut the wizard's leg out from under him, the smaller man turned his whole body, leapt, and launched a spinning kick right into Ashok's face.

Stinging, lip split, he took a step back, and spit a gob of blood onto the boards.

"Oh yes. You did me a favor coming here, Protector." Chatta-rak was smiling, enjoying himself, still thinking he had a chance.

Ashok had merely been trying to take him alive because he couldn't question a corpse. "Come on then."

Chattarak lunged, driving both blades at his chest. This time, Ashok dodged to the side, slicing as the wizard flew past. The cut went deep. Blood flew into the air.

"How—" Chattarak took a few halting steps, and then looked down at the weeping laceration. "Oceans."

"Where is Thera?"

The wizard roared and struck, twin katars flashing, constantly jabbing and cutting, moving with such speed that he had to be consuming whole chunks of demon at a time. Danger came from every angle, feet and knees coming from below, trying to trip him up, while steel came straight at him or from the sides.

Ashok stayed ahead of every attack.

Wizards could make their bodies faster, but their minds still processed information at the same speed. They had all the power in the world, but it did no good to deliver it in a manner that Ashok found predictable.

"What manner of demon are you?" Furious, Chattarak swung with all his might.

Ashok caught him by the arm, twisted it around until the elbow broke, and drove the wizard's own blade into his guts.

Gasping, Chattarak stumbled back. The handle of his katar was jutting from his stomach, embedded so deep it had to be sticking out his back. The other weapon, and the chunk of bone he'd been using to power it, dropped from his fingers to clatter against the wood.

"Speak quickly, wizard, or I will beat her location from you."

The wizard grabbed his belt, hand curling around dangling charms of demon bone. Ashok lunged for him, but it was too late. The moon disappeared as the dock was consumed by darkness. He had seen these wizards shape shift before, into great birds or a swarm of insects to escape his wrath, but there would be no escape this time.

Crashing through the dark, Ashok collided with whatever Chattarak had turned into, but it wasn't feathers or millions of husks, but rather the scales of a reptile. Then the moonlight came back, and he was entangled with a giant, hideous serpent.

It curled around his sword arm and tightened, so hard and fast that he couldn't even strike. The snake's head rose above him, solid black eyes gleaming as a forked tongue shot past fangs. It struck for his face, but Ashok got his other arm up in time, and the fangs pierced his wrist instead. Venomous fire shot through his muscles, but he was too focused on capturing this wizard to care. So Ashok used his own arm bones to lever the snake's head down enough so he could begin beating it in the skull with the pommel of his sword.

Only Ashok realized too late that the beast he was wrestling wasn't a magical facsimile of a land snake, but a *water* snake. It had wrapped around his legs, and they went down, rolling toward the edge of the dock.

They hit the river with a splash.

Beneath the surface it was a different world, the home of evil, where no man should ever willingly go. A river was just a finger of hell, reaching up onto land, searching for something to destroy. Beneath the water, it made the strongest arm weak, the sharpest eyes half blind, and the keenest ears deaf. Water loved to drown the brave and stupid.

The only time Ashok could remember experiencing fear was beneath the water. This remained true.

He did not like experiencing fear.

Holding his breath as the wizard tried to crush him, Ashok kept striking, but the evil water was slowing his movements too much. Ashok released the pathetic sword and let it sink to the bottom so that he could have that hand free to drive his thumb into the serpent's eye. He ground it in hard. The eye popped beneath the pressure, but the socket was too narrow to get his thumb into Chattarak's brain.

They twisted and fought as they spiraled into the deeps. The current was strong, and Ashok could feel the scrape of rocks and the impact as they hit the submerged timbers beneath the dock. They were being swept downstream. His precious breath was a stream of bubbles escaping toward the surface. The white moonlight of Canda was broken and reflecting above. His situation was dire. Even if he hadn't been wrestling a giant snake, he had been raised a whole man, and thus did not know how to swim.

Evil water rushed down his nose. All he could hear was the pounding of his heart. They struck the muddy bottom, which threw up a cloud that was nearly as blinding as the wizard's magic.

The snake was wrapped around one arm, his chest, and legs. Muscles tightened, trying to crush the life from him. All Chattarak had to do was outlast him, but the wizard was wounded and impatient. The fangs released from his wrist and bit deep into this shoulder. Ashok grimaced at the twin punctures, and regretted it as precious bubbles escaped from between his teeth.

As they rolled along the bottom being propelled by evil forces toward distant hell, Ashok knew he was running out of air... But if the Heart of the Mountain could beat for a Protector to get them through a crushed throat or punctured lung, then maybe it could stave off drowning for a time as well? Ashok focused on that, and since he didn't fade into unconsciousness, it must have worked. Only as he used the Heart for that, his body was no longer resilient enough to hold off the crushing pressure of the snake. His ribs creaked and his back popped, but the sacrifice bought him time.

When the snake had removed its fangs from Ashok's wrist, it meant he was now free to reach one of the knives on his belt. He drew a blade and plunged it through the scales, again and again. This knife was a mere four inches long, just wider than the palm of his hand, but sharp as a razor, and each time he twisted it hard before ripping it free, opening a massive hole in the beast.

He just kept on stabbing, over and over. Chattarak bit him again, but whatever manner of poison was contained in those fangs, the Heart of the Mountain had encountered it before, so it did nothing beyond burn and cause his muscles to cramp. The wizard was weakening and could no longer keep them stuck at the bottom. They floated along, locked in a battle to the death, the surface tantalizingly close.

Chattarak must have been growing desperate, because the death grip loosened. Either he was going to try and swim away, or come at Ashok from a different angle, but it didn't matter, because the instant Ashok's hand bumped into a better weapon, he let the little knife float away, and took hold of the katar still embedded through the snake. The river turned red as Ashok began sawing it back and forth through the serpent, splitting scales and the muscles beneath.

Then everything turned magically black.

They broke the surface and Ashok gasped for air. The snake was gone and Chattarak had returned. The wizard had either passed out or was dead, but Ashok still didn't know how to swim. He immediately turned the Heart back toward granting strength to his limbs, and grabbed onto one of the wizard's arms before he could be swept away.

The shore was near. They'd traveled surprisingly far on the current, but he could see the casteless's fires burning nearby. Ashok kicked and wallowed about grotesquely in the evil river, and his head kept plunging back below the surface. He was so tempted to let go of Chattarak, so that he could use both hands to flail, but he would not give the evil water that victory.

"Curse you, river! I am Ashok Vadal and I will not drown in you! Give me this wizard and let me go!"

His boot struck solid ground, just a toe, but it was enough. It took several tries to stand on the slippery rocks, but he slowly made his way ashore. The ground ahead was cold, clinging mud, but it was the most wonderful thing he had ever felt. Crawling, he dragged Chattarak all the way out of the river before flopping down next to him.

Ashok took several deep breaths and tried to compose himself. The cold had pierced him to the core. He couldn't stop shaking.

Chattarak was still breathing, but was missing an eye, there were a multitude of stab wounds scattered across his body, and the katar wound had gone from a single puncture to opening him from sternum to pelvis. The wizard coughed up river water and blood.

Ashok took hold of his collar and shook him. "Where is Thera?"

The wizard's teeth were stained with blood as he gasped, "I'm afraid to die."

"I am not," Ashok snarled. "Help me find her so I can."

As it to spite him, Chattarak died anyway.

Ashok roared in anger, drew back his fist, and with a single furious blow shattered half the bones in the wizard's face. He rolled off the body and lay on his back in the mud beside the dead man.

He tried to control his breathing. Red blood and black venom slowly dribbled from his arm and shoulder. The poison caused a great deal of pain, but was nothing compared to the terrible feeling of not knowing what to do next.

On the side of justice there was an answer to every question, even if it was a simple *because the Law requires it*. There was power in certainty. If the solution wasn't obvious, every man had a place, so there had always been a superior to tell him what to do. Now he had many followers, but had never been more alone. The *not knowing* was one of the harshest parts of his sentence.

The Law would give him no direction beyond obedience to his final orders. But how could he serve a prophet he couldn't find? He had followed the most tenuous of leads across the eastern third of Lok, pursued like criminal scum every step, only to kill the one man who knew the path.

Frustrated, wounded, damp, freezing, and lying in the mud, Ashok had nowhere else to turn. The wizard had said Sikasso was not a patient man. Thera's time was running out.

No one else would help him find Thera, so he might as well try the gods who'd supposedly chosen her.

"Heed me, Forgotten. I have made an oath I cannot break. If you are real and you want Thera found, I demand you show me the way... Also, your people keep flocking to me. If you give a damn about the fools who believe in you, then help me to not spend their lives uselessly. You are supposedly gods, so act like it." He waited a moment. Their silence just made him angrier. "If you do not, to the oceans with you, and I will do it myself!"

Satisfied that ought to do it, Ashok got to his feet. The coils of the snake had wrenched his knee, and he couldn't put his full weight on it. He pulled the katar from Chattarak's body so he would at least have a decent weapon, then started back toward the docks to see if Gutch was still alive.

He paused when he realized that he was being watched by two of the non-people. They'd come over from their fire to see what the commotion was about, and were just standing there, wide-eyed and silent. They were both male, and appeared stronger than most untouchables. If they thought he was just some foolish whole man who'd washed up on their shore, easy to be robbed, he held up the bloody katar to show them he was not in the mood. "What do you want?"

"All along the river, our people have been whispering about a hero," said one. "Could it be?"

"Are you Fall?" asked the other, hesitant.

It was pointless to deny his identity. Ashok lowered the katar. "That was my casteless name. How did you know?"

"You killed the barge master! Who else could do such a

thing?" They were awestruck. Thankfully they didn't start bowing, because he couldn't stomach that right now. "The barge master was a monster. A terrible, terrible devil."

"He took our women whenever he wanted, even drowned some of us for sport. But when we heard about Fall, who fights for the casteless, we prayed for the gods to send you to save us from him. And they did! They really answered our prayers!"

Ashok just shook his head. It seemed the gods were rather fickle about whose prayers they answered. Perhaps the casteless asked nicely? *What foolishness.* "At least someone is having a successful night." He muttered as he started limping away.

"Thank you, Fall! We'll tell the others about you. We'll sing songs about you! Tonight we celebrate for now we are safe. The whole men will give us a new barge master to pole for, but hopefully that one won't be so evil."

"Wait..." Ashok stopped. He thought back to his own time on the Martaban River with Keta and Thera, and how their barge had been driven by... *casteless.* "You rode on Chattarak's barge? Did you go with him downriver?"

The two exchanged a confused glance. "Of course. Whole men are too lazy to pole. He sat in the shade and drank wine while we worked."

It couldn't be. "There is a secret castle in the wilderness to the east, somewhere by the sea. Did he ever take you there?"

"Sure. The river don't go all the way to his golden house. There's more tributaries than I've got fingers and toes, but I know which he used to get close."

Ashok began to laugh. Sometimes it was too easy to forget about the casteless.

Chapter 27

Ashok sat alone by the river, sharpening his new sword. It was a Vadal blade, similar—not in power, but in style—to mighty Angruvadal. They had found it in Chattarak's warehouse along with several other fine weapons and pieces of armor from various houses, probably trophies taken off those he had defeated. This sword would replace the simple one Ashok had dropped in the river, but nothing would ever replace his ancestor blade.

From the hesitant footsteps upon the dock, Ashok could tell that it was Keta who approached. "You should not try and sneak up on a man like me in the dark, Keeper. It never ends well."

"Thera is the one who is good at sneaking. I wasn't sneaking. I was merely trying to be polite and not interrupt. May I join you?"

"Very well." Ashok went back to polishing the blade. There were a few spots of rust on it. Chattarak had never bothered to clean his trophies or store them properly, and that disgusted the ever meticulous Ashok. Since they had found a way to proceed without the wizard's help, it made Ashok glad that he'd killed him. Improper equipment maintenance was an indication of poor character.

"Why are you sitting by the water? You're constantly going on about how evil it is."

"Evil is what I deserve." Mostly Ashok had picked this spot because it was quiet. Back in the camp the new recruits kept trying to talk to him. He didn't like the way they looked at him with adoration, or spoke to him about their hopes.

"You are rather morose." Keta approached, carrying a clay jug and two cups.

"What do you have there, Keeper?"

"I don't know, but these eastern folk love to get drunk from it. Since we are going our separate ways in the morning, I thought we could have a drink together." Keta sat next to him. From the smell, the Keeper had already been doing quite a bit of drinking on his own. Ashok placed the sword on a cloth, and took the offered cup. "That's what men do, isn't it?"

"Legally speaking, neither of us is a whole man."

"Fine. Then that's what *friends* do."

Ashok began to respond, but then realized he didn't really know what to say. Oddly enough, Keta's words were probably true enough. So he just held out the cup so Keta could pour.

"How goes the preparations, Keeper?"

"Well, tomorrow the local casteless will ferry the women, children, and infirm across the river, and I will guide them to our refuge in the south." Keta proceeded to fill his own cup. "Jagdish is looting supplies from Chattarak's warehouse to outfit the Sons who are traveling east with you, while Gutch took the wizard's valuables into Haradas to sell at deep discounts to merchants who will ask few questions, so that you may have funds...I figure he'll bring you some, tell you that's all of it, while most of the notes end up in that greedy worker's pocket."

"How is his head?"

"Sore, but workers have exceedingly thick skulls." Keta lifted his cup. "May you find glory, kill many vile wizards, and bring our prophet back safe and sound."

Ashok downed the cup. It burned worse than the snake venom. Keta drank too. His face turned red and he began to cough violently. "That isn't drink. That is liquid cruelty!" After composing himself, Keta asked, "Another?"

"No thank you. I think I would be better off using the rest of it to remove the rust from this sword."

"Probably wise. The casteless I got it from warned me that this stuff can make you go blind." The two of them watched the flowing river in silence for a time. Keta poured himself another cup anyway. "I wish I was going with you, Ashok. Thera is my prophet. My responsibility."

"You feel guilty."

"Of course I do! But I can't neglect my people any longer. Thera and I left because the Forgotten wanted us to find you. I had to talk her into it. I had to pay her a lot in fact."

"I still do not understand having to pay your prophet for her services as a mercenary criminal to serve the rebellion she commands."

"Eh, it's complicated. There's the Voice and then there's Thera, and I've learned they're two very different things. I don't know why the gods chose her. The Forgotten tells us things through her, which she then ignores and does what she wants anyway. Thera doesn't care about the Law anymore, but she's made up her own code to replace it. I can't for the life of me figure it out. She'll come around eventually. If she's still alive that is... Not that you care. Sometimes I think you'd prefer she were dead, so that you'd be free of your obligation."

"At times," Ashok said truthfully. But at the same time, rebel or not, oddly enough he was fond of the stubborn woman. She had saved him from a river. It was only right to save her from wizards. "As you said, it is complicated."

"I worry constantly. What if Thera was tortured into giving up the rebellion's location and they told the Inquisition?"

"If everyone is dead when you reach your hideout, then you will know that answer."

Keta gave a long sigh. "You are a most melancholy drinking partner. Or what if in our absence, deprived of the Forgotten's guidance, my people have turned to wickedness?"

Ashok snorted.

"Don't you laugh at me, Ashok Vadal! Surely by now you know there's some truth to all this gods business!"

"I intended no offense." He thought about keeping it to himself, but what was the use? "I did not tell you before, Keeper, but after I killed Chattarak, I knew not where to go, so I demanded that your gods show me the way. Which is when these casteless approached, willing to help."

Keta got really excited. "You asked and the gods sent them to you? It's a miracle!"

"It is something." Ashok looked at the jug, thought *to hell with it*, and poured himself another cup of the disgusting drink. It reminded him of the stuff that some Protector acolytes would secretly make during training, fermenting odd vegetables in glass jars hidden behind the practice field. There had been no specific rule against acolytes making their own alcohol, but Ashok had been so devoted to following the spirit of the rules that he had not drunk any, until Devedas had ordered him to *maintain unit cohesion*. When Ratul had found out they'd all received a severe beating. *Good times.*

"I do not know what it is, Keeper. But it is . . . something."

"The gods smile upon you, Ashok. You are our new Ramrowan. That's why I know that I can take these people south. It is the gods' will that I make this rebellion succeed, just as it is their will that you protect Thera. Once we're reunited we will build our great army, and together, bring freedom to Lok."

Ashok said nothing, but if that was the case, perhaps failure was for the best? Maybe that was the lesson Omand had been trying to teach. Without Thera's gift, Keta's rebellion would fold. All who believed in their foolish dreams would be executed. Maybe their dismal failure would be so epic that it would long serve as an example to anyone else who thought about crossing the Law, and Ashok's participation would only add to their infamy.

"You seem so certain, Keta."

"I am. I know we are accomplishing great things."

"I was certain of things once." Ashok drank more of the poisonous swill. "I miss it."

"You were magically indoctrinated to be a perfect tool of tyranny, untroubled by fear or remorse. Of course you were certain, because they'd left you no capacity for doubt! Now that you've seen the truth, their construction crumbles!" Keta pounded down yet another cup of the vile drink. This time the coughing fit was rather short, and he quickly poured another. Most of it missed and splashed onto the docks.

"It is not so pleasant when your very mind is the crumbling construction in question."

"You feel doubt? Good! That means you're human after all! I'm glad you're questioning your conditioning."

Ashok had spent his life defending the Law, and when some of the highest representatives of the Law had put him on this path, he had immediately complied. He was still following those orders. Yet Sikasso had claimed to be working for the Grand Inquisitor too. Chattarak had not answered his question, but who else was in any position to promise *his sword* to criminals? Ancestor blades were sacred, not trinkets to be bargained with. The very thought of Omand being so selfish filled Ashok with an anger that only a bearer could comprehend.

No one was above the Law, but the Grand Inquisitor was a vital champion of it, and Ashok's final orders had been signed by some of the highest-status judges in the Capitol. Those people *created* the Law. Why would they damage the very thing they were sworn to protect?

Maybe it was the strong drink making him think this way, but if their paths ever crossed again, Ashok would ask Omand why he had given out a punishment that required loyal servants like Ishaan Harban to sacrifice their lives. For the Grand Inquisitor's sake, it had better be a damned good answer.

Keta had finished yet another cup of the potent substance, and he wasn't a very large man to begin with. His eyes had gone watery and he was swaying a bit. "You're quiet. What are you brooding about now?"

"I do not... *brood*."

"Ha! That's all you do. Brood and kill people! You, my friend, need a hobby."

"Your drunkenness has made you more annoying than usual. Besides, I already have a hobby."

"What?"

"Sword practice."

The Keeper of Names began to laugh so hard he threatened to topple off the dock. In his inebriated state, he'd probably drown immediately. Now that would be an ignominious end to a rebellion. Ashok stood, retrieved his new sword, and then helped Keta up. "Come on. You need to sleep. We both have long journeys ahead of us tomorrow."

"You know, Ashok," Keta's words were becoming slurred. "People keep asking me questions about how our religion works." He leaned in conspiratorially. "When I don't know the answer, or the Voice hasn't talked about that, I just guess and make up something that sounds good. It's a lot of pressure."

"I assumed it was something like that."

"I shouldn't be tellin' you this, but every day I pray to the gods that they'll help you find something more than just the Law to live for, so someday you could be more than just the black-hearted bastard killer they made you. That's why I tell you stories about heroes and ideals, hoping you'll be inspired to change, hoping you can become free! But then the gods don't answer my prayers, and I start thinking what if that's why they chose you? The gods don't care if you're a good man any more than the Law did. They just need a killer, and killing is all you'll ever be good for... And that just kind of makes me sad."

"Perhaps, Keeper..." Maybe he was right. After all, every man has his place. "Let's get you to bed."

The small man really couldn't handle his drink. Ashok had to steer the stumbling Keta back toward where the Sons had made camp. Surely the local warriors knew a large unknown group was camped near their casteless quarter, but they'd not ridden out to challenge the possible criminals who were obviously leaving soon anyway. There were not that many warriors in Haradas, but as a former enforcer of the Law, Ashok found their lack of commitment disappointing.

"Don't abandon the jug!" Keta gestured futilely toward where they'd left the alcohol.

"That stuff has made you stupid. I should throw it in the river."

"No! If it floats all the way to the sea then the demons will declare war on us!"

"They would be justified."

The casteless of Haradas were fully committed to assisting the Sons of the Black Sword. One of their barges would be used to ferry Keta and most of their number across the Nansakar to the Akershan side, where they would begin their journey south. They would be taking all their horses, as there was no use for the animals where Ashok's group was going. Since he still wouldn't let Keta tell him about the rebellion's secret hideout, he figured they'd probably end up snowed in and eating the horses to survive at this rate. Their other available barges would be used to take Ashok and the rest of them downriver toward the Lost House.

The casteless were overjoyed to provide their labor and expertise, and there was no longer a barge master to command them otherwise. As far as they were concerned, the gods had sent

the great hero Fall to deliver them from the hands of the devil
Chattarak, so the least they could do was help Fall destroy all
of Chattarak's vile friends.

Ashok did nothing to disabuse them of that notion.

In the morning, Keta had been too ill to give much of a
speech, a fact which Ashok was exceedingly grateful for. He
had mumbled some blessing from the gods upon those going
downriver, and then lurched to the side and vomited. The newly
arrived fanatics probably weren't too impressed with their new
priest, but he would have to do.

Keta approached him, looking gray and humbled. "Farewell,
Ashok, until we meet again in Akershan."

"If Thera lives, I will bring her to you."

"I know you will..." Keta's bloodshot eyes blinked against the
brightness of the morning sun. "By the way, do you remember
what I said last night?"

"You spoke honestly. It was appreciated."

"Oh, good. I was worried I'd embarrassed myself."

"I did not say that." He gave Keta a bow that would have been
appropriate between equals in status in Vadal lands. Surprised,
Keta returned the respectful gesture. "Good luck to you, Keeper."

Ashok walked to the end of the dock and stepped down onto
the waiting barge. He tried to hide his involuntary shudder as
it shifted beneath his feet. He was the last aboard. The casteless
used their poles to push them away from the natural safety of
the land and out into the cruel river.

With the addition of their new recruits, the Sons of the Black
Sword traveling east were thirty strong. Most of them were of the
warrior caste, and had never ridden upon a barge before. They
were not happy about their method of transportation, but Ashok
didn't give a damn about their happiness. The river was the fastest way to reach the Lost House. If they wanted to remain on
land with their dignity intact, then they shouldn't have become
criminals.

From somewhere, the casteless still ashore had produced
homemade instruments, rough carved flutes and drums made
from discarded garbage, and they began to play a discordant
tune. The fanatics ran along the bank after them, waving and
cheering. Some warriors were going south to guard Keta's group.
Those looked dejected to be left behind while the warriors on

the barges taunted their friends, loudly declaring that they were off to gain glory.

"May the gods watch over you and keep you safe!" Keta shouted after them.

Gutch was leaning on a spear a few feet from Ashok, looking amused at the whole spectacle. "You should have told Keta to keep his gods, because there's no safety where we are heading."

Chapter 28

〰〰〰

"Damn you, Ashok!" Devedas bellowed at the top of his lungs.

The window shattered as he hurled a chair through it. With an incoherent roar he kicked over the map table, breaking bottles and spilling plates. Then he took up the other chair and dashed it into pieces against the far wall. He cracked the bricks of the fireplace with his fist.

For a moment he spent his rage against the furniture and walls. Decorum was forgotten. The Lord Protector stood there in the middle of the destroyed room, chest heaving, knuckles bleeding.

Devedas picked up the crumpled note and read it again.

Ashok had killed Ishaan Harban.

A Protector had died on his watch, while following his commands, murdered at the hands of a former brother. Ishaan had been one of their best, a longtime friend of Ashok and Devedas both. This had to be a cruel joke. Devedas took a deep breath and composed himself. He needed to be calm once he started giving orders, or at least he needed to appear that way.

When this letter had been written, Bundit had still been in a coma, but would more than likely survive. Teerapat, the least experienced of the three, had taken up the chase, but he had been given faulty information by a local Inquisitor which had put him on the wrong road. By the time he'd discovered the mistake and doubled back, new snow had obscured their tracks. Ashok and his gang had been lost. Teerapat was deeply shamed by his failure, but Devedas very much doubted that the Inquisitor had *made a mistake.*

And not for the first time, Devedas felt the pangs of regret that came from entering a political alliance with a treacherous snake. If the Inquisition was covering for Ashok, what did Omand have to gain by prolonging Ashok's existence? It had to be more than merely embarrassing the Protector Order. Omand's ultimate goal was to overthrow the judges. He'd denied having any part in Ashok's current endeavors. But it was an Inquisitor who'd misled Teerapat, and it was another Inquisitor who'd claimed to have seen Ashok here in Shabdkosh.

He'd completed his investigation. The casteless had been inspired by tales of Ashok, but there was no proof he'd ever actually been here. He'd delivered his report to the new Arbiter, and more importantly, he'd shown his face so the Capitol knew the Order was taking this threat seriously. At least the occupants of this house had been murdered by the casteless during their uprising, so it wasn't like they'd complain about their broken furnishings.

It was time to go. Every Protector in the eastern regions of Lok would already be converging on Neeramphorn. They would probably find Ashok long before Devedas could travel all that way. He was so very tempted to ride to the much closer Capitol, to beat the truth out of Omand instead.

Only the Inquisition was currently far better favored than his own. Any overt move would simply get Devedas slandered and arrested. Regardless of what games the Inquisition might be playing, Devedas was better off keeping the Grand Inquisitor as an ally rather than an enemy. His conspiracy was too entrenched. Their success was inevitable. The judges would be overthrown, and rightfully so, it had been a long time since those useless curs had accomplished anything of note. All they did was collect taxes to build themselves bigger palaces and government buildings.

If he fought against Omand's conspiracy now, he'd only be protecting the gang of fools who held him in such contempt. Omand would slander the Protectors, and the judges would eagerly lap up his lies. If Devedas left the conspiracy alone, as per his agreement with the Grand Inquisitor, after the coup Devedas would be installed as their figurehead. A crisis required a strong hand, and the people needed someone to look to for leadership. Who better to unite the houses than a war hero and champion of the Law, who had no home, and thus held no bias toward any one great house?

Only Devedas did not intend to remain Omand's puppet king for long. He was done being anyone's servant. He intended to rule.

There was no other choice. Despite giving his whole life in service to the Law, when it was done with him, it would give him *nothing* in return. The Capitol would use him up and then toss him aside without a second thought. Outside the Order he would have no status. At most he would become a minor vassal to the Great House which had consumed his.

Firstborn of a Thakoor and a bearer, he'd been robbed of his birthright. He'd risen through the Order by the strength of his arm and the quickness of his wit, second in reputation only to a man with unattainable gifts. He'd given everything to the Law. Bled, suffered, and killed for it. Devedas understood it was the Law which was vital, not the men who wrote it. He'd been in the highest chambers of the Capitol and seen the judges in action. They were lazy, corrupt, vapid fools. But most of all, they were *replaceable*.

Other powerful men had come to the same conclusion. Change was coming. If Lok was destined to end up with a king, he'd at least make sure that king was a worthy one. If one man alone would wear a crown, better a noble Protector than a pawn manipulated by a merciless Inquisitor. Devedas had struggled with this, and it had kept him up many nights, but he'd come to terms with the necessity of his Law breaking. It was for the greater good, both for him personally, and for all of Lok.

But this plan became far less palatable when his Protectors died due to his ally's games.

Devedas had dislocated a finger punching the wall, so he popped it back into place. Then he picked up the map.

Where are you going, Ashok? What drives you now?

Ashok was a man of singular purpose. When that purpose had been the Law, he had been the most predictable man in the world. Now he was a mystery. Devedas had looked him in the eyes in prison, and despite his fury, he'd also felt pity. He'd seen in Ashok no reason to live beyond hoping his sword would find a good home.

Something had caused this drastic change.

Ashok was casteless. There was a casteless rebellion in Aker-shan. That had to be his destination. But why enter the busy city of Neeramphorn, where he was likely to be recognized? It made no sense.

His eyes lingered on the map for a moment. He wasn't too far from where he had hidden Rada. It said something, that his feelings for her were strong enough that he was briefly tempted to postpone his ambitions for a day so that he could go see her…But that was foolish. He had work to do now, so that they could all have a better future. Better to delay their reunion for a bit, so that he could spend the rest of his life with Rada by his side, as his queen.

Karno would keep her safe until the coup, and since Karno was one of the Protectors who was politically astute enough to piece together what was going on, it was better to keep him away from the Capitol. He was afraid that if Karno had to choose between their friendship and the letter of the Law, neither would like the answer.

Ashok's new purpose was a mystery, but Devedas understood his own. He'd make a much more convincing candidate for king if he was the man responsible for catching the most dangerous criminal in the world. Devedas folded the map and went outside.

Protector Abhishek Gujara, five-year senior, was waiting for him. Their horses were already prepared. He took one look at the broken chair lying in the yard, but said nothing about it to his superior.

"We ride for Akershan immediately."

"The word is there's big storms coming up the Ice Coast. We might not be able to cross the passes until spring." Abhishek was from the northern jungles and had no love of the southern cold.

"Then we'll ride until the horses flounder, and then we'll walk the rest." Devedas was from the harshest place in Lok, a land of endless brutal ice, where giant predatory bears lurked camouflaged in the snow, and volcanos perpetually spewed lava into the sea. The trek from the central desert to Akershan was nothing compared to that. The Heart would keep them warm enough to keep their fingers and toes. "Where is the Inquisitor?"

Abhishek nodded toward the barn, where the messenger was tending to his horse. "He was telling me how the Inquisition's wizards had done us a great favor, using up valuable demon to speed this message along to us, but then he heard you breaking things and decided to retreat."

"That was wise. Go inside and gather my things." He didn't want the other Protector to overhear what he had to say.

Devedas approached the Inquisitor, who was busy brushing down his tired steed. When he saw the Lord Protector approaching, he quickly pulled up his cloth mask to hide his face. It had the fangs of the Law stitched over his mouth. The metal or wooden ones made for a better show, but weren't as pragmatic for galloping across the desert.

"Greetings, Lord Protector Devedas."

"I have a message which you will deliver directly to Grand Inquisitor Omand and no one else." Devedas stopped, uncomfortably close to the Inquisitor, and glared at him. "Tell him I said *no more games.*"

Devedas turned and began walking away.

"Uh..." The Inquisitor seemed rather frightened. "That's all?"

"Omand will understand," Devedas muttered.

He had better...

Chapter 29

～～～～～

"What horrible need could wizards have for stolen children?"

The untouchable spread his callused hands apologetically. "Don't know, Fall. The barge master would drown us for talking to them, but they was children of whole men, and they'd cry their little eyes out for their mommies the whole way downriver."

There was nothing to do on a river journey except sit and wait. They couldn't even train without the risk of knocking someone over the side. So Ashok had passed the time by questioning the casteless about the nature of Chattarak's business. So far it had been more confusing than enlightening.

Ashok looked to Gutch, but the longtime criminal seemed to have no idea either. "I don't know why wizards would kidnap kids, General. There's no reason. Well...business reasons anyway."

"I know. In my years of enforcing the Law, I have punished men for acts of evil you can't imagine."

"Not surprising. I meet all kinds in my line of work. Just because you can smuggle magic, some folks ask you about smuggling *other* things. For those disgusting sods, it's a brick to the head and then a trip to the nearest deep hole to toss the body. There's crime because it's against the Law. And then there's *crime* because it's just plain wrong. Even smugglers have some standards."

Ashok had always seen things in black and white, but it seemed the rest of the world loved to wander about in the gray. "Yet, from Nod's description of these criminals, their dress, and their manner of speaking, the kidnappers and their victims came from every corner of Lok. Perversions would more easily be satisfied in places like the dark corners of Neeramphorn's pleasure district. Why bring children from the opposite side of the continent, as far away as Gujara or Uttara, all the way out here? It makes no sense." He turned back to the casteless. "How often would the barge master's associates bring these children to him?"

"Not too often, Fall. A few times a year, and never more than one at a time." The untouchable was called Nod. Apparently, just like in Vadal the non-people here were fond of simple descriptive names. "The barge master would stow them with the rest of the cargo, and whip us if we got caught lookin' at 'em."

He'd dealt with cults who believed there was power in human sacrifice, the more valuable the life, the better. Perhaps the Lost House believed in such superstitions as well? "You said they were children of whole men? Were they workers, warriors, or of the first?"

"It's hard to say, them not wearing their parent's badges, but they for sure weren't casteless!"

"How could you tell?" Gutch asked.

"They'd been eatin' good and weren't stunted and sick." Nod said that like it was painfully obvious. "You ever seen the state of casteless babies, worker? Only a dolt couldn't tell no difference."

"Dolt? Watch your tone with me, fish-eater," Gutch snapped.

Nod flinched, and immediately lowered his eyes, expecting to be struck. "Forgive me."

Every man had a place, and even outside the Law they seemed determined to find it. Gutch had no right to be here. Nod was at least fulfilling his assignment of poling this barge. Yet they were so certain of their roles that they all fell right back into them.

The moment struck Ashok as *incongruous.*

Within the Law, if a whole man took offense at any non-person, he could beat them for their insolence, and the only legal repercussion would be that he'd be required to pay their overseer for the value of any lost labor. If killed, then he'd be liable for the cost of a replacement and damages for the inconvenience caused...But here they were, violating other parts of the Law. Why were they all still compelled to spurn some things while clinging to others?

"Gutch, these casteless are here because I asked them to be.

They are the same status as I, and more Law abiding than you. Let him speak."

The big worker scowled, but was wise enough not to push the issue. "Sorry. It's being on all this water. Makes a man grumpy." The apology was directed at Ashok, not the untouchable. Because status aside, Ashok had killed a thousand men and Nod had not.

"Continue speaking," Ashok ordered.

Nod did so, looking a little bewildered that the legendary hero from the gods had just chastised a whole man on his behalf. "It's just that our youngsters are obvious. Skin and bones and sores. And these were scared of the barge master, but they'd get upset and show it, sometimes yell and kick and scream. Us casteless, even our little ones know better. We keep our heads down. Never know when a whole man will get mad for no reason." He gave Gutch a sideways glance as he said that.

"Is there anything else you can tell us?"

"Only the barge master got real eager when he had to make deliveries to his house made of gold. He'd whip us to pole faster everywhere the current gets slow. He hated Haradas. Made no secret of that. He wanted to live at the golden house. I think the ones who brought the stolen kids, they were the same. They called each other brothers. They'd talk a lot."

"About what?"

"Killin' mostly. Oh, they'd brag about the women they'd bed and the riches they'd stole, but mostly the killin' they done."

"Competitive bunch," Gutch muttered.

"Yeah. Like when me and Goat try to see who can push the barge harder. I always win."

"Your mother must be so proud."

"Silence, Gutch." Ashok wished Jagdish was here, but their risaldar was on the other barge. Jagdish had a mind for logistics and tactics. He would probably think of other important things to ask. "You said before that you've not seen the golden house, but you'd get close and then Chattarak would go the rest of the way on foot. How long did his journey take?"

"Depends. Fastest he went there and back was the same day. Usually he'd go for the night, and come back the next morning."

"Sadly his time means nothing to us. Chattarak could change into a snake. I assume when he was out of view he'd change, and who knows how fast a snake can slither through a swamp."

"We'd tie up and hope no demons came for us in the dark. It's real close to the sea." Nod shuddered. "*Real close.* The barge master would tell us not to stray from where he left us, 'cause demons probably wouldn't go there, but they wander all over the rest of the flooded forest."

"That's probably why they haven't been discovered. My former Order did not spend much time in this region. We seek out and destroy demons whenever they come on land, but when there are no people living there to report them, we have no reason to investigate."

"Oh, there's people who live in the flooded forest, Fall, and not just wizards. *Wild men.* We've seen them along the shore sometimes, wearin' furs and faces painted white like skulls, but the barge master said the wild men were afraid of him and his brothers, so they wouldn't raid us while he was away."

Ashok knew of a few groups like that who lived beyond the boundaries of civilization, heedless of the Law. Many years ago he had come across an isolated tribe living deep in the jungles of Gujara, in mud huts, probably descended from a lost settlement of whole men, but so forgotten by the Law and degenerate that their language had become gibberish. So he'd done as the Law required, and reported them to the Order of Census and Taxation. An expedition had rounded them up, declared them casteless, and shipped them off to various settlements around the peninsula to assimilate. Then their village had been put to the torch so they'd had nothing to flee back to.

That group had been relatively peaceful. The Gujaran warriors had only needed to make an example of a few of them before the rest had complied with the Law. Except he'd heard stories from Protectors about other tribes they'd encountered who were capable of great savagery. Since these wild men were surviving someplace demons freely roamed, Ashok had to assume they were dangerous.

"The barge master always said the wild men eat people and wear their skin, but I don't know if I believe him. He said the same thing about us non-people... But it's still a scary place. Least this time of year it's cold so all the alligators and poison snakes will be sleepy," Nod added helpfully.

"Lucky for us we've got a secret weapon for finding the Lost House." Gutch stuck himself in the chest with one beefy thumb. "I'm the best tracker in the business. That many wizards have got to be sitting on piles of magic. Get me close and I'll find the way. We'll be in and out of there in no time!"

Ashok was not so sure. These wizards struck him as clever. So many powerful users of magic successfully avoiding the Law like this suggested a great deal of intelligence and organization. He doubted it would be easy.

They drifted by day and camped on land at night. The caste-less knew of every spot along the way where it was safe to stop. Though Ashok was impatient, it was too dangerous to ride the river in the dark this time of year because of submerged rocks. When the snows melted in the mountains around Neeramphorn, then the river would become higher and faster, but now they would be asking for a late-night wreck and drowning.

To their north it was mostly forests of gnarly trees and low, rolling hills. To the south was an endless expanse of dead grass, the beginning of the great plain of Akershan. It was warmer here than in the mountains, but every morning they woke up with their blankets covered in frost. The air around Neeramphorn had been sharp enough to make their noses bleed, but here it was perpetually moist and foggy. Being on the evil river put the Sons in a bad mood, being perpetually damp and cold did not improve their spirits.

Unlike the well-traveled Martaban, there were no locks on the Nansakar. There were a few waterfalls along the river that required them to land, disassemble the barges, and reassemble them further downriver. Nod called it *portage*. He also said that usually Chattarak would nap during this process while the casteless did the work, until one year they'd been set upon by a pack of wolves and one of them had been devoured. Chattarak had laughed at their loss, but after that he had at least remained awake to be on guard.

The first waterfalls they crossed were obviously natural, but this one had once been part of a manmade structure. It was hard to tell since plants had grown all over it, but Ashok guessed that it had been a great dam. From the construction, it probably dated back to before the rain of demons, but like most things left over from the ancients, it had crumbled into rubble.

Ashok and Jagdish supervised the whole endeavor from a nearby hilltop, armed with bows in case the wolves or anything worse still lived nearby. When they had to take the barges apart, Ashok marveled at how quickly the warriors had joined in to help with the unfamiliar duty. Since they were all fitter and stronger than the casteless, they made quick work of moving the heavy logs, planks, and supplies.

"I did not know that warriors would so willingly lower themselves to tasks better suited for workers," Ashok told their risaldar.

"Sure, in town, with witnesses, you won't ever catch one of us getting our hands dirty. But out in the field there are no workers to carry our burdens for us. War's not all battles and duels like they sing songs about. It's making camps and building fortifications. A warrior can dig a trench as fast as any worker, especially when our lives depend on it...But don't let that get out. You'll ruin our glorious image."

That said, not all of their worker caste had gone south with Keta. For whatever reason, Jagdish had picked a few of them to go downriver too, including the miners who had been with them since Jharlang. There had been some bickering between the two castes. Then there were also men of several different houses, all proud, all with various grudges and history between them. There were tensions, but Jagdish had addressed those before the issue ever came to Ashok's attention...For the most part...

"I heard there was almost a knifing on your barge yesterday, Jagdish."

"It turns out the Somsak have led many raids into Kharsawan territory over the years."

"I did not know that."

"Neither did I, until Dilip tried to stab Abor over something his grandfather supposedly did. Something about the wasteful and dishonorable burning of a barn full of cows. I don't know. I got it sorted out though. It won't happen again."

Ashok didn't ask how. Jagdish was in charge of discipline. Which was good, since the majority of the discipline Ashok had handed out in his life had involved executions, so he lacked the patience for such things. "Good."

"I've not had to toss any of them over the side yet. I'll savor that small victory."

Ashok's heightened senses could hear no wildlife anywhere nearby bigger than a monkey, so he put down the bow and took a seat on a rock.

"I do not understand them," Ashok muttered as he watched the men work below.

"For you, that would be true of most people. I mean no offense."

"I seldom take offense at the truth. But the Sons in particular elude me. They've sacrificed their status to join us for something they can't know is real or not. They still fight over the honor of their houses, even when their very presence here brings dishonor to those houses. They all worship forbidden gods and are all equally criminals before the Law. You'd think that would be a greater bond than any petty family grudges."

"I don't know Ashok. To hear Dilip tell it, they were rather magnificent cows."

Ashok did not laugh often, but that made him chuckle. "You are right. I don't understand people. Their motives and decisions often baffle me. Like you, Jagdish."

Jagdish leaned against a tree and folded his arms. "What of me? I think I make my case rather clear."

"A man of integrity has thrown his lot in with criminals to achieve his goals. You vowed to avenge the men of Cold Stream. In a few days we should be at the gates of the Lost House. It will be death or victory. If victory, then what?"

"You've never struck me as the type to dwell on the future. But fine. If you must know, I'll take my revenge, collect some heads, then go home. Where I'll proudly reclaim my name, and get a new command, so I can raise my son as a proper warrior."

Jagdish possessed nobility that was rare among any caste. It saddened Ashok to think of that thrown away. "What will your house say when they find out you consorted with criminals to get this revenge? Or worse, that you served alongside me?"

"I suppose that'll depend on how much treasure I bring back. To justify working with the infamous Black Heart, those wizards had better be absurdly rich." Jagdish forced a grin onto his face. "Don't worry. I'll work it out."

"Hope is not a strategy."

"Hope's all I've got." Jagdish's smile died off. "Don't let my optimism deceive you. I'm no fool. I know what they'll say. But with my name ruined, no command would have me. It was spend the rest of my life being rented out as a lowly bodyguard for rich workers. Or worse, how long do you think I'd be willing to let my family go hungry before I swallowed my pride and ended up breaking knees to collect debts for some man like Bajwa? All while my son—who should be a warrior—was instead raised to be a baker, or a potter, or whatever mundane nonsense it is workers do."

"Your disgrace is my fault," Ashok muttered.

"Yes! Twice over. Which is why when fate gave me a chance to use you to get back what is mine, I took it! It was chase after you, or a safe dwindling into irrelevance. I chose boldness. I will not regret it."

"I may not understand most people, Jagdish, but I understand evil very well. Harta is Thakoor of Great House Vadal now, and his mother died because I exposed her crimes. He doesn't care about truth, only power. Harta lied to conceal my identity. He will blame me for the destruction of Vadal's ancestor blade, but I am currently beyond his reach. When he finds out that you were my ally..." Ashok paused. He didn't choose his words lightly. "That you are my *friend*...Then he will utterly destroy you."

"I'd be lying if I said that thinking about that hadn't caused me a few sleepless nights...I don't think I ever told you this, but after you escaped Cold Stream, when I caught Sikasso's wizards murdering my men, I was only there because I knew it was my last chance to challenge you to a duel for Angruvadal. I knew you were obligated to try your hardest, so I'd most certainly lose—"

"Without a doubt." Ashok wasn't being boastful, simply truthful.

"But regardless, what kind of man would I be if I didn't try?"

"A living one."

"It's the same reason when I found out Gutch could sniff out magic I went after you."

"I am glad it did not work out that way. It would have saddened me to kill you."

Jagdish nodded. "I appreciate that."

Ashok and Jagdish watched the men work in silence for a while. The workers had taken up a rhythmic song to make the carrying of the heavy logs easier. It turned out the casteless had a similar tune, and they'd joined in. The warriors tried too. It turned out they were truly awful at songs not related to marching or boasting, but they learned quickly. Their differences of house and status were temporarily forgotten, lost to the labor and distracted by aching muscles. It wasn't a belief in imaginary gods that united them, but rather heavy, water-logged lumber.

"To be frank, Jagdish, back when I thought the judges were going to execute me, my greatest fear was that Angruvadal would take offense and shatter because of such a dishonorable end. I hoped it would not, because I could think of two men who I thought might be worthy bearers. The first was Devedas, who was the son of a bearer, and the fiercest and bravest man I have ever known... The second was you."

Jagdish grew solemn, for there was great weight to Ashok's words. "Why me?"

"An instinct. Perhaps it was your conduct during Bidaya's duel, or your agreement to practice against me in prison. I don't know. The motives of swords are as inscrutable to me as the motives of men." Ashok still didn't understand why Angruvadal had picked him, a poor little casteless blood scrubber. Or why it had chosen to destroy itself in Jharlang, leaving him lost and alone. "It was just a hunch... Or perhaps, hope."

"You just said hope was no strategy."

"Then I suppose you are right. Sometimes hope is all you have. I believe with either of you, Angruvadal would have found worthiness."

Jagdish knew what an incredible honor that was. That was the highest compliment a bearer could ever give. "Thank you, Ashok."

The bearer of a great house's ancestor blade was automatically of the highest status, but more importantly to a warrior, being a bearer meant becoming a *legend*. Only Jagdish was not the sort of man to be consumed by melancholy, wondering about what might have been. Soldiers lived in the present.

"So if we come across any discarded ancestor blades lying around, you think I could take this Devedas fellow in a duel over it?"

"No." Ashok answered without hesitation. "You would die poorly. He is the only man alive I would not hesitate to call my equal in combat."

"I imagine he's humble like you too."

He shrugged. It was what it was. "Devedas was my brother and truest friend. He has also vowed should we ever meet again to kill me." Though he hated to admit it, Ashok was mourning more than just the loss of his sword. "Our kind do not make vows lightly."

"Sad," Jagdish agreed. "Come to think of it though, the other great houses still have their black-steel blades. That's what, at least eleven of them out there still. If one of those was to be in need of a bearer, you were found worthy once, couldn't you do it again? You could even challenge another bearer to a duel. If you won, even considering the true station of your birth, being chosen by not only one but two ancestor blades would be enough to convince anyone in the Capitol you were a whole and just man."

Ashok thought about that for a long time. Angruvadal hadn't merely been his sword, it had been the basis of his identity, his power, and his companion. Its absence had left nothing but pain and a sense of emptiness. Other bearers who'd lost their swords had been driven mad with grief. Like Devedas' father, who had leapt into the sea. Of course the idea of a being able to fill that void was tempting, but it was also wrong.

"It wouldn't convince me, for I am neither a whole man nor just."

"If that's what the Law declares, then maybe it's the Law that's wrong. Not you."

Ashok wasn't even offended, because Jagdish meant well. "I am what I am. My existence has already destroyed one black-steel blade. I would not deprive the world of another. They are more important than any one of us..." Yet, each of them could still be important in their own way, and not all of them needed to die humiliated. "Listen to me, rather than go back and be executed by Harta because of offenses I gave, you could try to earn a place in a different house. You'd have to start over, but surely some commander would appreciate your skills."

"Naw. I've shed too much blood and too many tears serving Vadal already. It's my home and my family. I was born to fight in the bronze and gray, and I'll die that way." Jagdish looked down at the stolen red uniform and shook his head sadly. "Hopefully... But come on, it isn't just other houses that need a decent officer. Who is going to keep your fanatics from knifing each other if I'm not around?"

"Of course, you will always be welcome among the Sons of the Black Sword. Your skills and your leadership are invaluable."

"Is that a request?"

"A request to a man of honor often results in him feeling some responsibility to help. I would not put you in such a position. You're not like me, condemned to this path. You're no fanatic like Keta or these men. I think they do what they want and then pretend it's because the gods told them to. As for you, there are no commands to hide behind, all you can do is what you think is right."

"What I think is right...Not what the Law demands?" Jagdish asked, incredulous. "You sure you haven't caught a fever?"

Ashok frowned. For once he hadn't thought of a decision in terms of the Law. *Strange.*

The last of the logs had been delivered to the bottom of the falls, and were in the process of being tied together. The casteless had done this so many times that it was a remarkably efficient process. Non-people were supposed to be stupid, but you wouldn't know that from watching them tie complicated knots. The first raft was nearly complete. It appeared they would be leaving soon.

"Assuming we don't get killed by the wizards, or eaten by demons on the way there, I'll have time to think about what to do after. We're a long way from home." They both knew Jagdish was on a dangerous course, but he was too proud to back down now. "If you'll excuse me, I'm going to rejoin the men and make sure all our supplies are accounted for."

"Very well. Carry on, Risaldar."

Jagdish gave him a casual salute, as if they were both in the army of Great House Vadal, and left to see to his responsibilities. Ashok might have struggled with understanding the motivations of most men, but there was no mistaking Jagdish's commitment to the ideals of his caste.

When the men saw him climbing down the hill, they greeted their risaldar warmly. He immediately began checking on each one of them, assessing their health and morale. Even though most of them had only known Jagdish for a few days, they already trusted him with their lives. They were wise to do so.

"It's too bad you perished while I lived, Angruvadal," Ashok muttered as he touched a hand to where the black-steel shard was embedded in his chest. "Because I really do think you two could have made a good team."

Chapter 30

"Most people don't realize it, but the land that belongs to the Capitol isn't limited to just the city itself. According to the Treaty of Annexation in the year 500, it includes all of Mount Metoro, the lesser peaks around it, and some of the surrounding desert for potential future expansion. Oh, and the aqueduct system which waters the Capitol falls under its jurisdiction as well, regardless of which great house border it may cross."

"Fascinating," Karno said.

"I know," Rada agreed.

"Not really. I was merely humoring you."

Karno was a terrible traveling companion.

Rada was tired and sore. She'd never been one for horseback riding. Her sister Daksha had taken lessons, but Rada had been too busy working at the library to engage in such frivolity. Usually when the first caste needed to travel it was by carriage, in shaded comfort. You climbed in, the workers or slaves took care of all the complicated parts, and then you got out when you arrived at your destination.

Only it turned out that horses required a great deal of maintenance. They didn't simply *go*. You had to feed them, water them, clean them—which was disgusting by the way—and even brush their hair to get all the sand and burs off which would worry into blisters beneath a saddle. Rada had never put that much effort into her own hair.

Karno expected her to do all this labor herself. He would demonstrate, but he never offered to help, though on the first day he had finally relented and fixed her saddle for her, because in his words "Cinched like that you're going to slide off the side and die." Luckily, unlike most women of her status, Rada understood the value of work. Which was why whatever section she was assigned to was always the most efficient and organized part of the library.

It was cold at night and warm during the day as they rode across the desert, avoiding the well-traveled paths. Sand got into everything. It was annoyingly soft to walk through, yet somehow still hard to sleep on. She had to keep an eye out for snakes and scorpions. Karno had warned her to always shake out her blankets before lying down, and to check her shoes before putting them on. She was a high-status daughter of the first caste. The first caste didn't normally have to *check their shoes for scorpions.* This was all new to her, and further proof that adventuring was for fools.

But she never complained. She listened to Karno's instructions and did her best to follow them. She'd let a wizard intimidate her into committing a terrible crime once, so as far as she was concerned, this was her penance.

"Well, Karno, even if you don't care, I do. Part of my obligation was reading old treaties and preparing reports for the judges about the current ramifications. It was lying about one of those assignments that got me into this miserable situation."

"I find the desert rather pleasant this time of year, myself."

They rode along in silence for a time, tired horses plodding along, trying to avoid the occasional prickly cactus that had grown along the path. Those nasty plants seemed to leap at you whenever the wind blew. Mount Metoro was to their right, red, brown, and bleak. It was so incredibly desolate here that it was hard to believe that the greatest city in the world was just on the other side.

This was such a harsh land that the Capitol shouldn't have existed at all. It had taken a multitude of expensive public works over the years to make the desert bloom. They didn't just have more fresh water than they needed, they had fountains, pools, and giant public baths to flaunt their excess. And since it was the furthest place in the world from hell, there was no stigma attached to this water. Like most Capitol residents, she'd taken such abundance for granted. It wasn't until you got out into the rest of the desert that you realized just how unnatural their situation really was.

She would've told Karno about some of the essays she'd read on that topic, about how it was an ostentatious show of wealth so when the representatives of the great houses came to visit, they would understand how powerful the Capitol was, but he'd probably just give her another noncommittal grunt.

Normally Rada didn't care for conversation or socializing. People made her uncomfortable. She much preferred the company of a book. Yet out in this terrible wilderness, with no way to read, and nothing to listen to but wind and hooves, she often found herself speaking aloud.

"You must think that I'm weak and soft, Karno. Well, maybe I am by Protector standards, but who isn't? You people tug of war with elephants for fun. I don't know how to fight, or ride, or live off the land. But I am very good at what I do. There's no one better in fact. I don't care what you think about the first caste, because I'm not like most of them. I didn't care about the parties or the dances. I didn't care about the nice clothing, or the concerts, or the banquets. I found the people who gravitated toward such activities to be vapid bags of noise, always talking just to hear their own voices."

"You don't say."

That made her laugh. "Point taken."

Karno actually seemed amused. "If it makes you feel better, I've guarded many members of the first over the years, and you whine far less than most. You've not yet annoyed me by breaking down in tears. You don't continually beg me to stop and rest, or bark at me like I'm a servant. Truthfully, you strike me as one of the least useless members of your caste that I've met."

Coming from Karno, that was quite the compliment.

"That does not count first-caste children who are obligated to the Protector Order, obviously. We toughen those up right quick...But I believe I understand what it is Devedas sees in you. Though, he's a fool to let feelings get in the way of his obligation."

Rada felt an instinctive need to defend her lover. "Devedas is a good man."

"I never said otherwise. Yet good men can be foolish. In fact, it is common. The best man I've ever known has turned into a criminal. The man who taught me to fight became a religious fanatic. And now my Lord Protector has fallen in love with a librarian."

Him putting it so . . . well, *bluntly*, made her blush. "Then what foolish thing are you guilty of, Blunt Karno?"

The Protector thought that over for so long that for a moment Rada thought he was purposefully ignoring her, but then he said, "Loyalty, I suppose." Karno pointed toward something in the distance. "There's the observatory."

Rada shielded her eyes from the sun and squinted, but she couldn't make it out yet. She needed glasses to read, but she'd always been able to see far away things just fine. "How can Protectors see so well?"

"Trade secret."

As they got closer, Rada was able to get a better view of the mysterious structure. It was simply a big rectangle with a single tower, exceedingly plain by Capitol standards. There was a small settlement around it, which Rada only knew by its odd reputation. It was said they allowed no lights after dark, not so much as a candle, so that the Astronomers could see better in the dark.

They continued onward. After a time, Rada went back to regaling Karno with the various facts she'd read. "The Astronomers are one of the smallest, and probably the most secretive Order in the Capitol. They're located here because they need to be shielded from the lights of the city to better look at the night sky, but still be close enough to report back to the judges when necessary. Otherwise, they're completely autonomous."

"I like looking at the stars. I could have been an Astronomer."

"It sounds terribly boring to me." Books were far more interesting than stars. You could learn things from books. Stars just sat there, twinkling. "Nobody really knows what the Astronomers do, and they only report to a few select judges, and never during an open session in the Chamber of Argument."

"The man we're looking for isn't part of that Order though. Why'd he build a home here?"

"I think Vikram just hates people." Rada could actually understand that. Karno even nodded at the sentiment. "He's a Historian. We Archivists deal with them often. We're supposed to cooperate, but that Order is a stuck-up bunch. We get the written materials, they get the artifacts, at least whatever the Inquisition decides isn't dangerous and in need of destruction. If someone discovers a carving, we claim it because it has words on it, but they'll get it because it's a rock... Can you believe that? You could say that we're political rivals. Sort of like you Protectors and those horrid Inquisitors. Only in our case everyone knows the library is superior to the museum."

"Clearly."

Compared to the vast stone structure of the observatory just a few miles away, the estate of Vikram Akershan was rather humble. It wasn't very big, and had been built right into the rocky mountainside. There was an outer wall made of clay bricks. Vikram may have been a high-status man, but his home had more in common with the goat farm Rada had recently fled than her father's nice estate.

The surrounding scrub brush had been cleared away to make room for vegetable gardens, some olive trees, and pens for livestock. There were servants tending the gardens. When they saw Rada and Karno approaching, they immediately stopped what they were doing and went inside the wall, not at a run, but at least a brisk walk. Once they were all in, a heavy wooden gate was swung closed behind them.

"They must not get many visitors out here," Rada explained. "I'll handle this. My father is a very respected man."

Karno just grunted.

There was a tarnished copper symbol of the Historians Order mounted on the wall. When they reached the gate, Rada raised her voice so that she could be heard on the other side. "Hello. We wish to speak with Senior Historian Vikram Akershan."

A woman on the other side shouted back. "There's no one here by that name. We've got no time for beggars."

"Beggars! How dare you? We are both of the First!"

"You don't look it! Go away. You're trespassing."

"I can't be trespassing. This land belongs to the Capitol. I know this is Vikram's estate. I've been here before. I'm Senior Archivist Radamantha, daughter of Durmad Nems dar Harban, Lord Archivist of the Capitol Library."

The woman on the other side of the gate actually booed

when she mentioned the library. "This is a Historian's holding. We don't want your kind here, librarian snob!"

"How rude!"

Karno seemed amused by the exchange. "May I?"

"Certainly." She fully expected Karno to take his fearsome hammer and smash the door into kindling, and frankly, at that moment Rada would have approved of such violence.

But instead, Karno spoke politely. "Please convey to your master that there is a Protector here as well. I wish to warn him that the Inquisition is offering a secret bounty for his capture. He can either speak with me now to clear this up, or he can wait for them to put a sack over his head and drag him to the dome for torture. I care not either way."

"What? There's got to be some mistake." The woman seemed really surprised at the mention of the more dangerous Orders. "Just a moment."

"Take your time," Karno said to her, before muttering to himself. "They're only Inquisitors."

A minute later a head appeared over the top of the wall. He was at least Rada's father's age, but with sharp hawklike features, skin that had been burned by the sun and wind, and long hair that had turned stark white. He looked at them rather suspiciously. "You say you're a Protector. I see no shining silver armor."

Karno nodded toward their pack horse. "In those bags. It chafes on long rides. But I have this." He reached into his shirt and pulled out a medallion bearing the face of the Law. Karno held it up to sparkle in the sun.

He squinted at it. "That could be fake."

"A forgery is possible, because criminals are stupid. However the penalty for impersonating a Protector is death." Karno shrugged. "Do I seem concerned to you?"

"You should leap over the wall and show it to him up close," Rada suggested.

The old man turned his attention toward her. "Wait... Salt water. Can it be? Rada? Is that you?"

"It is." She waved. "Hello, Master Vikram. It's been a long time."

"Ten years I think! Luckily you grew up to look like your lovely mother instead of your potbellied hunchback of a father. You, down there, open the gate. Come inside, and please forgive my wife's earlier rudeness."

"There's no offense taken." To be fair Rada couldn't blame them. If she had her own fort, she'd stock it full of books, and then probably never go outside again.

Vikram's slaves had warmed a bath for her. It was wonderful to be clean of travel dust and horse stink for the first time in days. A clean house robe had been left out for her. A Historian's symbol had been embroidered on the arm, but it was so clean and comfortable that she pretended not to notice that little indignity. While she had bathed, lunch had been prepared, and once she was dressed she had been invited to join them in the dining room.

It was a comfortable home, with large windows to let air flow. Gauzy curtains moved in the breeze. After a brief apology—the lady of the house obviously still held some lingering animosity toward the library—they ate. She must have wanted to make up for her earlier discourteous behavior, because the food was wonderful. Either that, or Rada's standards had slipped after weeks of unseasoned goat meat and handfuls of nuts eaten from a saddlebag. While she waited for the master of the house and Karno to arrive, Rada made polite and inane conversation with Vikram's family. He had two sons and a daughter, all far younger than she was, and all they wanted to know about was what was new and exciting in the Capitol. It was only on the other side of the mountain, but might as well have been on the other side of Lok for how little they seemed to know about it.

"Is your strong man really a Protector?" asked the youngest boy, who was probably only five or six. "I want to be obligated to the Protectors when I am older! How many people have you seen him kill?"

"Pranesh!" shrieked his mother.

Distracted, Rada answered their questions as best she could. "I've only seen him kill a couple, but each was very dramatic."

Again, Vikram's wife tried her best to apologize. "I still feel bad about my earlier outburst, but my family has long been Historians, and in the distant past they had some bad dealings with librarians. It was an instinctive reaction."

"Such things happen." Rada tried to dismiss it. She knew that everything in the Capitol was about politics. She'd always tried to avoid such things, but she'd been dragged into the worst of it anyway.

"Unfortunately for us, this is a first-caste grudge. When the lesser castes have a grudge they find a way to settle it. Warriors duel. They even make a big ceremony of the whole thing. Workers, being simple creatures, just brawl in the streets until they get the aggression out of their system."

"What do the casteless do, Mother?" one of the children asked.

"How should I know? Eat fish and breed like rabbits I assume. Regardless, the lower castes settle their grudges quickly and efficiently so they can go back to their duties. But not us. Oh no. The first caste never forgets a wrong. We savor our grudges. We pass them down to our children and grandchildren like family heirlooms. We walk around in a state of perpetual offense knowing that the great grandson of someone who once wronged our great grandfather is out there right now, not suffering for it, and that thought is simply unbearable."

Rada tried to say something polite. "I'd hope that those of our status could learn to set aside our differences so as to work together for the good of all the people."

"A noble sentiment, Senior Archivist. I hope such idealism works out for you."

As befitted his nickname, Karno had skipped the bath and spent the time speaking with Vikram about the bounty instead. When the two of them arrived in the dining room, the Historian seemed very grim.

"Everyone, please, leave us. I must speak with both our guests privately."

The children obediently complied without argument, which Rada actually found rather impressive. His wife briefly stopped by his side. He whispered something in her ear. She touched his hand gently, nodded in understanding, and then she left without another word.

Vikram sat on the cushions across from Rada. "Your friend has brought dire news. I'm very sorry to hear about your current situation."

Karno flopped down and began serving himself a plate of food. "What you do with this information is up to you, Historian. Normally, it's no business of the Protectors who the Inquisition wants to interrogate."

"I assure you, I'm no criminal."

"If I thought you were, I'd have dealt with you myself. Rada is no criminal either. They want her because she is a witness to a crime. Which makes me suspect you may have similar knowledge." Karno ripped the leg off a chicken. "You may explain while I eat."

Vikram put his palms together and gave the Protector a polite little bow, a gesture of acknowledgement and respect in Aker-shan. She couldn't help notice as he did that his hands were like scarred up pieces of leather. He seemed like a hardened desert creature, more warrior than scholar.

"I've already told you, I know of no conspiracies. My wife visits family there occasionally, but I've not been to the Capitol in years. I associate with no judges or arbiters. Most of my Order has forgotten about me. My work is here."

"What is your work?" Rada asked.

"I'm a caretaker of sorts. Beyond that, I cannot say. The nature of my assignment is secret."

Considering his rough appearance, Karno had remarkably decent table manners. For some reason she'd assumed he'd just toss the stripped bones on the floor with a loud belch, and hope Vikram had a dog. Instead he finished chewing and even wiped his mouth with a napkin before saying, "I promise that you'll tell the Inquisitors once they chain you to the dome. Secrets never last long up there."

"You'd be incorrect. There is a special section within my Order which takes our oath every bit as seriously as you do, Protector. I'd not reveal my obligation under torture any more than one of you would tell them about the Heart of the Mountain."

Karno's eyes widened. "Do not speak of that."

"Apologies." Vikram had the smile of a wise, old fox.

Rada had never seen the Protector shaken before. The idea that Karno could even be shaken at all was frightening to her. "What's the Heart of the Mountain?"

"A myth," Karno answered too quickly. Before he had been looking at Vikram dismissively, but his attitude had changed, and now he regarded the Historian warily. "The Heart is just a myth."

"There are many such myths in Lok. You'll forgive me. I've spent too much time in the hot sun and am easily befuddled. It can be hard to sort the truth from the legends at times. Like the one which got young Rada here in trouble, about who the casteless really are."

"You know about that?" Rada asked, surprised. "You read my report?"

"No. But I know which books you would've consulted to pre-pare it. Who can really say what is true? Did a powerful warrior really ride a ship made of black steel and fire out of the sky, to forge ancestor blades and teach magic to the people, so that they could drive the demons into the sea?"

"You are the Historian," Karno said. "Why don't you tell us?"

"The problem with history is that it is written by the victors. The Sons of Ramrowan *lost*. Our ancestors won. That's why officially all those old stories are considered propaganda left over from the Age of Kings. Yet every myth has some element of truth. In this case, what is true? Are the casteless really the descendants of the kings and their priests, and if so, are they truly the only ones who can save us all when the demons invade the land again?"

"That sounds dangerously close to illegal religion, but I do not grasp the significance of this."

"I believe Rada does, which is why they're so interested in her. Why don't you explain to the Protector, Rada?"

She was deeply ashamed. "I told Devedas this already. We know very little for sure about the time before the demons fell to the world, and much of it is clouded with religious silliness, but when the demons came, they destroyed nearly *everything*. There are other continents besides Lok, but we lost contact with them. Mankind was being hunted to extinction, until something stopped them."

"His name was Ramrowan," the Historian added. "The fanatics say the gods felt guilty because it was their war that had cast the demons out of heaven. They felt pity for us and sent their great-est warrior to save us." Vikram spread his hands apologetically as Karno glowered at him. "I am merely sharing the legends. I make no comment upon their validity."

"It's all right, Karno. If you want to understand this conspiracy, then you should probably know what they're trying to eradicate. Whatever the truth about this Ramrowan, all the histories agree that he was a powerful wizard, who united the survivors against the demons, and was afterward crowned the first king."

"We rarely speak of the Age of Kings," Karno said. "Mostly what we learn is so that we can more effectively root out the fanatics who still believe in those old gods. All I know is that it was a dark time."

"Not at first, Protector. On the contrary, Ramrowan had a reputation as a wise and just king. However, over time his descendants grew in power and pride, until they became utter tyrants. Any system will become corrupt once it gains power unchecked."

Karno didn't seem to like that. It was *almost* like Vikram was talking about the Law.

Vikram chuckled. "The problem was, with everyone believing that the demons were going to return to the land someday, and *only* the descendants of the first king could defeat them, then they'd better make sure they never run out of descendants. The Sons of Ramrowan each took a hundred wives, as did their sons, so on and so forth for generations. The people gave them everything they wanted, riches and power beyond imagining. They built a religion based around the necessity of their continuing lineage, and sent forth priests to ensure obedience. Their numbers became bloated, and their greed immense. It only took about three hundred years for the castes they created to serve them to decide the kings were such tyrants they'd been better off with the demons."

Rada stopped Vikram. "The important thing is, after the people rose up and deposed the kings, most wanted to slaughter them for their crimes, but a few were worried that the old stories were true, and if that bloodline was wiped out, if the demons came back we'd be helpless. So there was a great gathering of the wise men from the different houses, and they debated."

"The very first meeting of the judges," Vikram said. "Ah, you've read Ingragda's *First Volume of Historical Proceedings*. A brilliant work."

"Agreed. He had a most eloquent use of language—" Karno scowled at her, so Rada got back to the lesson. "A compromise was reached, their lives would be spared, but in exchange they'd be deprived of all their rights, and their descendants would be made to always suffer for their crimes, without dignity or caste. The princes and priests became the first non-people."

"I've been fighting for the Law my whole life, but I've never heard this."

"It's not just part of the Law, Karno. It was the very first part," Rada said.

"The Law started because of the casteless?" The Protector shook his bushy head and went back to his lunch. "That sounds absurd."

"Since they'd already gathered in what would become the

Capitol, they discussed how to rebuild and how best to prevent the injustice which had happened before," Vikram explained. "Each great house sent their wisest men to judge these new laws. A man could only have one wife. Since religion had become a tool of oppression, it was banned entirely. That took some doing, they couldn't just slap some plaster over every old mural, so they created what would become the Inquisition to systematically destroy it all. Except for a few select keepers of information—which would become our respective Orders—the old ways were to be purged, the gods forgotten. Groups were formed to see to these various necessary duties. The ruling families of each house and these new central diplomats became the new first caste. Three and a half centuries after Ramrowan was crowned, the Age of Kings had ended, and a new age, an age of reason and Law had begun."

"This coincides with what I learned," Rada said.

"Good." Vikram leaned back on his cushions, looking smug. "My wife wouldn't listen to me, but I assured her that not everyone at the library was a complete fool."

"I was foolish enough to lie to the judges! I didn't tell them about this, and now they're going to exterminate all the casteless because of me."

"Don't be dramatic, Rada. It's been 817 years since the creation of the Law. It's been a long time since anyone has been allowed to talk about our past at all, and this particular part has been severely limited even among those of us obligated to remember it. That's made it easy for them to slowly grind away the truth. If the judges had picked my Order to prepare the report instead of yours, I'm sure it would have been every bit as flawed."

"Still—"

"If you'd been braver, they would've just silenced you in a more permanent manner." Vikram seemed remarkably pragmatic about the whole thing. "Knowing your father, I bet he picked someone other than you to prepare this report. There is no way he would've put his own daughter in danger."

"How did you know that?" Was he trying to say her father was in on it? She looked toward Karno, because the Protectors had no patience for anyone breaking the Law, but he didn't seem to care. "My father is guilty of no crime!"

"I didn't insinuate he was. The Durmad I knew was a decent

and honorable man. However, in politics, decency and honor can get you in trouble."

Karno had finished his chicken, and leaned forward. "You said *them* and *they*. Who has been wiping out this information?"

"Sadly, I cannot give you an answer I do not have. Nor do I know why the Inquisition would be interested in a humble caretaker such as myself. Why does this bother you, Protector?"

"I've been tasked with protecting a witness. I've found the best way to do that is to kill everyone who would endanger them. It's a rather straightforward method, but it works."

"I cannot help you in your investigation, Protector. However in the meantime, since you need a place to keep your witness, both of you may remain here as long as you wish. Very few in the Capitol know where I live. We are self-sufficient, and other than trading the occasional basket of eggs with the Astronomers, have little contact with the outside world. We would be grateful for the company."

Karno put his hands together and made the same Akershani gesture of respect that Vikram had given him earlier. "Thank you, Historian. We will take advantage of your hospitality for a few days."

Vikram returned the gesture, and then stood up. Even though he was about the same age as her father, there was no groaning or popping knees. Harsh living conditions must keep one fit. "My home is your home. Now if you will excuse me, I have some business to attend to."

"Of course."

"It was a pleasure, Rada. I will enjoy having someone to talk about history with." Then Vikram left the room.

Rada waited until she was sure he was long gone before whispering, "I like him, but he's lying about something."

"I know." Karno had already helped himself to more food. "We're staying anyway."

She couldn't believe her ears. "The Inquisition is looking for him. Why stay here?"

Karno shrugged. "I'm curious to see who comes to kill him."

Chapter 31

The wizards of the Lost House seemed to be a solitary, unfriendly
bunch. In just her short time here, Thera had already seen how
they constantly plotted against each other. They made the rumor-
mongering, backstabbing, high-status ladies of Great House Makao
look like decent, honest, honorable folk. It was no wonder they
seldom gathered together for a feast, which made tonight a special occasion.

Her invitation had been more of an order. During their daily
training, Master Omkar had told her that she was expected to
attend or else. Sikasso had declared there would be a banquet in
the great hall, because he had something special to announce.

When she'd returned to her quarters, she'd found that the
slaves had left a dress hanging for her. It wasn't as ridiculous
and ostentatious as the silly outfits she'd been expected to wear
in her former husband's court, but it was also far less modest.
Thera didn't mind showing some skin, but it limited the places
where she could hide weapons. And she'd accumulated several
over the last few days, everything from a kitchen knife to a big,
rusty iron nail that could spike a skull. For the feast she'd have
to make do with wrapping the first shiv she'd fashioned in silk
and tying it around her waist beneath the dress.

Even though Sikasso had somehow been able to tell, Thera

always went armed if she could help it. Not that stabbing a wizard would get her anywhere, but it was the principle of the thing.

The great hall was a magnificent structure, with walls of intricately carved wood. A fire roared in a hearth surrounded by gleaming bronze plates, each engraved with the image of a wild animal. It was hard to believe that this place had once been partially ruined. She'd asked Omkar how they'd managed to get skilled artisans all the way out here, and he'd explained they'd simply kidnapped whoever they needed. The assassin had not shown the slightest bit of remorse about it. She hadn't asked what happened to those workers once the assassins no longer had need of their services.

She was glad for the big fire. The Lost House was always chilly, and her dress had no sleeves.

Every few feet a statue had been placed along the walls, but since they'd been collected from all over Lok, they were wildly divergent in style and size. The wizards flaunted the Law, so many of the statues were of the old gods. Though as far as she could tell, the wizards didn't venerate them, they just liked the images because they were illegal and expensive.

Several wizards had already arrived, all dressed in fine robes, and a few with colorful turbans. Some were young, some were old, fat, thin, short, tall, and everything in between. She only recognized a few faces, yet they were all dour. Nobody greeted her, or even acknowledged her at all. They either saw her as a threat or an unremarkable oddity. They noted her entrance, and then went back to their hushed conversations.

A silent slave caught Thera at the entrance and gestured for her to follow. As usual the slaves never talked or so much as made eye contact. The chair that was pulled out for her was practically a cushioned throne. There were thirty of those chairs around a long rectangular table. Golden goblets filled with wine were set in front of each seat, whether it was occupied or not. In the center of the table had been burned the same house symbol as hung from the banners on the wall. Slowly, most of the chairs filled.

As more wizards arrived, for the first time Thera saw a woman who wasn't a slave, but she was just as aloof and cold as the rest of the murdering bastards. They were eventually joined by two more women. Thera was unsure why there were so many more male assassins than female. From personal experience she knew that a woman could commit a sudden and unexpected murder just as well as any man. Successful murdering wasn't about physical strength, but rather commitment. Even the strongest warriors went right down when they never saw the knife coming. Perhaps men were just more likely to be born with the ability to use magic? Or maybe it was just the nature of the Lost House?

She would have to ask Kabir the next time he visited. Except after making their deal, he'd practically disappeared. Either he was regretting their arrangement, or he'd backed off because Sikasso was suspicious. Neither possibility was comforting.

Eventually Omkar was seated to her left. Kabir directly across from her. Even her teacher and her fellow plotter didn't acknowledge her existence. It was petty, but that insult bothered her more than the overt threats.

There were several empty chairs, probably belonging to assassins who were off doing something nefarious, or maybe they were empty because Ashok had killed their owners. She fervently hoped that Ashok would continue to free up seating around this particular table.

The most ornate chair was at the head, surely meant for Sikasso. It remained empty as the slaves silently brought in their first course. She had to admit that the wizards ate well, though from the amount of spice they applied most of it wasn't very fresh. Which made sense, there couldn't be very much in the way of farming out here. From the windows she'd seen slaves tending gardens and animals, but there wasn't that much space on the hilltop. Much of their food was delivered somehow. She'd given that some thought, because if things came in, then that meant there was a way for people to sneak out.

As usual, Thera paid careful attention to her surroundings, in the hopes of learning something that could prove useful. The conversations struck her as spiteful and competitive. They told stories about their assassinations. Laughing about how they'd pushed a victim out a window, or drowned one in their bath. It left a bad taste in her mouth, and not because of the killing. She'd grown up around warriors. A good killing was normal dinner conversation to her.

A warrior-caste feast would be filled with men bragging about their raids and battles, but long ago Thera's father had taught her a valuable lesson about such things. He'd taught her to be silent and watch. The more confident a warrior was, the less he felt the need to brag about what he'd done. His name would brag for him. When accomplished warriors talked about their business with each other, it tended to be matter of fact. And at a feast like this a truly great warrior didn't need to talk about his wars, but rather he talked about what he'd gone to war for.

There was none of that here. The assassins were all about self-aggrandizement. Kabir had told her about their desire to right the wrongs of the past, but their conversations never touched on anything so lofty. They talked constantly of killing, but not once did they talk about what they were killing for. It was a contest of cruelty. Their pride struck her as obnoxious. They were simply a more dangerous version of the bickering court ladies of Great House Makao.

It actually made her miss the company of Keta and the worshippers of the Forgotten. They were a wishful-thinking, but straightforward bunch. Her disdain for the wizards was thick enough she would have gladly traded the lot of them for the company of grumpy Ashok. Now he was a right murderous bastard, but also quite possibly the most honest man she'd ever known.

As the dinner went on, and more courses were served, she noticed an increasing number of glances toward the still empty seat at the head of the table. Sikasso's absence was causing unease among some, and joy among others.

The third course was the breast of some game bird, and it was delivered along with a decent knife to cut it. Thera would've stolen the knife if she thought she could have gotten away with it, but she kept feeling eyes on her. As much as the strangers pretended not to care, many of them were watching her.

Eventually, one of them actually spoke to her. "So does Sikasso's project talk?" He was thin, with a pockmarked face. "Or does she just sullenly peck at her food, while judging us with narrowed eyes."

Everyone was looking at her then. A few of the wizards seemed openly amused at her discomfort. Her powerlessness annoyed her.

"I talk. This conversation's just not to my liking."

"Why, girl? Do you not have the stomach for our business?" He laughed. Several of the others laughed at her too.

It shouldn't have gotten to her. Years of living as a criminal had taught her how to keep her head down. There was nothing to gain by provoking these murderers. Except for good or ill, Thera still had the fiery temper that came from having the blood of House Vane in her.

"I had stomach enough to put one of your kind in the dirt."

The pockmarked one had been taking a drink and nearly choked on his wine at her reply. That caused a few other wizards to laugh, but a couple obviously became angry. Across the table, Kabir tried to catch her eye, very subtly shaking his head in the negative, as if to warn her that she was playing a dangerous game.

"A tragic misunderstanding," Kabir said, explaining away the throat slashing of his best friend. "Our brothers who perished during those events will be greatly missed."

Thera glared back at Kabir, then cut a big chunk of bird, jabbed it with her knife, and stuck it in her mouth. To hell with these wizards.

"Speaking of what happened in Jharlang, I've not seen our host yet. He called us all here, but hasn't arrived himself," stated an older wizard with a red turban. He paused to take a sip of his wine, before wryly asking, "I wonder, has Master Sikasso not yet recovered from his terrible injury?"

"Meaning, you wonder if Sikasso is weak," said one of the women.

"I'm just thinking aloud. If he's too ill to attend his own banquet, then maybe he's not in any condition to manage the affairs of this house. It would be so very unfortunate if in addition to killing so many of our brothers, and not even getting a sword's worth of black steel as promised, that Ashok Vadal also cost us the illustrious leadership of noble Sikasso." He let that hang there.

"Truly, most unfortunate," Kabir replied without emotion.

That exchange caused the topic of the conversations to shift. The wizards all went back to their discussions, but now it was whispering about their leader, and some dancing around the idea of who among them would replace him. Thera had been wishing for something better than murder, but instead she got politicking. She'd have preferred the murder talk.

Surprisingly, Kabir didn't join in on any of those snide discussions. He may have been planning to overthrow his leader, but he was wise enough not to show his intentions beforehand. Thera still didn't trust him to keep his word to help her. He'd not taught her a thing yet about the secret laws of the Lost

House as promised. When she'd seen him since their deal he'd given her some excuses about how he couldn't meet during the brief times she wasn't being observed, because his absence would have been noticed.

"So, Thera, is it?" The wizard with the marked-up face addressed her again. "How goes your training? Have you unlocked that great and unknown magic that Sikasso swears is hidden inside your head yet?"

Omkar answered before she could. "We make steady progress."

"Of course you'd say that, old man. Your reputation depends on it. My question was aimed at the slave."

Thera's initial thought was to leap across the table and plunge her dinner knife into his heart. "I'm no slave."

"Semantics. If you reside within the House of Assassins you're either our property, or you've passed the trial to earn your status as one of us."

Kabir was sitting next to that wizard. "There is no need to provoke her, Hemendra. She is Sikasso's guest. Be careful you don't inadvertently give offense to him."

Hemendra smiled. He knew perfectly well that he was giving offense, but the man he was offending wasn't here to defend himself. That was when Thera realized that everyone was paying attention again. All of the other conversations had died off because this exchange was far more interesting.

"From your expression, you don't know of what trial I speak," Hemendra said to her, but then he shifted a bit so that he was addressing the group. "If Sikasso thought she was capable of passing the trial, he would have told her about it. Isn't that right, Omkar?"

Her supposed teacher clenched his teeth and said nothing. She knew enough about courtly politics to tell that Hemendra was using her presence as a way to attack their absent master. She had to tread carefully.

"What is this trial?"

The wizard had a cruel laugh. "You poor fool. How hopeless you must be for them to handle you with such kid gloves. We all had to pass the trial to earn our seat at this table. You merely manifest some odd abilities and just like that Sikasso thinks he can subvert our traditions? I think maybe the fallen Protector took more than just his arm."

There were some murmurs at that. Hemendra had just crossed one of their lines. Thera might not have understood their ways, but she recognized open rebellion when she saw it.

"The toxic fumes from your never-ending alchemical experiments have rotted your brain," Omkar said. "Master Sikasso would take issue with your accusations."

"My alchemical experiments have given us useful weapons and poisons. Meanwhile, Sikasso has been busy for selfish reasons, locked away in his study trying to regrow a limb—a pattern which has been lost for ages—while our deals lapse and our business suffers. Messages arrive from the Grand Inquisitor, asking about the status of the Black Heart, and what atrocities we plan to commit in his name, but Sikasso does not answer."

"Perhaps if the master wasn't so worried about usurpers pouncing on his temporary weakness, he would have more time for business," Omkar snapped.

"And I say if he's got no time to see to our business, then he should be replaced with a man who does." Hemendra banged one fist on the table.

The room was quiet except for the crackling fire. The wizards looked angry enough to fight, though Thera had no idea who was loyal to who. Regardless, if they started flinging magic at each other, she was going to use that opportunity to run for her life, swamp demons be damned.

Out of nowhere, a hand appeared resting on Hemendra's shoulder. The wizard flinched. There was a blur of shadows that hurt Thera's eyes as a man dressed in voluminous black robes appeared, and then the rest of Sikasso was standing directly behind Hemendra's chair.

"My apologies for my lateness." Sikasso's voice was cold enough to match his pale visage. His eyes seemed to glow as an aftereffect of the magic he'd used to appear so suddenly. "It seems you have begun discussing business without me."

The wizards were all surprised. It took quite a lot of skill to sneak up on an assassin, and from their expressions none of them had sensed Sikasso drawing near. Hemendra had sounded confident just a moment before, but now there was a bit of a tremor in his voice. He looked back over his shoulder. "We were just talking—"

"I understand." Sikasso patted his shoulder gently. "Why do

you tremble, Hemendra? Unlike you, I would not stab a brother in the back. Besides, how could I? I only have the one hand now, and it rests upon you as a symbol of friendship."

"Yes, yes. Of course—"

Another hand appeared from under Sikasso's robe, this one gloved and holding a loop of silver cord. In a flash Sikasso dropped the narrow rope over Hemendra's head. The other wizard reacted instinctively, grabbing at the garrote, but Sikasso pulled it tight with *both* hands.

"Oh, look at that."

Hemendra thrashed about as his pocked face changed colors. There were pouches containing bone or black steel on his sash, but he couldn't reach for them with his fingers trapped beneath the rope, yet they were the only things stopping Sikasso from strangling him immediately.

None of the others dared move. The ones who had been laughing along with Hemendra didn't rise to help him. Loyalty was an alien concept in this hall.

The master assassin's jaw clenched as he drew the rope tighter. "My other hand was hidden, like you hid that Fortress powder you've been brewing to kill me with." Hemendra kept trying to stand, but each time he was forced back into his seat. Sikasso was far stronger than he looked. "Shhhhh. Yes, I learned of your plots against me, old friend. I respect your initiative. I never expected one of you would try to do me in with something so clumsy as a bomb. Since you made such a vast quantity, it probably would have worked. However, I must bring your plot to an end, because right now unity is necessary for the good of our house."

Sikasso looked around the table, and spoke with a polite calm, as if he wasn't in the process of choking a man to death. "I noticed my guest had asked a question. *What trial?* Her question was rudely ignored, so I shall answer for all of us. Our secret agreement with the Inquisition which allows our survival requires that we limit our numbers, and self-preservation behooves us to honor this arrangement. When one of us dies—as is about to happen shortly—we must replace our number, yet our gift is rare, and not often passed down by blood."

Hemendra was trying to pull one hand free so he could reach for a weapon, but to no avail. He was making terrible, ragged, grunting noises and snot was bubbling from his nostrils all over his mustache. Sikasso was growing red faced from the strain of holding him down. The struggling wizard began to kick the bottom of the table, violently shaking everyone's plates and goblets. Kabir reached out and caught his wine before it could spill.

"We are spread across all of Lok. When one of us spots a child who has the gift, if their ability has not yet been recognized by their house, and they're not of high-enough status to be *too* missed, we take them, and bring them here to be trained."

Even distracted by the murder being slowly committed right in front of her, that revelation was so damned dishonorable Thera couldn't help but blurt out, "You steal babies from their mothers?"

"Hardly babies, Thera. That would be a logistical nightmare. Besides, the gift isn't easy to spot until they're old enough to understand patterns. We bring them here and train them in our ways. Most end up lacking the talent necessary. Those we scrub their minds—a process similar to what Kule of Vadal did to your friend Ashok, only without the painstaking rebuilding that wizard went through to turn that monster into the walking avatar of the Law—and they serve out their days as our slaves."

Thera glanced over at the nearest slave—the familiar one-eyed man—who was standing there holding a serving tray, seemingly oblivious to what was going on around him. This whole time she'd thought they were simply afraid to speak to her, not incapable of it. She'd underestimated the wizards' capacity for evil.

"How could you do that to them? That's terrible!"

"It is also an excellent motivator for the rest of us to study hard. For the select few with the talent and the hunger, once there is a vacancy in our ranks, we undertake the trial. Most perish. Those who pass earn our place in the House of Assassins."

With a shock, Thera looked around at the assembled wizards and realized what that meant. "You were all stolen children! You weren't born into this caste! This isn't your house!"

Eyes rolled back into his head, Hemendra had finally stopped kicking and gone limp. Blood was running down his beard from where he'd nearly bitten off his tongue. Sikasso kept up the pressure just in case.

"What does it matter where a man was born? That's one thing we have in agreement with your rebellion. Assassins are not born. We are *made*." Sikasso was no longer directing his words at Thera, but to the group at large. "Look around you. Omkar's father was a disgraced and drunken arbiter. Kabir and his brother were stolen from their pathetic dirt-farmer parents during a harsh winter when they would've starved to death anyway."

A dark look crossed Kabir's face as Sikasso said that, but he managed to hide it well. She didn't know if it was because of his worker roots, or... had the wizard she'd killed in Jharlang actually been his *blood brother*? No wonder he hated her.

"Our origins do not matter. This is our house, because it took us, claimed us, and molded us in its image. We were chosen. We were made powerful. It taught us to fight and thrive. All life is competition and only the strong survive. We were taught the dreams of those who came before and we swore a solemn oath to see them achieved. We do what we must. That is our way... But some of us forget our promises, and put our petty desires before the good of our house." Sikasso let go of the cord and stepped away from the chair. "It is good to be reminded."

Hemendra's head limply flopped forward and landed on his plate with a *bang*.

"I learned of his plans against me and I saw his cache of fortress powder. Impressive, to say the least. I shall not name his allies, but to you, be aware that as far as I am concerned Hemendra's conspiracy dies with him. All is forgiven and you remain my brothers. Let us stand united to bring about the goals of the Lost House." Sikasso made a big show of dusting his *hands* off.

"Master! Your arm is healed!" Omkar exclaimed. From his worshipful tone, Thera could understand why Kabir referred to the old man as Sikasso's dog. "That pattern was lost. What an incredible discovery."

"Partially." He held up the black glove and made a fist, so hard that they could all hear the leather creak. "I have reconstructed the old pattern enough to create a missing limb from the elements, but it is a work in progress and unpleasant to look upon. Once I've mastered the process I will share it with the rest of you. In the meantime Hemendra was a fool to insinuate that I would neglect my duties because of something so inconsequential as personal discomfort. To whoever doubted my commitment, let it be known that I never wavered."

"I tried to warn him that he was giving offense," Kabir said as he raised his goblet. "I would propose a toast, to the renewed strength of our visionary leader."

The rest of the wizards picked up their drinks, except for those who'd had theirs knocked over by Hemendra's kicking, but the slaves were already pouring replacements.

Sikasso was watching Kabir, expression unreadable. Thera assumed if he'd known the younger wizard was plotting against him as well, Kabir would be dead too. "Very well."

"To Sikasso. May he lead us to our glorious revenge," Kabir finished, and everyone raised their cup. Including Thera, because her mind was still reeling that she was surrounded by men grown from stolen children who were gleefully carrying out the plans of those who had stolen them, and she didn't particularly want to give offense and get strangled.

Their once again unquestioned leader took his seat at the head of the table. As he did so, more slaves came in and carried Hemendra's corpse from the room before the smell of his loosened bowels could upset anyone's appetite. Sikasso waited until they were gone before continuing. "Thank you for your loyal support. Now we must discuss why I have gathered you here."

Thera caught a few perplexed looks at that announcement, as if showing off a regrown arm—a feat no other wizard had accomplished in hundreds of years—and publicly executing a competitor to establish dominance weren't good enough reasons to throw a banquet.

"First, the Grand Inquisitor has sent several messages asking about our progress in observing and facilitating the rebellion of Ashok Vadal. He has heard rumor of the loss of Angruvadal and promised us an equal amount of black steel in compensation."

Thera dreaded hearing what would come next. All the wizards looked eager at their news. Despite stuffing their faces all night, there was still a hunger there. Their desire for magic reminded her of those she'd met who'd become addicted to the extract of the poppy. She suspected that was Sikasso's real secret. As long as he got them their drug, they would keep him in power.

"I have sent Omand a response assuring him that the House of Assassins remains vigilant. To demonstrate this, tomorrow morning most of you will fly for Neeramphorn, where Ashok was last seen by the public."

"I've worked that city. If you deem me worthy, I'll lead this force," one of the wizards said. He looked vaguely familiar to Thera. "You want us to find him again?"

"No, Yuval, I already know where he is. I want you to pick a vulnerable town somewhere in that area and slaughter its inhabitants in the name of his rebellion."

Thera stood up. "No!"

Sikasso absently touched a piece of demon bone hanging from his belt. There was a howl of freezing wind. He directed the wind against her and Thera was flung back helplessly. Her heavy chair struck the wall hard enough to break into pieces. She hit the floor, flat on her back so hard the breath burst from her lungs. It was like being trampled by a runaway horse.

The wind died and Sikasso continued as if he'd never been interrupted. "Don't kill all of them though, make sure there are survivors to tell the tale. Then pick another town, and do the same. Every three days I want another town in flames. Repeat this, over and over, traveling across the countryside until every whole man and woman in the east lives in fear that Ashok the Black Heart will be coming for them next. Kill the ruler, kill the warrior and the worker, but harm no casteless. Leave them untouched, so the Law will have someone to blame."

Thera was gasping for breath, dizzy, and trying to sit up. He couldn't do that! Those people had done nothing wrong. Keta's rebellion would be punished for Sikasso's crimes. *All* of the casteless would be punished. Thera knew her people. When the warrior caste felt threatened, its natural instinct was to attack. The rebellion was about the casteless becoming strong enough that the Law would have to leave them alone so that they could be free. It wasn't about indiscriminate murder.

"If the Grand Inquisitor wants the people to feel terror, then we will provide that terror."

"You expect us to believe that Omand really wants the Lost House to go to such extremes?" Kabir was trying his best to hide his incredulity. He must have done a good enough job that Sikasso didn't backhand him with a tornado.

"Omand has his own reasons, and he does not share them with me, but fortunately his nefarious goals benefit *us*. I did not make this agreement for the Inquisition's black steel alone. After a season, the bloodshed in the east will surely spread. Casteless will rise up, or warriors will preemptively exterminate them. All of Lok will be soaked in blood. What a glorious opportunity. We each have a list of important men descended from those who once wronged this house. Now is our chance to dispose of them. All we have to do is make sure to blame it on a casteless inspired by the Black Heart."

"Wait," said another wizard. "You said you know where Ashok is?"

"I do. I just received word that Chattarak was killed in Haradas. Ashok is more industrious than expected. He's even gathered a small army somehow. There are barges full of warriors upon the Nansakar now, and the rest of his forces went south into Akershan. It appears Ashok is on his way here."

The wizards seemed more shocked by that revelation than Sikasso killing their associate. There were a chorus of *whats* and *impossibles*. Thera was glad to hear their fear.

"Why would he come for us?" a female wizard demanded.

"Why do you think?" Sikasso answered. Every eye in the room turned on her again, only this time Thera was on the ground, bruised and bloodied, in a torn dress, trying to catch her breath. She'd have killed the whole gaggle of the wretched creatures right then if she could have. "Ashok and I have one thing in common. We do not leave things undone."

"You're nothing like him," she muttered. Ashok may have been a hard, stubborn, unfeeling bastard, but he was better than any of these animals. He'd promised to protect the prophet, but she'd doubted he'd even try once he realized it was merely her, a criminal and a fraud, not some great leader who knew the will of the gods. Except Thera should've realized just how powerful a vow was to someone like Ashok.

"Our location has kept us safe from infiltration for a century," another wizard declared. "There's no way Chattarak would've told him the secret path through the swamp, and Protectors can't change shape to fly. He doesn't even have his sword anymore. The demons in the swamp will surely kill all of them for us."

"Possibly, but we underestimated Ashok once in Jharlang, and bled because of it."

The wizard who'd spoken of Neeramphorn jumped in. "Then we shouldn't divide our forces. Burning towns can wait a few days. We can stay here until the Black Heart's eliminated."

Sikasso shook his head. "The Grand Inquisitor grows impatient, and Omand is truly the greater threat. Our business must go on. Plus, I still have more assignments to give. Do not worry about dividing our forces. To make up for our absent brothers, I have activated all of our Dasa."

"Ah...good choice, master. The guardian servants are deadly."

Thera had seen one of the thin, blue-skinned things only once. She didn't know their true capability, but from the approving nods, the assassins all thought the Dasa would be more than sufficient to stop Ashok. She hoped they were wrong.

"In addition, I will be sending a few of you after Ashok's allies who traveled south to silence them as well. We cannot afford to lose track of any who can claim to speak for the Black Heart, but more importantly we must assume they too know of our existence and location. They all must perish. Ashok Vadal will die here, but only we will decide how his legend lives on."

Within Akershan was the rebellion's hidden home. That had to be where they were going. Keta was probably among them, because very few knew the secret path. It was a slow journey this time of year, and they might even get snowed in. The wizards could turn into birds and fly. There was no way Keta could reach the safety of the Cove in time. Shaking, Thera managed to get to her hands and knees, and she crawled toward the table.

"Please. I beg you. Those people have done you no wrong. You can't do this, Sikasso."

"I can and I will. Isn't a true rebellion what the supposed god inside of you wants? You should be pleased by these developments... Either way, we've been overtaken by events. Your time is up."

"We had a bargain."

"Which you have failed to honor. Earlier I mentioned motivation. All of us were motivated to not end up as dimwitted slaves and to live through our trial. There is no greater motivator than survival." Sikasso looked over at Hemendra's empty chair. "We currently have some openings in our ranks. I declare that tomorrow we will begin a new trial. Thera will either master her power or she will die."

Chapter 32

They had almost reached the sea.

The great river had broken into a hundred smaller ones. In the endless fog and rain Ashok couldn't tell what was an island versus what was real land. Islands were not connected to the rest of Lok, and because of that he found them suspicious. How loyal could land be, when it was totally surrounded by water? The trees were choked with vines, and every rock appeared to be covered in a soft green moss. He could spot no landmarks, but the casteless knew exactly which narrow watery path to take them down. If it hadn't been for them, the whole men would have become hopelessly lost.

High in the tallest mountains of Devakula, the Protector Order had in its possession a map of the entire world, dating back to before the rain of demons. Ashok had first seen it as a young acolyte, while going before the Heart of the Mountain. His memory of the carving had remained sharp all those years, so he knew that there had been a huge city near here once. There was little evidence of it now, but every now and then they passed the rotting corpse of an old building, now completely overgrown, and only recognizable because there were a few too many straight lines for it to be natural.

The air in this region was moist and chilly, the sky perpetually grey. The mornings were cloaked in fog and the afternoons usually brought a cold rain. In the rest of Lok it was midwinter, and normally the further south you traveled, the colder it became, but not in the Nansakar river basin.

"I do not like this place. I do not like it all," Ashok whispered to himself.

Except one person was close enough to overhear him. "Me too!" The casteless, Nod, was at the front of the barge, using his pole to push them safely between partially submerged rocks and fallen logs. The rest of the passengers were sleeping, playing games of chance, or sharpening their weapons. "Bahdjangal is the worst part of the trip. But it's been a nicer trip with you than the old barge master, that's for sure. He was sure fond of his whip!"

Though it was cold, the casteless was wearing no shirt. He was probably used to the miserable damp. Ashok noticed that his back was covered in hundreds of long, thin scars. "Did it work?"

"Oh, it'd make us go faster. For a bit. But then we'd go real slow once he wasn't watchin' no more to make up for it." Nod grinned as he hoisted the dripping pole and then shoved it back down in one smooth motion, somehow striking a good solid spot to propel them along, simply by instinct. "Heh. We showed him."

"Acts of petty rebellion against your lawful master, just out of spite," Ashok muttered.

Nod froze, suddenly afraid that he'd gotten out of line. That kind of attitude out of a casteless could easily earn a beating or worse. He was obviously afraid that he'd gone too far, and become too familiar. "Sorry. I mean, I talked like you're a casteless too, but there's nothing really casteless about you."

"That is my legal status."

"You say so, boss." When Ashok said nothing else about that, Nod went back to work. "No spite for you though, Fall. You've been kind to us. We're happy to work hard for you, so we've made real good time."

Ashok looked across the evil water and the choking vegetation and sighed. These casteless had no obligation to him. They'd volunteered their labor on their own free will. He was no better than they were, and they were the ones helping him. He had only helped them by accident.

"I am sorry. I did not intend offense. It was not my intent to intimidate you." Despite his status, that was an incredibly difficult thing to actually come out and say to someone he'd spent his whole life feeling superior toward.

Nod appeared flabbergasted. He turned back to the river and kept poling. Apparently non-people weren't used to receiving apologies from supposedly god-sent heroes. "No need, master, no need."

"Regardless, you have my thanks. It would have taken me far longer to travel here without your aid and guidance. It is appreciated."

"It's the gods' will you be here now."

Keta's gods seemed to will a great many things, but it was men with sweat on their brow and calluses on their hands that did the work. But he did not argue with the poor casteless. Simply being treated with the smallest bit of dignity was such an unnatural experience that it seemed to overwhelm him. So Ashok went back to hating his surroundings instead.

"I do not understand this place. To the south it is winter. To the west it is winter. The rest of Lok has seasons, but this place seems stuck in a perpetual fall."

"That's your name. It should be a good omen," Nod suggested helpfully.

Though Fall was his casteless name, Ashok had no particular love of that gray season. "The north has a warmer climate. The further south you travel the colder it becomes, except here. I wonder why..."

"It's because in this low land where the Nansakar meets the sea, there's always a warm wind coming in off the ocean. It bumps into the cold wind that comes down from Neeramphorn through the valley Haradas. So it is always warmer here than on the high Akershan plain. That's why it rains so much here too."

Ashok was amazed. "That's the sort of thing learned men say when they're trying to predict the weather. How do you know about such things?"

Nod looked a little worried, like he'd gone too far again. "I've no learnin'. My whole life has been on this river. Just my father told me and his father told him. There's currents in the sky just like there's currents in the river. I guess we've known that forever."

"Huh..." Once he had started paying attention to them, he'd continually been surprised just how clever non-people could be. They had lives. Poor, brief, hungry, painful ones, but they were lives. There was a certain dignity that came from becoming very good at a task. Nod had deft hands and a keen mind for this river. He was probably as expert at poling a barge as Ashok was at fighting with a sword. It made him wonder, if Angruvadal hadn't chosen him, would he have been given his father's obligation? Instead of battle, would he have mastered cremation? There would never have been Protector of the Law, twenty-year senior, Ashok Vadal, just Fall, the cremator of corpses...

Certainly that would have been a lot simpler for a great many people!

Would he have been as good at burning the dead, or scrubbing blood, or whatever it was he'd have wound up doing, as Nod was at driving this barge? Only Nod was better at his job without a cruel and spiteful master there to torment him. Would young Fall have mastered a craft, or would he have been too busy cowering in fear?

"Nod, where is Chattarak's whip?"

The muscles of the casteless's back tensed up at the memory of the many times he'd been struck by that thing. He must have wanted to ask why Ashok wanted it, but was too afraid to do so. Instead he took one hand from the pole to gesture at a nearby wooden crate. "In there."

Ashok went over and opened the lid. It made a loud creak. He noticed that distinct sound made every casteless on each corner of the barge glance fearfully in his direction. Their flinch angered him. The sound even carried across the still water to the next barge twenty yards behind them, and he noticed the non-people there were all looking his way as well, conditioned to see who had drawn the barge master's wrath this time.

Ashok found the length of braided leather and pulled it from the crate. It was still covered in dried blood.

"That's it, Fall. We know it well."

Many of the warriors and workers had noticed too, and they were watching him, curious. Less than half of them had known him since Jharlang, and those barely knew him at all. To the rest, he was just an enigmatic figure spoken of by Mother Dawn. They were all interested to see what he intended to do.

"No more," Ashok said simply, and then he threw the whip into the river.

The casteless watched it float away. The whole men went back to their cards or sharpening their weapons.

Ashok knew his act changed nothing. Everyone and everything had its place. Theirs was at the bottom, property, worth no more than livestock. Eventually the Law would give these casteless a new master, and when they displeased him, they would feel the sting of the whip again.

But not today.

Ashok took his place beside the casteless at the front of the barge.

"Thanks," Nod said quietly.

They continued on in silence.

Chapter 33

Long before dawn, Thera stood in the courtyard of the Lost House in front of a group of wizards. The early hour didn't matter. It wasn't like she'd slept much that night anyway.

Sikasso was there. The normally unreadable man appeared rather solemn. The trials were serious business. Kabir and Omkar were there, as were many of the wizards she'd seen the night before. Only this time they weren't dressed in their fine robes, but rather for battle. Their armor was light and minimal, and their clothing was all in dark colors, better for sneaking in. They carried a wide assortment of weapons from every part of the continent.

Thera stopped in front of them. She had no idea what a trial entailed, other than a very good chance of dying, so she folded her arms and waited.

"The ceremony will commence," Sikasso declared.

"Why bother with the speeches?" asked one of the wizards. "There's real acolytes it'll matter to, but none of them are ready to test. It's just your oddity."

"Because we will honor tradition," Sikasso snapped.

Chastised, that wizard looked away.

"The House of Assassins mourns the recent loss of our brothers Lome, Choval, Bhorlatar, Vilsaro, Chattarak, and Hemendra.

We are lessened. For our great work to go on, their offices must be filled. Their oath must be replaced. Who among you has an acolyte who is worthy to test their place?"

Omkar cleared his throat. The others might have thought this was a joke, but Omkar took his duties very seriously. "I present one student before the House of Assassins. She will attempt the trial."

"Are there no others?" Sikasso knew damned good and well there weren't, but he stuck to his script. After a moment when no one spoke, he continued. "Acolyte, if you would take their oath and their place, come forward."

Everyone looked at Thera. She stepped toward the wizards.

"There are six oaths left unfilled. Whose oath will you claim?"

She didn't really know what to say. "I cut Vilsaro's throat. I suppose I should take his."

"That philosophy is more fitting than you realize," Sikasso muttered, then he went back to what must have been his regular speech. "The student will test to replace Vilsaro, may she prove worthy. The remaining oaths will go unfilled until the next trial."

"Just me then? You've no more stolen children to sacrifice?"

"Silence," Sikasso ordered. "You will not mock our ways. I wish I could be the one to guide you through the trial, because I would take a certain satisfaction watching the flesh ripped from your smug face if you fail, but you must pick another... Who from among the assembled members of the Lost House do you choose to be your guide?"

Fat Omkar was already stepping forward to accept the assignment, certain she would pick the man who'd taught her the tiny bit of magic she knew. The way he looked proud about it told Thera there had to be some prestige from the title.

So just out of spite she said, "I choose Kabir."

"With my wisdom I will guide—" then Omkar stopped, surprised, and sputtered, "What manner of insult is this?"

Sikasso looked toward Kabir, who was staring daggers at Thera. "The student has made her choice... Though it is a curious one."

"He's the prettiest one of you. If I'm to die at least he's easy on the eyes."

"I am unable to guide her, for I have duties elsewhere," Kabir said with forced humility. "I'm supposed to lead the group in pursuit of the friends of Ashok Vadal who are traveling into Akershan."

"The student has made her choice," Sikasso repeated. "Tradition is clear. I shall send Omkar in your place. Apparently his presence here is not as necessary as he thought."

Neither Omkar or Kabir looked happy at this development, but Kabir gave a small nod and said, "Then with my wisdom I will guide the student through the trial."

"The choices have been made. To replace the oath of fallen Vilsaro, the student and the guide will depart immediately. You will return worthy of the House of Assassins or not at all."

"Row faster," Kabir hissed at her.

"I've never rowed a bloody boat before!"

"I don't care. The longer we're in the open the more likely we'll attract a demon."

Thera didn't know why they were whispering. Demons seemed to sense prey just fine without ears. They were on fresh water, but it was mighty close to the sea. If there happened to be a demon nearby surely it would sense their little boat or the splashing of the oars against the water.

"You could row too."

"I'm not allowed to actively help you achieve your goals, merely guide you in how to do it yourself. Most students wouldn't have to take a boat because by now they've learned how to change shape to make the journey quick and silent. We could have flown or swam across the lake. Only a fool would ever undertake the trial without being able to shape shift into at least one or two different forms."

"Damn your rules, wizard. If I could turn into a bird or a fish I would. Your rules won't mean salt water when a demon comes from below and flips us over." Her arms were burning. Rowing was far more difficult than the casteless made it look. She was strong, but her muscles weren't used to this sort of awkward repetition. "Grab an oar."

"It's not that easy. I guarantee one of my brothers is high above us, watching with the eyes of a hawk to make sure our rules are followed. Don't even think of trying to run away. If I help you cheat, he'll swoop down and kill you, and report me, assuming it isn't Sikasso himself. You've surely damned us both. Sikasso has to be wondering why of all the wizards you picked me."

"You were supposed to help me."

"That was before your maniacal Protector showed up and shat all over my carefully laid plans. I thought we had more time. You'd gain skill enough to do this right, and then at the beginning of the trial you'd make a claim for Sikasso's living oath instead of one of our dead. He'd have had no choice but to follow tradition or lose respect. He'd have to remove most of his magical defenses to compete against you. Then I could have struck somewhere out here while he was vulnerable."

"You didn't tell me that!"

"I said there was no time. You were being watched too closely." Kabir seemed to mull it over. "Unless, Sikasso suspected such a ploy, but he knew that none of us would dare make a move against our strongest member while most of us were off pillaging villages and the murderous Ashok Vadal was on his way here… If that's the case, then he's even shrewder than I thought."

Thera just growled and kept on rowing. Now her back was killing her too. Boats were absurd and rowing one was a bloody stupid endeavor. It was one thing further inland, but this close to the sea it was ridiculous. They were a slow target. Plus when a demon did finally come and rip her apart, she'd die tired and sweaty.

Kabir glanced around nervously at the fog. "We should be fairly safe until we land on the opposite shore. Demons don't usually get this close to the Lost House. The Dasa patrols normally keep them away."

"Those blue scarecrows are really that effective?"

"The Dasa were constructed during the days of Ramrowan, before man forgot most of what he taught us about magic. Yes. They're incredibly effective." Kabir sounded nearly in awe of the things.

At least his talking distracted her from the exertion. "What makes them so special?"

"They're not alive, so they can't really die. If they're dismantled you simply put them back together, or if any of them remain, they'll find all the pieces and repair their broken allies themselves. The Dasa can be set to work at different levels. They can go seemingly forever at their slower settings without tiring. They can only go a short time at their higher setting, then they have to sleep for a long time afterward, but at that level they can fight off a demon."

Sikasso was going to send several of those things against Ashok. The swordsman was good, but he couldn't be that good. "Is there a way to put them to sleep?"

"Yes, but only a few of us are given the secret commands. I am not among them yet." Kabir gave her a sideways glance. "Why do you ask?"

"No reason."

"You still think Ashok can save you! Foolish woman. I've never seen Sikasso this furious before. He's the greatest assassin the Lost House has ever produced, and he's usually downright dispassionate about most he kills. This is personal. Ashok is doomed. He isn't going to save you. Thera, listen to me, you need to realize your friends are already dead, and you will be soon if you don't focus."

Kabir was right about one thing. She couldn't count on anyone. Not Ashok, certainly not Kabir; she was on her own. Gritting her teeth, she lifted the oars and then thrust them back through the water. She had no clue how to row, but she'd sort of figured it out, so that they were being propelled along at what seemed to be a decent pace. That's what she always did when faced with a new challenge, she struggled along until she figured a way out. This trial would be no different.

"Why didn't you tell me any of this before? We had an agreement, Kabir."

"I had to tread carefully. Sikasso is a suspicious man."

"I can't believe you were all taken from your homes. That's barbaric. Now you do to others what was once done to you."

A sneer appeared on Kabir's handsome face. "What we do to a few is no different than what the Great Houses do to all. They assign everyone a place, including wizards. We're all merely another commodity to be used up. Be obligated to this duty or else! Do what you're told or die! Only do approved magic when and how the Law allows it or burn atop the dome! You think wizards are given this much freedom beneath the Law? No. We'd be slaves there far more than we are here. We do our kind a favor by bringing them here."

"Tell that to the poor bastards you've turned into drooling imbeciles to cook your food and make your bath."

Kabir looked away for a moment. "That's different."

"How?"

It was obvious he didn't like speaking about this topic. "They couldn't develop the skill or mindset necessary to become one of us, and we could never risk letting them free. What if they talked? If certain groups within the Capitol found out we still lived, then we'd be destroyed. It is either cloud their minds, or kill them in self-defense."

"I've got no stomach for your excuses. From which house were you stolen from a cradle in the middle of the night, Kabir?"

He gritted his teeth. "I do not wish to talk about ancient history."

"Sikasso said you and your brother were taken. Was that him in Jharlang? Is that why you hate me, Kabir? Because I killed your own flesh and blood?"

"Vilsaro was my...he was my friend. That is all." Kabir seemed ashamed, but that shame seemed to compel him to continue. "My brother, my *real* brother...He was a few years older. He watched out for me, protected me in training, even got disfigured once stepping in front of a whip meant for me...But I'm afraid he didn't have what it took to become one of us."

"He died on this trial?"

"He's alive." Kabir stared off into the distance. "His mind was sharp, his focus second to none, but his heart was too soft to take a life. Dattu was no killer."

"Oceans!" Thera couldn't believe it. She even fumbled the stroke and spun the rowboat sideways. "They made your brother a slave? He's still there? Wait...The one-eyed slave with you in the hall that night? That's him!"

For a brief moment, Kabir's tormented look told her that was right.

"How could you let Sikasso destroy his mind?"

"He didn't. Sikasso ordered me to perform the ritual myself. It was that or they would've killed him. I had no choice."

Thera was tempted to take the oar out of the water and brain the wizard with it. "You miserable bastard! You turned him into a mindless drone. How could you do that to your own family?"

"*How could I not!*" So much for being quiet enough to not attract demons. "At the time I thought it was a mercy, leaving him as unthinking and obedient as one of the Dasa, but at least Dattu's life would be spared. We are still together...Only I've seen there's still something of him left inside after the process, plaintive glimmers of understanding, so at times I am unsure." Kabir shook his head, dispelling the temporary weakness, and just like that he was back to playing the callous and unfeeling wizard. "I will speak of this no more."

Thera didn't even try to hide her disgust. "Then do your job, *guide*, and tell me about the trial."

"You will more than likely die," he said sullenly.

That wasn't particularly helpful. Thera had managed to hide all of her stolen and improvised weapons beneath her traveling clothes that morning. She was sorely tempted to surprise stab Kabir in the neck and then shove him over the side, but that wouldn't do anything about the wizards watching from above.

"Normally the trial would only be undertaken by a student who has spent years learning our ways. Of those I've trained, I've always told them to have at least two or three useful patterns mastered before attempting it."

"How many of your students have passed?"

"None. Before you insinuate that I'm a bad teacher, that is not so odd. Four out of five of us who attempt the trial fail, and perish in the process."

"Oh, yeah! You're doing those kids a huge favor bringing them here!"

Kabir was defensive, and growing angrier by the second. "There are only allowed a hundred of us in the world, a number which allows no room for weakness. You think we are unaware that we do evil? We do what we must so that someday *all* wizards may be free of the Capitol's chains. This House was the only one in all of Lok that allowed wizards to experiment in the manner they saw fit, and the Law drowned us for it. But enough of this. I don't need to defend our actions to the likes of you. How many patterns have you mastered?"

"None," she answered truthfully.

"None." Kabir sighed. "Just as magic is only part of what makes an effective assassin, it is only part of the trial. You will be expected to use stealth and cunning as well."

"That I can do."

"For your sake, I hope so. There is the other possibility though, that Sikasso is right, and the danger will force your strange gift to surface."

Thera gave a bitter laugh. "The Voice doesn't care! It only

shows up at the worst possible times. It's never done a thing to keep me safe. On the contrary, it's gotten me into all sorts of trouble. I think Sikasso's going to be disappointed."

"*He won't care.* He regrew an arm—an unheard of feat—and publicly executed his most outspoken critic to show it off. Don't you get it, Thera? My opportunity to take over has passed."

"I'm terribly sorry that after I die horribly in a swamp you'll be inconvenienced like that."

"How dare—"

She had no time for bickering with wizards. "Shut up, Kabir. I've got bigger things to worry about than your stupid house politics. Tell me about the trial."

Kabir was a tricky, murderous bastard, who'd given his own brother amnesia, but he must not have been *all* bad. Since she was facing near-certain death, he let the offense pass. "Fine. First you must understand the basis for the trial. It takes a lot of resources to teach someone how to be a proper wizard. Our students burn through a great deal of demon parts over the years. To pass the trial, you've got to replace those precious resources. The more you've used up, the more you're expected to bring back."

"That's easy enough. I've not been here long. I can't have used much."

"That is the only thing you have going for you. The end of a finger or even a tooth should meet the requirements. Except you can't bring back just any magic, the trial requires it to come from a specific place. To get in unseen, and to escape in one piece, requires the skills of an assassin. If you survive, you have demonstrated that you are truly worthy."

Thera couldn't do magic worth a damn, but she'd spent a lot of time sneaking in and out of places she wasn't supposed to be in, and stolen quite a few valuables in the process. How much worse could this be? "What is this place?"

"It's where demons go to die."

Chapter 34

〰〰〰〰

They called it the graveyard of demons.

When there had still been a network of dams and sea walls left behind by the ancients, this valley had been submerged, becoming an artificial reservoir to sustain a great city. It wasn't until the Capitol had destroyed those great constructions that the rivers changed paths, the waters receded, and the graveyard beneath was revealed.

The forces of the Law were long gone by then. It was a few survivors of fallen House Charsadda, hiding in the wilderness, who had discovered the great field of bones. *Demon bones.* No one had ever seen or heard of such a thing before.

Among the refugees were wizards who realized that there was wealth incalculable there, easily enough to reclaim their house and status. Except when they went down to claim their newfound treasure, they discovered that though this place was now on dry land, the demons still claimed it as if it were beneath the sea.

Many of them lost their lives. Yet a few made it out, packs bulging with bones. They'd survived not through battle, but by using their magic to hide, to move quickly and quietly, and to attack with surprise and overwhelming violence. These survivors would be the first to sell their skills they'd learned by grave robbing hell. They were the first to take the blood oath.

Thus began the House of Assassins.

Thera hadn't particularly enjoyed that history lesson. Now that she was slinking along through the reeds, trying not to make a sound, she wasn't having much fun either. In fact, she was scared to death, and hoping that demons couldn't smell fear.

When they'd landed their little rowboat, Kabir had given her a satchel with a few pieces of demon inside, as was prescribed by their rules. It was the final gift from the Lost House, the last magic that would ever freely be given rather than earned. The student was supposed to use those bits to walk through the shadows, or move like the wind, or turn into a snake to slither unnoticed through the mud, or some other useful pattern that would let them get in and out safely with their satchel filled with valuable new magic.

That was the theory at least. For Thera, all of those remarkable abilities were unattainable.

So she crawled through the mud on her belly. To the ocean with wizards and their fancy tricks, she'd do this the old-fashioned way, like a warrior scout, low and slow.

Kabir was waiting at the shore of the lake. She'd thought about making a run for it, but every now and then she'd caught a glimpse of the sky through the fog, and there had been birds circling every time. Some of those were bound to be wizards. From way up there they could probably watch her as well as Ashok's progress.

Maybe she'd get lucky and live long enough that the crazy Protector would simply kill all the wizards, and then she'd be free to go on her merry way. Maybe Keta would reach the hideout before Omkar caught him too. And then they'd all live happily ever after.

Not bloody likely that.

Thera crept up on the edge of the reeds but didn't touch them. There wasn't even the slightest breeze, so if the reeds swayed they were bound to look out of place. She took her time. The fog was hugging the damp ground, so hopefully that would provide her extra cover. This would be easier if anybody understood how demons could see and hear and smell without eyes, ears, or nostrils, but they sensed prey somehow.

In front of her were a bunch of puddles. There was very little cover. Judging from the height of the grass growing out of the water, it couldn't be more than a foot or two deep. Ahead, the valley which held the graveyard was just a round indentation, slightly lower than the surrounding area. Nothing moved or made a sound. Not so much as a bug or a frog. At least there was no sign of any demons yet. Maybe she'd timed this just right, and none of them would be home? That was about as likely as Ashok beating a bunch of Dasa and rescuing her.

Patience was her weapon as she picked the best route forward. There was a fallen log that she could hug the ground next to, that would get her to the next patch of tall reeds. *Low and slow.* Thera slid into the cold muck. Her long leather coat was harvest brown, rather than the grey-green of the pond scum and lily pads, but it got darker when it was wet. Hopefully it would be close enough in color to camouflage her, but she didn't even know if demons could see colors.

Kabir hadn't known why demons came to die here. Surely there were plenty of places for them to die in the ocean. Corpses washed up on shore all the time. What made this place special to them? He said the Lost House had been coming up with theories for a hundred years, but none of them really knew.

There was a splash on the other side of the log. Thera froze in place.

There was another splash. That was far too big to be a frog.

Something heavy rubbed against the bark.

Terrified, she let her body sink deeper into the mud, until her mouth was submerged in the fetid water, but she kept her nostrils free so she could still breathe. Her hair was floating around her face. Hopefully her leather hood would appear to be a rock.

Heart pounding, her instincts were screaming for her to get up and run. But she forced herself to hold perfectly still instead.

She couldn't see it, but she knew it was a demon. It *felt* like a demon. It reminded her of being in the ocean, helpless. If it wanted her dead, she would die. It was that simple. There was another splash as the demon moved away from the log, and then a sucking noise as it slid up onto land and across the mud.

Thera waited a long time. Her hands were sunk deep into the muck and her fingers were freezing. She was wearing gloves, but once soaked, they provided little warmth. A kink formed in her neck from the awkward angle and her muscles began to shake involuntarily. Hopefully the demon had moved on.

She began slinking forward again.

Hours passed that way. The sun climbed. The fog thinned. Thera's life condensed down to nothing but cautious movement or frozen waiting. This could take a while. Kabir had better have packed a lunch.

She remembered the advice her father had given her about stalking prey. Andaman Vane had been legendary at silently removing enemy sentries during raids. *Sudden movement draws the eye. Breathe through your nose, it's quieter. Always listen.* Focusing on his words gave her something to dwell on rather than the discomfort and the mind-numbing terror.

Then she reached the graveyard.

This had to be the place, because there were hundreds of scattered bones and dried-out husks wreathed in shredded, hanging, black skin. Trees had grown up here over the last century, lifting old carcasses into the air, and bones and skin hung from the branches cloaked in wispy gray moss. Some of the remains were ancient, partially dissolved into dirt, the magic probably long vanished. Others were obviously newer. It was hard to tell because of the moist decay but some of the corpses couldn't have been here for too long. The visible bones were still white instead of crumbling gray and plants hadn't covered everything. Those should still contain magic.

It was an eerie place. Some of the monsters had died sitting up, or leaning against trees, but they'd died so long ago that now they were just green, demon-shaped piles of vegetation. What could possibly compel them to come here to die?

No matter. Thera picked out the nearest body, but then she thought better of it. That one was still mostly in one piece, and even sawing away at it, demon hide was notoriously difficult to cut through. That meant noise and movement. This was just like when she'd first learned how to pick pockets, surviving as a criminal after Ratul had hidden her away. Some Protector he'd been! You didn't try to take the purse tied to the cautious warrior's belt. You took the purse from the oblivious Firster who'd had too much to drink. She may have been terrible at working magic, but that didn't mean she was uneducated.

Thera changed her approach so that she would reach one of the more mangled bodies first. That made her wonder, what manner of scavenger was strong enough to rend apart a demon? Regardless, the connective tissue had long since rotted away, making for a much easier grab.

Reaching the corpse, Thera grabbed a handful of bone fragments and dirt and then crammed that into the damp satchel.

Though it had no eye sockets, the weird skull was staring at her anyway. Dead demons looked as emotionless as the living ones. Would those fragments be enough? Some of the teeth had fallen out, so she hurried and grabbed those as well, but she'd forgotten just how sharp demon teeth were, and one sliced right through the end of her glove. Red blood spilled from her fingertip.

Damn it. After hours of caution, she'd made one hasty, sloppy mistake. She didn't know if demons were actually attracted to blood or not, but Ratul had been certain they were. She stuck her finger in her mouth, then put the teeth in the bag and made sure it was tied shut. She'd not done all this to have her loot fall out during her escape. Tasting blood and swamp, she removed her finger from her mouth. The end of her glove was dangling, and she could see the water logged skin beneath. She tried to squeeze the cut shut, but it was too deep and her flesh too soft from the moisture. So she jammed her hand into the mud to coat it fully, because filling the hole with dirt might stop it, or at least keep it from dripping everywhere.

Forty feet away, something pitch black appeared between the reeds.

Thera hugged the ground, hoping the demon would go away. But it just lay there, darker than the shadows. Too scared to breathe, she couldn't even risk turning her head to look. She could barely see it from the corner of her eye.

Soundlessly, it rose to its full height, far larger than the man-sized demon that had nearly ended her life years ago. It breathed in, expanding a chest big around as a barrel, and then slowly turned in her direction. Thera resisted the urge to scream.

The demon moved toward her.

She had to make a choice. Had it spotted her? If it had, her only hope was to run. If it hadn't, and she moved, it would give chase, and it was said demons could outrun horses.

Thera decided to stay still. Or maybe she was just so terrified that her muscles were frozen and the decision was made for her.

Regardless, it proved to be the correct call, because the demon wasn't coming for her. It went to the more recent corpse she had passed up. Now that she could see it clearly, this demon had to be eight or nine feet tall, and was so thick that it must have weighed seven hundred pounds. Only it stepped so lightly that she could feel no vibration in the earth she was clinging to. Its shoulders were vast, the featureless head just a lump set too low on its chest, its waist too small, its limbs too long. There was no natural proportion about this thing.

The demon squatted next to the newer body, a mere twenty feet away.

And did nothing.

Thera waited for it to move on, but the demon just remained there, perfectly still, head tilted downward as if it were studying the dead.

Was it mourning? *Do demons feel?*

Suddenly, the creature drove its claws into the corpse. It happened so fast that it took everything Thera had not to gasp or flinch. The sharpest knives dulled against demon hide, but the claws tore right through. Then the demon grabbed hold of the black skin with both hands and tore it open like a piece of fabric. The hide made a terrible sound as it ripped.

Now she knew what manner of scavenger it was that could tear apart corpses this tough.

Only the demon wasn't just attacking the body, but rather it seemed to work with a methodical purpose. It wasn't scavenging, because it wasn't eating anything. Bones snapped, flesh tore, but there was nothing savage about the process. The demon was simply rearranging the parts and stacking them. The act seemed more ceremonial than anything.

It would have been curious if she wasn't so damned terrified.

The demon stopped working. Its head lump abruptly twisted upward. Then it slowly turned toward her.

Thera's eyes flicked down. The mud on her fingers was stained red. Her cut had bled through.

The demon stood, dropping the leg it had just effortlessly wrenched off a body denser than an ox. Its manner changed. It was on the hunt.

Now Thera ran.

The demon gave chase.

Terrified, legs pumping as fast as possible, Thera tore through the graveyard. Leaping over bodies and ducking beneath branches, she could feel it gaining on her with each giant stride. She moved between the trees, thinking that its bulk would slow it down, but it crashed right through, shattering limbs and hurling demon bones in every direction.

There was only one way for her to go, deeper into the graveyard.

She crashed through the brush, hoping that it would trip up the demon, but it barely slowed. Branches slapped her in the face and cut her skin. She didn't dare look back, but it had to be right on top of her.

Then Thera stumbled into a field of hard white.

It was a clearing piled high with bones. *Filled* with bones.

She rushed into the open, the demon almost on her. Thera tried to keep running, but the bones slipped and tumbled beneath her feet. She fell and desperately began to crawl across the clattering ground. But here were bones everywhere, some stacked in piles, deep as her waist.

In the middle of the circle was a monument.

The monster stopped at the edge of the field.

Gasping for breath, Thera looked back toward the demon, but it was just standing there, watching her silently. Then she looked back toward the thing in the center of the clearing, and her mind rebelled at the sight.

It was an idol, wide as a wagon and ten feet tall. It was a statue like the multitude which decorated the House of Assassins, just as ancient, just as religious, only this one hadn't been fashioned by the hands of man. At first she thought the idol was made of some dark green stone, speckled with black moss, but this was something else entirely. It didn't feel carved, but rather grown.

Thera couldn't understand what she was looking at. It wasn't the image of a demon, but of something else entirely. Was this an image of *their* god? Nervous, she looked over her shoulder, but the quiet demon was still watching, and seemed unwilling to enter the circle.

There was a strange logic to where the bone piles had been placed around the idol, geometric, like a mandala. The wizards had tried to help her see the patterns that made up all things. Apparently demons had patterns too.

The idol *spoke*.

It didn't use words. It used noise and pain, but it got its message across.

It had been waiting a millennium to deliver its ultimatum to someone like her.

The world shook. Bone piles toppled. Crazed images flashed through Thera's mind as ancient gods collided inside her head.

Chapter 35

The Sons of the Black Sword made their way across the treacherous land.

Ashok knew to never trust a swamp. A swamp was an in-between place. It only pretended to be real land. He'd worked in swamps before, mostly on the Gujaran peninsula, far to the north. But Bahdjangal was different. A Gujaran swamp was where their endless jungle hit a low spot and filled with water, but they remained as hot, miserable, and loud as the surrounding jungle.

It was nothing like that here.

Bahdjangal—as the casteless called it—was cold, but not nearly cold enough for the water to freeze. It was quiet. A Gujaran swamp was filled with the noise of screaming birds, and the impossibly loud buzzing of millions of stinging insects. Here, there were no animal calls, and not so much as a breeze to make a branch creak. Occasionally there was a mysterious splash as something slithered into the muck, but other than that it was still.

It took him a while to realize the most glaring difference of all. Gujaran swamps were bright green with life. Here, everything seemed tinted gray. There was too much death—fallen trees and scattered animal bones—and every living thing appeared diseased and soft. The air was heavy with the scent of decay.

Regardless, the men's morale was high. They were not a real

military unit. Most of them had never trained together before. They weren't unified by an official Order or even caste. Until a few days ago they had been strangers, and the men of the different houses still held an ancestral animosity for each other. Yet they moved swift and sure across the muddy ground, united by their odd faith. Even those who hadn't a few days ago known that there was a prophet, believed they were doing their gods' work saving her now.

Ashok also suspected that some of the warriors were just trying hard to impress him. When he'd been a Protector he'd become used to such behavior from the warrior caste. It was illegal to worship gods, but warriors loved to worship heroes. Not to mention, if a Protector spoke highly of an individual's service to their Thakoor, it could go a long way toward boosting that warrior's name and status. Ashok could no longer do that, but he wondered if some of these fanatics thought he was in a position to put in a word with their gods instead... If that was the case they were going to be sorely disappointed.

Perhaps they were just happy to be off the damnable swaying barges, but whatever it was, the Sons of the Black Sword were looking forward to a fight.

It was customary for a risaldar to break his paltan into two to five squads, with a havildar overseeing each. They were thirty strong now, so Jagdish had chosen two. Previously, he had picked Shekar of the Somsak, to oversee the original Sons of the Black Sword recruited in Jharlang. Eklavya of the Kharsawan—the young man who had spoken for the fanatics on the road—had been picked as their second havildar to oversee the newcomers.

Both of them seemed to be doing well as junior officers, though their styles were very different. Shekar was smarter than most Somsak, but was still basically a bloodthirsty savage. Like most of the Kharsawan, Eklavya seemed orderly and composed. What manner of odd god could appeal to such wildly divergent warrior cultures? Ashok assumed that all fanatics were like Keta, and their god was a blank canvas for them to paint whatever motives and traits they desired upon it.

If that were the case, then Ashok hoped one of those traits was courage, because if this swamp really was infested with demons, then these warriors would need all the courage they could get.

Where the water was moving, it was too dark to see through.

Everywhere the water was still, scum and soft green pads grew on top. It was fresh water, not salt, but demons didn't seem to care much about the difference, and often swam up rivers when they were in the mood to rampage.

"Can your gift sense the presence of demon?" Ashok whispered to Gutch. "They're magic."

Their tracker was at the front of their column. Since there was no road or sign of any path, Ashok had told Gutch to lead them toward the strongest magic. The worker had been reluctant to be on point, but Ashok had said he would stay by Gutch's side to keep him safe. Ashok was not the sort to lead from the rear anyway.

"Maybe. Sometimes. When they die they rot and stink like everything else. But demons are strange when they're still alive. Their magic is inside them and kind of blends into their surroundings. I don't really know. I've done my best to avoid living demons! Did I mention yet I don't like being in front?"

"Do not worry. In my experience, when demons ambush, they let the lead pass, then attack the middle in order to inflict maximum carnage in the shortest amount of time. Once a coherent resistance is broken, then they devour the stragglers at their leisure."

Gutch swallowed. "Oh . . . I don't know if there are demons close, but I can feel a lot of concentrated magic that way." He pointed with his spiked club to the east. "Two, maybe two and a half miles. Hard to tell since there's so much magic there, black steel and demon both. But there's something else in this place, confusing things."

"What do you mean?"

"I don't know. I've never felt nothing like it before, like a fog hangs over something to the north."

"To the place with the black steel first. Let us make haste."

They had set out as soon as there was enough light to keep from tripping and breaking their necks. They'd been marching for hours. It was slow going across this muddy terrain. If Gutch was right they could reach the wizards while the sun was high. Ashok really didn't want to be stuck in the swamp overnight. Demons killed just fine in the sunlight, but in his experience they seemed to prefer striking in the dark.

The Sons were covered in filth and soaked to the bone. Even

the warmest clothing became useless once it was sodden, so many of them were shivering. There was no dry path, so they constantly had to wade through the water. Everyone in Lok knew that if a man went into water deep and dark enough to hide his feet, demons could be lurking. Yet the men showed no fear and gave no complaint as they slogged along. If he'd still been a Protector and this had been a lawful mission, then he would've given their Thakoors a glowing report.

Sadly, even with their good spirits, Ashok knew that he could have abandoned them and made far better time. Among the Sons were many strong men, but none of them were as agile as one who'd touched the Heart of the Mountain. This close to the wizards, it was tempting... But Ashok had to check his pride. He no longer had Angruvadal. Without it, there would no longer be any easy victories. And he had not come all this way just to get killed at the wizard's doorstep.

Their feet seemed to get heavier at every step as more and more mud clung to them. Gutch was red faced and breathing hard from the exertion. "Hang on ... There's something odd." He stopped to lean against a tree, and then thought better of it, and slid down until he sat on the ground. Surprisingly, inside Chattarak's warehouse, Gutch had found an armor shirt made of chain and woven leather plates, big enough to fit even him, though it was snug. He was probably regretting the decision to wear it now. Workers didn't realize just how heavy armor got after a while.

"What is it?" Ashok held up his fist, indicating the column should halt. He didn't want them too bunched up. He'd once seen a leaping demon plow right through an entire shield wall, scattering half a dozen spearmen in every direction.

"Just... I don't know." Whatever it was seemed to have struck him dizzy. Gutch rubbed his hands down his face, but all that did was smear mud everywhere. "There's some kind of weird magic being used, but in a different spot, where that odd sensation was coming from. Give me a moment."

It was good Ashok was there to guard Gutch, because he was too weary to pay much attention to his own safety. Gutch didn't even see the viper that came out from under the tree he was sitting against. And he never did, because Ashok quickly crushed its head beneath his boot.

"How is this magic different, Gutch?"

"I don't know. It doesn't feel like black steel or demon. I can't puzzle it out. Whatever it is just came out of nowhere, and it's real strong. Like ancestor-blade strong. It's clashing against..." Gutch blinked a few times, obviously confounded. "The strongest demon I've ever felt! What in the salty hell is that thing?"

"Thera," Ashok muttered. Then he grabbed Gutch by the straps on his new armor and effortlessly hoisted the big man out of the mud. "Which way?"

Gutch nodded. "That way." It was hard to tell since there were no landmarks and the sky was too cloudy to see the sun, but it seemed to be north.

"Jagdish!"

The risaldar shouted back, "What is it?"

They would not be able to keep up. "You are in command. Continue toward the Lost House. I will find you." He called upon the Heart of the Mountain to grant him speed as he leapt through the flooded forest.

Ashok had a Prophet to protect.

The Protector Order would be ashamed to know that the precious magic of their Heart of the Mountain was being so heavily drawn upon to save the life of a rebel, but Ashok didn't care. A vow had been made. That vow would be kept.

The ground was treacherous, but Ashok barely touched it as he flung himself through the forest. With great bounding strides he moved, trying to hit logs, roots, and solid dirt, in order to not waste any precious momentum. It was commonly said that a Protector could outrun a horse over short distances, but what most never witnessed was that through terrain this rugged, a Protector could chase down a fleeing deer.

Ashok pushed himself to his limits, and then beyond. His real heart was pounding. His breath was ragged fire. The Heart of the Mountain made up the difference muscle could not, and swamp passed by in a flash. If there were demons hidden here, none of them tried to stop him, perhaps because he'd gone by too quickly for them to realize he was even there.

The leaves on the trees ahead of him were shaking. *Earthquake?* He skidded to a halt in a clearing, breathing hard, but trying to listen. The black earth vibrated beneath his boots. There was an odd buzzing in his ears, like insects, but this sound was made by no living thing, but rather from some strange energy building in the air.

In the distance, a woman screamed.

Thera! Ashok adjusted course toward the sound and took off again.

Breaking through reeds and splashing through puddles, Ashok ran along the edge of a lake. There appeared to be only one semisolid path across, and he'd already proven that he was a terrible swimmer. He had to cross an open expanse, but did not hesitate. The water was knee deep, and the mud beneath sucked at his boots.

Then from the reeds ahead appeared a man. Or at least he thought it was a man, until he saw that it had blue skin.

Ashok had encountered such creations before. The first time was as an acolyte, when he and Devedas had battled them at the top of the world to prove themselves worthy. They had been a mystery then, but Lord Protector Ratul had educated them about the Dasa after they'd attained senior rank. Ashok did not understand what a guardian servant was doing all the way out here, and did not have time to ponder on it. He kept running.

The Dasa moved to block his path.

Then Ashok realized a second one had risen from the water to his side, and a third from behind. They did not breathe. They could lie beneath water indefinitely. The ones that belonged to the Order slept beneath the snow until someone intruded onto the Heart's peak, and then they reacted with overwhelming violence.

He stopped in the center of a triangle created by three very dangerous foes.

The Dasa were covered in muck, but from the shape and the gleam of metal, they were dressed in armor. Two were armed with axes, and one held a spear in its seemingly delicate blue hands.

They did not speak as they approached. The triangle shrank. "Let me pass."

The spear Dasa struck first. It was nearly as fast as he was, which meant it had been set to its most dangerous setting. The setting one lower than that had easily defeated him and Devedas all those years ago.

But Ashok was no longer a child. Coat whipping, he spun around the spear thrust, and slammed that Dasa in the side of the head with his elbow. He dodged beneath a falling ax, and kicked that one in the chest. It crashed back into the water.

As the last one struck, Ashok shouted a command. *"Arret!"*

It was an old word, from before the Age of Kings, when there had still been different languages in the world. Ashok didn't know what the word meant, only that Ratul had taught it to the Protectors who might have to deal with the guardians of the Heart. It would stop those Dasa in their vengeful tracks.

The axe froze, inches from his face.

Ashok was pleased to see that these Dasa spoke the same language as the ones that belonged to the Order. *Good.* Ashok didn't have time to fight them. The magic just ahead had grown so incredibly strong that even he could sense it.

In fact, he could *see* it. A hazy light was glowing through the trees, and it was becoming more visible because the sky was rapidly darkening. Ashok looked up and was surprised to see that the clouds above were circling, like they were being sucked toward the ground. Lightning cracked across the sky.

Something caught his eye, and he called upon the Heart to sharpen his vision. In the distance was the sea. The flash had reflected off *several* black shapes rising from the surf that had turned a violent foaming red.

"Salt water," he muttered.

The demons were still far away. The only reason he'd noticed them with his unaided sight was because one of the demons was the size of an elephant. It was by far the biggest demon he'd ever seen. It was a good thing he could not feel fear, because any normal man would've been left trembling and helpless before this army of hell.

All the demons were slowly converging on that light.

The three Dasa were still eerily still, each stuck somewhere in the process of trying to kill him. The wizards had probably placed them here along this narrow path of land to keep him from reaching Thera. They had no way of guessing that the Protector Order knew how to control Dasa too, or at least some of them did. Those who reached Lord Protector rank were taught all the commands. As a senior, Ashok only knew three. *Stop, sleep,* and . . .

Attack.

Chapter 36

"Sikasso! Sikasso!"

The leader of the House of Assassins looked up from his vital experiments. Even though his project was going through her trial, and Ashok Vadal was only a few miles away, his current efforts could not wait. He had undertaken a great personal risk, and risks had to be managed or else. But the wizard sounded panicked, so Sikasso removed the needles from his new arm, and hid the bags of ground ingredients and beakers of medicine beneath a cloth, before rising.

He pulled his glove on to hide his crime, and then opened the vault door. "What is it?"

It was Waman, a tiny, fragile man, who despite his size—or perhaps because of it—made an excellent spy. He was among those Sikasso had ordered to fly high above the swamp, observing Ashok's approach, as well as Thera's progress... And since Waman was loyal, to also make sure that the ambitious Kabir did nothing to cross him.

"We need you!" Waman was nearly out of breath. Magic still lingered upon him. He had just finished changing back into his normal form, and had run the rest of the way.

"Ashok shouldn't be here for hours."

"He's not coming here. You guessed right. Somehow he sensed Thera and went after her alone. He left his men behind."

"That is excellent news." Sikasso had been prepared for that, so he'd left more than enough Dasa in place to ambush and kill Ashok. There were only so many ways to the graveyard, and he'd doubted Ashok would lower himself to swimming. His greatest disappointment was that he wouldn't be there to see the damnable Protector expire, but his current magical and medical efforts could not be postponed. "Is Ashok dead then?"

"No! Ashok commanded the Dasa! Just as you do! And they obeyed him!"

"What?" The secrets to controlling the ancient servants were closely held, and only handed down to a few select members of the Lost House. "Impossible."

"There's more. Something strange is happening at the trial. It's as you hoped, her magic has appeared."

Sikasso was still reeling at the idea a Protector could command his most loyal servants. His defenses were ruined. Thera was inconsequential compared to that. "Good, before they left I ordered Kabir to record the images so even if she gets eaten by a demon, at least in the process we could still learn what possessed her." He was more preoccupied thinking about how to change the command words for the remaining Dasa than gaining access to Thera's powers.

"But the demons aren't killing her. That old thing in the dead center of the graveyard, we thought it was just a statue they worshipped, but it's not! It's some sort of ancient device, and it's awakened. They're fighting!"

"What? Who?"

"Thera and the idol! It's like a magical contest of wills. Only from the wild power emanating from it, I don't think it's Thera at all. She's just a vessel to hold it, no different than a chunk of black steel." Waman was actually terrified. "It's the gods! One of them appeared in the light, wrestling the darkness! I saw him!"

Sikasso's new hand shot out and he grabbed Waman by his scrawny neck. He squeezed and Waman's eyes nearly bulged out of his head. "Calm down and speak clearly." A sudden rage came over him, and it took all of Sikasso's will not to rip Waman's throat out. Then he released the pressure. "Explain."

Waman gasped. "I can't! It's the old gods returned! It really is."

This was not the time for fairy tales.

"Your spy tells the truth." There were several heavy footsteps, and then Kabir appeared in the doorway, muddy and scratched. He was dripping swamp water all over the nice rug. "It's no illusion. There's been a manifestation of power the likes of which none of us have ever seen, and it's clashing with an unknown form of ancient demon magic."

"What are you doing here? You're supposed to be observing her!" Sikasso snapped.

"I was, but I flew back as fast as I could when I saw *five* demons coming out of the sea!"

He had to be mistaken. That number wasn't just impossible. It was outlandish. Except Kabir was grim, and though he was a treacherous one, he had nothing to gain from lying about this. A couple demons could raze a town. Five demons was an unstoppable nightmare. If they turned their attention against this place, their house would be lost again. The wizards would be forced to flee. Everything they'd built would be destroyed.

"Sikasso," Kabir said gently. "I hate to interrupt your contemplations, but..."

He realized that his new hand had involuntarily tightened on its own, and he was choking Waman to death. He forced the fingers to unclench, and Waman dropped to the floor, coughing.

Sikasso took a furtive glance at his experiments beneath the cloth. He couldn't afford to abandon them for long, and if he had to retreat, he wouldn't be able to recreate them elsewhere in time before the side effects began.

"Omkar and Yuval's forces are already long gone." Sending away most of his assassins had been a terrible miscalculation. He'd done it to appear confident, but he'd had no way of knowing the Protector could command their deadly guardian servants. "We can't communicate with them until they land, and by the time they turn around it will be too late. Summon every other wizard still in the region back to the house. While you do that I shall place new patterns upon our Dasa so the rest can't be compromised. If the demons turn their rage against us, we will hold here. These walls will not fall a second time."

"That's madness. I didn't exaggerate the number of demons I saw. No fortifications in the world can slow a determined demon for long. We should send the slaves and students inland while we gather our most precious treasures and prepare to evacuate."

Sikasso's voice was a deadly whisper. "Do you challenge my rule, Kabir?"

He could tell the younger assassin was thinking about reaching for one of the strips of demon hide hanging from his belt. If he made a move, Sikasso would rip Kabir's heart from his chest and eat it in front of him while it was still beating. The look Sikasso gave him must have conveyed that fact, because Kabir's survival instincts overcame his pride.

"I do not challenge... But I fear for the future of our house."

"Of course you do," Sikasso snapped. "You've lived your entire life in fear. You hide it well, Kabir, but your doubts plague you and render you weak."

"Regardless, have your spy give those orders. I'm needed elsewhere. I've given my warning. Do with it as you wish. Now I must return to the graveyard."

"Do not think you can shirk your oath, Kabir."

"On the contrary, Master Sikasso, it was love of my house that brought me here briefly. Until Thera returns or dies, I am still obligated to be her guide."

Sikasso gave him a patronizing smile. "Tradition demands no less."

"Tradition is everything." Kabir backed out of the vault. He did not turn his back to walk away until he was in the hall, well out of striking distance. That was an insult, but Sikasso let it pass.

He kicked Waman in the leg. "Get up, you whimpering slug. We have an invasion to repel."

Chapter 37

⌇⌁⌁⌇⌁⌁

Jagdish held up one hand signaling for the Sons to halt. They immediately complied, weapons raised, nervously watching their surroundings.

"Something's not right," he whispered.

"The part where there's a bleeding magical funnel cloud just over thataways? Or where our illustrious leader ran off leaving us on our own?" Gutch whispered back.

Ashok knew what he was doing, and besides, Jagdish had this under control. "Come now, Gutch, if you'd had your way it would just be me and you here."

"I didn't realize what a stupid idea that was at the time."

Jagdish waited for the big man to quit his bellyaching as he surveyed the area. They'd found a patch of relatively solid ground and had been making good time when the hairs on his arms had stood up. The whole place was eerie enough to set his nerves on edge, but something about this particular spot was nagging at him.

It felt like they were being watched.

Turning around, Jagdish signaled Shekar and Eklavya to get ready, who in turn warned their men.

He'd spent a year sparring against Ashok in prison. In between him getting soundly beaten, Jagdish had asked a lot of questions about combat, because Ashok had lived through more of it than anyone else alive. Not to mention that his sword had provided him with the martial memories of generations of his ancestors. He was a walking encyclopedia of battle. So of course Jagdish had asked how best to fight demons. What warrior wouldn't? They were the most dangerous thing in the world after all.

Ashok's first answer had been to have an ancestor blade, since it was the only thing that could easily slice through their incredibly resilient hide. That was handy advice—for about a dozen men in the whole world—but as for the rest of them, there was no good answer, because there was no sure way to beat a demon. Regular steel could occasionally cut them, but that required a near perfect strike, which was difficult considering how ferociously demons fought. Since their white flesh was rubbery and the bones beneath hard as rocks, they were resistant to bludgeoning as well. The concentrated force of a narrow spike on a mace or war hammer that could pierce a steel breastplate usually just bounced off a demon. Fire, even magical fire, did not burn them. You couldn't run one down with cavalry, because horses—even war elephants—refused to go near a demon.

Whenever regular warriors did manage to kill one, it was usually at great cost, with many men giving their lives until a few lucky shots landed. These were the sorts of victories that resulted in warriors becoming legends, with people singing songs about them, and holding feasts in their honor for generations after, because Grandfather so and so had once cut down a demon to save their village and only twenty of his friends had died in the process!

Of course songs and feasts were no comfort to the warriors who died before the killing blow landed.

Shekar Somsak made an abrupt gesture to get Jagdish's attention, and then he pointed across the swamp. It took Jagdish a moment to pick out what he'd seen. Then his blood ran cold. You'd think that something so pitch black would stand out against the dreary browns and sick grays of Bahdjangal, but the demon was surprisingly well camouflaged in the shadows.

It was a hundred yards away, wading through a stream they had just crossed. The water had come up nearly to Jagdish's waist. It barely covered the demon's knees.

He'd never seen a real live demon before. The fearful tales

didn't do them justice, because they were far more bone chilling in the flesh. It was said that no two demons were alike. This one was sort of shaped like a man, upright and walking on two legs, except the thing was easily a foot taller than Gutch, even walking hunched over in a manner that suggested it had a badly twisted spine. Even with that deformity, there was nothing that suggested it was crippled.

As the demon glided through the water with an eerie smoothness, Jagdish forced himself to look away from the terror to check on his men. Beneath the mud streaked on their faces, every single one of them had gone pale. But nobody screamed. Nobody broke and ran.

It was heading in the same direction that Ashok had gone, seemingly drawn toward where the clouds were swirling. It had surely seen them, but the deadly thing looked willing to pass them by for now. Jagdish signaled for the men to remain still, not that they needed the encouragement.

Gutch was kneeling next to him. The big man was so scared he was shaking. He could hear the jingle of chain armor. And then Jagdish realized that it wasn't just Gutch. He was trembling too. Jagdish had seen many battles, and he'd always thought of himself as a brave man, but being in the presence of a demon was so much worse. He was so scared it was making his stomach hurt.

They might have been fine, it was possible fate—that fickle bitch—could have spared them, if one of them hadn't made a mistake. A weapon slipped from someone's wet, cold fingers. The wooden spear shaft made a clunk as it struck bark, and then a splash as it landed in a puddle. The demon froze. Its head was revealed to be a featureless lump, set too low between its shoulders, as it slowly rotated in their direction.

The warrior bringing up the rear of their column was only forty yards from the demon. It focused on Murugan Thao, who'd joined them on the road, proud and bold, but who was now reduced to crouching behind a tree praying to his illegal gods.

The demon's path changed, and now it was heading directly toward them.

Don't move. Don't move, Jagdish thought at Murugan as hard as he could, but he didn't dare make a sound.

No warrior could take that unflinching, hungry gaze for long. Murugan bolted.

The demon might have been more interested in the magical forces gathering in the distance, but when prey ran, predators chased. With an explosive burst of speed, it leapt from the stream and went after Murugan.

"Attack!" Jagdish rose and charged. "Attack!"

The Somsak were quick, and their large crossbows made a distinct sound when they released. Some bolts missed the speeding demon, but a few struck it, only to bounce right off. There were archers among the Kharsawan and they let fly with their long bows, not faring much better.

"Archers hold. Spearmen up!" Jagdish bellowed at the top of his lungs. The warrior who'd dropped his spear in the mud was huddled there, too frightened to move, so Jagdish snatched up the weapon as he ran past.

The demon had already caught up with poor Murugan. It casually kicked out with one long leg, black toes striking the warrior in the heel. Murugan tumbled, momentum taking him on a face-first slide through the mud. It bent over, reaching down for him.

Except another warrior had been hiding nearby. Abor Somsak came out of the bushes, swinging an ax with a berserker scream that would make his raider house proud. He struck the demon in the arm hard enough for weird sparks to fly from its hide.

The demon backhanded Abor across the swamp.

"Spear wall! Spear wall!" The other spearmen were trying to catch up with Jagdish, but since he was going to get to the action before them, he just set the shaft against his side, locked his elbows, and drove the steel point into the demon's back with all his might.

The spear ground to a halt. The shaft flexed and the shock of the impact traveled back into Jagdish's cold, numbed hands. He might as well have charged into a brick wall for the all the good that had done. Jagdish hurried and scrambled back as the demon turned toward him. He barely flinched out of the way as claws whistled past his face.

Murugan may have run, but Jagdish could not call him a coward, because from on his place on the ground, he'd drawn his sword, and hacked at the demon's feet. The demon casually kicked him into the stream.

The other spearmen had reached Jagdish. He held up his own

bent and blunted weapon and shouted. "Spears up!" Warriors and workers of three different houses followed suit. It was almost orderly. If he'd not been scared to death it would've brought a tear to his eye.

"Strike!" The spears were thrust into the demon, retracted, and then thrust again. The monster seemed almost bewildered as the steel blades crashed against it. Reaching for them, it quickly discovered that the spears were slightly longer than its arms. Each time it tried to strike a spearman, that warrior would withdraw, and two others would stab instead.

"Keep it up! Swords and hammers, to the flanks!" Jagdish shouted. His gut told him to fight, but his brain told him to lead. *Damn it.* He was the risaldar, not some pissant footman infantry. He needed to be able to see what was going on.

The warrior he'd taken the spear from, Dilip, had returned to his senses and followed. "I'm here!"

"Take your place and do your bloody job, Nayak." Jagdish tossed the spear back.

The demon was not stupid, so it changed tactics. Since the spears weren't breaking through its hide, it simply pushed into them, then started swatting shafts aside. Wood splintered. Men were knocked down. But the rest stood, and their brothers got back up. It grabbed hold of one man's spear, but the warrior refused to let go, which was a terrible mistake since the demon used it to lever him over its shoulder and toss him through the air.

But the men had heard their orders, and those armed with shorter weapons had moved around the sides. They came at the demon, hacking, stabbing, and cutting.

The demon responded, but each time it did, it got hit in two other places.

"Strike and move out of the way! Rotate through. Let your brothers have a turn."

The demon hadn't been prepared for this.

"You're not showing off for your gods. This is business. Strike and move! Keep those spears up!"

Even a surprised and overwhelmed demon was still dangerous. It moved away from the spears and lunged to the side, sending swordsmen flying. Claws flashed and warriors screamed.

They were past orderly and organized combat now. There were no commands to give in a brawl. Jagdish drew his sword and went into the fray.

Another warrior went down. Jagdish couldn't even tell who it was through all the mud and blood. The demon opened its head and fell atop him, biting deep into the warrior's shoulder, and then shaking him, like a dog with a rat.

Half a dozen warriors were on it then, slashing and striking the demon. Maces rebounded off its back. Swords turned against impenetrable skin.

Since the casteless of Haradas had sworn there were demons near the Lost House, and Jagdish had access to a well-stocked warehouse, he'd made sure the Sons were armed with a variety of weapons. Ashok had said demons came in all sorts of different shapes and sizes, so it made sense that some things would work better than others.

Nothing seemed to work.

With a roar Jagdish struck the demon in the back of its head. The edge of his sword left a visible dent.

Soundlessly, the demon rose. Red human blood was running down its chest. Bits of tattered cloth and flesh clung to its blank face. It was hell, come to dry land.

None of them fled. Jagdish was proud.

Then suddenly the demon lurched to the side.

The lump of a head twisted down to see a sword was stuck *into* its belly. Demon blood—white as cream—spilled from the hole.

The surprised warrior who'd delivered that blow shouted, "I got it!"

In return the demon ripped his face clean off. His body went spinning away in a shower of blood.

But the rest of them saw the wound, and they knew...Demons could die. They just died hard.

The Sons of the Black Sword went after the beast, striking madly at it. Only so many of them could strike at the creature at one time. Jagdish kept them from getting in each other's way. "You're an army, not a mob!" When Jagdish saw men faltering, he dragged them away. "You'll get another turn!" And whenever there was a gap, he took it himself, striking at the demon until the calluses on his hands ripped and bled.

Jagdish had never fought this hard in his life, and it was because he wasn't just fighting for himself, but for *his* men. When it swung at one of them, Jagdish was there, putting his sword and his body in the way. Several times he collided with the beast, and it was surprisingly hot to the touch. The first time, its skin seemed almost soft, the second time he hit it against the grain, and it cut him.

He got knocked down. And got back up. He got knocked down again. And this time one of his men dragged him up. He didn't have the breath left to give directions or orders. This was nothing but brutality.

The demon lifted a struggling worker into the air, claws stuck into his chest. It sunk its other hand into his pelvis, and pulled him *in half.* Though they stood in a rain of blood, the Sons did not falter. Then another wound appeared on the demon's back. And a moment later, one of its arms was spraying milky blood.

The demon was still clawing and biting, but it was slowing down. Then there was a sharp *crack* and it stumbled. One of the multitude of hammer blows had finally broken a bone, and its leg flopped about useless. Then the great beast toppled over.

Gutch was standing there, covered in blood, holding the great spiked club that had finally shattered the demon's knee. He seemed amazed that something had finally worked, before the demon's other foot struck him in the chest and sent him flailing into the mud.

It was down. That's what mattered. And it knew it was beaten! The demon had changed tactics from destruction to escape, and had begun dragging itself toward the safety of the stream. He shouted a command to stop it. What came out of him was more anger than coherent words, but the men understood, and they piled on. One enterprising miner wrapped a rope around its broken dangling leg, and his brothers all grabbed hold. The rope snapped tight, and they dragged it away from the stream.

Jagdish didn't know at what point he'd lost his sword, but he found a discarded mace, and proceeded to club the demon over the skull with it. The mace rose and fell, striking over and over and over, until he forgot what he was doing. In that moment, he was more worker than warrior, it was just repetitive movements. He might as well have been digging a ditch.

The demon made no sound as it was beaten to death.

Jagdish finally stopped when he realized the mace was coated in white, and black bits of hide were stuck to it. The demon's skull was a flattened, splintered mess.

Panting, he looked around the forest. His vision was blurry, so he had to wipe the milk from his eyes in order to see his men. Half the Sons were still standing, covered in blood and demon filth. There were many wounded and many dead.

The forest had fallen quiet except for a rhythmic thumping noise. It took Jagdish a moment to figure out what it was. Murugan, who'd first run, and then been thrown in the stream, had come back fighting. He'd managed to impale his sword into the demon's back, and had picked up a rock to beat against the pommel, like he was driving a tent stake. From the depth, by now he'd put it through the demon's chest and was pounding it into the ground. Jagdish reached out to grab Murugan's arm. The warrior flinched, and was so consumed in the moment he appeared as if he were about to strike Jagdish with the rock, before he realized who it was and what was happening.

"It's over, Nayak."

"I'm so sorry, Risaldar. I caused this."

Jagdish rested one hand on his shoulder. "Go and tend to the wounded."

The Sons of the Black Sword had just killed a demon. That was the stuff of legend.

They were all too stunned to cheer.

Chapter 38

"What manner of evil is this?" Ashok demanded as he approached the field of bones.

The *thing* in the center was an abomination. Not just before the Law, but before all of existence. Dark magic was practically pouring off it in waves, so foul that it made his skin crawl. It was a device of hell and a corruption festering upon the land. He may have no longer been a Protector, but he didn't need to be a perfect servant of the Law to understand that this disgusting demonic creation did not belong in this world.

It had to be destroyed.

The ground was rumbling. Thunder rocked the sky as Ashok started toward the light, and his three Dasa followed.

There were two kinds of light, an unnatural jade glow coming from the abomination, and a hazy white light coming from the other side of it. They seemed to roil and clash against each other, pushing back and forth. The air felt charged, as if lightning had just struck here.

Then Ashok found what he'd come for.

Wreathed in the strange white light, Thera stood in front of the abomination...No...Not standing. She was *hovering* a few inches above the ground, as were hundreds of bits of bone swirling around her feet. Her palms were pressed together before her, head down, eyes closed, almost like she was meditating. Her hair and long coat were floating about her, weightless. There was a whirlwind of clashing colors, lights, and sparks between her and the abomination.

"Damnable witchcraft."

As he got closer, he realized Thera wasn't meditating. Her face was closer to that of someone who was trying to close their mind to resist torture. Thera was in pain. That realization filled him with a great and terrible wrath. The demonic abomination was trying to break her. Though the method of warfare was beyond his understanding, he could tell this was a battleground.

As he went to enter the circle, he crashed against a wall.

There was nothing there. Ashok reached out, but when his hand crossed the boundary, it struck something invisible, yet hard as stone. He pushed. He threw his shoulder against it. He kicked it. There was no give. He moved along the perimeter, searching for a hole, but the air remained solid, from the ground to as high as he could reach. He drew his sword and struck it as hard as he could. It clanged off uselessly.

"Damnable witchcraft!" Illegal magic was keeping him from fulfilling his oath.

He'd already spied a large demon nearby. It had seemed oblivious to his presence, and was watching the conflict from just outside the circle. Its casual presence on dry land offended him, and he wanted nothing more than to go over there and punish the trespasser, but that was no longer his mission.

The demon had heard the commotion and started toward him.

The Dasa must have been set to attack demons on sight, because they lifted their weapons and moved to intercept the monster.

Ashok slammed the tip of his sword into the hardened air. Trying to find some seam that he could pry open, except there was no texture to it. He was used to water being treacherous, but it angered him to have other elements be so vindictive.

"I am Ashok Vadal and I must protect that woman. Get out of my way."

Desperately, he picked one spot and went to work against it. Over and over he struck, concentrating force sufficient to shatter bricks. His knuckles split open. His blood just seemed to hang there in the air, seemingly attached to nothing.

"It will do you no good."

Ashok spun around. A man had seemingly appeared out of nowhere, and he'd been smart enough to appear sitting high in the branches of a tree, so that Ashok couldn't just simply cut him down by reflex. He reached for a knife to throw instead.

"Hold, Ashok Vadal!" The stranger lifted his hands to show they were empty. "I mean you no harm."

Muscled and fit, this one looked more warrior than wizard, but his sudden arrival way up there suggested that wizard was far more likely. Ashok pointed his sword at the man's chest. "I mean you great harm if you do not remove this wall!"

"The barrier is not my doing. I tried to break through myself, but it's a powerful pattern that goes all the way around the grave-yard of demons, from the sky above to the ground below. Look."

As if to prove his point, it had begun to rain, a great crashing downpour. The drops were striking the invisible wall and rolling down it. His bloody knuckle prints became diluted and runny. Cloaked in water, the force around Thera and the evil took on the appearance of a great glass dome.

"I am here to protect that woman." Ashok looked toward where Thera was floating, unmoving, yet locked in a deadly battle all the same.

"As am I. My name is Kabir. I have been obligated to be Thera's guide. She was forced here against her will by a man called Sikasso."

"I know of the Lost House wizard."

"Yes, he's been rather surly ever since you cut his arm off." Kabir looked over at the sound of a crash as the demon hurled one of the Dasa against the invisible wall. He turned back to Ashok. "I wish to help you, but there's not much time."

"Indeed, wizard. There's a multitude of demons converging on this place now."

"I saw them. That's why I landed in a tree! They climb quickly, but not as quickly as I can change shape. Now listen to me carefully. This barrier is the creation of Sikasso. He hoped exposure to demon magic would force the god in her head to come out and fight, and he's trapped her inside until it does, or she dies. Sikasso is the only one who can remove the barrier. If you want to save Thera, you must kill him."

Illegal wizards disgusted him. "Why should I believe you?"

"Do as you see fit. Those Dasa can hold off one demon, but

they'll be destroyed by several, as will you eventually. Even the legendary Black Heart has his limits. Yet those limits are greater than mine. You can defeat Sikasso. I cannot."

The two men studied each other in the crashing rain.

"Why would you help her?"

"Sikasso is my adversary, and I support the idea of her rebellion. Plus, I must admit I've become somewhat fond of Thera." Kabir spread his hands apologetically. "She's direct."

"That she is." He looked back toward the magical conflict and sharpened his vision enough to see that there were tears streaming from her eyes, which were clenched hard shut. Veins stood out in her neck. Then something changed in the battle, and Thera let out a scream of agony.

The abomination was winning.

"Where's Sikasso?"

"He hides within the Lost House. It is that direction, but there is a lake in your way. Go toward that thicket of dead trees and you will find a secret foot path which will take you directly across the marsh."

"When I kill him and the barrier is broken—"

"Then I will fly Thera from here before the demons can get her. You have my word."

An illegal wizard's word was worth salt water, but Ashok saw no other way. "If you have crossed me, Kabir, then nothing will save you from my wrath."

Chapter 39

When gods collide, the last place you wanted to be was caught between them.

Thera couldn't explain what was happening. The Voice had come upon her again, but for once she hadn't been pushed aside. She still had control of her mind, but it was also there inside her head, screaming.

From the outside—trying to get in—was an inconceivable darkness.

Her god was afraid.

The two gods were fighting, but she didn't understand their words. The Voice used a language that was unlike anything she'd ever heard before, and the demon god spoke in colors and madness.

What she could understand was their hate for each other. It burned hot as the sun. That hate extended to their children, for the Voice hated the demons, and the darkness hated humanity. The gods had grown old and weak, a tiny fragment of what they'd once been, but all their hatred remained. If they couldn't destroy each other, they'd use their children to destroy in their name.

These weren't even the real gods, they were partial gods, shadows of shadows, distorted echoes of a sound that had happened a long time ago. Images flashed through Thera's mind. Things that she'd never seen, nor imagined, but were terrifyingly real.

She saw the War in Heaven, forces beyond her comprehension clashing. That was when this piece of the darkness had been torn from the rest of itself, and hurled down in a ball of fire, amid a rain of demons. It had struck the ground so hard that it had dug a crater which had filled with water. Broken, it had died. Its children had sensed its presence and come to worship. Some of them chose to die here next to the piece of their fallen god, because its darkness reminded them of home.

It had lain there, unthinking, until it had sensed a small part of its ancient enemy hiding inside Thera, and its hate was strong enough to wake the dead.

It was hard for her to understand what was going on, but Thera realized that the evil wanted to seize the Voice from her, and consume its power to grow strong again. Tendrils had reached into her mind to rip it out. The Voice had reacted, throwing up walls of fire to repel the invasion. If it couldn't kill her mind, then it would rip apart her body instead. The darkness had no body of its own, so it called for its children to destroy her. The Voice threw up another wall, this time in the real world, to keep out the demons.

This duel would remain between gods. The darkness was satisfied by that. Its hate alone was sufficient to kill another god.

The darkness cut the Voice. It bled stars.

The Lost House appeared through the rain.

It was on a patch of high ground, overlooking the flooded forest. Ashok had sprinted past many ruined buildings half submerged and rotting along the way, but the great house was a thing of restored beauty. Though much smaller, it was styled like the one in Vadal, the place where his fraud had begun, but unlike it, this one had no exterior fortifications. The high walls around it had collapsed during whatever catastrophe had swallowed this city. *Good.* That was one less thing for him to climb.

There was no time for subtlety. He ran as fast as the Heart could drive him, climbing the old trade road, heading straight for the front doors of the House of Assassins.

The foot path had led to a once respectable road, now cracked and overgrown with weeds. There were fields, orchards, and pens of livestock where great government buildings had once stood. Humble homes had been built along the way, and these were obviously lived in, but they were of no interest to Ashok. The man who could free Thera would be inside the big one, along with an unknown number of powerful wizards, who would not look kindly upon his trespass.

He did not know what fate awaited Thera should the demonic thing defeat her, but he would not—could not—allow that to happen.

There were more Dasa guarding the house.

The doors behind them were closed, sure to be locked, and they were solid enough to hold off a battering ram for a time. And a ram would be difficult to use, since the only way to reach those doors was up curving stairs. There were no windows along the first floor. The mansion houses built for the tribal rulers back before the Age of Kings had been designed to be beautiful and defensible.

Like the great house of Vadal, it would have been constructed with other entrances for house slaves and those not important enough to warrant entering through the main hall. Only Thera did not have time for him to search for one of those.

The Dasa started toward him.

Ashok shouted the old command for them to stop.

They kept coming.

There were five of the ancient constructs. Functioning at their highest level, without Angruvadal to help him, Ashok did not know if he would be able to defeat that many at all, and even if he could, surely by then Thera would be dead.

So instead of slowing to fight them, Ashok ran right through them.

He ducked beneath a sword, and rammed his shoulder into a Dasa, driving it back into one of its companions. The three of them fell onto the road, but Ashok used his momentum to roll off them, and sprang back to his feet. He narrowly dodged a hurled spear. Another Dasa got ahold of his long coat as he passed, but Ashok shrugged out of it and kept running.

The Dasa chased after him.

They ran through the rain likes wolves on his heels. He'd fought these things before, but he didn't know if he could outrun them for long.

The house loomed ahead of him. Rather than aim for the solid doors, he'd go for the stained-glass windows far above it.

Even a Protector could not leap that high, but the stone work was rough enough to climb. He just needed to get close.

The Heart made his legs strong, and he launched himself at the wall. Ashok then concentrated its magic into his hands and arms before impact. He slammed into the stones, but with fingers that could bend nails, latched on, and immediately began to climb. With the fresh rain and slick moss, it took everything he had not to slip.

The Dasa skidded to a halt beneath him, and looked up with their blank blue heads. It took them a moment to process this development, but then they latched onto the wall and began climbing after him. They were fierce, but they weren't nearly as agile as he was. He had a lead.

Ashok pulled himself up next to the window. It was made of thousands of colorful bits of leaded glass, held in an intricately twisted iron frame, forming a beautiful picture of some ancient Thakoor, now forgotten by the world. He smashed a hole with his fist, grabbed hold of the central iron bar, and pulled with all his unnatural might. With a roar he wrenched it from its mortar.

The window exploded. Colorful glass rained down on the pursuing Dasa. Rather than just toss down the bar, Ashok hurled it like a spear, knocking the closest servant from the wall. Then he stepped inside the House of Assassins.

Below him was the great hall, and there were wizards there. *Surprise, lawbreakers.*

Ashok jumped down from the window ledge. His boots hit the stone with an impact that would've broken a normal man's legs, and he immediately started toward the nearest wizard.

"Where is Sikasso?"

"Intruder!" That shocked wizard grabbed hold of a piece of magic hanging from a sash around his chest, but Ashok was already on him. He grabbed a handful of hair, and smashed the wizard's face into a nearby statue. Blood from his shattered nose sprayed everywhere.

There were two more on the other side of the hall. He'd obviously interrupted their conversation. "Where is Sikasso?" Ashok was still holding up the dazed wizard by the hair, so he brained him again, this time hard enough to leave a chunk of blood and hair on one marble corner. "*Where?*"

It was said that there was nothing more terrifying than a Protector when he was angry, and Ashok had been the most frightening of them all. They were momentarily taken off balance by his sudden appearance and violence of action, but these were not normal lawbreakers. They were professional killers. They reacted. Hands flashed. Knives flew.

Ashok swung the unconscious wizard around, and his human shield caught the blades instead. Dropping the body, Ashok drew his sword and lunged toward the wizards. They'd only been twenty feet away. He covered that in two steps.

These wizards fought like Chattarak had, using magic to make themselves incredibly fast. Only they were not as experienced as the barge master had been, and he only needed one to question. Ashok had nothing left to live for except his final vow. No office, no ancestor blade, he had lost every purpose except *protect the prophet,* and he had just seen her in mortal danger. It was hard to keep a man of such dedication from his goal. It would take a legion of wizards to stop his rampage.

The first wizard had drawn a short sword as he backpedaled. Ashok caught it with his longer blade and steered it aside, then he kicked that wizard's legs out from beneath him. The other lunged at him with a pair of daggers, but Ashok rolled around them, and then turned and slashed into the wizard's body as he passed by. Steel bit deep into muscle.

The first hit the ground. The second's out-of-control momentum carried him into another statue. The impact toppled the ancient artwork from its perch, and it cracked in two when it hit the floor. That wizard tried to push himself off the wall, but Ashok slashed again, this time aiming for the back of his legs. He screamed and went down.

Ashok stepped on the first one's sword, and then he stabbed him in the shoulder as he tried to rise. "Where is Sikasso?" He looked back to see that the door was shaking, but it had been barred from the inside. Except that locked door wouldn't matter for long, because a blue head appeared in the broken window. The Dasa were excellent climbers.

Turning back to his interrogation, the wizard had reached for some demon bit on his belt, but Ashok twisted his sword, widening the puncture, and the wizard's face contorted in agony. "I will not ask again."

"The vault! Sikasso's in the vault. Back over there. Down the hall, down the stairs."

Ashok pulled his sword from the wizard's shoulder. A gout of blood spurted from the hole and the wizard cried out. He would have finished them on principle but he lacked the time, and besides, they were out of the fight. The Dasa however, would never quit. He saw one of them climbing through the broken window, and it was trying to figure out how to climb down. So Ashok picked up the broken chunk of statue, cocked back his arm, and threw. The stone hit that Dasa in the side of its head, and since it was already precariously balanced, it slipped from its perch, and fell outside.

As he ran down the hall he could hear more wizards shouting. They knew they'd been invaded. The rest of them would have their magic ready and would be hunting him in number.

He found the curling stairs, and he heard a few sets of footsteps rushing up. His first instinct was to hurl himself down into them, and stab as many times as possible as they tumbled to the bottom, but these men were not his target. Only Sikasso was. So Ashok stepped behind a hanging tapestry and waited. If Sikasso was among them, he'd strike, if not, he'd let them pass.

He heard a panicked voice. "It's got to be Ashok!"

"It can't be yet. He can't fly and no one is that fast. There's got to be a demon in the house!"

Same result for your kind either way, Ashok thought idly as he waited for the wizards to rush past. Once they were gone he moved silently down the stairs, bloody sword in hand.

The basement was cool. There were decorative lanterns hanging from the walls, but there was enough distance between them that it was a gloomy, shadowed place. The vault was obvious, because the metal door was like something from the Capitol Bank. Unfortunately, it was closed. He'd run all the way here because he couldn't break through a magical barrier, only to find another made of iron.

Ashok snarled at the sight. He hadn't thought to torture the location of a key from the wizards above. If the gods wanted him to protect Thera so badly, they were certainly making it difficult. *Those ungrateful bastards.*

The brass wheel on the vault door turned, as someone opened it from the other side.

Maybe there was something to this prayer *nonsense after all?*

The heavy door swung open. There was a diminutive wizard

standing there, obviously in a hurry, arms wrapped around a heavy sack bulging with demon parts. His eyes widened when he saw Ashok standing before him. Before he could react, Ashok slammed his fist into the side of the wizard's head hard enough to stun a horse. The little man hit the ground, spilling the sack. Bits of demon wrapped in cloth rolled across the floor.

Ashok stepped into the vault.

It was cold inside. The room was so large that the dim light cast by the few burning candles was insufficient to reveal most of it. Chains dangled from the ceiling, and each of those ended with a big metal meat hook. Many of the hooks were filled. He'd gone inside a worker's slaughterhouse once, and its storeroom had felt similar to this, only it wasn't goats and sides of beef hanging from these hooks, but partial demons. White flesh and black hide dangled.

Along the walls were shelves, filled with books, scrolls, glass beakers, and wooden boxes. There were dried plants, both whole and ground into powder. At the back of the room was an alchemist's work station, where bottles of mysterious liquids boiled atop torches.

And there was the wizard Sikasso.

They'd never really been introduced before he'd turned into a bird and Ashok had removed his wing with an axe, but he recognized his target. Sikasso was a plain-looking, unremarkable man, of average size and build, who'd have no problem disappearing into any crowd. But here, in his home, he wore fine robes and carried himself like a proud Thakoor.

"Ashok Vadal," the wizard said as he took up a sheathed sword that had been leaning against the desk. Sikasso drew the blade and tossed the scabbard aside. "I knew you would come. I have been eagerly awaiting the day I could repay you for taking my arm."

He seemed to have both arms now, but Ashok did not pretend to understand the strange ways of wizards. He stepped over the unconscious man and started toward Sikasso. "I've come for Thera. Remove your magical barrier or else."

Sikasso might have been dreaming about his revenge since their last meeting, but of the many things he might have expected Ashok to say, apparently that had not been among them. "What *barrier*?"

"The dome of hardened air you have placed around Thera and the demon thing. *Remove it!*"

"I've done no such thing. I don't even know a pattern like that."

"The wizard Kabir said it was your creation."

"You believed deceitful Kabir?" Sikasso laughed, genuinely amused. "He sent *you* to kill *me*? Oh, that's good. A bold play from the lad, I can respect that. No, foolish Protector, such a potent shield pattern would have to come from the idol inside of it...or perhaps, the power within Thera is defending itself. If that's the case, then maybe I can salvage something of use from her after all. Either way, you're wasting your time with me."

Ashok hated many things, but liars especially galled him. The wizard's surprise seemed real, and he still needed to free Thera somehow, but Sikasso might just be trying to save his miserable life.

"I'm already here. I will kill you just in case."

"A logical choice, except you will not find victory so easy this time, Black Heart. I've made a few changes since last we met."

Every candle in the vault was snuffed out, plunging them into darkness.

Chapter 40

The gods were trying to tear each other apart. They attacked and countered each other a million times between each of Thera's pounding heartbeats. She was helpless to stop them.

No. She was a daughter of Vane. She was *never* helpless.

There was nothing she could do in a battle between gods that was moving too fast for her to comprehend. But there was still the real world. Maybe she could do something there?

Her muscles seemed frozen. She didn't think that was the evil's doing. It was more likely the Voice trying to immobilize her so she didn't injure herself, like sometimes happened during the damnable seizures it had inflicted upon her.

Let me go, she pleaded.

Her god wasn't merciful. It had used her cruelly and given her nothing but misery. But they were in this together. If she died, it would die.

Let me help, she commanded.

Suddenly, her joints unlocked and her limbs responded. But with that freedom came *unbelievable pain.*

Thera fell in the mud. It was as if her body was on fire, and a giant metal screw was being turned through the bone of her forehead. She'd been wrong. The Voice closing most of her senses off had been an act of mercy.

She could barely see. Light scalded her eyes. There was cold mud beneath her and everything else was made of pain. Trying to look away from the light, she could make out black shapes hurling themselves toward her. *Demons!* Except they were being turned aside, again and again, their bodies squishing like watching a thumb press against the side of a bottle. Only no glass in the world could withstand a demon. For a moment she thought that maybe the pain had driven her mad, because a black shape appeared that was *gigantic,* the size of a house, and it was coming for her.

The great demon crashed against the Voice's wall. It was larger than an elephant, big as the legends had said whales were supposed to have been. When it hit the blackness seemed to flatten against an invisible wall, from ground level to over twenty feet in the air. It didn't break through, but the impact shook the whole world. The massive thing slowly picked itself up, and began plodding away. It was going to make another run.

Something cold struck her burning skin. It was rain water falling through from above. That impact had put cracks in the magic. Nothing could hold for long against a demon so vast.

Thera turned back toward blindness. The idol was just ahead of her, its hate the only thing burning hotter than her pain. She knew this thing was just a container for a splinter of the real evil, a receptacle, like when Omkar had tried to show her how to send visions from one piece of bone to another. She needed to break the container. Her hand fell on a thick leg bone, heavy as a club. It would do.

Forcing herself to her feet, Thera stumbled toward the idol. She crashed against it, cold and waxy to the touch. She drew back and began striking it with the bone. She didn't know what she expected it to do. Her muscles were racked with so much pain she could barely move. This thing had fallen from the sky in a fireball and hit the ground so hard they'd eventually turned the hole into a reservoir. Her feeble efforts wouldn't even scratch it.

Thera kept on hitting it anyway.

The wizards had tried to teach her about the patterns that made up magic, but none of it had made sense to her. They'd gone into that dark area just outside of the real world, where the patterns were made plain, but she'd still been nearly blind. Only the most powerful magical creations had registered to her at all.

The pattern that suddenly appeared before her eyes was nothing like what she'd seen before. This wasn't some hastily drawn afterimage a wizard had scribbled into a book. The Voice was showing her exactly what to do and how to do it, down to the smallest particle. She could see the elements moving into place. The purpose was clear. The gods were showing her how to make a real weapon.

Thera concentrated on that pattern, just as Omkar had shown her, and then she applied it to the raw material in her hands. All of the latent demon magic that still resided in that piece of bone awoke at once. It turned from a lifeless club into a *molten spear*.

She'd never felt so powerful.

The ground rumbled as the massive demon began a new charge. It was going to blast right through the Voice's wall this time and flatten her into a red mess beneath its giant webbed feet.

Thera lifted the spear high and shouted a war cry she'd not used since she was a little girl playing at Dirt War. *"Vane is here!"* Then she drove the concentrated point of magic down into the idol. It struck in a shower of sparks and burned a hole right through it.

The battle in her head abruptly ceased. The light vanished.

There was nothing left to block the rain, and it all came crashing down.

The supernatural agony of the gods' war was gone, but it was suddenly replaced with torn muscles and burned hands. The molten magic had burned right through her leather gloves. Thera looked down at her palms, scorched, as red blood spilled between blackened skin, and screamed.

The idol was dead, truly dead this time, with a glowing, molten hole burned clear through it. Something like the white demon blood poured out, and where it hit the glowing metal, it hissed into steam.

The rumble was growing stronger. Thera looked up from her ruined hands to see the great demon barreling her way. There was no longer a wall to stop it. She'd never get out of the way in time.

Another pattern appeared before her eyes. This one was familiar, because Omkar had tried to teach it to her. She'd failed then, because she'd lacked focus and the wizard's version was childish garbage in comparison to this. She concentrated, ripped the magic from the bones scattered around her feet, and imagined the world around her changing to fit the Voice's pattern.

Everything went black as Thera went to the space between.

The great demon's pattern was gigantic as it bore down on her. She flinched and covered her head as she was surrounded by a storm of glowing sparks. The mundane elements that made up her body passed cleanly through the magical elements which made up the demon.

Then she fell back into the real world.

The giant had crashed past. Bones had been pulverized into splinters or driven into the dirt in its wake. It had even knocked over its idol, but that didn't matter, since it was just a broken, empty vessel now.

The shaking of the ground was too much, and Thera lost her footing. What little strength she had left was rapidly leaving her. The pain in her hands was too much to bear. The clear connection to the Voice was gone. Magic did not come easily to her, so using it left her weak and sick. She went to her knees beneath the rain.

More demons were approaching, sleek and deadly, and probably angry that she'd just speared their tiny god.

No more patterns appeared before her eyes. Her god had gone quiet, worn out from its battle. She was on her own again. She stuck her burning hands into a puddle, quenching the flames that still danced on her gloves.

A black shape loomed over her. She couldn't even curl her burned fingers around one of her knives to fight back. Thera had fully accepted death when she realized that demons couldn't fly, and the black thing streaking toward her was in the shape of a giant hawk.

Talons latched onto her shoulders an instant before a demon reached her. Everything lurched violently as Thera was yanked from the ground. The demon was right behind them as they streaked along, her feet dangling in the reeds, but with a few mighty beats they climbed higher, leaving the vengeful demons behind.

The ground flashed by below as she faded in and out of consciousness. The talons were locked tightly upon her so she wouldn't fall, hard enough to bruise her but Kabir was being careful not to pierce her skin. The experience should have been frightening or exhilarating, but compared to being a gods' battleground, she was too wrung out to notice. She closed her eyes. The wind froze the swamp water on her face and made the pain in her hands even worse.

Thera awoke when she hit solid ground.

There was a blur as the hawk disappeared and Kabir stepped from the darkness. Eyes still glowing, he shouted, "I need help! Bring water and bandages." Then he knelt next to her. "Can you hear me, Thera?"

Flat on her back, weak as a babe, she managed a feeble nod. She didn't know where they'd landed exactly, but the floor and walls were rough stone, overgrown with vines and moss. She realized they were high up, atop a ruined tower. Then she turned her head and saw the tall roof of the House of Assassins not too far away.

"Drink this. It's extremely potent and will numb the pain," Kabir said as he put a vial to her lips. The liquid was incredibly bitter. "Rest now. We will care for your wounds. You survived the trial, and it was like none that has ever happened before." Kabir actually sounded excited as he whispered to her. "If anything, Sikasso underestimated what you can do. You're more valuable than he ever imagined. With you among us, we'll finally be able to crush the Capitol!"

A female wizard had come running up the stairs, followed by a muscular slave. "Kabir! You must hurry! Ashok was seen inside our house."

"I'm aware," he stated. "I told Ashok that killing Sikasso was the only way to save his beloved prophet."

"What? Why would you do that?"

"Because Sikasso's time is done, sister. He's gone mad. This is our time to seize control. Now help me with her. There are more than enough bones in her satchel to satisfy the trial, so she's one of us now. Even if she wasn't, we must keep her alive. She's far more valuable than you can imagine."

"I defer to your wisdom, Kabir," the woman said, as she went to retrieve a pack that had been stashed in the corner.

"Don't worry, Thera. This is one of my fellow conspirators. I'm sorry to use your devoted follower like that, but Ashok is the only one who has a chance to defeat Sikasso, or at least weaken him enough that I can finish him off. Before, I thought I could do it myself, but I just learned how he managed to get his arm back."

The slave began using a wet cloth to clean her hands. She realized it was the one-eyed slave who was really Kabir's blood brother...*Dattu was his name.* She screamed when the fabric touched her burned palms. Dattu flinched at the sound, because somewhere in his magically addled brain, kindness remained.

Kabir leaned in close to whisper in Thera's ear. "There was a demon arm in the vault, I knew it because I was the one who retrieved it. Perfect condition, almost exactly man sized. The left...Same as Sikasso's lost. The arm was there before Sikasso's revelation, but when I went to speak with him in the vault earlier, the hook which had held it hung empty. A melding of man and demon! Such wild magic is forbidden, even to us. When the others learn of this, they'll be enraged. Sikasso was so desperate to maintain control that he's done the unthinkable."

Even in her dazed state, Thera realized what that meant. It was widely said there was nothing in the world more dangerous than a demonic hybrid. One had nearly killed Ashok in Jharlang, and that was when he'd still had his magic sword. Kabir had just sent Ashok to his doom.

"No." She tried to sit up. "You can't."

"It's all right. It's for the best." Kabir gently pushed her back down. He looked at her burned palms. "Don't worry. If you lose your hands, the wizards of the Lost House can serve as your new hands."

"Evil hands," Thera mumbled as the female wizard returned with the supplies. She stopped just behind Kabir and pulled something from the pack.

"Your magic is like nothing we've ever seen before, Thera! With such power combined with our knowledge, not even the Capitol could stop us! We could rule the world!"

Kabir's triumph was premature, because just then the other wizard reached around, long knife in her hand, and she slashed his throat.

"I'm sorry, Kabir. Sikasso found us out. I had no choice."

Kabir never knew what hit him. She'd opened him from ear to ear, and deep. The arteries had been severed. He grabbed for his neck, but his hands were instantly drenched in blood. It rolled down the front of his coat in great rivulets.

The look on his handsome face was one of denial, then terror, and then nothing.

The woman stepped away from Kabir as he gradually slumped over.

"He said you passed the trial. Then welcome, sister." She looked down at Thera, almost apologetically, as she wiped her bloody knife on a rag. "It is unfortunate about your guide, but Sikasso made me a far better offer. Kabir would've done the same to me."

There was no honor within a House of Assassins.

Trembling, Dattu looked toward Kabir, lying there dead. The wizards may have called each other brother and sister, but those were just words. Only Thera could see that in that broken, cursed man, the realization that his real brother, his *little* brother, had just been murdered. Kabir had betrayed him and destroyed his mind, but the slave still remembered *family*. He knelt there, stunned.

"Now let's get you back to the master so he can decide what to do with you. Hurry up, slave."

Poor shaking Dattu obediently went back to wrapping Thera's hands, until he bumped the piece of metal she'd hidden in her sleeve. As Dattu realized what it was, Thera could see the wizard's construction crumbling. Kabir had said his brother didn't have the heart of a killer, but he was wrong. Anyone could kill. They only needed a good enough reason. She looked the poor broken slave in the eye and nodded.

A single tear rolled down Dattu's face as he pulled the shiv from her sleeve.

Chapter 41

Ashok's eyes adjusted quickly. Sikasso had seemingly vanished. The vault was dark, but it wasn't absolute. The odd torches beneath the alchemical ingredients were casting some light, and the big metal door leading to the hall was still open.

Expecting a wizard's trick, Ashok shifted his weight to the balls of his feet, raised his sword to a defensive position, and waited.

The shadows were deep. Sikasso had to be hiding somewhere within them. The wizard had changed their environment for a reason. Then Ashok would adjust for that change in a way the wizard wouldn't expect. He used the Heart to sharpen his hearing. A stream of artificially cool air caused a vibration of chains and the creak of meat hanging from hooks. He listened for breathing or the movement of living flesh, but there was only the hanging dead.

Had Sikasso fled? *No. He is here.* Sikasso seemed more pragmatist than coward, but this had become personal. The wizard was playing a game. Time was on his side. The longer he forced Ashok to wait, the more likely Thera was to die.

"Come out, Sikasso, so I can remove the rest of your limbs." He moved forward, slowly, still listening.

The vault door slammed shut. He turned to look and saw the brass wheel was still spinning, but there was no one there. Ashok cursed himself. Had he just been locked in? Was the wizard out in the hall, calling for reinforcements, and having a laugh?

There was a small movement behind him, the sole of a shoe rubbing on stone, and the whisper of silks. Ashok turned just in time to dodge the sword point that had been aimed for his spine. The attack had come out of nowhere. Sikasso followed with a flicking jab for his eyes, but Ashok parried. The wizard darted back into the shadows... and was gone.

How had he done that?

There was another noise, this time from the opposite side. Sikasso came out from behind a hanging demon, swinging for Ashok's lower leg. He lifted it in time, but it had been so close that steel touched the leather of his boot. He countered, swinging for Sikasso's ribs, but his sword passed through nothing.

Sikasso had vanished again.

"Impressive. A normal man wouldn't have been able to react in time." Sikasso's voice seemed to come from all around him. "My old master once told me, make a Protector blind and he'll still fight with his other senses." One of the hanging demons was pushed. It collided with another, causing a chain reaction. The rattle of chains was deafening to Ashok's augmented hearing. Then Sikasso used his wizard's trick to cross the room, and he set the dangling limbs over there moving as well. "Overwhelm those senses, then strike."

Unfortunately, Sikasso's old master had been a clever one. There was too much movement and noise for Ashok to pick out the subtle shift of air as Sikasso came out of the shadows behind him. Steel zipped through the muscles of his back. Ashok reacted, dropping onto his shoulder, and rolling forward. He came right back up facing his foe, who was already gone.

Ashok winced. He'd been cut. Not deep, but the sting reminded him he was mortal.

So this was the wizard's game... If he'd still had Angruvadal he would've been warned of the attacks sooner and cut Sikasso down. Without it, and deprived of his superior senses, Ashok would become a creature of pure reaction. The power of the Heart flooded through his limbs.

The sword pierced his shirt, only Ashok moved away from it near instantly, fast enough to avoid spilling blood. Sikasso followed with a kick, that barely caught Ashok's side. He crashed against a hanging demon. Ashok guessed what was coming next, pushed off, and was out of the way before Sikasso's sword raised green sparks off the demon hide.

Sikasso kept coming at him. It was as if he could enter any shadow, and come out another at will. It took all of Ashok's knowledge and all the speed the Heart could muster to keep him ahead of the attacks.

The voice came from all around again. "Oh, you're fast. I've killed a few of your kind over the years, but you make them look like sloths."

So far Sikasso had been fighting like a man, coming at Ashok from angles he could predict and defend. He should've known such a powerful wizard wouldn't limit himself to the predictable. This time the sword came from above, slicing deep into Ashok's shoulder as Sikasso fell from the rafters. Ashok had jumped ten feet to the side by the time the wizard disappeared through the floor. Solid things were mere distractions for him.

He had to be using an incredible amount of magic to do so many tricks so quickly, but Ashok had not seen the wizard holding onto any vessel. With most wizards, all you had to do was stay ahead of them until they exhausted their bodies or the supply of magic they had stored in demon parts. Was Sikasso drawing magic from the stores around him?

Sikasso came up out of the floor behind him. Ashok felt the blade bite his calf, but he moved with blinding speed, turning down into the attack. His knee slammed into solid muscle and Sikasso let out an audible gasp before he dropped back into the shadows.

That hit bought him a second to think. There were too many angles. Half blind, Ashok ran to the side, until he crashed against a shelf. Bottles clattered and fell, shattering on the ground, spilling pungent fumes. But at least he had his back against something solid.

An arm came out of the wall, encircled his neck, and dragged him into the dark.

Ashok had never gone in between worlds before. It was too still, too quiet. His senses were dulled. Everything seemed slower. It reminded him a bit of being underwater, and that thought made him extremely angry.

Then he was flung out the other side, where he smashed into the desk. Beakers shattered. Alchemical ingredients spilled. Some of them burst into flames. At least that would provide more light.

Sikasso stepped out of the darkness. "I can move between with impunity now, easy as breathing. If I'd realized the potential, I would've made this improvement a long time ago."

Ashok sprang to his feet and attacked. Surprisingly, this time Sikasso did not flee. Their blades crossed. In the fire light, the wizard's eyes were wide, fevered. Ashok tried to hurl him down, but Sikasso didn't budge. He shoved back, and Ashok was thrown violently against the wall.

"Oh yes. Such power. All magic is addictive, but this..." Sikasso made a fist with his gloved hand. "This is godlike."

Ashok winced as he got up. Something had popped in his spine. Every second he listened to this criminal blather was a second that Thera was closer to death. Ashok struck. Sikasso was incredibly fast. Protector fast. And far more skilled than any wizard Ashok had faced before. Their blades moved back and forth in a razor-sharp blur.

But Sikasso overextended, Ashok got past his guard, and slammed the hilt of his sword into the wizard's mouth with a blow sufficient to tear a regular man's jaw off. The wizard dropped his blade.

Sikasso stumbled back, spitting blood. Ashok went after him, raising his sword high, and cleaving downward at Sikasso's head. The wizard reacted instinctively, raising his arm to block. Which Ashok was fine with, since he had already declared his intent to remove them.

The edge hit true. Ashok had delivered such a blow many times. Skin and muscle should have parted with ease, the twin bones of the forearm should have exploded. And the blade should have continued on, barely slowed, to be planted deep into Sikasso's skull.

The sword bounced off his arm.

Ashok stared at his weapon, incredulous. The fine Vadal steel had curled on impact. He'd hit so hard it had stung his hands. That hadn't been like hitting armor. That was like hitting *demon*.

Sikasso slowly lowered his left arm, the sleeve cut and hanging. The fire reflected off the obsidian black below.

"Hybrid abomination!" Ashok shouted.

"That's a secret you'll take to your grave, Protector." Sikasso launched himself forward.

Twisting, Ashok drew his sword back, aiming for the heart. Sikasso slammed right into the point, his momentum shoving the steel clean through his ribs. But that didn't even slow the wizard down. He drove Ashok back into the wall. They hit so hard that a century of collected dust was knocked from the ceiling.

Sikasso slammed his fist into Ashok's face, hard enough to put a thin crack in his skull, from his teeth, through his nose, and into his eye socket. The back of his head slammed into the wall. The next shot, Ashok ducked, and demonic knuckles pulverized that bloody stone into powder. Ashok twisted his sword, trying to widen the hole, grinding steel against ribs. Red and white fluids poured from the wound, but with a roar, Sikasso lifted him into the air, turned, and hurled him across the vault.

He crashed through the chains, before he hit the floor hard, skidding across it.

Sikasso pulled the Vadal sword out of his chest, dropped it, and started after him, pushing through the swinging demons. "I did what I had to do. I was born to rule this house. No one can take that from me. I made an oath. I will do whatever I must to see it done."

"By becoming a monster?" Ashok struggled to get up. He was seeing double. There were two Sikassos coming to kill him. That blow to the head was making his brain swell.

"We're all monsters to someone. How many thousands of widows and orphans cry themselves to sleep at night because of the murders committed by Black-Hearted Ashok? You are the monster. This is your fault. I was looking for another way, but your arrival forced me to take the more dangerous path. It's because of you I used this arm, and it's because of you that I sent Thera to her trial."

Ashok put the Heart to healing the crack in his skull. He needed to buy time for it to work.

"How have you not lost control?" Hybrids were normally driven insane with bloodlust. Sikasso seemed angry, but rational. Their sickness quickly became obvious, because it caused terrible mutations of the flesh. Obviously, the new arm had sent veins and arteries crawling to his heart to feed it, which was why he bled demon blood, but other than the telling hole in his chest, Sikasso looked completely normal. "What kind of illegal magic is this?"

"I am far from the first to try to blend human and demon, but I am the first who will succeed. Through the arcane knowledge my people have gained, and by the strength of my will, I will not allow it to corrupt me. Living demon flesh never runs out of magic. It renews continually. With that power, I can create the patterns necessary to keep it under control."

"Not even criminals will follow an abomination."

"As long as I do my part, they'll never know."

"You'll go crazy eventually." Though Ashok did not find this amusing, he forced himself to laugh, just because he thought it might enrage his foe, and rage causes mistakes. "We'll see how loyal your assassins are once you lose your mind and start drinking blood and eating babies. You're the one who cursed Nadan Somsak. You know I'm right."

"Then they'll accept my affliction because I'll be unstoppable. I'll return this house to glory and burn the Capitol to the ground. My people will love me for it. They will appreciate my sacrifice."

Ashok got shakily to his feet. He could almost see and think clearly again. Sikasso stopped a few feet away.

"I'm not a monster. I am a seeker of truth and a solver of mysteries. I am the leader of the Lost House and the taker of lives. But most important of all, I will be the man who killed Ashok Vadal."

Sikasso swung, but Ashok had been ready for that. He ducked as he pulled a dagger from his belt. He came up and slammed it into Sikasso's guts, hard enough to lift him off the ground. Ashok shoved him back, stabbing the whole way. Sikasso hit the wall, and Ashok kept on stabbing.

"You're nothing but an abomination," Ashok bellowed as he perforated Sikasso's torso another half dozen times.

"So are you." Sikasso smashed a fist into Ashok's chest, sending him staggering back. "There is black steel inside you. I can smell it. We are both hybrids of a sort."

Fiery pain radiated out from the impact point. Ribs had broken. Ashok struggled to breathe. Sikasso struck him with a mighty overhand blow that sent Ashok to his knees, dazed.

Sikasso continued speaking, unperturbed by the multitude of what should have been fatal wounds. "I couldn't before, but I can see it now. The black steel is in your blood. It intends to use you the same way this arm will try to control me... Only I'm better than you, stronger, smarter. I will bend the demon magic to my will. You've been nothing but an unwitting pawn your whole life."

Sikasso's demon hand shot out and clamped around the back of Ashok's neck, hard as a worker's vise. He effortlessly lifted Ashok high into the air.

"And now that life is over."

Ashok saw the danger coming, but there was nothing he could do in time. The wizard swung him around and he was impaled on one of the dangling hooks.

Ashok screamed as the curved steel slid into his chest.

"You know what else my old master taught me about Protectors? The best way to kill one is to cut his heart in two." Sikasso let go.

His body dropped. The chains snapped taut. The hook pierced Ashok's heart and burst out his back.

Not even the Heart of the Mountain could save him from such a wound.

Ashok dangled there, boots inches off the ground, helpless... dying.

"Now the mighty Ashok Vadal is just another dangling piece of meat."

There was a banging against the vault door. "Master Sikasso!" The voice was muffled. "Demons approach! We need you!"

"Deal with them! I'm busy!" Sikasso roared, never looking away from Ashok. "Before you go to the endless nothing, I need you to realize you've failed. You only had one thing to protect, Protector, and you couldn't even do that. Once I've dealt with these trespassers, I'm going to rip Thera's magic out of her. Then I'm going to skin you, and pluck every piece of black steel from your corpse, so that even the broken remnants of your sword serve me. I need you to understand this."

The world was fading away. Ashok could not fear death. There was just an emptiness where the fear should have been.

Death cannot take me. I am not finished.

Had Ishaan Harban had similar thoughts go through his mind before the darkness had taken him? It had done him no good either after Ashok had stabbed his brother in the heart.

He could no longer keep his head up. Blood ran down Ashok's limp fingers to splatter against the floor below. That red puddle reminded him of a long-ago memory, tiny casteless hands scrubbing blood from the floor. Then that too was gone...

The wizards in the hall were still pounding on the door, but Sikasso waited, watching Ashok until the light faded from his eyes.

"It is done," Sikasso hissed once he was certain.

Ashok Vadal was dead.

Chapter 42

Demons to the left. Wizards to the right. And Jagdish once again wondered why fate was such a stone-hearted bitch.

He'd sent the wounded back to the barges. Their leader, Ashok the unstoppable killer, was still missing. That left Jagdish with only fifteen men to storm a fortification held by an unknown number of enemies with dangerous magic.

It was a good day to be a warrior.

"Sons of the Black Sword, heed my words! We are mighty! We have already defeated a soldier of hell today! Compared to that, what are some cowardly wizards?"

His men roared. The battle fever was on them. They were from different houses and even different castes, but they'd done the impossible together. And they'd had time for that realization to sink in while he'd run them across the rest of the swamp.

"It's just a little bit further now. Eyes up. Double time!"

Now they were nearly at their journey's end. Jagdish would have his revenge. Gutch would have his treasure. The Sons would rescue their prophet. Or not, and they'd all die out here on the edge of nowhere, and no one would ever know of their heroic exploits. But such was life!

Shekar rushed out of the trees. He'd ordered the Somsak to range ahead as scouts. Say what you would about their barbaric nature, but those men could run through a forest like deer. Murderous, tattooed, raider deer. Jagdish moved to the side and stopped to hear Shekar's breathless report.

"Bad news, Risaldar. The big demon is swimming across that lake directly towards the wizards' house."

"How can you be sure?"

"The lake isn't that deep, so it's more like wading than swimming."

"Salt water..." The scouts had seen the group of demons a few minutes earlier. He'd been hoping they'd head back to sea, but they were plodding along up the coast instead. The normally swift creatures seemed inclined to proceed at the pace of their slowest ally, which was unfortunately the biggest demon he'd ever heard of.

"We'll get there first, but the demons won't be far behind. There are some warriors with blue-painted skin waiting to fight them at the shore. I don't think they'll hold for long though."

Going in at all was suicide. They'd be better off running away and letting the demons tear the place apart. The logical thing to do was to return to the barges and give the demons a few days to satisfy their bloodlust, then sneak back in to loot the place afterward.

"I know what you're thinking, but we've got to save our prophet first," Shekar begged.

"She's not my prophet, Havildar."

"You didn't get to hear her in Jharlang, or see one of the gods appear that day. Believe me, sir, she speaks for the Forgotten. It's true! We came so far to find her, if we abandon their chosen servant now, the gods will forsake us forever."

At times Jagdish had to remind himself that, though he was very proud of this little group he'd helped mold into the semblance of a functioning military unit, they were still a bunch of religious fanatics who believed in tall tales.

"Please, Risaldar, I beg you. We must do the right thing."

Jagdish mulled it over. *What would Ashok do?* Probably something insane that would instantly be the death of a normal man. That was no help. "How much time do we have before the demons arrive?"

"At this pace, by the dots of that pocket clock you're so fond of, fifteen minutes at most."

Regardless of what had brought Jagdish here, it was not what these men were fighting for. Their mission was to serve their gods. He had no doubt at this point they'd follow his orders because they trusted him, but a good leader never put his own desires first. It was about the mission and then the men.

"Then we'd better go faster." Jagdish raised his voice. "Sons! Full run! Don't slow until we're knocking on the wizard's door. Move! *Move!*"

The men picked up the pace. Shekar's marked-up face split into a delighted grin. "The gods will bless you for your faith, Risaldar!" Then the scout took off through the trees.

Jagdish just shook his head, and set out at a run to catch up. It was easier going now since the treacherous swamps had given way to pastures, and thankfully the rain had stopped as suddenly as it had begun. The warriors were used to running long distances, but his handful of workers were struggling to keep up. There are different kinds of strength, and strong arms did not necessarily make for strong lungs.

It didn't take Jagdish long to catch up and then pass most of the men. "Come on! We're almost there," he shouted, encouraging the workers in the rear. Poor Gutch was so red faced that he looked like his heart was about to rupture. "This is why you don't see many round bellies in the warrior caste, Gutch!"

Gutch didn't have the wind sufficient to insult him back, but he still managed to give Jagdish a vulgar gesture.

"That's the spirit, friend. Just think about all that treasure up there and keep going." Jagdish left the workers behind and pushed harder. It had been months since he'd thought about Ashok breaking his leg, but that bone was really beginning to hurt, warning him that he needed to slow down, but Jagdish would be damned if he wasn't the first of them to reach the Lost House.

The column ran past crumbling ruins of once great buildings, now serving as mere corrals for livestock. The pigs and goats were snorting and panicked by the smell of nearby demons. There was a cluster of wooden houses. These were of newer construction, simple, humble dwellings, probably for servants or those who didn't rate a spot inside the great house.

They saw no one. No warriors tried to stop them. No wizards lurked in ambush. The forces of the Lost House were otherwise occupied. There was nothing more distracting than a pack of rampaging demons, but Jagdish wasn't about to thank the foul oceans for anything.

The path curved uphill. With burning legs, even some of the warriors began to falter. Jagdish didn't need to shout encouragement to them. He just put one boot in front of the other until he was past them. It was a universal truth across every house, that proud young warriors did not like being shown up by anyone, especially an officer. So seeing Jagdish get ahead of them made them push harder to keep up.

The top of the hill opened onto wide flat. A few hundred yards ahead of them was a magnificent building, but Jagdish didn't pay any attention to the lavish decorations or intricate carvings. He focused on the fact that the Lost House had a very solid-looking set of reinforced doors and no ground floor windows. It wasn't like they'd carried ladders or siege equipment through the swamp.

It didn't matter. They'd come this far, and he was getting in there if he had to dig a hole through the wall with his fingernails.

There were spots along the roof where archers could be hiding. If they ran up in a strung-out line, they'd be easy pickings for arrows, or since these were wizards, something worse. So Jagdish held up his fist. "Slow!" He'd let the hounds catch up with the gazelles, or in the case of Gutch, the ox. "Group up!"

The Somsak raiders immediately began turning the hand cranks to cock their powerful crossbows. Of course, leave it to the mountain barbarians to outrun Jagdish. If he was a few years younger he would've showed those tattooed maniacs what's what.

"Remember, lads, no mercy, no quarter. You fight a wizard, you gang up and kill him quick. Don't give 'em an inch. The longer you fight, the more tricks they'll pull."

As the rest of the men reached the crest, Jagdish gave them directions. They'd lost so many men to the demon that the two squads he'd organized them into had basically ceased to exist. It was easier to address them by their houses than by name in the heat of the moment. "Somsak spread out, watch for archers. Thao, Akershan, on me. Kharsawan, as soon as the workers catch up, bring up the rear with them. Go."

They started toward the house at a quick walk. There was a ruined tower nearby which would be a fine spot for an observer. Jagdish thought he caught a bit of movement up there, so he got Shekar's attention and pointed. Satisfied the Somsak had it covered, Jagdish turned back to his men.

"Risaldar!"

Jagdish looked back just in time to see a woman plummet from the top of the tower. Limp, she tumbled through the air. The fall was soundless until the abrupt wet *thud* at the end.

Shekar held up his crossbow to show that the bolt was still there. "Wasn't me."

Jagdish drew his sword as he approached the corpse. The fine clothing indicated she was probably one of the Lost House. Her limbs were twisted in odd directions, but it was fairly obvious it wasn't the fall which had killed her, but rather the chunk of metal sticking out of her bleeding ear canal.

"Think that's a wizard?" Shekar whispered.

"I certainly hope so."

Shekar approached cautiously, then squatted next to the woman. He grabbed hold of the weapon that had killed her, slid it right out of her head, and held it up to examine it. The Somsak was so nonchalant about it that even jaded Jagdish grimaced.

"It's not even a real blade, Risaldar, just a sharpened chunk of pot metal."

"I told you wizards aren't that tough," Jagdish said with forced bravado, because really, nobody was tough once stabbed in the ear hole. Yet who had killed this wizard? This didn't look like Ashok's work. Did they have other allies here?

He got his answers a moment later when two people descended the broken tower's stairs. One of them was a woman, as filthy with swamp muck as the Sons, so covered in mud that it was hard to tell what she looked like, but from the way the man was supporting her, she had been wounded. He was dressed in drab worker's garb, bald, and missing an eye. Her hands were wrapped in gauze, and even though she was practically being carried down the stairs, she met Jagdish's gaze, head up, proud as any warrior.

"She murdered my guide," the woman seemed a little out of it as she explained herself, almost as if she'd been drugged. "He was a treacherous bastard, but he was my treacherous bastard. Serves her right."

Shekar and the other Somsak must have recognized her, because they immediately went to their knees. One of the workers from Jharlang cried out, "It's the prophet!"

That answered what would have been Jagdish's next question.

"Who are you people?" Thera demanded, confused why a bunch of strangers were suddenly bowing before her.

"I am Risaldar Jagdish. These are the Sons of the Black Sword." He answered on behalf of all of them, since most of his fanatics had gone to bowing. Jagdish wasn't about to bow to some outcast, regardless of how many imaginary gods she had in her head. "These men have come a long way to find you."

"Really?"

Jagdish could see it plain upon the faces he'd come to know so well. They truly believed this woman spoke for their gods. This was devotion unfeigned. It made Jagdish a little sad. This was no longer his unit to command, in a way it never had been, but it had been an honor to be their steward for a time.

"They're here because they believe in the Forgotten. This is your army, Thera. They're not many, but they are good men, strong and true. They are yours to command. Please, command them well."

"*I* have an *army*?" Thera seemed rather surprised by this development, but then a malicious grin slowly spread across her face. "Then I want to burn this place down."

"We've got to loot it first!" Gutch interjected.

"The wise thing to do now is retreat," Jagdish said. She might speak for them, but the gods hadn't taught this woman a damned thing about tactics. "There are demons on their way."

"Risaldar," Thera was battered and exhausted, but there was steel in her voice. "There's always time for arson."

Chapter 43

Ashok was truly dead.

Once, he'd thought he died in Jharlang, but that had merely been close, on the edge between life and death. This was something different entirely.

He had been promised that death was nothing. This was not *nothing*.

Death was indescribable.

Until the gods spoke with a voice as thunder.

Hathiyaar Punarjanm.

The black steel embedded in his chest turned into molten fire.

His heart couldn't beat split in half, but Angruvadal gave him strength, and then it shocked him with a bolt of lightning.

Life came rushing back.

His eyes flew open. Ashok still hung from the meat hook stuck in his chest.

Angruvadal had conquered death, but did nothing to dull his pain. Such agony was like nothing he had ever experienced before, but he traded pain for a cold fury as he assessed his situation.

Sikasso had shed his blood-soaked, tattered robes. His left arm was a sleek shadow. Black veins were visible spreading from his armpit and across his chest. The multitude of stab wounds across his body had already sealed. The abomination went to a shelf, dried off some of the blood with a rag, and then pulled on a new shirt to hide his evil arm from his subordinates, who were still pounding on the door and begging for their master's aid.

"Stop your infernal knocking. I'm on my way."

With quiet determination, Ashok filled his lungs again. *Thank you, Angruvadal.*

Sikasso spun the wheel and opened the heavy door. "What?"

"Master Sikasso, a few demons are crossing the lake, including the biggest one we've ever seen. We've sent the Dasa to slow them but they'll be here any—" The wizard stopped when he realized that the vault had been torn apart and covered in blood. He noticed the first wizard Ashok had knocked out, and moved over to help his moaning brother. "What happened to Waman? Are you all right, master?"

"Ashok Vadal came for me," Sikasso said with false modesty as he tied his sash. "So I killed him."

The younger wizard looked toward where Ashok was hanging. "He doesn't look very dead to me."

Ashok had begun struggling, but his feet couldn't reach the ground. He needed to get his weight off the hook to free himself. So reaching high, he grabbed hold of the chain, and pulled himself up. Just taking his body weight off the hook was an incredible relief.

Sikasso's head snapped around. "Impossible."

Once Ashok pulled to where his face was even with his hands, it gave him enough slack to work with. He held onto the chain with one hand, bicep straining, while he reached down with his other hand to pull the hook out of his chest. It was rather slippery, and made a sucking noise as it was drawn free. Once the hook was out, he let go, and dropped, flopping uselessly prone.

"*Why won't you die?*" Sikasso roared.

"Truthfully, I wouldn't mind." Ashok lay on the floor and laughed as Angruvadal welded his heart back together. This time his laughter was real. "But I too, am bound to an oath."

A fury rolled over Sikasso. No matter what medicines he'd taken or potions he'd brewed, nothing could hold back a frustrated demon for long. His face contorted with murderous rage as he ran for Ashok.

Good. Rage makes you foolish.

Ashok let the abomination take hold of his shirt to yank him from the ground, but before he could be thrown, he grabbed onto

Sikasso's human hand and twisted, grinding the joints. Protector acolytes spent hundreds of hours learning various ways to break limbs, and hundreds more practicing on each other. Ashok used his leverage to snap Sikasso's wrist. The wizard bellowed in his ear. Then, still locked onto that wounded hand, Ashok turned, throwing his elbow on top of Sikasso's and shoving down. There was a *crack* as the wizard's elbow broke.

There would be no fleeing through the darkness this time, because Ashok was not going to let go of him until every part of Sikasso was broken.

The wizard tried to hurl Ashok away, but he'd latched on. They slid through the puddle of blood and crashed against the wall. His burning heart was pounding, but it felt *strong*, as if Angruvadal had lent him some of its righteous might. Ashok got one hand free, and used that to slam Sikasso's skull against the stone.

He kept hitting Sikasso in the head, trying to keep him too rattled to use magic. Even with one arm dangling, the demon blood pumping through his body made Sikasso far stronger, so it took all of Ashok's skill to grapple him. The wizard's fine shoes slipped in the blood, and they both went down. Instinct and training enabled Ashok to stay on top. He got one arm beneath Sikasso's chin, tightened his grip, and twisted. Sikasso thrashed about as they kept rolling across the slick floor.

The other wizard reacted to seeing his master being thrashed by drawing a throwing knife and hurling it at Ashok.

Since both of his hands were occupied, all Ashok could do was grimace as the blade stuck him in the side. "Idiot! Can't you see I'm fighting a demonic hybrid?" But then he thought better of it, risked letting go with one hand long enough to pull the throwing knife out, and then went to carving up Sikasso's face with it.

The young wizard lacked either courage or commitment to his master, because he turned and ran, screaming for help. "Ashok's in the vault murdering Sikasso!"

Ashok didn't care if help came, because nothing was going to stop him from slicing this abomination into ribbons. Then the neck he was twisting collapsed into thousands of tiny, scurrying things, and the knife was cutting through beetles. His opponent had dissolved into a man-sized pile of insects.

It failed to take him by surprise. That trick was how Sikasso had escaped him last time.

Calm, Ashok got to his feet amid the spreading cloud of biting flies and stinging wasps. The swarm was scattering, but they were near the alchemical desk. The fire had gone out, but Ashok had seen that some of the substances had burst into flame when they'd touched air. There wasn't time or light enough to read labels, so Ashok upended the entire desk and flipped it atop the squirming pile.

One of the bottles caught fire. The swarm made a high-pitched screech as some of the fliers flashed into sparks. *Insufficient...* Unsatisfied with that paltry amount of destruction, Ashok tore the entire alchemical shelf from the wall and hurled the whole thing—containing dozens of bottles—into the swarm.

Glasses shattered. Some of mixtures burned, orange, red, or even blue, but it turned out that a few of them, when mixed... the result turned out to be rather *robust*. There was a sizzle of growing sparks and spreading smoke, then a bright flash. The explosion knocked Ashok across the vault.

Thousands of insects burning made a terrible noise as their fluids boiled into steam and their bodies burst. Ashok picked himself up as a caustic green smoke began to fill the room, burning his eyes and lungs, and forcing him to retreat.

Ashok stumbled out into the hall, coughing. He'd never cared much for alchemy.

The short wizard he'd knocked out with a blow to the head had come to at some point, and was dragging himself away. He seemed too dazed to be much of a threat, so Ashok simply kicked him over and took his sword.

He tried to run for the stairs, but it was more of a lurching walk instead. He was just too badly injured. The sensation of molten black steel and the strength he'd temporarily gained from it was gone. His injuries and fatigue remained. There was a hole in his chest big enough to insert his thumb. So he put the Heart of the Mountain to work sealing his wounds so he could face his next challenge. He didn't know if that alchemical fire was sufficient to destroy something like Sikasso, but even if it wasn't, it was certain to take the fight out of the abomination for a while. In the meantime, wizards were coming for him, and demons were coming for the wizards.

To the oceans with all of them, he had a prophet to protect, and not even death would keep Ashok Vadal from her.

Chapter 44

It might have been Thera's army now, but she wasn't in any shape to walk, let alone lead. She'd told Jagdish that her wizard rescuer had given her some drug for the pain. At least he hoped that was what was causing the slurred speech and slow wit, and that his men weren't following the whims of a drunk. So Jagdish just did what came naturally and started giving orders. The smartest thing to do was flee, but Jagdish had come a long way to avenge the Cold Stream garrison.

"I want a Somsak to climb that tower and watch for demons. As soon as they reach this hill, we have to retreat or we're good as dead. Murugan, stick with your prophet. You're her shadow." He pointed at some workers. "See that barn? You two go find something in there to make a litter so we can carry her. She's in no shape to walk. The rest of you, let's go kill some wizards."

"I volunteer to be in charge of robbing them of valuables," Gutch insisted.

"That goes without saying, my friend."

"Try not to harm the slaves." Thera nodded toward the silent man she was leaning against. "They're unwitting captives, stolen children. Apparently now that I've passed the trial they'll obey my commands." Jagdish's expression must have indicated he had no clue what she was talking about. "Never mind. It's a long story."

361

"Anyone else you don't wish killed, best say so now."

"The only one here I thought might be an ally got his throat cut. Slay them all."

The Forgotten must have been one of those *wrathful gods* he'd heard about! "You heard the lady. Move out."

There was no sign of living wizards as they ran toward the house. His scout said that five blue-painted warriors were still down by the lake, waiting to engage the demons. Those men had to be incredibly brave or insane. Either way, Jagdish was glad those warriors were trying to slow the demons instead of him. One demon was enough for him today.

"Movement above!" Eklavya warned, pointing toward the top floor. Giant birds, gleaming an unnatural black beneath the dim sunlight, began rising into the sky.

"Take them down!" Jagdish shouted.

Crossbow bolts and arrows flew. Most of them missed, but at least one struck true, because the last bird's wings folded, and it spiraled downward to crash onto the roof, out of sight.

The other shape-shifted wizards continued to climb away. They weren't coming out to fight. They were running away. *Good. Cowards.* "Let them go. Take the entrance."

They ran up the curving stairs. The doors were a solid affair. They had a few axes and hammers between them, but these looked really sturdy. Jagdish didn't know if they'd have time to breach—

But then the doors burst wide as a body was hurled violently through. The man flipped over the railing and onto the grass, where he came to a bloody, eviscerated stop.

Solves that problem.

More men appeared in the doorway, desperately fleeing whatever was inside. The first was looking back over his shoulder, so frightened by what was chasing him that he nearly ran right into Jagdish. He was dressed in fine silk robes and had demon bones jangling from his sash, so Jagdish assumed he was a wizard and let him run right into the point of his sword.

The wizard gasped as steel punched through his belly. He turned to face Jagdish, eyes wide and afraid.

"Greetings from Cold Stream." Jagdish twisted his sword hard, and then yanked it out through the man's guts. His victim dropped to his knees, done for, but knowing better than to take chances with someone who could use magic, Jagdish drew back his arm and smoothly lopped his head clean off. It went bouncing down the stairs and across the neatly trimmed grass, colorful turban unraveling behind.

There had been two other wizards behind this one, and they didn't fare much better as the Sons of the Black Sword fell upon them. The first caught a hammer to the shoulder that shattered bones, and then he was impaled on two spears and driven back against the wall.

The last at least managed to grab hold of some of his magic, making his body incredibly fast for a moment. With a sword in each hand he swatted away the incoming blows, snarling at his unexpected attackers. Even outnumbered, such speed made him a deadly opponent, but then a sword hurtled through the doorway, end over end, to slam into the wizard's lower back. The blow must have severed his spine, because his legs suddenly went useless and he flopped down, easy prey. Four of the Sons immediately surrounded him, swords rising and falling as they brutally chopped the cripple into pieces.

That had been lucky. He'd fought wizards before. They were far easier to put down when they were distracted and didn't see you coming. Jagdish had a sneaking suspicion what they'd been running from, and it was confirmed when the bloodied form of Ashok Vadal appeared in the doorway. The Protector looked like death walking. Jagdish had never seen a man gone so pale, but nevertheless, a smile split Ashok's face when he saw them.

"Nice of you to leave us some, Ashok!"

"Don't worry, Jagdish. I'm sure there's more where that came from." Ashok staggered down the steps, unusually clumsy, almost as if he was drunk from blood loss.

"Good to see you, brother." Jagdish put one hand on Ashok's shoulder to steady him. "You look like you need to sit down."

"It's rare an honorable man would call a criminal 'brother.'" Ashok cocked his head to the side and squinted at Jagdish. "But thank you...I think I died but Angruvadal brought me back to life."

"Now I know you need to sit down."

"No. I must go back to the swamp for Thera."

"She's safe." Jagdish nodded toward the tower. "Over there."

Ashok blinked a few times, as if he couldn't believe it. "Safe?"

"Temporarily. At least until the demons get us. Whatever

this mysterious oath is that binds you, you've done your duty. Go to her, Ashok."

Their lookout atop the tower began waving his arms and yelling. Murugan was at the base, and he began relaying what the Somsak was saying by shouting loud enough for Jagdish to get the gist of it.

"*The big demon is ashore and killing all the blue warriors.*"

"Time to go then," Jagdish muttered.

"*More demons have come through the swamp to cut off our escape.*"

They were surrounded.

Chapter 45

Inside the House of Assassins, the Sons of the Black Sword prepared their defenses. It appeared all the wizards who could flee had, abandoning their home and their treasure to the demons, but since none of the Sons could turn into birds and fly away, escape was not a possibility. The demons had last been surrounding the base of the hill. Now they were out of sight. Only a fool would believe they'd returned to the sea. The idea of them on dry land, trespassing with impunity, flaunting the Law, left Ashok furious.

The wizards must not have been a loyal bunch, because they'd left behind a few of their wounded, including the one Ashok had put into a coma by beating his head against a statue, and the short man he'd knocked out downstairs. He'd hoped to find a body, but Sikasso was no longer in the vault. There had been thousands of scattered ashen bits—all that remained of the burned insects—but Ashok didn't know enough about shape shifting for that to tell him if Sikasso was alive or dead.

The house slaves had been left behind, but they all seemed to be dumb and mute. They offered no resistance, but also no help. He'd been told that Thera had ordered them not to be harmed, she'd said something about them just being poor victims of the Lost House, so the Sons had honored her command. They'd herded them all into one room, so at least they'd be out of the way when the demons started ripping everyone apart.

Ashok found Jagdish near the front entrance, trying to figure out how to reinforce the doors. Two of the men were attempting to drag a huge bronze statue in front of it.

"I figure since everyone who worshiped this fellow is long dead now, he didn't do them much good, but he might help us now."

"That won't even slow the big one." A few years ago seeing this many illegal images would have moved him to tear the place down. Now he was ostensibly serving the speaker for an illegal god. It was strange how things worked out. "The regular-sized demons will climb the walls and breach from the upper floors."

"I wish this place had better defenses," Jagdish muttered.

"For demons? It would make no difference."

"Well, barricading the door's better than nothing." Jagdish shrugged. "This is my doing. I should've retreated as soon as we found the prophet. I didn't think of demons as being smart enough to circle around in order to cut off our escape."

"Take no guilt from your decision. They were there long before your spotter saw them and would have intercepted you on the way out regardless."

Jagdish didn't seem convinced, but if it made the risaldar feel better to have someone to blame, so be it. "Any idea why they haven't attacked yet?"

"In my experience demons prefer to rampage in the dark. They'll wait until they can see and we cannot. Anyone who gets past them then will be easy pickings in the swamp."

The risaldar pulled out his pocket watch and checked the odd little device. "Then we've only got a couple hours. That's not much time."

"Time for me to heal enough to fight them." He needed it. Ashok had never felt so weak and weary in his life. Getting a steel hook through the heart was rather brutal, even by his standards.

"Even the legendary Black Heart can't fight five demons."

Two had nearly killed him, and that had been with mighty Angruvadal in his hand. "I might not defeat them, but I can draw their attention long enough for the rest of you to run for the barges."

Jagdish chuckled. "All those times we sparred together in prison, whenever you talked about how the judges might order you to commit suicide, your voice would get a little wistful. I was hoping you'd find a better purpose and move past all that."

Ashok did not fear death. He'd done it once already today, though he doubted very much that Angruvadal would be able to bring him back if he was in pieces being digested in a demon's stomach. "It is what it is."

"There's got to be another way out."

"Then find it. Wishful thinking will not stop that clock from ticking. The Lost House must have planned for various contingencies." He turned toward the men wrestling futilely against the statue. "Leave that be and bring us the prisoner."

While he waited, Ashok leaned against the wall. It wasn't very dignified, but he was so tired he could barely stand. Getting killed took a lot out of you. A moment later they dragged the short wizard into the room. He'd been stripped of his clothing, searched for magic, and bound by the wrists and ankles. From the bruises, the Sons had been rather rough about it too. The warriors unceremoniously dumped the assassin at Ashok's feet.

The little man twisted his neck to look up at Ashok. "As I was waking up, I saw you die, then I saw you come back." He seemed rather awed by that.

"Indeed. Yet if I kill you, it will be permanent. Remember that fact as you answer my questions. What is your name, wizard?"

"I am Waman."

"In their rush to escape your brothers abandoned you."

"Of course they did. Most flew off to save their own skins." Waman spat on the floor. "They've no love of me! I was always loyal to Master Sikasso. If he were here we'd all stand and fight. Without him *and* with you killing a bunch of us, the rest have run off to hide until the demons leave."

Jagdish stepped in. "I could waste time torturing you, or we can make a simple trade. Help us find a way to escape and we will take you with us. Hinder us, and we'll leave you tied up for the demons."

This wizard struck Ashok as a sniveling coward, but he wasn't a fool. "I'll gladly join your cause. Untie me and give me a bit of magic. I'll help you fight."

Jagdish scoffed. "Arm an assassin in his own house? Hardly. No, it is you that'll be arming *us*."

While Jagdish questioned the wizard and the Sons searched the rest of the building, Ashok approached Thera. She was being guarded by one young Thao warrior who was remaining a polite distance away. There was a muscular slave nearby, but he was sitting there, staring blankly off into space with his one remaining eye. Their long-lost prophet had been put on an improvised litter and placed on the floor. Both of her hands had been bandaged. He couldn't tell if she was awake, asleep, or somewhere in between.

"Hello, Thera."

Regardless of how poorly she felt, she opened her eyes when she heard his voice. "Ashok?"

They had not spoken in a long time. He'd chased her across a third of the continent and killed many men to find her, and now he didn't really know what to say. "How are your hands?"

She sounded weary. "The only reason I'm not screaming is Kabir gave me a drug. Everything's numb. I can wiggle my fingers a bit though I'm scared to look at them... But I'm still alive. I can't believe you actually came after me."

"When we were traveling together, I told you I intended to serve the prophet." Muscles aching, he put his back against the wall, and slid down until he was sitting next to her. He needed to give the Heart of the Mountain time to do its work anyway. "You'd think by now people would know that I always do what I say I will do."

"I guess we just get used to most people breaking promises rather than keeping them."

"I am unlike most people. As are you, it turns out."

The two of them sat there together, battered and exhausted. He'd cheated death and she'd thwarted a demon god. It had been a very long day.

"My promise to serve the prophet would've been easier if I'd known I'd already met her. I wish you would've just told me the truth to begin with."

"You were the Law's greatest killer and I inspired a rebellion against it. Of course I didn't tell you. I thought you might murder me."

"It crossed my mind," he said simply.

"I could tell!" She gave him a sad little laugh. "I didn't particularly trust you much then."

"You were going to roll a bomb onto my blankets while I slept."

"Think that would've worked?"

"Perhaps. Have I earned your trust yet?"

"After spending time among these backstabbing assassins, I'm thinking you might just be the most honest man I've ever met." Thera sighed. "Not that it matters. We're going to die here anyway."

"Normally when demons come ashore, they kill in a frenzy then leave, they don't lay siege. Something has caused a change in their behavior. I witnessed your struggle in the demon's graveyard. I thought it was Sikasso's magic keeping me and the demons out, but it was you, wasn't it?"

"That was the Voice trying to protect itself."

"Do you think you could call upon that power again?"

"I don't know." An involuntary tear rolled from her eye and cut a line through the dried mud on her face. "I'm sorry...I shouldn't show weakness." She tried to rub her face with one wrapped hand, but the movement was too numb and clumsy.

Ashok reached out and gently wiped the tear away with his thumb. It was an unconscious gesture. He awkwardly took his hand away. "We are all weak at times."

"These warriors came here for me, and they're going to die here because of it. I saw things during the trial, inside my head, visions from the demons, from the past, I don't know. That thing I fought, it was like hell's version of the Voice. There's more of them out there, hiding, waiting. But I killed this one. Now hell wants revenge. These demons are here for me. Leave me here. Then the rest of you might get away."

Criminals were supposed to be without honor, yet Thera was willing to sacrifice herself in the off chance it might save others. Ashok found it odd sometimes, the places you found such dignity. Powerful wizards abandoned their wounded brothers, while a lowly outcast rebel was selfless on behalf of men she'd just met.

"I don't think you understand the nature of the Sons of the Black Sword. They will not abandon you. I suspect Gutch will fill a sack with treasure and run as soon as the demons are busy eating us...But the rest of them would rather die for you." Strangely enough, Ashok could respect that. He would be here regardless, because obedience was the very fiber of his being. The others had chosen this illegal, yet bold, path.

"The Voice is a curse. Oh, why do I keep inspiring good men to do stupid things?"

"I am neither good, nor inspired."

He hadn't meant for that statement to be amusing, but it made Thera smile. For some reason that made Ashok feel a little better.

"Where is Keta? I've not seen him. Please at least tell me that Keta isn't trapped here too."

"The last I saw of him, Keta was safe. Many fanatics joined us along the journey. We couldn't bring them here. He wanted to come after you, but he was the only one who knew the path to your rebellion's hideout, so he led the noncombatants south."

Thera groaned. "No! Sikasso knew about that group. Omkar has gone after them. He's a sadistic killer. They're doomed."

Ashok scowled. He was very good at what he did, but he could only be in one place at a time. "Keta will find a way to escape. He is clever, like you."

"That's the nicest thing you've ever said to me, Ashok..." Her voice was growing tired and weaker. She was quickly fading back into a drug-induced slumber. "I don't want to die here."

"I will do my best to keep that from happening."

"Doesn't your precious Law say all us criminals deserve to die?"

Ashok found himself in disagreement with the Law on that point, and he didn't even feel guilty about it. "While it is no longer my place to judge, it is still my obligation to protect... Now sleep, Thera."

She could no longer keep her eyes open. Her voice was a whisper. "Will you be here when I wake up?"

Since Ashok wouldn't lie to her, instead he said nothing, and waited for her to drift off. He sat there, silent, listening to the breathing of the woman he'd sworn to serve. She needed to rest. Regular people did not have the Heart of the Mountain to repair their wounds or stave off fatigue. Except even the mightiest Protector had his physical limits, and a few minutes later, Ashok nodded off as well.

When he came to, the light coming through the stained glass windows had turned orange. The sun was going down. The Heart had done its part while he'd rested. His wounds were nowhere close to fully healed, but he was feeling stronger than before. Thera was still next to him, unconscious. When the drug wore off, she would awake in terrible pain.

He whispered so as to not wake her up. "You have done your part, and now I must do mine."

The Thao warrior was still standing a respectful distance away, keeping watch over them. Ashok approached him. "What is your name and rank?"

"Nayak Murugan of Great House Thao. Risaldar Jagdish told me to keep an eye on her."

"Good. Your orders haven't changed." He already knew the answer but he needed to ask anyway. "Are the demons still out there?"

"Yes, sir."

Ashok looked the soldier over, he was young and skinny, obviously inexperienced, but he seemed determined enough. "When the time comes I will make a path through the demons and she will be carried back to the barges. Do not leave her side. While I am away, you will protect her at all costs. You cannot fail. Do you understand me?"

"But, sir, I failed before, in the swamp I panicked and ran! I'm not the one to—"

Ashok grabbed him by the collar, dragged him close, and growled, "There is only one man in Lok who does not know fear. Of course you're afraid. Fear is the tool that keeps most alive. Now you must be afraid for her as well." Ashok shoved him away. "Do not fail me. Do not fail her." And since they seemed to be actively involved today, he added, "Do not fail your gods."

The young warrior gave him a grim nod. "I won't."

The slave was also still sitting there. "Who is this?"

"The prophet called him Dattu and said he'd helped her. He wouldn't go with the other slaves. But there's something wrong with his head. I think he's simple."

Ashok went over to the slave, who seemed oblivious to everything around him. "You helped Thera?" There was no response. He'd been scarred with a whip across the face. Curious, Ashok lifted the eye patch and confirmed that it had really been sliced in half by the wound. He dropped the patch. "If you can understand me, demonstrate it."

Slowly, the slave turned to looked at him, and Ashok thought that maybe there was some tiny measure of understanding still in there. Slowly, painfully, he tried to speak. It was obvious that it had been a long time.

"Evil has been done here."

Ashok nodded. "I agree."

"My walls crumble..." Poor addled Dattu stared right through him. "I can see it. They made you like me once, but more. Now your walls are falling too."

"Perhaps." Ashok gave the broken man a respectful nod. "Regardless, thank you for aiding Thera. Her safety is very important to me."

"General! General!" One of the workers ran up to him. "I was sent to wake you. Come quick. Risaldar Jagdish and Forge Master Gutch have a plan."

"Very well." Any plan had to be better than his idea of just walking up to the largest demon and picking a fight. He took one last look at their sleeping prophet and then followed the worker.

The Sons had been busy. Last he'd seen, the warriors had been futilely pushing at the big bronze statue, but the far more efficient workers had taken over with ropes and pulley, and arranged a trap that Ashok found most ingenious. From the piles of weapons, the armory must have been cleaned out. Several large wooden barrels had been brought in and stacked along the wall. There were sacks, bulging with what had to be demon parts, ready to be carried off. Gutch threw down another sack, and from the opening in the top, Ashok saw that this one was filled with Capitol banknotes.

"What's all this?"

"Well, General, in the unlikely event any of us actually escape, we might as well escape fabulously wealthy. Don't scowl at me! I know you don't care about such mundane things, but the rest of us have got to eat. Besides, I've found a rare treasure in their armory you're sure to appreciate." Then Gutch saw that some of the warriors were struggling with one of the heavy barrels. "Careful with that!"

One of them slipped, and the barrel made a loud *thunk* as it struck the floor. From the way everyone cringed, Ashok could tell it was extremely dangerous.

Gutch shook one meaty fist. "Even static can set that off! You fools slip up again and we'll all be raining down on the ocean in bloody chunks!"

"What foul magic have you stolen this time, Gutch?"

"A common misconception among the upper class, but that stuff's not real magic. Just nature mixed together differently. *Chemistry,* it's called. My caste uses chemicals all the time for different industrial processes. We just have to get the Order of Technology and Innovation to give permission for new formulas and inventions first to make sure it isn't something we could turn against the Law. Since they're so picky us workers call them the Order of Stifling Innovation, but anyways, from the look of things these wizards love experiments. Theirs are just a bit more energetic and a lot more illegal is all."

"I saw some alchemy downstairs."

"Ah, that was nothing. Waman said Sikasso wouldn't let them store any of the really volatile stuff in the vault where it might damage their valuable demon bits. Which gave me this idea. See, this is the rest of their supplies. They had to keep it out back in an underground bunker. Turns out that one of their number, wizard by the name of Hemendra, was fixated on replicating the formula for Fortress powder."

Ashok stared at the barrels, offended. This was one of the most brazenly illegal things he'd ever seen. "The Capitol has placed the harshest of penalties upon anyone who possesses Fortress magic, let alone in such an obscene quantity."

"Do these folks strike you as the kind who'd give a damn what the Capitol declares? Anyways, that little snitch thinks Hemendra was making lots of the stuff because he intended to assassinate Sikasso with it. Since it's not really magic, their master wouldn't be able to detect a bomb, which would make for quite the surprise. But Sikasso strangled him first... They sound like a right lovely bunch. Makes me happy to rob them and blow up their house. Though losing all this artwork is a shame. Do you have any idea how much some of these pieces would fetch in the underground markets of Vadal City?"

"This evil must be destroyed," Ashok muttered, but then he realized in the process that such a devastating force could be turned against an even greater evil. "You're preparing a welcome for the demons."

"Now he's catching on!" Gutch slapped him on the back. Ashok frowned at the too familiar gesture, and Gutch quickly removed his hand. "Sorry."

Jagdish came over to join them, looking grim. "So Gutch told you. The wizard showed us a secret door in the basement we can use to escape while the demons are occupied. He's rather forthcoming, since he doesn't want to get eaten."

Ashok understood their plan, and also its key. "Reaching the barges will still require crossing the swamp in the dark. Blind and on rough terrain, a single demon could still kill everyone.

Someone will need to draw all of them here to be consumed by the Fortress magic."

"The bad news is whoever lures them in here probably won't make it out. And I don't suppose you'd be willing to let anyone else have that honor, would you Ashok?"

"I say this without intending offense against your courage or martial skills, but none of you would last long enough to make a difference. I will."

"I figured you'd say something like that." Jagdish smiled. "Looks like you might just get your suicidal wish after all."

Ashok mulled it over. One criminal life in trade for five demons? And death would come while fulfilling his obligation? "This outcome is acceptable to me."

"It's decided then." Jagdish looked toward the windows and the dying light. Like a proper warrior, he tried not to let his emotions show, but even the hardest of them didn't like losing a friend. Even unflappable Gutch seemed a little uncomfortable. "I doubt we've got time for long good byes."

"It's been an honor, Risaldar Jagdish."

"Agreed, *Protector*. Since the sun's nearly down, don't waste my time arguing. As far as I'm concerned you've earned that title forever. Now let's get you properly kitted up so you go out looking the part too."

Curious. "What was this other treasure you spoke of?"

Chapter 46

As darkness fell, the soldiers of hell crept from their hiding places, sleek and deadly.

"Demons incoming," a lookout shouted.

It was time to bring some measure of Law to this lawless land.

The massive doors of the House of Assassins swung wide, revealing a tall figure in heavy armor. The construction of lamellar plates, leather, and cord had been made by the best craftsmen in Lok. Upon his head was a conical helmet, covering his face was a mask of fine chain, and on his breastplate there was a golden ornament, the judgmental visage of the Law.

With torch held aloft in one hand, and a pole arm in the other, Ashok Vadal walked down the steps to declare war on hell. There was guilt in donning the armor of the Protector Order again, but it would help him survive longer, and in an odd, selfish way, being clad in steel and silver felt *right*. They'd found it in the armory, along with uniforms and insignia stolen from every house and Order imaginable, to be used as disguises to help the assassins complete their nefarious missions. Whichever Protector had been murdered for them to obtain this suit, surely he would be offended to know that unworthy criminals had donned it, but Ashok hoped he would also be pleased that it would be used to slay demons one last time.

He stopped in the middle of the courtyard and raised his

375

voice to a commanding bellow. "Heed me, demons. I am Ashok Vadal. You are guilty of trespass. Return to the sea now and I will spare your lives. Stay and I will kill you all."

The Sons were watching from the windows. They needed as many demons as possible to commit before they made a run for the barges. It had taken thirty men to beat one demon while losing half their number in the process. The math did not favor Jagdish getting Thera to safety with only three fighters to each demon. They'd try to take the house slaves with them, but the only help they were likely to provide was that the demons might slow their pursuit long enough to devour them.

Thinking of those slaves though... The door to one of their nearby quarters had been ripped from the hinges. While waiting for the sun to go down, the demons had probably slaughtered everyone caught outside the walls of the great house. The live-stock had screamed and bleated as the demons had torn them to bits, but the mute servants had never made a noise, never begged for help, or mercy. Those people had done no wrong, broken no Law, they were simply victims, first of the wizard's cruelty, and then the demon's hunger. Ashok's righteous anger grew hotter.

"I have changed my mind. Your opportunity has passed. I will allow none of you to run back to the sea to hide. I will show no mercy to demons tonight. *Come out and face me!*"

There was a line of braziers set out along the path, Ashok dropped the torch into one, and took up the pole arm in both hands. There was movement near the base of the ruined tower. A dark round head rose over the rocks to peer at him. A second demon appeared, crouching on the roof of the slave barracks. With the helmet covering his ears, and only a narrow slit for his eyes, Ashok focused his senses to make sure there were no others sneaking up on him. It was just the two for now.

Insufficient.

"Who will contend with me first?"

The rooftop demon leapt down soundlessly and started toward him, while the tower demon waited.

"Excellent."

This one moved with a strange fluidity, going to all fours and nearly disappearing into the tall grass. It was not a large one, merely man sized. He aimed the pole arm at the nearing threat, surely it couldn't be stupid enough to use its own momentum to help impale its body upon the blade. Of course, it wasn't, and the demon came to a smooth stop, just outside the reach of the dim firelight.

Alone among the Protector Order, Ashok had wielded an ancestor blade, the only thing in the world which could easily pierce the hide of a demon. The others had fought them with regular steel. Master Ratul had allowed Ashok no crutch in training though, so he'd learned to fight demons like everyone else. Their skin was incredibly resilient, but a perfect strike *might* cut them. Their bones were impossibly hard, but a powerful enough blow *might* break one. Jagdish and the Sons had dispatched one by striking it a multitude of times, until they'd gotten lucky. Protectors relied on cold calculation and skill.

Still on all fours, the demon began to circle. This one had a thin torso, and arms and legs that seemed too long, sticking up above its body, then bending sharply at the knees and elbows to shoot downward. Unlike the others he'd fought, it seemed shaped more spider than man.

Ashok began to spin the reclining moon blade between his hands, picking up speed until the foot of steel on the end was whistling through the air. He was not as skilled with this particular weapon as Bundit Vokkan, but they'd trained together, and given room to maneuver, Ashok knew its blows could generate an incredible amount of force.

The demon lunged at him. Never interrupting the rhythm of the spin, Ashok slid back, and brought the heavy blade straight down on that featureless head.

It bounced off, but with a resounding *crack*. The shock traveled up the haft to sting his palms. Against a man that mighty blow would have split a helmet, the skull beneath, and launched brains from the hole. It merely made the demon wobble a bit.

Only Ashok never hesitated, never let up for a second. Only an ancestor blade could drop a demon in one blow, and even that was rare. Using the momentum of the blade rebounding, Ashok whipped around the haft and slammed it into one planted arm. Of course wood wouldn't break demon bone, but that hand slid across the damp grass, and the demon dipped forward, off balance. The blade was already coming back down, and it slammed into the demon's spine.

Surely it felt *that*.

Ashok had to leap back to avoid a claw, and then the toes—which were just as sharp—as the demon rolled forward through the grass. Smooth as a Capitol acrobat, it came up on its feet, rising to its full height, reaching for Ashok's face.

Only he'd ducked back while rotating the shaft so that the back of the reclining moon blade was pointing toward the demon, and he dragged the steel hook into its ankle and pulled hard. That leg went out from under it, flying forward, and off balance again, it crashed against the brazier, knocking it over and spilling torch and sparks.

Before it had hit the ground, Ashok had spun the pole arm overhead to build speed, and he brought it straight down, stabbing for the demon's chest. The point struck true, and with all of Ashok's unnatural might behind it, the hide gave way.

The demon made no sound as its chest was pierced. It grasped for him, but Ashok brought the blade down again. This one didn't hit as clean, and glanced off its shoulder, but the first wound had been dealt. Blood had been shed, and it was white rather than red.

Perhaps they would take him seriously now.

The demon from the tower was headed his way, and another had appeared, leaping over the fences, from where it had been spitefully tearing apart the wizard's livestock. *Good.*

Ashok had time to slam the blade into the wounded demon a few more times before the others were upon him. The tower demon turned out to be bigger, similar in build to the ones he'd fought in Gujara, with shorter legs, longer arms, and a massive chest. It seemed demons came in many different shapes and sizes, but experience had taught him that this type was *exceedingly* dangerous.

Unlike the first, this one didn't slow its approach. There was no caution, no strategy, simply destructive might. Ashok braced the pole arm against his hip to aim the blade, roared, and met charge with charge.

He planted the blade into its chest so hard the shaft bent, but nothing being certain with demons, the steel slid off. Ashok had to duck and roll beneath a mighty swing. With the rattle of metal and jangle of chain, he came right back to his feet, spinning the pole arm so that the hook struck demon arm. Green sparks rose from magical flesh, but it accomplished nothing.

With shocking speed, the demon struck back. The impact pulverized the wood into splinters, and the reclining moon blade went flipping away into the dark. The claws had left deep scratches across his armored chest.

He still had a sword sheathed at his side, but the third demon was nearly here, and the wounded one was back up. *Jagdish had better have gotten everyone to the basement by now,* Ashok thought as he ran for the House of Assassins.

They were right behind him, but the Heart of the Mountain provided him with a burst of speed. He leapt up the stairs and bolted through the doorway. He didn't even bother trying to close it behind him.

The demons pursued him right into the killing field Gutch and the workers had prepared.

The plan required him to hold them as long as possible. Weapons would break faster than a Protector, so they'd scattered the assassin's tools around the great hall. Every lantern had been lit. Little would the demons realize that they'd been positioned to light the barrels or trails of Fortress powder they'd poured on the floor.

For now though, Ashok was mostly interested about the statue they had suspended from the balcony over the entrance. Made of solid bronze, the ancient deity had to weigh at least five hundred pounds. It hung there, creaking, dangerous. Ashok picked up the battle axe which had been leaned against the marble pillar securing the taut, easily severable ropes.

It turned out workers were surprisingly creative.

The demon was tall enough it had to duck to get through the doorway. Once through, it came for him, arms spread wide, as if it wanted to embrace.

Ashok cut the ropes.

The statue landed on the demon. Bronze bent, but bones shattered. White blood sprayed across the entrance as it went down hard.

It lay there, twitching, head pulverized between metal and the stone. The smiling fat man seemed pleased. Ashok did not think the smiling fat man was the Forgotten. The Forgotten did not strike him as a kind god. Anyone who would choose Ashok Vadal to be his warrior would never be portrayed as *kind*.

The other demons made their way up the stairs, slower, cautious this time. The spiderlike one twisted through the doorway, head lump aimed upward, checking for more falling gods. It was bleeding down its chest, but still seemed capable enough. The one behind it was shaped like a gangly, thin man, but over seven feet tall.

There was a scraping noise from above, demon hide brushing against broken glass. The fourth had climbed the wall and was upon the balcony.

All he needed to do was draw the ire of the big one. Then he could die, oath fulfilled.

Ashok lifted the battle axe. "Fight me, demons."

They did.

The spider demon rushed him. Ashok slammed the axe into it, spinning it aside. The thin one attacked, claws flashing. It was far stronger than it looked. He struck it with a mighty overhand blow that it simply shrugged off, but then it backhanded him into a marble pillar. Green sparks rose from its claw as it tore into the steel of one shoulder plate. Ashok ducked beneath another swing that left marks on the marble.

There was a spike on the end of the axe. He drove it into the thin demon's side. It didn't penetrate, but the shock of the blow made it step back. That gave him room to set up another blow, this one coming in from the side, at waist level, striking the demon in the pelvis. *Nothing.*

Rolling across the floor, the spider demon reached for his ankle, but Ashok moved away. If they pulled him down, it was over.

The demon which had climbed through the window leapt down from the balcony. He heard it land behind him, surprisingly lightly. Ashok moved to the side, narrowly avoiding claws, and he spun against that attacker, axe low, instinct telling him to go for its legs. Sure enough, it wasn't a big one, and the blow was sufficient to sweep the feet out from beneath it.

Had that been his instinct, or was Angruvadal helping him again? At this point, he couldn't even tell the two apart.

He was hit again and a claw pierced his side. It didn't feel deep. *Let it bleed.* He needed the Heart to give him speed. Moving quickly between the statues, Ashok made distance. The three demons were all coming for him at once, getting in each other's way. There was a war hammer leaning nearby, and none of these demons were particularly dense, so he might do better with bludgeoning than cutting. So he hurled the axe into the nearest demon, and scooped up the heavier weapon.

The demons were relentless. The Heart of the Mountain gave him incredible speed, but these things were just as quick, and far more resilient. For creatures of the ocean, their bodies seemed to exude a dry heat. They traded blows back and forth. His breath couldn't keep up. The muscles of his arms burned.

He'd sparred with Blunt Karno using hammers the same

way he'd trained with Bundit on the pole arm. His whole life, whenever possible, he'd sought out those who were better than he was at some certain skill, so he could learn from the masters. By this point there probably wasn't a tool in the world Ashok couldn't be lethally effective with.

He slammed the hammer into one, sending it flying back, but the spider demon immediately swept around behind, striking at him. Chain broke, leather tore, but the armor saved his life. Ashok whipped the hammer around, cracked it into the space where the demon's face should be, and sent it skidding across the floor.

A glistening black fist crashed into his helm. An indent of linked chain was crushed into his cheek. But Ashok broke away, rolled past that demon, and hammered it square in the back.

The Protector this armor had belonged to had been a bit larger in stature than Ashok, so the fit wasn't exactly right. It was slowing him down slightly, but he knew he already would be—at minimum—severely injured without it. Gutch had promised that if they lived through the night, give him a hammer and an anvil and he'd be able to adjust it to perfection. An easy job for such a skilled smith, he'd bragged. But up to his neck in demons, Ashok sincerely doubted Gutch would ever have the opportunity.

The spider demon started to rise, and for just a moment Ashok had a perfect opportunity. Driven with all his might, he brought the hammer down on the back of its head with a blow that could kill an elephant.

It hit the floor, but it wasn't finished. Temporarily stunned, the lump of a head was resting against the unyielding stone. There would be no give this time. No neck acting like a spring, no distance to absorb energy. Ashok lifted the hammer high overhead and roared.

It was like smashing a melon.

Bleeding and breathing hard, Ashok stumbled away as the demons paused. They were expressionless as usual, but he hoped that these things could be shaken by the death of a comrade. If they were troubled, it wasn't for long, because they started toward him again.

Now there are two.

Then the front wall bulged as the biggest demon in the world collided with it. Dust rained from the ceiling.

Three, Ashok corrected himself.

He began backing toward the nearest hanging lantern. Beneath it had been poured some of the black Fortress powder, the beginning of a trail that led back to the stacked barrels. Gutch was no architect, but he'd directed them to be stacked against a vital interior wall, in the hopes of collapsing the whole front of the building.

Jagdish had better not waste this.

It was like being in an earthquake. The entire House of Assassins shook as the great demon battered its way inside. It was hitting the building so hard that Ashok might not even need to break a lantern, the demon would probably do it for him. But he wanted it inside first, catching flying debris and falling roof beams, not outside, sheltered from the blast by stone.

The big demon didn't bring the whole wall down, it simply punched a hole big enough to squeeze its bulk through, and then slid inside. Ashok had never imagined such a thing could be. There were whispered rumors of such vast beasts, small parts of them occasionally glimpsed by witnesses way out in the surf, but he'd always dismissed such things as rumors. Besides, as long as the demons didn't trespass on dry land, he didn't care what they got up to beneath the waves. Hell had been out of his jurisdiction.

It was black as oil, same as the lesser demons; it was on all fours to squeeze through the gap, but the way its claws were curled like fists, and it was walking on its knuckles, he could tell it was meant to stand. There was a line of a mouth, and as he watched, fascinated, it spread open, four feet wide, and filled with teeth like black daggers. There was a sick gurgle, and then it regurgitated the mangled blue remains of a few Dasa servants and their weapons and armor into an acidic puddle across the floor, probably to make room in its belly to consume him.

Rising to its full height, its dome of a head easily cleared the second floor balcony. It casually shoved the fallen bronze out of the way, and heedlessly crushed its fallen brother beneath its giant webbed feet as it stomped toward him. A hanging banner of the Lost House got in its way, and the great demon tore it down and flung it aside.

Though strangely tempted, he knew it would be impossible to fight such a being. Ashok knocked the burning lantern from the wall.

The glass shattered. The oil rolled outward, catching fire. There was a sudden, alien hiss, and a gout of orange flame as the Fortress alchemy erupted. Belching smoke, that fire ripped across the floor, following the trail laid by Gutch and the workers.

The demons didn't seem to know what to make of the strange magic. They simply stepped out of the way, heads swiveling to watch as it burned past them. The little fire moved with startling speed, leaving a trail of smoke and scorched stone.

"I warned you there would be no mercy," Ashok said as he awaited their inevitable destruction.

A sudden gust of wind howled through the great hall. Banners whipped about. Furniture toppled. Ashok had to shield his eyes as he was blasted with grit. Then the wind passed as suddenly as it had begun. Most of the other lanterns had been extinguished, plunging them into darkness.

The trail of Fortress powder had been blown from the floor. With nowhere else to go, the little fire sputtered and died.

"Treacherous magic!" Ashok roared. "Is that your doing?" he demanded of the demons, but of course, they didn't answer.

A voice came out of the darkness. "Did you think I would let you so easily destroy that which I've built?"

"Sikasso," Ashok snarled.

Across the great hall, the abomination stepped from the shadows. It was hard to tell in the dim light, but he seemed *less*. As he got closer, Ashok could see that the Lost House's ruler was ragged and disfigured, with strips of flesh missing from his face. He was covered in red holes where the insects that had been burned to ash should have gone, a few so deep they showed white bone beneath. His teeth could be seen through the hole in his cheek. He was like a puzzle that had been put together, but missing pieces.

But then Ashok had to return his attention back to the demons, who were once again trying to eviscerate him. The hammer was swatted from his hands. He drew his sword as he fell back.

"We reclaimed this house from the sea. We rebuilt it with our own hands. We rediscovered our old ways and grew our numbers. Through murder and intimidation we founded a secret empire which will someday overthrow the Law itself! And you think you can come in here and take that all away? You killed my men. The rest have fled like cowards. And now you think you can use a traitor's alchemy to burn my home? *How dare you?*"

Sikasso's angry shouting had caught the great demon's attention, and it had turned his direction.

"And you, champion of hell, I could feel your god begin crawling around inside my mind, trying to tell me what to do, but I will never obey, for I am Sikasso, master of the House of Assassins. I would not bow to the Capitol and I will never bow to you." He opened his tattered robe, and threw something on the ground.

It was his demonic arm. Long thick veins hung from the jagged stump, bleeding white. The wizard had *torn* his corruption off.

Ashok could respect that.

"Better to die a cripple, than a slave." With his remaining hand, Sikasso lifted a long strip of demon hide. He bit the end to hold it in place, and then wound it tightly around his hand. Once supplied with magic, he drew his sword. *"Now get out of my house."*

The great demon went after Sikasso, covering the distance in a few great strides. Only when it reached for him, the wizard stepped back into the shadows and was gone. Ashok knew how that game was played, and sure enough, Sikasso came out of the demon's own shadow, futilely slashing at its legs.

To the oceans with demons and wizards both, Ashok was going to bring this house down if he had to ignite those barrels by rubbing two sticks together. He clashed against the demons, but they were between him and his goal. Claws struck at his armor. An elbow knocked a dent in his helm. He was brutally kicked back against the wall.

The demons were no longer getting in each other's way, they were working together, taking turns striking at him, giving him no lulls to take advantage of. It was almost as if the presence of the large one was somehow making them more organized. There was a shield on the wall, bearing the symbol of the Lost House. Ashok snatched it up and ran his left arm through the straps.

It didn't matter if he was mortally wounded in the process, but he had to reach that powder. He shield slammed the lighter of the two demons, trying to drive it out of his way. He knocked it over, and then drove the other one back with a hard thrust to the gut. It didn't break the skin, but it was close, and the demon was forced to move back. That small gap was all he needed.

Ashok ran for the barrels.

Sikasso was still disappearing and reappearing around the big demon. He couldn't damage the thing, but even though demons had no expressions, he could tell it was infuriated. Ashok certainly had been when facing such trickery.

Unfortunately, Sikasso must have realized what Ashok was trying to do, because this time when he came out of the darkness, it was at his side. The wizard's sword glanced off his shoulder plate. Ashok turned in time to catch the next blow with his shield.

"I won't let you do this," Sikasso spat.

"You can't stop me," Ashok said as they crossed swords.

"No, but he can," the wizard vanished.

The big demon was heading right for Ashok.

He dove to the side as a giant fist pulverized the stone floor. Rolling, he barely managed to avoid being crushed beneath a massive foot. He came up on his knees, shield between him and the incoming foot.

It kicked him *across* the great hall.

Ashok hit the far wall and bounced off.

His helmet had been torn off. Bones had been broken. The shield had been snapped in half. When he tried to stand, his knees buckled beneath him. He had to turn the Heart of the Mountain to controlling his wounds, or the sudden rush of internal bleeding would have dropped him.

He was nowhere near the barrels.

The three remaining demons were moving toward him.

Sikasso stepped out of the shadows on the balcony above him. He shook the spent demon hide from his hand and it crumbled into ash. "A noble effort, Ashok, but it was all for nothing. The demons will kill you, but eventually they'll have to return to the sea. Then my people will come back. We'll rebuild. We'll find more gifted children and bring them here. The strong will replace those we've lost, and the weak will be our slaves. We will survive this. It's what we do."

Ashok coughed up blood. "Evil."

"Perhaps."

The demons were cautious in their approach this time. They'd already lost two of their nearly indestructible number to the Protector, and the wizard was an unknown power to be reckoned with. They probably didn't understand that Sikasso would merely flee, and that Ashok was now too broken to be a threat.

But he would fight to the end, because that was his way. He'd landed near a fireplace, so he used the stone of the hearth to pull himself upright. At least he would die on his feet.

"One question, Sikasso. Did Grand Inquisitor Omand promise you Angruvadal?"

"That's what matters to you now?" The wizard studied him,

visage grisly, skull gleaming through the pattern of holes on his
face. "He did."

"Why?"

"Because Ashok Vadal is a name that invokes terror, he will
use your legendary crimes to justify a war of extermination
against all the casteless."

"There are millions of them."

"I don't know why Omand wants what he wants, but what
I do know is that long after this demon digests you and shits
you out at the bottom of the sea, the Lost House will still be
committing atrocities in your name...After how much you've
offended me, I might even do them for free."

The demons were closing. The two smaller ones spread out
to the sides to cut off his escape.

"Farewell, Black Heart."

There was a flicker of light at the opposite side of the great
hall. Someone was standing next to the powder barrels. He couldn't
tell who it was, and he couldn't sharpen his vision without releas-
ing his wounds, but then the light grew as the match was used
to light an oil-soaked rag.

Through blurry eyes, Ashok recognized the one-eyed slave,
Dattu.

Sikasso's patchwork head snapped up. "What are you doing?"
He reached for some demon bone hanging from his belt to blow
out the fire. Only before he could grab hold of the magic, a knife
blade pierced his hand and pinned it to his hip. "Aaaaah!"

Ashok's aim had been perfect. *Now that was worth calling upon
the Heart*, he thought as the sudden blood loss overcame him.
Knees buckling, he collapsed into the cold ash of the fireplace.

"No!" Sikasso screamed at his disobedient slave. Without
another hand to pull it free, all he could do was try to tear his
hand *through* the blade. "I command you to stop!"

But Dattu just shook his head and said, "No more."

He dropped the flaming rag onto the barrels.

The giant demon was a black silhouette shielding Ashok from
the brilliant flash. Then everything was wiped away.

Chapter 47

Thunder boomed across the swamp. Jagdish turned around in time to watch a massive plume of fire rise into the sky and roll into black smoke.

Running from demons or not, all of the Sons stopped to gawk. From their position they could only see the roof of the Lost House. Much of it had just been blown off, leaving only the main beams looking like the ribs on a skeleton. The rest of it was raining out of the sky as fiery debris. It was awe inspiring. It was such a destructive power that no wonder the warrior caste had given up on trying to conquer the island of Fortress.

And then it hit him like a punch to the gut what this meant. Ashok was dead.

"Now that's a worthy death," Jagdish said, and really, what more could a warrior ask for? It would be a crime to waste such a magnificent sacrifice. Ashok had given his life to protect this woman. Jagdish didn't know what oath Ashok had sworn to, but getting her out of this awful place was the least he could do in honor of his memory.

"All right, men. Blowing up a wizards' house full of demons is the sort of thing they'll sing songs about for generations, but those songs will never get written if we don't survive to tell the tale."

But they seemed too stunned to move, staring back at the fire, eyes wide on their dirty, exhausted faces. Even Gutch, struggling beneath the weight of sacks full of notes, seemed shocked. Only the slaves they'd herded along with them seemed not to care, but they looked so blank and dimwitted that he doubted they cared about much at all.

A few of these warriors had fought Ashok in Jharlang. And their tales had grown in each telling, as they'd told the newer recruits about how Ashok was a superhuman warrior drafted by their gods, who could duel whole armies. At this point they probably believed in Ashok nearly as much as their damnable Forgotten. He was the greatest warrior in the world. It was like they'd actually expected him to survive this suicidal last stand, kill five demons, and come walking out of the fire, no worse for wear, so that he could lead them to glory like their strange prophet girl had declared he would.

Maybe, in a way, Jagdish had held onto the same naïve hope.

"I know you're tired, Sons of the Black Sword. Ashok had a mission. Now it falls upon us to fulfill it. We have to keep going."

No.

The word was inside his head, louder than the explosion which had ripped apart the Lost House.

Turn back.

Jagdish wasn't alone. Men shielded their ears, or cried out in fear. Even the befuddled slaves seemed to have been woken up by the great and terrible voice. The Somsak and the workers from Jharlang recognized what it was right away, and had gone to their knees before Thera. The surprised slaves nearly dropped the stretcher.

The prophet sat upright, her eyes *glowing* as the strange power took over.

I am not finished with him yet.

Getting his own words past the power intruding into his mind was incredibly difficult, but he had to speak the truth. Jagdish grimaced. "What if he's finished with you?"

Had Ashok not done enough? The man so despised living as a criminal that he yearned for death. These gods were fickle and selfish. In the exceedingly unlikely event he had survived, why couldn't they just leave him be?

Then all of mankind will perish.

The gods made a compelling argument, as they pounded his brain like a drum.

Turn back.

The noise in his head cleared. The eerie light faded, and Thera once again appeared to be a normal woman, seemingly confused about what had just happened.

"Oceans, woman, you could have just asked nicely."

Thera lay back down, exhausted. "I truly don't get much say in the matter."

His ears were ringing as Jagdish rubbed his temples with his fingers. There could still be demons lurking up there, but if there was any chance Ashok lived, then they'd bring him out. "Alright, lads, you heard the...I don't know what. Let's go."

Before they'd made it twenty feet, Jagdish realized they were completely surrounded.

He held up one fist, but it was too late. Figures appeared from the swamp all around them. Not demons thankfully, but men, dressed in furs, hair long and wild, exposed skin covered in mud and white ash. Only with the number of arrows and spears aimed his way, these men didn't seem any friendlier than the demons.

The Sons lifted their weapons. "Hold," Jagdish warned. They were outnumbered, and since their approach had been so stealthy that even the Somsak hadn't seen them coming, he didn't know how many more were out there that he couldn't see. They couldn't afford this fight. "Easy."

The ashen faces had been smeared in a way to resemble skulls, white cheeks and foreheads, with dark hollows around the eyes. The casteless on the barges had warned them about a tribe of wild men who lived in the swamps. Jagdish had dismissed it as a rumor started by the barge master to keep his foolish non-people from wandering off. Apparently, Jagdish had been the fool.

He tried not to sound nervous. "Hello, friends." Jagdish lifted both hands to show they were empty and that his sword remained at his waist. "We're just passing through."

One man approached, the mud sucking loudly at his boots. He was nearly as big as Gutch, only without so much as an ounce of fat upon him. His head had been shaved, so the skull effect was rather complete all the way around. Charms of bird bones and alligator teeth hung from a cord around his neck. He stopped a few feet away from Jagdish, and spoke, voice low and guttural.

"Which of you killed the old god in the graveyard of demons?"

That question was nonsense to Jagdish, but Thera raised her voice. "I did."

"Then the gods have gone to war again." The wild man gave them a savage grin. "*Excellent!* The Mother of Dawn warned us this day would come."

Chapter 48

Rada had discovered there was one nice thing about hiding out in a Historian's fort... *Books!*

Vikram Akershan had an excellent personal library. Apparently each time his wife went to visit her family, she'd returned with a copy of whatever was the latest mass-printed volume circulating in the Capitol. Plus, he had several hand-scribed works, two of which she'd never seen copies of before. One was a collection of essays about great house politics from the mid-600s, and the other was a guide to Akershani-style sword fighting. She had no clue if any of the technical information was correct, but the illustrations were lovely.

Vikram had granted her access to his study. She'd built a warm fire in the hearth that provided plenty of light to see by. It was the middle of the night when she heard the polite knock at the door. As was her custom whenever she'd found something new to read, Rada had simply lost track of time. Her father had often found her half passed out over a book in some corner of their estate. *Go to bed on time, girl,* he'd order. *Or you'll be too cranky to read tomorrow.*

The advice remained sound. She just had a hard time following it.

Rada carefully put her reading glasses in their case for safe keeping. When she answered the door, it wasn't surprising to see the master of the estate. Vikram had probably finally grown tired of her taking up his couch, and was going to throw her out. Before she could greet him, the Historian shook his head, and held one finger to his lips, silencing her.

He kept his voice at a whisper as he closed the door behind him. "I just received a message from the observatory. Inquisitors came by asking for directions to this estate. My friends sent them up the wrong trail, but that will only buy us a little time."

Rada cringed. They were going to have to run again. "I've got to wake Karno."

"First I must show you something."

Still not fully trusting the Historian, she hesitated.

"I've sent a slave to wake the sleeping giant, but the Protector Order doesn't know about this. They *can't* know about this. The Law enforcers are not among the knowledge keepers. That's limited to a few of us, a handful of you Archivists, and the Astronomers." Vikram went to his bookshelf, moved his family genealogy out of the way, and pushed against a specific brick. It made a *click*. Then he pulled against the shelf and the whole thing swung open like a door.

Rada gawked at the secret passage. There was a flight of stairs leading downward. She'd read about such things, there were even rumors of there being tunnels like this hidden inside the Capitol Library, but she'd never actually seen one.

"Your father learned about this when he was promoted to his current office. I'm justifying my decision to show you because I can only assume that he intends for you to someday take his place. If the Inquisition kills me tonight, someone else will need to keep it safe. When Karno told me about the Inquisition's bounty, I sent a message to my Order requesting aid, but I've not heard back from them yet. My wife, wonderful woman that she is, lacks the temperament, and my children are too young to take up my obligation. So if I'm dead, it must fall to you." Vikram picked up one of the candles and started walking. "Are you coming or not?"

Anything that provoked her curiosity that much made for an easy decision. Rada grabbed another candle and followed him into the dark.

Vikram hurried down the stairs. Even though she was much

younger, she had to hurry to keep up. Then she realized that the old man was wearing a belt, and from it hung a scabbard holding a forward-curving sword. Apparently that illustrated guide to sword fighting hadn't just been a decoration. Come to think of it, she'd not looked at the bound genealogy, but she was beginning to suspect that Vikram hadn't always been of the first caste. But why would the judges have obligated someone born of the warriors to be a Historian?

The stairs had to be ancient, far older than the house which had been built on top of them. They went down for a long time, carved straight into the rock of Mount Metoro.

"What is this place?"

"The museum has locks and guards, but since everyone knows it's filled with treasures, thieves still find a way in. The greatest vault of all is secrecy. No one tries to steal something they don't know is there."

Vikram's candlelight kept getting further away. They had to have gone down at least three stories worth of stairs before it stopped. When she caught up, there was a large door there, made of a shiny metal unlike anything she'd ever seen before. The Historian's symbol had been painted on it in red.

"What lies beyond this door is every bit as important as every book in the Capitol Library."

She doubted that very much, but since Vikram seemed so intense, she didn't scoff aloud.

"This is history. *Real* history. It's the reason I've spent the last twenty years living in this awful desert. If the Inquisitors capture me, you must take it from here and keep it safe until it can be turned over to another caretaker. You can't tell the Protectors. You can't even tell your fellow Archivists. And above all, whoever it is who is trying to kill the casteless, you can *never* let this fall into their hands. Our people have lost far too much already. Swear it. Swear you will protect our history."

Vikram was beginning to scare her. He looked haunted in the flickering light, but always too curious for her own good, Rada nodded anyway. "I've already made a solemn oath to protect our knowledge. I failed once, but never again."

"That'll do." The door made surprisingly little noise as Vikram swung it open. "Come then."

She'd not known what to expect, but it was just a room,

about the same size as the study that hid the entrance. It had
been cut from the red stone of the mountain, perfectly square
and smooth, rather impressive actually, considering how deep
beneath the surface they were. However, there was nothing inside,
no treasure chests, no shelves full of relics, no valuable scrolls...
Just what appeared to be a small hole in the center of the floor.

So the Historian's big secret was a room with a drain? She'd
been so nervous that she actually laughed aloud.

"Look at it again," Vikram suggested.

Rada did. The thing in the middle wasn't a hole...It just
looked that way because it was so incredibly black that her eyes
had tricked her. As she stared, she realized it was darker than
shadows. Darker than night. In fact, as she watched, the perfect
circle seemed to hungrily devour the light of their candles.

"Black steel..." she whispered. It had to be four or five inches
across, and an inch thick. "That's got to be worth a fortune."

"A fragment that big, yes. But that's no mere shard. It is a
device."

"What?"

"You may examine it if you wish, but don't let it touch your
skin."

"I'm fine." She wasn't going to go anywhere near that thing.
She'd read enough about black steel to know that it was the most
dangerous substance in the world. She wasn't about to *touch* it. That
was wizard business. "What would happen if it touched my skin?"

"It would taste your blood, and then somehow judge your
character and intentions, an effect similar to when someone
attempts to pick up an ancestor blade."

She flinched and took an involuntary step back. Everyone had
heard stories of ancestor blades angrily lopping off the limbs of
those found unworthy of picking them up.

"Don't worry. It isn't nearly as destructive or volatile as an
ancestor blade. This was designed for a purpose other than war,
though I'm sure if it fell into the wrong hands, it could be used
to cause incredible destruction. If I'm gone, and you need to move
it, use leather gloves to place it into some sort of container, and
then make sure that's securely tied."

"What?" Rada had dealt with a few ancient treasures in the
library, but none of them had actively wanted to harm her. It
was said that black steel was *alive*. "Why?"

"Over the last eight hundred years quite a few Historians have lost careless fingers to it," he explained as he set down his candle and pulled on a pair of thick workers' gloves. "The Mirror can be very unforgiving."

"It's a mirror?"

"Of a sort." Vikram knelt next to the thing, and gently, ever so gently, reached out and took hold of the edges. He slowly lifted the piece of black steel, rotating it so that she could see what was on the other side.

Rada saw her reflection in the mirror. Perfectly smooth, clear as the glass she used to read. *What manner of force did it take to polish the hardest substance in the world?*

She could see herself, and the stone wall and open door behind her, but the background grew darker and darker, until it was just her alone. It was as dark as the space between the stars. And then, oddly enough, there were stars.

The longer she stared into it, the deeper it seemed to grow, until she felt like she could reach out...and *through* it...

Then there was something else in the mirror with her.

Rada gasped as she spun around, but there was no one standing behind her, like there had been in the reflection.

Vikram saw her reaction, nodded grimly, and then placed it back on the floor, reflective side down. *Thankfully.*

"So you saw it too?"

"Saw what?" she shouted. "What was that?"

"The Asura." Vikram rose, and quickly pulled the gloves off. "Now I know you'll do. We must go."

Knees shaking, Rada followed him back to the stairs. Vikram closed the door, locked it, and then held out the chain toward her, key dangling from the end. "Here."

However, she didn't reach for it. "Not until you tell me what that thing inside the black steel was."

"Have you ever stopped to wonder why in ancient times, man was so quick to believe in ghosts and gods, yet today we're not?"

She shook her head. "No."

"Because it's easier to believe in things when you can see them."

She stared at the dangling chain for a long time. Then, grudgingly, too curious for her own good, Rada reached out and took the key.

Chapter 49

The tiger ran through the snow with effortless grace. The night air was freezing, but the excitement of being so near his goal kept him going. As he approached the assassins' camp fire, darkness gathered around the tiger as matter was rearranged, and out walked a man.

Inquisitor Javed adjusted his coat and pulled his wide-brimmed hat down low. *Now* he was cold. Honestly, he'd not been truly warm since his last night in the Capitol, in the bed of Arbiter Artya. That memory made him smile as he began walking toward the light, crunching through the deep snow.

The assassins had sensed his magic approaching and prepared themselves accordingly, swords in one hand, demon in the other. There were two of them, an unmatched pair, one tall, thin, and young, the other short, fat, and old.

"Who are you, wizard?" The fat one demanded.

"Calm yourself, Lost House. I'm no real wizard, just an amateur who likes to play at magic."

"So you say, but the tiger pattern is a difficult one to master."

"If it's not difficult, then what's the point in trying? Speaking of which, what did you two do to draw Sikasso's ire so much that he would send you out here to freeze?"

The assassins exchanged a nervous glance. Very few people in all of Lok knew of the existence of the Lost House, and fewer still would so brazenly name their master. "You're Inquisition," the fat one muttered.

"You possess a swift mind. Yes. I am Inquisitor Javed, Witch Hunter, fifteen-year senior, on a mission from the Grand Inquisitor himself." He gave them his most disarming smile, difficult to do when his beard was already covered in blowing snow. "Mind if I warm myself by your fire?"

"I am Omkar," the fat one said as he unhappily sheathed his sword. "What're you doing here?"

They'd said nothing about joining them by their fire, but Javed closed the distance anyway. "I'm hunting a group of fanatics. I picked up their trail north of here. They were easy to follow, what with all those frozen bodies you two have left along the way. I was looking for Ashok Vadal, but since you're both still alive, I can safely assume the Black Heart isn't here."

"They're ours," snapped the thin one.

Javed held his hands out over the fire, letting the heat soak into his leather gloves. "Not anymore. You will leave them to me. In this weather, you ought to be grateful for my taking over."

"But they're friends of the man who destroyed our—"

"Silence," Omkar snapped at his companion. "I'm afraid you've made a great journey for nothing, Inquisitor. Their lives belong to us."

Curious. "The Inquisition needs these fanatics alive."

"Why?"

"Normally slaves do not demand answers of their masters." Javed kept his voice jovial as he insulted them, but he could already tell how this would unfold. These wizards had developed some personal stake in tormenting these rebels, and they wouldn't relinquish such an investment easily. Javed knew what he had to do. "Don't forget that it's the Inquisition which holds your leash. Now the time has come to call off Sikasso's dogs."

The thin one had never put away his sword. "You're a long way from the Capitol, witch hunter."

"And you're a long way from your swamp, dog."

Omkar opened his big mouth to say something else, and Javed promptly stabbed him in it.

The Keeper of Names shivered by the campfire, tired, cold, and afraid. He didn't look into the fire, but rather kept his back toward it. Recent experience had taught him that looking at the fire would ruin his vision in the dark and make it easier for the assassins to get him.

There was a noise out in the darkness. Keta instinctively turned his head in the direction, as did everyone else who was still awake. His hand went to the big cleaver he kept beneath his blanket and waited.

After the first few nights of being picked off one by one, now they slept in shifts. Keta was supposed to be asleep, but rest no longer came easily for him. These people—these brave followers of the Forgotten—were his responsibility, and that weighed heavy on a man.

The noise didn't come again. It might just have been a branch breaking beneath the weight of the damnable fresh snowfall that had slowed their progress and trapped them upon the Akershan plain, still many miles from their hideout... Or it might have been the murderers sneaking up to slit more throats again.

Keta prayed once again for help, begging the Forgotten to protect his faithful, and to deliver them from these killers. *Why must you test us? Have we not suffered enough? What would you have us learn from this nightmare?* Then he tried to go back to sleep, but he kept his hand on the worn handle of his meat cleaver.

They didn't know for sure who was hunting them. Keta had only caught the briefest of glimpses of a man with a gray beard, corpulent yet nimble for his build. Whatever their motivation, the killers were methodical and cruel. Worst of all, Keta had a terrible suspicion that they were enjoying the process. Like they could have easily been wiped out by now, but they liked making them linger.

The warrior caste that Jagdish had sent to guard them had done their best, but the most capable among them, the murderers had targeted first. They'd find them in the morning, heads missing, or bowels spilled and frozen, and the ground was too hard to even bury them.

Then, in a move that shouldn't have surprised him, they'd started attacking the animals. They'd kill, or wound them so that they'd start screaming during the night and have to be put out of their misery. Deprived of their horses they were slower and more vulnerable. They had all the meat in the world, with no good way to carry it.

During the days, all the group could do was keep trudging on through the too deep snow, hoping to reach the hideout. The warriors had tried to hunt down their attackers, but they never left behind tracks to follow. And those who'd gone off to search for them had never come back. They'd either been murdered by their quarry, or fled back toward civilization. They only had a few of their sword swingers left, and those brave men wouldn't even wander off to take a piss alone.

The column of the faithful had lost warriors, workers, and casteless, both male and female, but so far the killers hadn't targeted the children. Some of the parents called that a blessing from the Forgotten himself, but Keta suspected it was because the children were their weakest members, and as long as they were alive, being carried, or trying to trudge through deep snow with their little legs, the group would remain slow, easy victims. Once the adults were dead, the killers could just leave and the winter would take care of the young for them.

By day they marched, making awful time through the unusually deep snow. By night they waited to be murdered. The fatigue and tension were getting to everyone, and many of the faithful had begun to fight among themselves. Keta had done everything in his power to keep them united and calm, leading them in chants and prayers, telling stories of bravery, and giving encouragement, but even he was beginning to fray, unable to defend against a threat that seemed to move effortlessly from one shadow to another.

The mountains were achingly close. If it hadn't been for this miserable storm they would've already reached their goal. Once they got to the secret path beneath the stone, they would be safe. He'd even told the others about what landmarks to look for, that way if he got picked off the rest could reach the Creator's Cove without him.

There was another sound, clearer this time, and Keta bolted upright.

"Someone's coming!" their lookout shouted. Everyone grabbed their weapons. Even the children had knives.

It might be a trick. It wouldn't be the first time the killers had tested their defenses, making enough noise to wake them all up, before retreating, that way the next day everyone would be even more tired and irritable. Keta actually hoped they would come out and fight.

"There. I see someone!"

Then Keta spotted it too, a single dark spot on the white snow trudging their way. This part of the Akershan plain was not nearly as flat as it looked from a distance. There were swells and gullies that you could really only see by their shadows when the sun was setting, but whoever it was wasn't sticking to those, they were walking out in the open, not even trying to hide. The only reason he'd even gotten this close without being seen was the falling snow.

Keta couldn't take it anymore. He threw down his blankets and began to shout. "Come out and fight us, wizard pig! We are the faithful. The Forgotten will punish those who have wronged us! He is the god of the sky. He is the god of war! And he will deliver us from your evil! Come out, bloated coward who slinks about in the dark! Oh, nightmare of the plains, *show yourself!*"

"Hello. One approaching your camp," the stranger declared. "I'm not a bandit. I'm a friend."

If this was a trick, it was unlike the others. "Come toward the fire," Keta shouted back. Then he whispered to the others. "Be ready to cut him down."

The man did as he was told, slowly. He had a sack over one shoulder and a sword at his side. He looked around at the array of readied weapons, and then meekly approached. His manner was contrite, his voice humble. "I am Javed, rice merchant of House Zarger."

"You're a long way from your desert," said one of the workers suspiciously.

"Only because the gods told me I needed to come here." There was a great deal of muttering at that, but his answer wasn't so different than theirs. One of the warriors rushed over and shoved him from behind. Javed went to his knees in the snow. "Please, I beg you. I heard your challenge. If you are who I think you are, then you'll know I speak the truth."

"A bold answer, when worshipping illegal gods will get you killed," Keta said. "Search him."

The warriors roughly pushed Javed down, tossed his pack and sack to the side, and removed a short sword and hunting knife from him. He made no effort to resist.

"I know it's bold, but I've walked too far to lie. My friends and I worshipped in secret, until we were told of the resistance of Ashok Vadal. We came to join his army."

"Where are these friends of yours, huh?" asked a warrior as he glanced around nervously.

"Set upon and killed by a foul wizard." Javed began to weep. "Not too far from here. It was terrible, but we prevailed."

"You *what?*"

"The wizard bragged about how they'd been slaughtering the faithful, but the gods gave us strength. I was the last. I'm no warrior, only granted a sword by the First to guard my wares is all, but I caught him by surprise. I brought you a trophy so you'd know I speak true."

The warriors dumped out the sack. A severed head fell into the snow. There were gasps all around the fire.

"That's him!"

"It's the murderer!"

Round and heavy, Keta rolled it over with his toe. With the long gray beard over soft chins and doughy cheeks, it certainly looked like the magical killer who'd been hounding them across the plains.

"Does this please you?" Javed asked.

"You have no idea! I knew the Forgotten would deliver us." He had prayed for a miracle, and once again the gods had provided one. Nearly overcome with emotion, Keta went over, took the newcomer by the arm, and dragged him to his feet. "Welcome, brother."

The faithful cheered as Keta embraced their savior.

Chapter 50

Grand Inquisitor Omand was in the secret chambers far beneath the Inquisitor's Dome when he received the report. As planned, Senior Arbiter Artya Zati dar Zarger had taken the podium at the Chamber of Argument and given a speech, once again proposing the eradication of all the casteless in the world. The observers described it as *moving*, *visionary*, and *heartfelt*. The woman certainly had a gift.

Of course, Omand knew it was too early to push for a final count. It took time to reshape public opinion. He had counted the great houses' votes, both those he was certain of, like his fellow conspirators or those he knew to utterly despise the great embarrassment which was the non-people, and those who were certain to vote no, like the soft hearted, or those who'd resist simply to spite him. It was the undecided he still needed to convince.

But there was some unexpected good news, and Omand smiled as he read the report. Artya had gotten the judges so fired up that they'd actually obligated a commission of high-status warriors to study the logistical feasibility of this endeavor.

The proposing judge had called it a War of Extermination. But Artya had moved to amend that title, and her name had stuck. It couldn't be an Extermination War, because *war* implied the enemy was capable of fighting back, thus it would be known

403

simply as *The Great Extermination* . . . as if the untouchables were nothing more than vermin, rats who'd crawled up from the sewers, spreading disease and disgust.

Like everything else involving the Capitol, things would move forward with ponderous slowness. The warriors' commission was supposed to deliver its report within ninety days. That gave him plenty of time to make things certain. As he'd done with the librarians and the Historians, Omand would see to it that this report said exactly what he wanted it to.

The judges would be informed that the Great Extermination would be a simple endeavor, easily completed in the span of a season. Omand had studied this topic his whole life, so he knew that it would most certainly plunge the whole continent into war until every river ran red with blood. The judges would fall, a king would rise—he'd already found a perfect candidate. The people would get their strong man to follow, while Omand controlled everything from the shadows.

All of this was necessary, for *progress.*

In some of the lowest, darkest chambers, far beneath the dome, a fire burned in a smith's forge, because the special Inquisitors who worked here needed to keep some of their tools red hot. So Omand crumpled the coded report and dropped it on the coals. He watched long enough to make sure the incriminating evidence was totally consumed before continuing with his duties.

The Inquisition's single most important prisoner was waiting to see him.

The prisoner had no name. For thirty years he had been in Inquisition custody, so incredibly dangerous that they'd sawed off his arms and legs, and smashed out each tooth with a hammer.

Omand continued deeper beneath the ground, to a hidden, protected place. Within the secretive Inquisition, very few knew of this chamber, and even fewer knew what was really inside of it. Only a select group had ever seen this prisoner, and only one Inquisitor—in the entire history of their Order—had ever learned to effectively communicate with him.

The prisoner had originally been captured in Vokkan. A massive, destructive tidal wave had struck the northern coast, and in the aftermath he had been discovered far inland, trapped, badly injured, yet still alive. The Inquisitors there had been quick to claim such a rare prize.

It was humid in here. The air always stank of mold. Omand had ordered the construction of this facility after he had grown tired of traveling back to his homeland for interrogations. When needed, pipes brought in clean water, and more pipes sent the filthy waste off to the Capitol's sewer system. In the center of the room was a great metal tank, filled with thousands of gallons of murky water. The guards had been instructed to keep it as salty as the ocean.

There was a single window in the wall of the tank, made out of the thickest glass in the world. On the other side, gray muck swirled and bits of rotting flesh floated by.

Omand took up a piece of demon bone in one hand, and pressed his other against the glass. It was cold to the touch.

The glass vibrated. Ripples appeared across the top of the tank.

Something dark and hideous appeared in the water.

No Cut No Cut No Cut

The Grand Inquisitor grimaced against the painful noise inside his head, and the awful images forming behind his eyes. Demon speech was a terrible, unnatural thing. If he could bottle demon speech, and give it to his torturers, even the hardest criminal would spill his guts when bombarded with this.

"Each time your claws start to grow back, we'll chop them off. This will continue until you give me what I want."

It was hard work, having a sea demon as a pet. Even keeping him starving in filth, their kind was so resilient that they could grow new limbs in a month. It did give the Inquisition a nice reliable supply of the freshest demon magic. In fact, they'd simply called the old facility in Vokkan *the farm,* since they'd continually harvested the demon's flesh there. It had been Omand who had figured out how to interrogate their prisoner. He had even taught the demon a few of their words.

Pain Blood Burn Cut Beg No

"Then it is simple. It doesn't have to be this way. Give me what I want and I'll send you back to hell."

The prisoner floated closer, until it pressed its odd bulbous head against the glass beneath Omand's hand. The demon presented his counter offer.

Ramrowan Revenge Suffer Death Death Death

They'd had this discussion many times. "He wronged your kind, and now his descendants are beyond your reach. But you know they are not beyond mine. If you want them to suffer and die for the crimes of their blood, then you know what I must receive in exchange."

The demon slowly drifted back from the glass, dark and malevolent, thinking. Demons spoke mind to mind, so it could plainly see his conviction and intentions.

The answer came in the form of a vision. Omand saw all of Lok, as if he was looking down upon it from high above, green and brown, shrouded by white clouds, and surrounded by blue ocean. This must have been how wizards who could turn into birds saw the world, only no bird could fly this high. Suddenly, the vision jerked, as if he were speeding downward. Omand could tell what region he was heading for, but then the vision abruptly ended before he could discover his destination.

Remainder Upon Kill

"Very well. When the blood of Ramrowan's children has begun to water the land, we will speak again."

The Grand Inquisitor removed his hand from the glass and began walking away from the tank. That vision had brought him tantalizingly close to the location of the ancient source. The gods were a myth, but their powers were real. Man may have forgotten about the great and terrible forces they had controlled in the days of old, but the demons remembered. One thing he had learned... demons never forget.

Omand had known the prisoner for a very long time. He was a simple, cruel, focused, vengeful creature. Their capacity to hate was awe inspiring. He had learned much from this demon over the years. In a way, he could be considered one of Omand's oldest friends. On the way out of the room, he commanded one of the guards, "Drag him out and cut him."

The Inquisitor looked uncertain. The demon wasn't due to be harvested again for another week. The process was difficult and dangerous, involving harpoons and chains.

"Do it. And skin some of him too."

As Omand returned to his duties, he thought about how his careful plans were finally coming to fruition. In a season, war would come. The Capitol would fall, and be born again. Millions would die. It was a small price to pay for progress.

Truly, he did not mind making Devedas king, because Omand intended to become a god.

Chapter 51

—◇◇◇◇◇—

Before him was the symbolic face of the Law, carved into the eternal stone of the Capitol, unyielding, unflinching, seeing all and forgiving none. There was no mercy, no middle ground. Cruel perfection, it appeared spotless, unmarred... But he understood now that beneath those carved lines was a seething corruption. It dispensed order, but at a terrible price.

He touched his hand—the hand which had so faithfully served—to that perfect face. And when he took it away, there was left a smear of blood.

The Law had been stained by his rebellion. The illusion of perfection was ruined.

Good. Let them all see.

Ashok awoke from his dream to a world of crushing pain and total darkness. His broken limbs were trapped beneath fallen rubble. There was absolutely no give. He didn't know how long he'd been out... hours? No... It had been days. But the Heart of the Mountain had been working on him the whole time. What a waste of precious magic. It could have been better spent helping a loyal servant of the Law, rather than on a criminal who was just going to perish, buried alive. Better to save it for someone who deserved it. He let go of the Heart.

His mouth and nose were mostly filled with dust and dried

407

blood. There was so much weight pressing down on him that he could barely breathe, but there was enough air flow he wouldn't asphyxiate. The armor had kept his ribs from being crushed. Death by dehydration then? With as much blood as he'd lost, that wouldn't take too long. Who would have ever guessed that the mighty Ashok Vadal would die of thirst beneath a pile of bricks? If it had been physically possible, he would've laughed at the irony of it.

He was glad that the House of Assassins would be his grave. He'd spent his entire life serving the Law. He'd thought he'd die a humiliating criminal death, rebelling against the Capitol. But instead he'd been able to strike one last blow against lawless evil. Such a death was a greater honor than he'd allowed himself to hope for in a very long time.

Forgotten. You are probably not real, but I have no one else to talk to. If this was the end you intended for me all along, I am grateful. May the others live. My work is done.

As consciousness faded, Ashok was content.

When it returned, there was torch light above. Dust rained down as bricks were lifted away.

"Over here! I've found him!"

Ashok should have known he wouldn't be able to shirk his duty so easily. Grudgingly, reluctantly, he once again called upon the Heart to sustain his life.

It took a very long time, drifting between awake and asleep, for them to dig him from his tomb. Through his grit-clouded eyes, he recognized some of the Sons, but there were many others, strangers with ashen faces. As they pulled him free, whenever his broken bones banged against the rubble, the pain brought him back. Someone put a rag soaked in water against his mouth and wrung it out so it could run across his cracked lips and down his parched throat. It seemed the greatest kindness he'd ever known.

As the sun rose over the sea, he found that it was Thera who was peering down at him. The wind was blowing her hair so that he could see the long scar, from which the gods had cursed them both.

"Rest for now, Ashok. I don't think they're done with us yet."

No. Their rebellion was just beginning.